TWO MEDIEVAL MERCHANT GUILDS OF SOUTH INDIA

SOUTH ASIAN INSTITUTE
NEW DELHI BRANCH
HEIDELBERG UNIVERSITY

SOUTH ASIAN STUDIES NO. XVIII

Two Medieval Merchant Guilds of South India

MEERA ABRAHAM

MANOHAR
2026

First published 1988
Reprinted 2026

ISBN 978-81-85054-48-3

Published by
Ajay Kumar Jain *for*
Manohar Publishers & Distributors
4753/23 Ansari Road, Daryaganj
New Delhi 110 002

Printed and bound in India

Contents

Acknowledgements

I particularly wish to thank G.S. Dikshit, formerly of Karnatak University for his long hours of advice, discussion and assistance in the very early stages of this project. I also wish to thank those who in Jawaharlal Nehru University, New Delhi provided the intellectual stimulus which enabled me to initiate this work. The department of history and the library of the University of Peradeniya, Sri Lanka, the library of the University of Bern, Switzerland, the Pontificio Istituto Orientale, Rome, the Connemara library, Madras and the library of the School of Oriental and African Studies, London have all provided assistance in ample measure. The staff of the office of the Chief Epigraphist of the Archaeological Survey of India have been generous with their help. It is impossible to thank individually all those other scholars who have helped with comments and criticism and I take this opportunity to emphasize that I owe much to them. Prof. Burton Stein now in London and Prof. H. Kulke of the South Asia Institute, Heidelberg have given me very valuable advice and also the support necessary to bring a research project finally to fruition. Although neither of them is to be held responsible for the interpretations and ideas contained in this book, without them my work would have been much more difficult.

My project has almost completely been self-financed even though it included trips to London and Singapore and much travelling in India. My family do not expect an expression of gratitude from me nevertheless it would not be fitting if I did not mention that but for them I probably could not have completed a research project of this nature.

Tamilnad Printers and Traders have prepared the South India maps under the expert guidance of R.P. Arya. The Sri Lanka map was prepared by U.P. Ratnatunga and is the result of hours of discussion and of painstaking identification of medieval place names. A. Lawrence of Printers Plates gave invaluable help in the final stages of typesetting of this book.

Glossary

ācārya	–	Preceptor.
aghil	–	Aloeswood.
agrahāra	–	Settlement intended primarily for Brahmans.
ādi-vaṇikēsan	–	First or chief merchant.
aiññūṟṟīśvarar	–	The deity of the Five Hundred.
aiññūṟṟuvar	–	The Five Hundred.
ambalam	–	Temple.
araiyan	–	Title of an "official" in Tamil areas.
ardha-maṇḍapa	–	Pillared hall which is also ante-chamber in temple.
avarai	–	A lentil.
banajiga	–	Trader in Kannada areas.
banañju-paṭṭinam	–	Trader's town or market town in Kannada areas.
bhaṭṭan	–	A Brahman.
bhūmi	–	Land, the earth.
brahmadeya	–	Grant of incomes to Brahmans — thereby usually village or land granted to Brahmans.
cadjan	–	Palm-leaf.
caturvedi	–	Brahman who knows the four Vedas.
cheli	–	*Chelai* — a sari.
dagoba	–	Buddhist temple, a relic chamber.
dēvadāna	–	Usually grant to temples or religious establishment.
devale	–	Temple, used primarily in Sri Lanka.
dharma	–	Religion.
doāb	–	Land between two rivers.
erivīrapaṭṭinam	–	A fortified trading settlement.
gahapati	–	A householder and/or landowner.
gavuṇḍa	–	*Gauṇḍa, gauḍa*, an agriculturist, village headman also a hereditary office in Kannada areas.
ghi	–	Clarified butter.
gopura	–	Storeyed structure over gateway to temple.
heggaḍe	–	*Pergaḍe*, an "official in districts". *Nāḍ-heggaḍe*- a paid official probably answerable to ruler in Kannada areas.
honnu	–	A gold coin, *pon*.
inām	–	A gift, term used to describe a form of land tenure.
jaggery	–	Unrefined product of the sugarcane.
Kaikkoḷar	–	A warrior group who also took to weaving and trade.

kaḷanju	–	A weight.
kāśu	–	A unit of currency.
kottalis	–	Representatives of guilds
kudirai-ceṭṭis	–	Horse traders.
kula	–	Family.
kūṟṟam	–	A territorial unit in Tamil areas.
mahāpradhāna	–	An important "official" in Kannada areas.
maṇḍalam	–	A large territorial unit in Tamil areas.
maṭha	–	A religious educational foundation.
maṭṭar	–	A land measure.
meykkīrtti	–	Eulogy, often appearing at head of inscription.
nāḍ	–	Territory.
nāḍu	–	A territorial unit in both Tamil and Kannada areas.
nagaram	–	An assembly of merchants.
nagarattār	–	Member of *nagaram*, also member of Nattukottai Chettiar community.
nakara	–	In Kannada areas appears to be merchant member of urban association.
padineṭṭu	–	Eighteen.
paḷḷi	–	Church, Buddhist or Jain temple, mosque.
perumpalli	–	Large *palli*.
pandit	–	Brahman and learned man.
pattanasvāmi	–	Literally, "lord of the town". A person appointed to take care of specific aspects of administration in urban settlements.
peraraiyan	–	Title of an "official" in Tamil areas.
perumbadai	–	A military unit.
perunteruvu	–	A large street.
prabhu	–	Literally, lord, master. An official with administrative duties (in Kannada speaking parts).
praśasti	–	Eulogy, *meykkīrtti*.
sabhā	–	An assembly of Brahmans.
sālai	–	A *maṭha* or a charitable feeding hall.
samaya	–	An association.
samudāya	–	A group, a society.
śāsana dēvata	–	Deity of the order or rule.
seṭṭi	–	Merchant.
sthānapati	–	Temple "executive"
svāmi	–	Literally, lord, master, a Brahman.
tambula	–	Betel leaf.
tirukkāvanam	–	An (auspicious) thatched shed, a courtyard.
toddy	–	Liquor distilled from palm tree.
tope	–	A grove

tuvarai dāl – A lentil or pulse.
Ugura 300 – Association of betel leaf pickers in Kannada-speaking areas.
ūr – Village, *ūrār*, people of the village, *ūrāḷis*-headmen of the village.
valanāḍu – A territorial unit — *Cōḷa*
vaṇikēsan – A merchant.
Veḷḷāḷa – Agricultural land-owning group (Tamil).
vīrakal – Hero stone.
visa – A measure.
vyāpārī – A trader.

Abbreviations

ARE	*Annual Report on (South Indian) Epigraphy*
BEFEO	*Bulletin de l'Ecole Française d'Extrême-Orient*
BJRL	*Bulletin of the John Ryland's Library*
BK.	Bombay-Karṇatak (contained in *South Indian Inscriptions)*
BSOAS	*Bulletin of the School of Oriental and African Studies*
CHJ	*Ceylon Historical Journal*
CJHSS	*The Ceylon Journal of Historical and Social Studies*
CTI	*Ceylon Tamil Inscriptions*
Cv.	*Cūlavaṃsa*
EA	*Etudes Asiatiques publiées à l'occasion du vingt-cinquième anniversaire de l'Ecole Française d'Extrême-Orient.*
EC	*Epigraphia Carnatica*
EI	*Epigraphia Indica*
ET	*Epigraphia Tamilica*
EZ	*Epigraphia Zeylanica*
FMJ	*Federation Museums Journal*
IA	*Indian Antiquary*
IAL	*Indian Art and Letters*
IATR	*International Association of Tamil Redearch*
IESHR	*Indian Economic and Social History Review*
IHQ	*Indian Historical Quarterly*
IHR	*Indian Historical Review*
JA	*Journal Asiatique*
JAOS	*Journal of the American Oriental Society*
JAS	*Journal of Asian Studies*
JASB	*Journal of the Asiatic Society of Bengal*
JBBRAS	*Journal of the Bombay Branch of the Royal Asiatic Society*
JESHO	*Journal of the Economic and Social History of the Orient*
JIH	*Journal of Indian History*
JKU	*Journal of Karnatak University*
JKUH	*Journal of Karnatak University Humanities*
JMBRAS	*Journal of the Malaysian Branch of the Royal Asiatic Society*
JOR	*Journal of Oriental Research*
JRAS	*Journal of the Royal Asiatic Society* (Gt. Britain)
JRASC	*Journal of the Ceylon Branch of the Royal Asiatic Society*
JSBRAS	*Journal of the Straits Branch of the Royal Asiatic Society*
JSEAH	*Journal of Southeast Asian History*
JTS	*Journal of Tamil Studies*

KI	*Karnatak Inscriptions*
KR	*Kannada Research* (Nos. assigned to inscriptions)
MAR	*Annual Report of the Mysore Archaeological Department*
MJLS	*Madras Journal of Literature and Science*
MTB	*Memoirs of the Toyo Bunko*
NDI	*A Collection of the Inscriptions on Copper-Plates and Stones in the Nellore District*
PSI	*Inscriptions of Pudukkottai State*
PSSMSI	*Peasant State and Society in Medieval South India by Burton Stein*
QJMS	*Quarterly Journal of the Mythic Society*
SII	*South Indian Inscriptions*
SITI	*South Indian Temple Inscriptions*
SLJH	*Sri Lanka Journal of the Humanities*
TAS	*Travancore Archaeological Series*
TBG	*Tijdschrift voor Indische Taal-, Land- en Volkenkunde uitgegeven door het Koninklijk Batavia-asch Genootschap van Kunsten en Wetenschappen*
TOCS	*Transactions of the Oriental Ceramic Society*
UCR	*University of Ceylon Review*

Introduction

This is a case history of two medieval merchant guilds of South India, the Maṇigrāmam and the Ayyāvoḷe. Both these associations are well-known by name to historians of medieval South India although no sustained analysis of their activities in the peninsula has been attempted so far.[1] The Maṇigrāmam and the Ayyāvoḷe originated independently of each other, but from the mid-thirteenth century onwards the Ayyāvoḷe association became so powerful that the Maṇigrāmam functioned in a subordinate capacity to the Ayyāvoḷe, virtually as an adjunct to the Ayyāvoḷe group. Geographically, the area in which these associations operated in the past corresponded, more or less, to the territory of the present-day states of Karnataka and Tamil Nadu, as well as southern Andhra Pradesh, particularly the Coromandel strip. Both these guilds also functioned, during certain periods, in some parts of Kerala, when the west coast of South India attracted foreign trade and was actively part of the medieval, maritime trading arc connecting China, Southeast Asia, India, Sri Lanka and West Asia.

The time frame chosen for this study is approximately the ninth to the mid-fourteenth century. In Tamil-speaking areas this was the period in which two dynasties, the Cōḷas and later the Pāṇḍyas dominated the scene, while in Kannada areas the important ruling dynasties were those of the Rāṣṭrakūṭas, the Western Caḷukyas of Kalyan and the Hoysaḷas, and to a lesser extent the Yādavas and the Kākatīyas. In the Tamil south the first of the imperial Cōḷas who came to prominence was Vijayālaya who captured Thanjavur about the mid-ninth century. The greatest and best-known of the Cōḷas were Rājarāja and Rājēndra whose reigns covered the period from about the final years of the ninth century till approximately the end of the first half of the eleventh century. Rājarāja and Rājēndra placed emphasis on trade and conquests outside the South Indian peninsula. Kulōttunga I who ruled from 1070 – 1122 A.D. also showed considerable interest in the outside world judging both by epigraphs which showed that he maintained relations with Southeast Asia and also by the evidence of the Chinese chronicles which speak of a special trade mission that he sent to China.[2]

From the thirteenth century onwards the Cōḷa power was on the wane. The second Pāṇḍyas took their place and during their rule the South Indian

[1] A resumé of the history of one of these guilds is contained in M. Abraham, "A Medieval Merchant Guild of South India", *Studies in History*, 4, No. 1 (1982), 1-26.

[2] *EI*, XVII, pp. 281-84; *Sung Shih*, 489, 22, courtesy, a group of Chinese South Asian historians in Beijing.

peninsula was again outward looking, alive with contacts with the trading world of West Asia and Southeast Asia and China.[3] Under both the Cōḷas and Pāṇḍyas events in South India had repercussions on Sri Lanka and Sri Lanka was often an active participant in the dynastic disputes that arose on the mainland. But more important were the trade rivalries that precipitated some of the major conflicts between the two areas. Many aspects of the economic history of South India and Sri Lanka were linked in this period.

The Rāṣṭrakūṭa Kriṣṇa III of Karnataka in the tenth century invaded and conquered part of the Cōḷa kingdom. His armies proceeded along routes to the south which were probably used by traders travelling between the two areas in earlier times. It was near Manyakheda, one of the capitals of the Rāṣṭrakūṭas that the important Ayyāvoḷe trading guild originated. The Caḷukyas of Kalyan, their successors, and the Hoysaḷas had close dealings with this important merchant guild. During the long reign of Caḷukya Vikramāditya III (1076 – 1126 A.D.) the Ayyāvoḷe merchants were very active in what are now the modern Dharwad, Shimoga, Bijapur and Kaladgi Districts.[4] The Caḷukyas remained in power till the end of the twelfth century. In their place came the Hoysaḷas, the Yādavas and Kākatīyas. The Hoysaḷa kingdom was based in the south of the Kannada country. Nilakanta Sastri has described the decades 1220 – 1245 A.D. as the period of "Hoysaḷa hegemony in the South."[5]

Events in the heartland of North India began to affect the South dramatically in the early fourteenth century. In 1310 Malik Kafur a general of Ala ud-din Khilji raided the kingdoms of the Hoysaḷas and the Pāṇḍyas, and returned with immense booty to Delhi. The gold and the horses he came back with may have been acquired partly in the far south where merchants were engaged in active foreign trade and horses were regularly imported.[6] The pearls he is said to have brought back may have included pearls from the fisheries of the Gulf of Mannar.[7]

The origins of Vijayanagar, the last great kingdom of the south, may be traced back to the mid-fourteenth century. The capital city of Vijayanagar was founded in the central plains of Kannada-speaking territory on the Tungabhadra. By the end of the fifteenth century, many of the southernmost areas which formed part of the Pāṇḍya kingdom were absorbed into the empire of Vijayanagar. With the establishment of Vijayanagar there is no explicit evidence of the continued existence of the Maṇigrāmam. The Maṇigrāmam probably ceased to function in Tamil areas by the

[3] K.A.N. Sastri, *A History of South India* (Madras, 1966), p. 222.

[4] See Appendix A.

[5] Sastri, *op. cit.*, p. 214.

[6] These points are elaborated in Chapter V.

[7] See note on "Pearls" in Chapter V.

mid-fourteenth century. The Ayyāvoḷe appeared either to have changed character completely, or to have been supplanted by a new organization founded in imitation of the Ayyāvoḷe, under Vijayanagar. It used the same name Ayyāvoḷe. But it was clearly dominated by a new set of merchants and their *modus operandi* was dissimilar to that of the earlier group.

With the recent revival of scholarly interest in the Vijayanagar empire it may be possible, at some later date, to come to some conclusions regarding the relationship of the Vijayanagar merchants with feudal chiefs, with the king or with other categories of people in urban settlements. At the present moment all the indications are that their role in the towns was not comparable to that of the original, earlier Ayyāvoḷe merchants. There were occasions when the Vijayanagar Ayyāvoḷe merchants were active in trading settlements stretching right across the peninsula from coast to coast. But primarily the association in late Vijayanagar and in post-Vijayanagar times — even as late as the end of the seventeenth century — appeared to be concentrated in the cotton textile producing areas of what is now Andhra Pradesh.[8] It is clear that in this region some of these merchants had close connections with the weavers who produced the cloth. As a matter of interest a list of inscriptions referring to the Vijayanagar Ayyāvoḷe is included in Appendix A. Nevertheless no further discussion on their activity is undertaken in this book partly because our understanding of the social fabric of Vijayanagar, or of its urban centres is still so limited. In contrast, a great deal of scholarship, some of it quite recent, has been expended on South Indian history in pre-Vijayanagar days. This background of research has made it possible to bring some degree of precision to the conclusions arrived at and has been an important factor behind the decision to concentrate here on the period prior to the rise of Vijayanagar.

The chief source of information on Ayyāvoḷe and Maṇigrāmam is the corpus of inscriptions. The inscriptions most frequently consulted here have been those of Kannada and Tamil-speaking areas and include most of the published inscriptions as well as some unpublished inscriptions in which these two guilds are mentioned. They are generally recorded on stone and also occasionally on copper plates. These inscriptions on stone are often located in or near temples and are intended as records of the taxes in cash and in kind levied for the benefit of the temple, from merchant groups and from townspeople, on commodities produced in the area, or on goods in transit. Occasionally, they record public services in villages or in urban areas which were initiated or maintained by merchants. And on a few occasions they record details of what appears to be an agreement between ruler and merchant, demarcating merchant townships, or in one case, a contractual agreement recording trade rights granted to a group of foreign traders, as

[8] See Appendix A.

well as to local trade groups, and also including a grant of some privileges and immunities within the "foreign enclave," in this case, the precincts of an East Syrian church in Quilon, Kerala.[9]

Of the published inscriptions used many are abbreviated. Several portions have been omitted in publication. Therefore very frequently it has been necessary to trace the original estampage and transcript in the office of the Archaeological Survey of India at Mysore. This exercise, painstaking and time-consuming though it was, has paid off in that it has been possible to look at the total inscription afresh instead of at very early translations, or abridged versions. Most often the portions omitted in early published versions have been those of interest to social and economic historians and have been of special value in this research project. The location, chronology and the full contents of the inscription are of importance in any serious attempt at analysing medieval South India. Also the *praśasti* or eulogy of the ruler or merchant guild which often appears at the outset of the inscription has been taken note of and studied in this work in the beliet that the wording of the *praśasti* had considerable significance. The *praśasti* was in part standardized and in part composed for the occasion. Both from the standardized phrases and from the newer interpolations one obtains indications of intricate factors such as the relationship of merchants with the state (or ruler), or the position of a guild in relation to other corporate bodies, or the religious affiliation of its members at a particular time and place. The inscriptions used in this book are mentioned with comments in tabulated form in three appendices, and it is hoped these will be useful both to those who wish to re-examine the assumptions I have made and to those who wish to pick up the threads and proceed further.

An important detail carried in Appendix A, wherever possible, is the list of commodities of trade which are mentioned in many of the inscriptions. These, in most cases, are not found in the published version, but have been gleaned from the original transcripts and estampages. From these details regarding the commodities traded it is possible to draw some conclusions regarding the nature of trade and to determine whether it was primarily a luxury trade or whether it catered to basic needs for food and clothing. This study for the first time shows that from the end of the twelfth century there is clear evidence both of increasing foreign trade in luxury goods as well as a thriving, local internal trade in basic necessities including grain and pulses. These points are amplified and illustrated both in the text of this work and in Appendix A.

Apart from inscriptions other sources used have been published chronicles and an old manual on ship building as well as a survey recorded on palm

[9] *TAS*, II, 9.

leaf.[10] Through extensive surveys of the Pudukkottai and former Ramanathapuram Districts much information has been obtained on the Nattukottai Chettiar community. And it has been possible for the first time to link the ancestors of these Chettiars with the Ayyāvoḷe association. Early Christian ecclesiastical sources have also been used with satisfying results since in Kerala the Maṇigrāmam is known to have collaborated with Christian immigrants from the littoral of the Persian Gulf in the ninth century. Most important are the translations of Chinese dynastic histories and topographies that have been used, in most cases published translations, but in a few cases translations undertaken by Chinese scholars at Beijing.[11] Relevant aspects of Chinese histories illuminate aspects of Cōḷa and Pāṇḍya external trade in a remarkable fashion. But much work still remains to be done on this score. Here only a portion of this reservoir of information has been utilised.

A case study such as this is generally limited in scope and narrow in focus. This work follows in general the normal pattern for a case study. It concentrates on the Ayyāvoḷe and Maṇigrāmam, the two most important of the merchant associations of the medieval South engaged in both long-distance and in local trade. With them were associated other associations of craftsmen such as weavers, basket makers, potters, leather workers, market gardeners and important groups of peasant farmers. All these groups receive mention and some attention in this book, but no detailed analysis of these groups has been attempted. For others who wish to work on South Indian history this remains a largely unexplored field. These aspects have been omitted here because an attempt to enlarge this work would have meant further delay in publication. But the decision to concentrate on Ayyāvoḷe and Maṇigrāmam has also been conditioned by the belief that in the present state of research on South India limited micro-studies aiming at precision rather than range still have their uses.

Despite this self-imposed limitation the investigation of the history of

[10] C.M. Ramachandran Chettiar, ed., *Kongadēsa Rājākkaḷ* (Madras, 1950); C.M. Ramachandran Chettiar, ed., *Cōlan Pūrvapaṭṭaiyam* (Madras, 1950); T.P. Palaniyappa Pillai, ed., *Kappal Sāttiram* (Madras, 1950). Also the *Statistical Account* of 1813 of Pudukkottai, prepared on palm leaf.

[11] See P. Wheatley, *The Golden Khersonese* (Kuala Lumpur, 1966) particularly Chapters XIII and XVIII. See also K.A.N. Sastri, ed., *Foreign Notices of South India; from Megasthenes to Ma Huan* (Madras, 1939). Also F. Hirth and W.W. Rockhill, ed., *Chau Ju-kua, His work on the Chinese and Arab trade in the twelfth and thirteenth centuries, entitled Chu-fan-chï* (St. Petersburg, 1911); W.W. Rockhill, "Notes on the relations and trade of China with the Eastern Archipelago and the coasts of the Indian Ocean during the fourteenth century," *T'oung Pao*, 14 (1913), 473-6; 15 (1914), 419-47; 16 (1915), 61-159, 236-71, 374-92, 435-67, 604-26, especially 15 (1914), 430-437 and 438-443 in which the missions from the Pāṇḍyan kingdom, and Quilon to China and *vice versa* are listed from the *Yüan Shih*. See also Ma Tuan-lin in Hervey St. Denys, *Ethnographie des peuples étrangers à la Chine* (Geneva, 1883), pp. 573-575.

these two guilds has very often necessitated a fresh look at many aspects of political and economic history. In the course of this research it became clear that these guilds were active in the handling and distribution of commodities of foreign trade and also in some instances may themselves have procured these goods at source. Yet medieval maritime trade is a field of study very little worked on. In order to relate the evidence on foreign trade available from Indian sources with what is known in general about Asian maritime trade an attempt is made in this book to reconstruct in broad sweeping terms certain aspects of Asian maritime trading history which appear relevant. To broaden perspective, some parallel, contemporaneous economic events in the medieval Islamic world and in medieval Europe and North Africa are also mentioned. Justification for taking this macro-look at trade is sought on the ground that while we are not yet in a position to quantify or assess the importance of medieval long-distance trade the facts are that both overland and by sea, commodities of trade were transported over surprisingly long distances, sometimes traversing the whole breadth of the Eurasian continent. At certain times in the period under review goods of Chinese origin were taken, by land or by sea, as far as Europe as well as to closer destinations in Southeast and South Asia.[12] Some Southeast Asian aromatics were marketed in North Africa.[13] Manufactured goods from South Asia as well as raw materials were sold both in the East as well as in the West.[14]

In his important paper "Proto-Industrialization and Pre-Colonial South Asia," Frank Perlin says, "I argue that India, like Europe, was affected by profound and rapid change in the character of its societies and economies, and state-forms, from at least the sixteenth century, and secondly that a fundamental aspect of that development was a local merchant capitalism which emerged independently of that in Europe, but with a common international theatre of societal and commercial changes."[15] If Perlin's argument is

[12] For example in A.D. 1340 "... the agents of the Frescobaldi company (the great Florentine rival of the Bardi) imported into London China silk, 'serico nominato Catewy'". R.S. Lopez, "European Merchants in the Medieval Indies; The Evidence of Commercial Documents," *Journal of Economic History*, 1 (1943), 166. The thirteenth century *Chu-fan-chï* of Chau Ju-kua describes admirably maritime trade, with special reference to commodities of trade in Southeast and South Asia and the market for Chinese exports in those areas.

[13] S.D. Gotein, *Letters of Medieval Jewish Traders* (Princeton, 1973), p. 103. A merchant writing from Tunisia in the eleventh century requests a shipment of "odorous wood." E. Ashtor, *A Social and Economic History of the Near East in the Middle Ages* (London, 1976), pp. 105-106 cites Ibn Khurdadhbih's work of the ninth century in which the activities of the Jewish merchants, the Radhanites are described. They carried into Christian Europe from the East, musk, aloeswood, camphor and cinnamon. Ashtor points out that this may not have been a regular trade.

[14] See section on "Commodities" in Chapter V.

[15] Frank Perlin, "Proto-Industrialization and Pre-Colonial South Asia," *Past and Present*, 98 (1983), 33.

acceptable then a study of the commerce of the period preceeding the sixteenth century becomes doubly important. The medieval trade of peninsular India with the outside world has not been examined before in any detail. The ambiguities of a study of commerce in an era in which quantification and the use of statistics is not possible are great, but to some extent this is compensated for here in the detailed analysis of commodities of maritime trade included at the end of the last chapter. The distribution of the bulk of these commodities in India was handled by the Ayyāvoḷe. Commodity analysis has been possible through the use of a wide range of sources including Chinese texts in translation. The examination of these commodities shows that luxuries such as precious stones, pearls, aromatic woods, resins and perfumes were traded as well as commodities such as dyes, textiles, processed iron (*wootz*), livestock, spices, and medicinal plants. Of these the manufactured goods, the textiles and processed iron became increasingly important from the thirteenth century onwards. This new emphasis was dictated by changes in commodity demand within India as well as outside India.

Speaking of Anglo-Egyptian trade in the late Middle Ages, R.S. Lopez says, "At least we must be prepared to assume that such international trade as may have existed in the Middle East was linked to trade conditions in other areas, and that basic changes in England, Italy, India and China had some repercussions on Middle Eastern commercial trends."[16] Similar comments could be made about medieval Asian, foreign trade. A global perspective despite the inevitable inaccuracies is not one believes, out of place and provides a frame, a possible explanation, for the ups and downs of Asian maritime commerce, a trade with which the South Indian guilds were intimately involved.

Precise evidence of Indian inclusion in the medieval maritime trading arc connecting China, Southeast Asia and India and West Asia really appears only in the important inscriptions of the Ayyāvoḷe guild in which long lists of commodities clearly of overseas origin were mentioned and the taxes levied on them were specified. Although commodities of both West Asian and Southeast Asian origin were listed in these inscriptions the direct involvement of the Tamil merchant and of the Cōḷas and Pāṇḍyas was with the eastern end of the trade. There is very little evidence of Tamil activity in West Asia.[17] Although there is inscriptional record of Kannada-speaking

[16] R.S. Lopez, Harry Miskimin, Abraham Udovitch, "England to Egypt, 1350-1500: Long-term Trends and Long-distance Trade," in M.A. Cook, ed., *Studies in the Economic History of the Middle East* from the rise of Islam to the present day (London, 1970), p. 93.

[17] At the excavations at Quseir Al-Qadim a Tamil inscription was found. It is held that "Its context-within poorly constructed rooms and in association with an iron forge-may indicate 'that Indian merchants, perhaps even iron workers, may have lived here.'" The quotation is from D.S. Whitcomb and J.H. Johnston, *Quseir Al-Qadim 1978 Preliminary Report* (Cairo: American Research Center in Egypt Inc.); *Quseir Al-Qadim 1980 Reports*, cited in M. Gittinger, *Master Dyers to the World* (Washington, 1982), p. 57. It has not been possible for me to obtain a copy of the inscription.

merchants of the Ayyāvoḷe guild handling the distribution of imports there is no indication in this period of their activity overseas.[18]

In the early centuries A.D. the sailing guide, *The Periplus of the Erythraean Sea* describes very clearly the active trade between the Romans, the Arab world and India.[19] Archaeology testifies to some of the trade links with Southeast Asia as far as the borders of China. The Arab trade between Southeast Asia, India and China in the eighth and ninth centuries is described in Arab topographies and G.F. Hourani gives us a graphic account of the Arab voyages.[20] The Indian role in this trade whether in the early centuries of the era or in medieval times has remained largely a matter of conjecture based on some Sanskrit and Tamil references, on some inscriptions and on incidental references in Arab and Chinese works. The spread of Indian influence in Southeast Asia is a reminder that active links were once maintained between these regions. In this work for the first time it has been possible to present tangible evidence of Indian participation in medieval, maritime trade by showing the circulation of imported goods of West Asian, Southeast Asian and Chinese origin within the South Indian peninsula. It seems quite certain the Ayyāvoḷe and Maṇigrāmam were involved in this trade.

Sri Lanka was in medieval times an area of involvement for South Indian merchants. Ayyāvoḷe merchants were to be noted in strength in some areas of the island. This has necessitated a fresh look at the political history of South India and Sri Lanka. The politico-religious historiography of Sri Lanka of which the Buddhist chronicle, the *Cūlavaṃsa* is a good example, depicts the Cōḷa invasion of Sri Lanka as an assault on the Buddhist establishment.[21] Seen within the context of the functioning of the Ayyāvoḷe guild the Cōḷa wars appear to have been inspired both by the desire for booty as well as the desire to corner the trade with Southeast Asia and to capture the pearl fisheries of the Gulf of Mannar. Investigation of the patterns of medieval maritime trade which were undertaken in order to understand further the role of the South Indian merchant, has also led to a better understanding of some of the other compulsions of medieval Sri Lankan history. One of the causes for the dramatic movement of the Sinhalese people in the thirteenth century away from the northern plains of Sri Lanka to the "wet zone" and the coastal plains in the west was undoubtedly the desire to enter

[18] *EC*, VII, Shikarpur 118 c. A.D. 1150; *EC*, V, pt. 1., Belur 177, A.D. 1167; *EC*, V, pt. 1, Arsikere 22, A.D. 1188, *ARE* 277 of 1934-35, about mid-thirteenth century; *EC*, IV (new), Kollegal 97, A.D. 1323.

[19] W.H. Schoff, trans. and ed., *The Periplus of the Erythraean Sea* (Philadelphia, 1912).

[20] G.F. Hourani, *Arab Seafaring in the Indian Ocean in Ancient and Early Medieval Times* (Princeton, 1951).

[21] *Cūlavaṃsa*, trans., W. Geiger, Vol. I (Colombo, 1953), 55, 16-22.

into the new and active thirteenth century trade with Egypt and the intermediary states in the Arabian peninsula. Gujaratis and ships from the Malabar and Konkan coast of India, as well as Jewish merchants were already active in this trade. Plantation products, cinnamon, pepper, dyes such as brazil-wood, pearls and textiles were among the staples of medieval maritime trade in the late twelfth and early thirteenth centuries. Many of these were "wet zone" products and it is very probable that the availability of these products as well as proximity to the new trade centres conditioned the Sinhalese move to the west.[22]

Some new ideas have also emerged in the course of this study on the commercial organisation of the south of India, particularly on the origin of urban settlements and these have been incorporated in this work. They do not conflict with the descriptions of urban settlements in the studies of Hall and Stein.[23] Put together all these views enlarge our vision of the nature of towns and of urban life. Stein lays emphasis on the role of temples and sectarian movements in urban development. In my view, trade played an equally important role. At ports such as Quilon, Kodungallur, or Nagapattinam merchants and the requirements of commerce were of predominant importance. In the interior of the country, in the twelfth century, trade contributed to the growth of settlements — market towns. Some stimuli for both the growth of the ports and the market towns may have come from external trade. At some urban settlements one is not able to determine which factor was more important, the religious or the commercial, or which came first. The sacred and the economic geography coincided. Along with the proliferation of urban-type settlements in the twelfth and thirteenth centuries one notices the increase in the number and influence of landholders and agriculturists, and these landholders were not necessarily Brahmans. Karashima speaking of the thirteenth century in Tamil areas says that ". . .among the landholders in the villages of the Lower Kaveri were many influential figures who possessed large tracts of land and who held important positions in the local or even central administration".[24] He contrasts this with the early Cōḷa

[22] See Abraham, "A Medieval Merchant Guild", where for the first time it has been suggested that the changes in patterns of maritime trade conditioned the Sinhalese move to the west in medieval times. Other causes suggested for this move may be found in K. Indrapala, ed., *The Collapse of the Rajarata Civilization in Ceylon and the drift to the South West* (Peradeniya, 1971).

[23] K.R. Hall, "The *Nagaram* as a Marketing Center in Early Medieval South India", Diss. Michigan Univ., 1975; Burton Stein, *Peasant State and Society in Medieval South India* (Delhi, 1980).

[24] N. Karashima, *South Indian History and Society Studies from Inscriptions A.D. 850-1800*(Delhi, 1984), p. 20. In M. Abraham, "The Ayyāvoḷe Guild of Early Medieval South India", M. Phil. Diss. Jawaharlal Nehru Univ., 1978, I had laid stress on the increase in power of the landowning class in the late twelfth and thirteenth centuries.

period when individual landholding among non-Brahmans was rare. The present study shows that both in Kannada and Tamil areas there was a surge of self-confidence and evidence of growing influence and power among landholders in the late twelfth and in the thirteenth centuries; in Tamil areas members of this new grouping were not Brahmans.

The Ayyāvoḷe inscriptions reveal a close link between these groups and traders in the late twelfth and in the thirteenth centuries. This link may have grown as a result of the need for food in developing urban areas, a need which only the agriculturist was able to meet. In the same social group the landholder also became important in Sri Lanka in this period.[25] The twelfth and thirteenth centuries were also marked by the increasing involvement of the South Indian peninsula and Sri Lanka in overseas trade. Karashima believes the growing importance of the landholding peasant farmer in Tamil areas was the result of "an accumulation of wealth brought about by the imperialistic expansion of Chōḷa power during the reigns of Rājarāja I and Rājēndra I, which was distributed to the people in the heart of the Chōḷa country, the lower Kaveri Valley."[26] He feels that "an increase in agricultural productivity was made possible by the introduction of new techniques such as the construction of dams, the maintenance of water tanks and channels etc." This he suggests was an added cause for the growth in power of the farming interests. The overseas imperialist expansion of Rājarāja I and Rājēndra I may have been undertaken to increase the share of the Tamil kingdoms in overseas trade. The channelling of profits whether acquired through pillage or as revenues from trade may have contributed to increased prosperity in the Kaveri valley. Improvements in agriculture, "imperialist expansion" and the expansion of trade both local and foreign were all probably inter-connected causes of the social changes of the thirteenth century. But these changes are to be noticed not merely in the Kaveri valley, but also in Kannada areas and in Sri Lanka. One is therefore inclined to attach the most importance to trade as being the original catalyst since both in the peninsula and in Sri Lanka expansion of trade was the common factor during this period.

So far the use of the word trade has not been defined partly because a reading of the text of this work is in some ways self-explicatory on this particular point. The content and nature of trade changed, and this is reflected in this work. There was a dramatic expansion of local and foreign trade in the thirteenth century. When the texts of the Ayyāvoḷe inscriptions are analysed commodity-wise,it is apparent that in some areas of the peninsula, household or village self-sufficiency may have existed.[27] But the predominant

[25] See Abraham, "A Medieval Merchant Guild", p. 21.

[26] Karashima, *ibid*.

[27] See table of inscriptions, Appendix A. The commodities circulating in the area where the inscription was recorded are mentioned in the section "Remarks".

impression (and quantification has not been attempted on this point yet) is that the majority of villages were by no means self-sufficient isolated units. The nature of the commodities exchanged can be verified by the taxes levied on them which are recorded in the Ayyāvoḷe and the Maṇigrāmam inscriptions.[28] These commodities at least from the latter half of the twelfth century onwards included a wide range of luxuries and important basic commodities. The range of commodities indicated a quality of life which in no way accorded with the early impressions of a 'stagnant' society in India.[29] The word trade then in this work and in the context of our understanding of the state and society in medieval times approximates closely to R. McC. Adam's definition of modern trade as being "the act or business of exchanging commodities by barter or sale".[30]

Scholarship on the history of South India has been and still is dominated by K.A. Nilakanta Sastri, Burton Stein and Noboru Karashima. Burton Stein's article on "Coromandel Trade in Medieval India" contains valuable and seminal ideas on merchants and trade and the impulse to undertake this project owes something to that article.[31] K.A.N. Sastri's emphasis on the importance of maritime trade led to the detailed investigation on that topic in this work.[32] Noboru Karashima's valuable conclusions on the existence of a "bureaucracy" in Cōḷa times have been accepted here.[33] Previous research on the merchant guilds is limited but K.R. Venkatarama Ayyar's "Medieval Trade, Craft and Merchant Guilds in South India", needs to be mentioned, as also G.S. Dikshit's "Constitution of the Trade Guilds in Medieval Karnataka" and K. Indrapala's "Some Medieval Mercantile Communities of South India and Ceylon" and "South Indian Mercantile Communities in Ceylon, circa 950-1250".[34] The works of these scholars provided the basic groundwork for my current research.

[28] *Ibid.*

[29] See Karashima, *op. cit*,p. xvii.

[30] R. McC. Adams, "Anthropological Perspectives on Ancient Trade", *Current Anthropology*, 15, No. 3 (1974), 239.

[31] Burton Stein, "Coromandel Trade in Medieval India", in J. Parker, ed., *Merchants and Scholars* (Minneapolis, 1965), pp. 49-62.

[32] K.A.N. Sastri, *The Cōḷas* (Madras, 1975), p. 219, says "As in ancient times, this trade was part of a flourishing maritime commerce between the countries of the Western world and China, in which Arabs, Indians and the people of the Malay peninsula and Archipelago acted as intermediaries." While I disagree with Sastri's description of this trade as being solely between the Western world and China while other countries acted as intermediaries, I agree with him that this trade was important to the Cōḷas and indeed to most parts of the Indian peninsula. The vitality of this sea trade constituted a real difference between the North Indian plains and the South Indian peninsula in perceptions of the outside world, a difference which remains a feature of the Indian "world view" to this day.

[33] Karashima, *op. cit*.

[34] K.R. Venkatarama Ayyar, "Medieval Trade,Craft and Merchant Guilds in South India", *JIH*, 25 (1947), 269-80; G.S. Dikshit, "Constitution of the Trade Guilds in Medieval Karnataka", *JKUH*, 3 (1959), 53-57; K. Indrapala, "Some Medieval Mercantile Communities of South India and Ceylon", *JTS*, 2, No. 2, pt. 1 (1970), 3-15 and "South Indian Mercantile Communities in Ceylon, circa 950-1250", *CJHSS*, n.s. 1, No. 1 (1971), 101-113.

Chapter I

The Maṇigrāmam Guild of Traders

One of the earliest inscriptional notices of the Maṇigrāmam guild of traders appeared in the ninth or early tenth century at the port of Quilon on the Kerala coast. The contents of this inscription, as well as of many others which will be referred to subsequently, indicate that the Maṇigrāmam association was undoubtedly a merchant guild. The evidence that this corporation of merchants was functioning at this port, at that time, needs to be viewed in its wider context as part of a larger pattern of overland and maritime commercial activity which included areas bordering the Persian Gulf and the Arabian peninsula, parts of north-west India, the east and west coasts of India, Sri Lanka, some parts of south Burma, the Thai-Malaysian peninsula and many areas of Southeast Asia and China. This wide-ranging trade was a recurring feature of Asian history and was particularly important in medieval times.

A. *The Persian Gulf, Northwest India and the Malabar Coast: Harappans, Greeks and Christians from West Asia*

The commercial transactions that took place, in very early times, in one particular section of the trading world just described, is of relevance to this study and we may take a brief look at it. Across the Arabian Sea and from the Persian Gulf long-distance trade with the Indus valley, northwest India and the west coast of India, including the Malabar coast is to be noticed in several phases of Indian history. The Harappan trade with the regions bordering the Persian Gulf has been described in a definitive study by S.Ratnagar.[1] In a later period some of the *Jātaka* stories describe trade between these two regions. The *Bāveru Jātaka* tells of merchants who set out to trade by sea with Babylon (Bāveru) and who carried with them a land-finding crow (*diśa-kākā*) as a navigational aid.[2] The *Jātakas* may be dated in the period from around 400 B.C. to the first century A.D. but in them may be preserved far earlier traditions.

1 S.Ratnagar, *Encounters: The westerly trade of the Harappa civilization* (Delhi, 1981).

2 *Jātakatthavaṇṇanā*, ed., V. Fausbøll and trans., T.W.Rhys Davids, *Text*, Vol. III (London, 1883), *Bāverujātaka*, pp. 126-128.

It is fairly certain that voyages were being made regularly between the Persian Gulf and the Indian subcontinent around the mid-fourth century when Alexander invaded India. The invasion by Alexander was primarily a land expedition but on the return journey the sea route between India and the Persian Gulf was also used. Part of Alexander's army returned along the coastal route under the command of his admiral Nearchus. Alexander's interest in sailing was considerable. He encouraged shipbuilding on the Euphrates as well as the transport of Phoenician ships in sections to be re-assembled there. For the return coastal voyage Nearchus obtained the services of a local guide on the Makran coast (Greek Gedrosia) to conduct him as far as the Gulf of Hormuz.[3] Portions of the *Anabasis* of Arrian give the impression that local sailors had some knowledge of monsoon winds.[4]

The establishment of the Indo-Greek kingdoms in northwestern India in the second century B.C. may have given an impetus to the sailing between the Indus delta, Kutch-Kathiawar and the Persian Gulf. The Greeks gained control of Saurashtra and the Gulf of Cambay in addition to the coastal settlements at the delta of the Indus. Patala, founded by Alexander, or rebuilt by him on the site of an earlier settlement, may have been used in the time of the Indo-Greeks. Further south Bharuch as the terminus for trans-peninsular routes was probably a focal point for trade. Ships may have coasted along northwards from Bharuch calling at settlements on the way up the Makran coast till they arrived at the Gulf of Hormuz. Here, it has been suggested, there was a Greek trading station, an intermediate port, from where the goods were transhipped to Seleucia on the Tigris.[5] Land routes to Seleucia were important after the Indo-Greek kingdoms were established as a result of the increase in trade.[6]

In the first century A.D. much of the territory of the Indo-Greek kings was in the hands of the Śakas from Central Asia and the Parthians. In the early centuries A.D. the movement of traders along the land and water routes connecting what are now modern Iraq and Iran with northwest India may be inferred from the many references to trade and merchants contained in the literature of the early Christians. The merchant accompanied the missionary or the merchant himself was an agent of proselytization. Early ecclesiastical traditions of the East link the Persian Gulf ports with northwest India and the Malabar coast. The *Acts of Judas-Thomas*, the apocryphal account of the mission of the apostle Thomas in the first century A.D. was probably composed in the city of Edessa either at the end of the second century A.D.

3 J. W. McCrindle, trans., *The Commerce and Navigation of the Erythraean Sea and Arrian's Account of the Voyages of Nearkhos* (London, 1879); Arrian, *Indika,* XXVII, I.

4 *Ibid.* Arrian, *Anabasis*, XXI. See also Arrian, *Indika*, XXI-XXII.

5 W.W. Tarn, *The Greeks in Bactria and India* (Cambridge, 1951), p. 93, p. 261, pp. 481-485.

6 *Ibid.*, p. 261.

or in the early years of the third century.[7] It speaks of the mission of Thomas to the Parthians and the Medes after which he proceeded to northwest India accompanied by the merchant Habban. Portions of the *Acta* have been proved to be historical. Numismatic evidence shows that the Indo-Parthian king of "India" Gondophares, who, it is claimed in the *Acta* was converted by St. Thomas, did exist.[8] There are many literary references to St. Thomas in India and to the merchant who, it is claimed, accompanied him and later brought back his bones. The fourth century hymn composed by Ephraim, doctor of the Syrian church, says of the death of Thomas in India:

> Thomas, whence thy lineage,
> That so illustrious thou shouldst become?
> A merchant thy bones conveys;
> A Pontiff assigns thee a feast
> A King a shrine erects.
>
> The bones the merchant hath brought,
> Over them an outward watch he kept.
> They from within guard over him keep.
> Since in divers trades he embarked
> Nothing so priceless did he acquire.[9]

There is frequent mention of merchants in contemporary Christian religious literature and these confirm the view that the trader was very often an agent of conversion and that early Christianity in these areas spread along the routes used by traders. For example, in *The Hymn of the Soul* which was probably composed in the third century and is found in *The Syriac Acts of St. Thomas* one notices phrases in the hymn that seem to indicate that the author himself was a trader for he speaks of a journey and says, "I passed the borders of Maishan the meeting-place of the merchants of the East." Elsewhere he writes of a friend and says,

> "And I made him my intimate, A comrade with whom I shared my merchandise,"

lines which undoubtedly could not have been composed except by a

7 E.Tisserant, *Eastern Christianity in India* (Calcutta, 1957), p. 2.

8 *Ibid.*, p. 3; A.E. Medlycott, *India and the Apostle Thomas, An Inquiry with a critical analysis of the 'Acta Thomae'* (London, 1905),pp. 1-17.All the evidence points to a mid-first century date for the coin of Gondophares. See also J.N. Farquhar, "The Apostle Thomas in North India," *BJRL*, 10 (1926), 80-111, reprinted in *The Apostle Thomas in India According to the Acts of Thomas*, ed., Jacob Vellan (Kottayam, 1972).

9 From Medlycott, *Apostle Thomas*, pp. 27-28. Medlycott bases his translation on *The Breviary according to the Rite of the Church of Antioch of the Syrians*(Mosul, 1886-1896), Vol. VI, p. 635 and Mon.Lamy, *S. Ephraemi Syri Hymni et Sermones* (Mechinlae, 1902), Vol. IV, col. 704. S. Ephraem lived in the fourth century at Nisibus and at Edessa. Lamy bases his translation on manuscripts held in the British Museum and believed to be of the eighth or ninth century. See Medlycott, p. 25.

merchant.[10] The *Acta S. Maris* probably composed in the seventh century describes the conversion to Christianity of Persian traders who returned from the "west". And it described further that,

> ...as these Huzites and Persian converts used to return from the west they used to make numerous conversions in the neighbouring countries; and from that time dates the origin of the Church among the Huzites and in Persia. When Mar Mares reached the country of the Huzites, and found believers there, and heard of the conversion of the Persians, his heart was filled with joy to find a small quantity of wheat in extensive fields of tares. He preached through that country and converted many. Then he descended still further (or went still further) until the perfume (or odour) of Mar Thomas the Apostle was wafted unto him: and there also he added great numbers to the fold, and left behind a disciple named Job to minister to them.[11]

While the total historicity of the *Acta S. Maris* is very much in doubt, the descriptions of trade and proselytization in the first few centuries A.D. probably reflect actual conditions as also the account of the direction in which some of these traders moved, from Persia and Iraq westward, and then eastward towards northwest India.

According to the tradition of the Syrian Christians St. Thomas the apostle left north India, sailed across to Socotra and from Socotra to Cranganore (Muziris) on the west coast of India.[12] The island of Socotra according to *The Periplus of the Erythraean Sea* was a trading halt on the return journey from India for Arab and Persian traders and it is well within the bounds of possibility that the route ascribed to Thomas the apostle was correct.[13] The St. Thomas traditions represent events which were contemporary, or near contemporary, with the sailing patterns in the Arabian Sea as described by the author of the *Periplus*. The Egyptian Greek Agatharchides writing about 110 B.C. mentioned the presence of Arabs, Greeks and those he called "Indians" at Socotra.[14] Socotra may have been an entrepôt of some importance

10 *The Hymn of the Soul* contained in *The Syriac Acts of St. Thomas*, ed. and trans., A.A. Bevan, Cambridge, 1897 in *Texts and Studies, Contributions to Biblical and Patristic Literature*, ed., J. Armitage Robinson, Vol. V, No. 3 (Cambridge, 1899), p. 15. The hymn was probably composed before the first quarter of the third century.

11 J.B. Abbeloos, *Acta Sancti Maris Assyriae Babyloniae ac Persidis Seculo I Apostoli* (Leipzig, 1885), pp. 83-84, also Medlycott *Apostle Thomas*, pp. 36-37.

12 Tisserant, *Eastern Christianity*, p. 6; J.N. Farquhar, "The Apostle Thomas in South India", *BJRL*, 11 (1927), 21-24.

13 G.F. Hourani, *Arab Seafaring in the Indian Ocean in Ancient and Early Medieval Times*(Princeton, 1963), p. 22; W.H. Schoff, *The Periplus of the Erythraean Sea* (Philadelphia. 1912), pp. 133-139. Hourani and Schoff argue a great antiquity for Socotra as a meeting place for seamen from many places. (The name Socotra may be derived from the Sanskrit *Dvīpa Sukhadāra*, in Greek, Dioscorida, a translation of the Sanskrit.)

14 *Ibid.*

in the second century B.C. The halt at Socotra and the voyage of St. Thomas from Socotra to the Malabar coast, his stay in South India and martyrdom in Mylapore are part of the generally accepted traditional history of the Syrian Christians.[15]

If we agree that the Christian missionary and the merchant often went hand in hand then we may also obtain some idea of commercial trade routes and in particular the movement of traders into western India by pinpointing the location of Christian communities in early times. Mingana in his careful and well-documented study has said, "The quickest way to India from Persia and Mesopotamia lay through the Persian Gulf and the Arabian Sea."[16] He has shown that

> all along on the Persian and Arab side of the Gulf, there were considerable Christian communities from very early times. Pherat-Maishan, the modern Basrah, at the northern end of the Gulf, was a Bishopric since A.D.225, and further south, on the Arab side of the line, the country of the Katars on the highway of the sailing ships from the Persian Gulf is spoken of in history as having also bishops as early as A.D. 225. In the Persian tableland, situated on the eastern side of the Gulf, and best known in Persian history under the name of Fars, ... Christianity had also made great headway at the very beginning of the third Christian century....[17]

Khuzistan, the province neighbouring Fars he says had an important Christian community at Baith Lapat in the third century.[18]

The persecution of the Christians under the Sassanids may have been responsible for an exodus of Christians to Malabar in the fourth century led by Thomas of Jerusalem. In an eighteenth century account in Syriac script and some use of the Malayalam language the traditional history of the St. Thomas church in Malabar is narrated and in it the visit of the merchant Thomas of Jerusalem is described.[19] The Bishop of Edessa according to the manuscript had a dream in which he learnt of the unfortunate condition of the St. Thomas church in India. So he spoke to the Catholicos of Seleucia—Ctesiphon and through his intercession the merchant Thomas was sent to India and with him, according to the account, went many from Baghdad, Jerusalem and Nineveh. The story stresses the continuing link between Malabar and West Asia. It must be noted that no scholar of repute is prepared to vouch for the total accuracy of the account describing the visit of Thomas of Jerusalem. What one may stress again here is the persistence of

15 Tisserant, *op.cit.*, p. 5.

16 A. Mingana, "The Early Spread of Christianity in India", *BJRL*, 10, No. 2 (1926), 3-81.

17 *Ibid.*, pp.5-6.

18 *Ibid.*, p. 6.

19 *Anecdota Syriaca*, ed., J.P.N. Land, Tomus primus (Leiden, MDCCCLXII), pp. 124-125.

the tradition linking the spread of Christianity to India with traders and with merchants.

B. *The Romans in the Indian Ocean*

Except in this study, the movement of Christian traders towards northwest India and towards the Malabar coast has so far received very little attention. The entry of the Romans into the Indian Ocean in the early centuries of the Christian era on the other hand is better known. The foundations for Roman maritime activity in the Indian Ocean were laid with the Roman conquest of Syria, followed by their conquest of Ptolemaic Egypt in 30 B.C. The Romans had received luxury goods from the East at trade termini such as Alexandria, the ports of Syria and the Black Sea ports. Some of the land routes leading to the west had partially been penetrated by merchants from the Roman world, but they had not travelled into India. An increasing demand in Rome for luxuries, coinciding with disturbances in intermediate areas, focussed attention on the development of trade through Alexandria.

The beginnings of Roman trade with India were tentative, hesitant and exploratory. Trade intensified when the Graeco-Romans became aware of the periodicity of the monsoons and learnt the use of these winds for voyages across the Arabian Sea. The use of monsoon winds, known and in use by Arabs and Indians, was a trade secret not revealed to the Romans, and exploratory voyages were made over a period of time before they hit on the use of the southwest monsoon for speedy passage across the sea, particularly to Bharuch (Barygaza) and to Malabar. The northeast monsoons were used for the return voyage. Several reconstructions have been made stage by stage of the sailing routes followed by the Romans before the discovery of the monsoon. Pliny's *Natural History,* and *The Periplus* , a sailing guide probably composed in the first century A.D. provides the background for the early stages of the sailing.[20] It appears most likely that the earliest voyages were coastal sailings around the Arabian peninsula as far as the entrance of the Persian Gulf. Ships then turned in the narrow straits, proceeded along the Baluchistan coast, and then made for the Indus ports.

Following the Arabian coast, at some stage, the Romans desirous of shortening the voyage may have noticed the Arab ships returning from India put in at Moscha halfway along the coast. Moscha is situated beyond Syagros where there is a deep indentation in the coast line. Therefore, at this point, from Syagros (Ras Fartak) they will most probably have first struck out across the sea to arrive at the Indus delta, or to points on the Gujarat coast.

20 *The Natural History of Pliny*, trans., J. Bostock and H.T. Riley, 6 Vols. (London, MDCCCLV), and the *Periplus*, already cited. The *Periplus* is used for the reconstruction of sailing routes outlined in the next two paragraphs.

During these voyages, it may have occurred to the Romans that spices such as pepper and many of the other commodities they wanted could be obtained at source further south. Possibly for this reason the final stage was evolved in which after Aden they veered south and headed towards the Malabar coast. The voyage to the Malabar coast by this route sometimes took only forty days. The heyday of the Roman trade with India appears to have been the latter half of the first century and the second and the third centuries. The commodities they picked up in South India included pepper, pearls, ivory, silk, spikenard, malabathrum, precious and semi-precious stones and tortoise-shell.

C. *Some Aspects of Sixth Century Trade*

The voyages already mentioned of the Christian traders, in the Arabian Sea, took place during the peak period of the Roman trade, and also continued in later times. By following the trail of Christian trade with the west coast we are better able to understand the first Maṇigrāmam inscription of Quilon in Kerala, which was a record of a contract between emigrant foreign Christians and local authority.

In a sixth century unpublished version of the life of a monk Abraham of Kashkar who probably lived in a monastery in the region around present-day Oman the monk is reputed to have said, "I was a merchant of the number of those who trade and travel on the sea. It happened to us that on our way back from the country of the Indians, our ship broke up...."[21] This active trade in the sixth century between the regions bordering the Persian Gulf and the west coast of India is vividly described by the Nestorian monk Cosmas, who also details the commodities exchanged in this trade. Cosmas wrote of Sri Lanka, and the west coast of India:

> The island being, as it is, in a central position, is much frequented by ships from all parts of India and from Persia and Ethiopia, and it likewise sends out many of its own. And from the remotest countries, I mean Tzinsta and other trading places, it receives silk, cloves, sandalwood and other products, and these again are passed on to marts on this side, such as Mále, where pepper grows, and to Calliana which exports copper and sesame-logs, and cloth for making dresses, for it also is a great place of business. And to Sindu also where musk and castor is produced... and to Persia and the Homerite country and to Adulê. And the island receives imports from all these marts which we have mentioned and passes them on to remoter ports, while at the same time exporting its own produce in both directions.[22]

21 Mingana, "Early Spread of Christianity", p. 23.f.n. 7. Based on Fol. 26b of Syr.MS. Mingana, No. 252, in Rendel Harris Library, Birmingham.

22 J.W. McCrindle trans., *The Christian Topography of Cosmas an Egyptian Monk*, Hakluyt

Cosmas noted that the ports of Malabar exported pepper as did the ports of the south Konkan coast.

D. *The Inscriptions of Sthāṇu Ravi: Foreign Trade and the Kerala Coast*

The first half of the seventh century saw the beginnings of Arab forays into western India. The Arab conquest of Sassanid Persia, Egypt and Sind gave them the control of a long area of strategic seaboard including the Persian Gulf and the Red Sea and through them the approaches to the Mediterranean. In the ninth century there are records of long voyages made by Arabs which, with halts and possible changes of shipping, terminated in Canton. The long Arab route is described in the anonymous work the *'Aḥbār as-Sīn wa'l-Hind.*[23] The sailings commenced at Muscat or Sohar in Oman and ships went straight to Kulam Mali which has been identified with Quilon in Kerala (Malayalam, Kollam). Rounding Cape Comorin ships then went directly to Kalah-bar an entrepôt port most probably located northeast of present-day Singapore. Ships then went through the Straits of Malacca, past Pulao Tioman, before proceeding towards China. The extract from the writings of Cosmas, quoted earlier, described the voyages of Persians and other sailors from ports on the Persian Gulf to the west coast of India and to Sri Lanka.

It is in the context of this seafaring and commerce that we may look at the evidence of the ninth to tenth century exodus of Christians from the regions bordering the Persian Gulf to the Kerala coast which is contained in the inscriptions of Sthāṇu Ravi, a series of inscribed copper plates in which the Maṇigrāmam guild of India is first mentioned.[24] In the second half of the eighth or in the early ninth century Christians may have come to India led by Bishop Thomas of Cana.[25] Later in the ninth century another similar group came led by two bishops, Mar Sabrīsho and Mar Peroz. It is the second immigrant group which is mentioned in these copper plates.

We may first examine the written evidence for the arrival of this second group as it is contained in the same Syriac document of the eighteenth century earlier quoted, written by a Jacobite priest from Malabar. The account as translated by Mingana says:

> Then in the year 823, the Syrian Fathers, Mar Sapor and Mar Parūṭ

Society, Vol. 98 (London, 1897), p. 365.Book XI of the *Topography* from which this extract is quoted is not found in the manuscript known as the the Vaticanus. It is considered very likely that this book was added by Cosmas himself at a much later date. Taprobane is mentioned in the earlier books as well.

23 J. Sauvaget, *'Ahbār as-Sīn wa'l-Hind; relation de la Chine et de l'Inde*, rédigée en 851 (Paris, 1948), pp. 8ff; Hourani, *Arab Seafaring*, p. 66.

24 *TAS*, II,9.

25 Mingana, "Early Spread of Christianity," p. 44, f.n. 1, p. 49, pp. 64-65.

> (Piruz), with the illustrious Sabrisho‘ came to India and reached Kullam (Quilon). They went to the King Shakirbirti, and asked from him for a piece of land in which they could build a church for themselves and erect a town. He gave them the amount of land they desired, and they built a church and erected a town in the district of Kullam, to which Syrian bishop and Metropolitans used to come by order of the Catholicos who sent them.[26]

A portion of another Syriac manuscript of the mid-sixteenth century Cod.Syr. Vat., N.iv, quoted by Mingana and translated by him speaks of a document composed by a priest in India which the priest claims was written in "... the holy Church of Mar Shapur and Mar Yapot (Piruz?)."[27]

The Quilon copper plates mention a Maruvāṇ Sapīr Īśō which Mingana says is the Syriac *Maran Sabr-Īsho*. He says: "*Mar* is the Syriac title of all bishops, and *Sabrisho* is a very common Syriac name meaning 'Jesus is my hope'".[28] The patriarchs who came to Quilon (Kollam) may possibly have belonged to a church in Persia which was under the "jurisdiction of the East Syrian (Nestorian) Patriarchate of Ctesiphon."[29] There is evidence that in the seventh century an Indian church existed formally under the Patriarch of Ctesiphon, a patriarchate which included the provinces of Persia such as Fars.[30]

The Maruvāṇ Sapīr Īśō mentioned in the Sthāṇu Ravi plates may be identified with the Syrian Father mentioned in the traditional Kerala account just referred to, and in Cod. Syr. Vat., N. iv. The Sthāṇu Ravi plates have appended a list of signatures of witnesses in three languages, in Arabic, using the Kufi *fleuri* script of the ninth to tenth century and in the Pahlavi and Hebrew scripts. The use of the Syriac titles for Maruvāṇ Sapīr Īśō and the use of Arabic, Pahlavi and Hebrew scripts are in conformity both with the traditional Kerala accounts of church history and also with the East Syrian ecclesiastical tradition with its known links with Persia. The evidence linking the Persian branch of the Patriarchate of Ctesiphon with India in the seventh century has already been referred to. Fr. Khalil Samir believes that the names in the Arabic list could be of witnesses who were either Christians (Syrian) or Muslims, and in the Hebrew list of those who could have been Arab Jews or Christians.[31] These witnesses could have been either Christians who came along with Mar Sapīr or Christians along with Muslims and Jews who were cooperating with Mar Sapīr's group for purposes of trade. As the examination of the text of the inscription shows, many aspects of buying

26 Land, *Anecdota*, p. 125; Mingana, "Early Spread of Christianity", p. 45.

27 Mingana, "Early Spread of Christianity", p. 70.

28 *Ibid.*, p. 76.

29 *Ibid.*, p. 32.

30 *Ibid.*

31 Father Khalil Samir, *Pontificio Istituto Orientale*, Rome, 1 October, 1983, oral communication.

and selling at Quilon were entrusted to Mar Sapīr and the Tarisa church of Quilon in the ninth to tenth centuries, the peak period of the Arab trading voyages to India and China.

The most satisfactory published interpretation of the signatures in Pahlavi is that of Prof. H.W. Bailey who believes that of the witnesses whose signatures are in Pahlavi, some were Zoroastrians.[32] The Arabic names read are "...Maimun son of Ibrahim, and Muhammed son of Mani, and... (? Sulk) son of Ali, and Uthman son of Al-Marziban, and Muhammed son of Yahyd, and 'Amr son of Ibrahim, and Ibrahim son of At-Tay and Bahr son of Mansur, and Al Kasim son of Hamid, and Mansur son of Isa and Isma'il son of Ya'kub."[33] In Hebrew the names deciphered are Hasan Ali, Ishaq son of Michael, Ibrahim and Isma'il.[34]

The inscriptional record of this merchant group by name is of great value. Elsewhere evidence of commerce between West Asia and the west coast of India in the ninth century is of a more general nature, consisting largely of mention of trading stations and commodities of trade contained in Arab sailing guides and topographies. The importance of the Sthāṇu Ravi record for a study of ninth or tenth century overseas trade cannot be over-emphasized. As has already been mentioned, the port of Quilon is frequently mentioned in Arab works as the main halt for Arab seamen on the way to Southeast Asia and China. The Quilon record is therefore not merely evidence of emigration led by Christians, but is to be seen also as the movement of a Christian group with trading interests to a port that was rapidly becoming a major Asian entrepôt. The signatures appended to the grant including those of Zoroastrians and Muslims and also possibly Jews and Christians tell us something of the composition of this group of foreigners, traders, who were either established in Quilon, or who had commercial links with the city, in the ninth to tenth century.

Apart from the signatures in Pahlavi appended to the Quilon grant, other Pahlavi inscriptions found in Kerala are the inscriptions, nearly identical, on crosses found at Kaḍamuṭṭam, Kottayam and Muṟṟucira. There are wide divergences in the way the inscriptions have been read. The early translation of J.J. Modi suggest a direct connection between the inscriptions on the cross and the arrival of the foreign prelates in Quilon.[35] The cross found by

32 L.W. Brown, *The Indian Christians of St. Thomas* (Cambridge, 1956), pp. 87-89.

33 *Ibid.*, p. 89, f.n. 1, "Burkitt quoted in *Malabar Christians and their Ancient Documents*, by T.K. Joseph". Father Khalil Samir reads Yahya for Yahd. He believes the script used is Kufi *fleuri* of the ninth to tenth century.

34 *Ibid.*, and personal communication, Father Khalil Samir 1 October, 1983.

35 J.J. Modi, "A Christian Cross with a Pahlavi Inscription Recently Discovered in the Travancore State", *JBBRAS*, 2, No. 1 (1926), 1-18. See also A.C. Burnell, "On Some Pahlavi Inscriptions in South India", *IA*, 3 (1874), 308-316; T.K. Joseph, "Another Persian Cross in Travancore", *IA*, 52 (1923), 355-356; A.S.R. Ayyar, "A New Persian Cross from Travancore", *The Ceylon Antiquary*, 9, pt. iv (1926), 188-196.

the Portuguese and now installed at St.Thomas Mount, Madras, bears a similar inscription. It has been suggested that the others were copies executed after the Portuguese re-installed it in the mid-sixteenth century.[36] On paleographic grounds the Pahlavi used has been dated the seventh to eighth century by Dr. Modi and the ninth century by E.W. West.[37]

Returning to an examination of the copper plate inscription of Sthāṇu Ravi it may be noted that some plates are missing but what remains is long and elaborate.The record merits attention both for the incidental information it gives about an embryo township and for the information it contains about the ninth century conduct of trade. There are two sets of copper plates and they are inscribed, except for the signatory portions, in Vaṭṭeḻuttu characters of the ninth or early tenth century. The language of the text of the inscription is Tamil. The second set may be a copy of the first, as the palaeography suggests that it was inscribed somewhat later. Some of the plates are in the possession of the Mar Thoma church at Thiruvalla and the remaining plates are with the Jacobite Syrian Seminary at Kottayam. The reconstruction of the two sets, and the reading by Gopinatha Rao are here followed in preference to the earlier reading of Gundert.[38]

According to Gopinatha Rao, inscription I shows that in the reign of the king Sthāṇu Ravi the governor of Vēṇāḍu granted to the church, the Tarisāppaḷḷi at Quilon, built by Esō dā Tapir (later on in the same record the same name appears as Maruvāṇ Sapīr Īśō), the rights over certain families handed over to the church, presumably in order that their services might be utilised by the church. These consisted of four "families" of Īḷavar a toddy drawing caste, along with eight Īḷakkaiyar who were perhaps women of the same caste.[39] It is possible that these were people originally from Sri Lanka. One family of the washerman caste was also included. The ruler withdrew his right to collect within the settlement taxes such as *taḷaikkāṟam*, imposed on toddy tappers, and *ēṇikkāṇam* (a similar tax) from these groups donated to the Tarisāppaḷḷi. In addition the right to collect some other taxes within this area on these groups was also renounced, taxes such as the tax on thatches of houses, and the poll tax levied on toddy tappers. The ruler or his deputy, also waived the right to a tax known as 'polippon' which Gopinatha Rao suggests may have been a tax on "heaps of paddy, pepper etc." Inscription I goes on to say,

> These Īḷavars may...bring their carts into the market and within

36 T.K. Joseph, "Christian and non-Christian Crosses in Ancient India", *JIH*, 28 (1950), 112-122.

37 E.W. West, "Inscriptions around Crosses in South India", *EI*, IV, 21, pp. 174-176.

38 H. Gundert's analysis appears in "Translation and Analysis of the ancient documents engraved on copper in possession of the Syrian Christians and Jews of Malabar", *MJLS*, 13, No. 30, pt. i (1844), 115-46.

39 The interpretations and translation of Gopinatha Rao have been followed in this paragraph, *TAS*, II, 9.

> the (fort) walls and ply their trade. The washerman also may, by coming into the market and within the (fort) walls, do his work.[40]

Headmen of the community and the 'master of the fort' were not to interfere with them, and the church was granted certain rights of jurisdiction (phrased in vague terms) over them. The inscription goes on to record that these rights were secured through the efforts of Maruvāṇ Sapīr Īśō. We have here then also in this inscription a picture of a walled settlement of the ninth century. The Christian community, in this case, under the leadership of foreigners, was permitted to send the families whose services were assigned to them into the walled settlement or fort. These families were permitted to ply their trade within the precincts of the fort.

The second inscription shows more clearly that the church, the Tarisāppaḷḷi (known today as the Kadisha church), was not located within the precincts of the 'fort'. This inscription gives more details on the land grant made to the Tarisāppaḷḷi showing that the Tarisāppaḷḷi had as its boundaries cultivated land on one side, the backwaters of Quilon and the fort on another side, the sea to the west and to the north and northeast the land belonging to two local families mentioned by name. One of these families was the Punnaittalai family which may have been a prominent family of indigenous Christians. They were mentioned in the first inscription as being part of the group present when the "governor" of Vēṇāḍu formulated the agreement with the church. Within this foreign settlement (the lands of the church) the foreigners and those dependent on them were to be tried by the church in cases of misconduct.[41]

Three other groups were mentioned by name.

> The members of the community known as the Six Hundred, the Añjuvaṇṇam and the Maṇigrāmam were enjoined to do everything in their power for the good of the church and its land, in accordance with the conditions laid down in the copper-plate document, as long as the earth, the sun and moon endure.[42]

The Six Hundred may have been a group of indigenous Christians, or a local group with some administrative duties. Two groups in Kerala numerically identified were known to be Christians.[43] The identity of the Añjuvaṇṇam and the Maṇigrāmam has caused much speculation in the past. They were probably trading associations. This view should now be increasingly acceptable since the reconstruction of the history of the *aiññūṟṟuvar* or Ayyāvoḷe trading group of Tamil and Kannada areas has now been widely accepted, as

40 *Ibid.*

41 *Ibid.*

42 *Ibid.*

43 *Ibid.*, p. 75.

has also the idea of effective corporate association among traders in the medieval period in South India.[44] Gundert has quoted an old Malayalam song the Payannūr Paṭṭōla which describes these groups and which he translated to read:

> Strong guards ... are now required (to) take the children of the Govatala Cheṭṭi, of Añjuvaṇṇam and of the Maṇigrāmam people, who together with ourselves, are the four (classes of) colonists in the four towns.[45]

Gundert eventually concluded that the Añjuvaṇṇam was an organisation of foreign traders.[46] If the signatures appended to the Sthāṇu Ravi grant were those of members of the Añjuvaṇṇam, then as already pointed out they could have been Arab Jews, or Arab Muslims, Christians or Persians or a mixed group.[47] In a later Ayyāvoḷe guild inscription of the eleventh century found at Vishakhapatnam on the Andhra coast, there is a reference to *añjuvaṇṇattu-vyāpārī*, the merchants of Añjuvaṇṇam.[48] A mid-thirteenth century inscription from Tittandatanapuram, former Ramanathapuram District, not far from the old site of Tondi mentions the Añjuvaṇṇam and Maṇigrāmam and groups of other traders meeting to discuss the levy of cess on articles of trade.[49] A hero stone of A.D. 1427 at Kaikini, South Kanara refers to the *hañjamāna* and from the description and context it is clear they were Muslim, Arab or Persian.[50] *Hañjamāna* may be similar to Añjuvaṇṇam. The location of the *añjuvaṇṇattu-vyāpārī* and of the *hañjamāna* at commercially important points on the coast buttresses the argument that they were outsiders, foreign traders, not as Gopinatha Rao and D.C. Sircar suggest, indigenous group consisting of members of five sub-castes.[51] V. Venkayya believed the Añjuvaṇṇam were traders, a semi-independent group.[52] It has been suggested that the term *hañjamāna* is linked with the Persian *anjumān*, an association.[53] There were other inscriptions found in

44 See M. Abraham, "A Medieval Merchant Guild of South India", *Studies in History*, 4, No. 1, (1982), 1-26.

45 H. Gundert, "Hebrew version of the Jewish Sasanam with translation into English; together with a notice of an ancient Malayalim Poem, called the Song or Legend of Payanur", *MJLS,* 13, No. 31, pt. ii (1844), pp. 11 ff.

46 *Ibid.*

47 See supra f.n. 31.

48 *SII*, X, 651.

49 *ARE*, 598 of 1926-27.

50 *Annual Report on Kannada Research in Bombay Province*, No. 48 (1939-40).

51 *TAS*, II, 9; *EI*, XXXV, pp. 291-92. K.V. Ramesh, *A History of South Kanara* (Dharwar, 1970), pp. 252-253 does not accept D.C. Sircar's opinion equating *hañjamāna* with *pañchavaṇṇa* Sk. *pañchavarṇa*. Dr. Ramesh suggests that they were Arab-Persian merchants. He points out that there were many inscriptions in South Kanara referring to the *hañjamāna*.

52 *EI*, IV, p.294.

53 *ARE* 1926-27, para, 48; *IA*, XLI, pp. 173-76.

Kerala which mention the Añjuvaṇṇam and these are detailed in subsequent portions of this chapter.

When the inscription was first read there were several interpretations of the term Maṇigrāmam. Gundert first believed it was a Christian principality.[54] It was held also that the Maṇigrāmam could have been a group of Manicheans, that is Christians following the heresy of the "School of Manes."[55] Another theory was that the Maṇigrāmam consisted of Christians who were reconverted to Hinduism by Mānikkavāćakar.[56] The Sthāṇu Ravi plates undoubtedly indicate a close connection between the Maṇigrāmam and the Christian community. All other epigraphic evidence, located in other parts of the peninsula, and referred to in subsequent portions of this chapter, shows that it was an association of Hindu traders.[57] In the late nineteenth century Maṇigrāmmakār were still to be found at places in Kerala such as Quilon, Kayamkulam and Kattamaṟṟom (Kadamuttam) and they appeared even then to have had ties with the Syrian church which they were anxious to break.[58] As late as the mid-nineteenth century the Maṇigrāmmakkār at Kayamkulam were obliged to pay fees to the church on the occasion of a marriage.[59] In the early twentieth century they were classed as *śūdra* Hindus in Quilon, but by the mid-twentieth century had achieved the status of Nayars.[60] The Syrian Christian tradition about the Maṇigrāmmakkār is that they were a group who had originally come from the Cōḷa country.[61] The Maṇigrāmakkār were most probably Hindu traders who in Kerala worked in cooperation with the Syrian church. The Sthāṇu Ravi plates suggest the church sponsored and engaged in trade and in particular overseas trade. Evidence of another period suggests the Syrian Christians continued to be involved in overseas trade in the later medieval period. A Chinese source suggests this as also the Mārgam Kaḷi song of the Syrian Christians, chronologically quite inaccurate but containing in it a combination of oral tradition and legends of the community from which useful perspectives are

54 Gundert, "Ancient Documents", pt. I, p. 116, but Gundert later held other opinions about the interpretations of the term Maṇigrāmam.

55 C.M. Agur, *Church History of Travancore* (Madras, 1903), pp. 10-11.

56 *Ibid.*, see also Gundert, "Ancient Documents", p. 121.

57 T.A. Gopinatha Rao, "A Note on Maṇigrāmattār occurring in Tamil Inscriptions", *EI*, XVII, 9, pp. 69-73. See also V. Venkkaya, "Kottayam Plate of Vīra-Rāghava", *EI*, IV, p. 294.

58 L.W. Brown, *The Indian Christians*, p. 77 and T. Whitehouse, *Lingerings of Light in a Dark Land* (London, 1873).

59 *Ibid.* Brown says Whitehouse noted that the Maṇigrāmakkār at Kayamkulam received a cloth from the church on the occasion of a marriage and a funeral. At Quilon apparently at that time there were thirty families of Maṇigrāmakkār whose priest was buried in the same position as the Syrian bishops, not cremated.

60 Brown, *ibid.*

61 *Ibid.* Brown has relied on tradition recorded on palm leaves and published in T.K. Joseph's *Malabar Christians and their Ancient Documents* (Trivandrum, 1929).

obtained.[62] The song includes the suggestion that St. Thomas the apostle after performing many miracles in the Cōḷa country, went to Malacca and China and then returned to Kerala. The Mārgam Kaḷi song links thereby key places on the medieval, maritime trade route, Quilon, the Cōḷa country, Malacca and China, all of which appears to be additional confirmation of the description contained in the *Yüan Shih* of the participation of the Syrian Christians in overseas trade.

Analysis of the copper plates of Sthāṇu Ravi (II) shows that greater honours were granted to Maruvāṇ Sapīr Īśō than in the first record. In the second record it was recognised that he had established the prosperity of the city of Kollam (Quilon) the translation in English being "... Maruvāṇ Sapīr Īśō, who founded the city of Quilon."[63] Since the word translated as city is *nagaram* we may question whether the founding or enlarging of the township is described or the establishment of a successful *nagaram*, an assembly or association of merchants and the organizing of successful commercial enterprise at Quilon. Maruvāṇ Sapīr Īśō was also granted the rights of *pārakkōl* or *pārkkōl* and the *paiñcha-kkaṇḍi* on behalf of the church. The first term has been interpreted by Gopinatha Rao and Gundert as meaning either a staff of honour or a staff signifying entitlement to a "share", or a sceptre (*pārkkōl*). In the earlier inscription *pārakōl* and *paiñcha-kkaṇḍi* had been held by the "governor" of Vēnāḍu. The *paiñcha-kkaṇḍi* may have been a symbol of honour.

62 T.K. Joseph, "The Saint Thomas Traditions of South India", *Bulletin du Comité International des Sciences Historiques*. No. 20 (1933), 563.
W.W. Rockhill, "Notes on the relations and trade and China with the Eastern Archipelago and the coasts of the Indian Ocean during the fourteenth century", *T'oung Pao*, 15, pt. i (1914), 434-435, *Yüan Shih*, 210, 16b-18a, refers to the mission sent by the Chinese to Kollam (A.D. 1282). "At the same time (the head of the) Yeh-li-k'o-wen Wu-tsa-erh-sa-li-ma and Mohammed the head of the Mussulmans and others of the country, having heard of the coming of the Imperial envoy, all came and requested that they be allowed to send yearly presents to the Court. They therefore sent a representative to be received at the audience". *Yüan Shih*, 12,8a, 9b, says the chief of the Christians sent a messenger with gifts to the Yüan emperor, 'a gorget set with different kinds of jewels, and two flacons of drugs,' also in A.D. 1282.The messenger formed part of the official delegation from the kingdom of Kollam. (Rockhill, p. 437). Rockhill's scrupulous scrutiny of the use of the word transliterated 'Yeh-li-k'o-wen' and his conclusion that the word here refers to the St. Thomas Christians is contained in pp. 434-435. Rockhill quotes Duarte Barbosa who says of the Syrian Church at Kollam that it was "endowed by the king of Coulam with the revenues from the pepper, which remain to it to this day". From *A Description of the Coasts of East Africa and Malabar in the Beginning of the Sixteenth Century* by Duarte Barbosa, trans., H.E.J. Stanley, Hakluyt Society, Vol. 35 (London, MDCCCLXVI), p. 162.

63 The analysis in this paragraph and the subsequent paragraph and the quotations of translations of the grant are from *TAS*, II, 9.

Several trading rights were granted to the church in the second grant. These are detailed here.

> The churchmen might collect eight *kāśus* (a kind of coin)during the passage into or out of the jurisdiction of the church (?) of merchandise brought in loads *(vayinam) by land (?) and four kāśus* per boat every time it came in or went out of the harbour (*vediyilum?*).
>
> Customs duty should be levied on all dutiable articles only in their presence and with their cooperation.
>
> The fixing of the prices of these commodities and every other business of the king (perhaps only those pertaining to trade and not his private business) should be done only with the help of the people of the church.
>
> The customs collected day after day should be taken care of by the members of the Añjuvaṇṇam and Maṇigrāmam.

Also it was noted,

> If any complaints arose among the Añjuvaṇṇam and Maṇigrāmam peoples and others the former two would stop the *ulgu* and *tulā-kkūli* on the merchandise that were (sic) exported to the countries beyond the king's realm, and the differences settled amicably between them and their aggressors.

Ulgu has been translated as "sea-customs", an interpretation which another distinguished epigraphist has accepted.[64] Further, it is recorded that the "weighment-charges" were to be made over by Sapīr Īśō to the church.

The most notable feature of the above extracts are the distinct references to incoming and outgoing trade and to trade with foreign countries. No specific mention of commodities is made but here we may infer that pepper was an important commodity. In the mid-fourteenth century John de Marignoli wrote of the "very noble city of India called Quilon where the whole world's pepper is produced."[65] He also says the St. Thomas Christians owned the pepper which was available for sale there and also that they were "masters of the public weighing office."[66] The privilege of weighing and the right to the "weighment charges" given to Maruvāṇ Sapīr Īśō apparently continued to be held by the Syrian Christians for many centuries, but by the time the Portuguese came they no longer held the "seal and the standard weight of the city."[67]

64 K.G. Krishnan, personal communication, 3rd August, 1979.

65 *Cathay and the Way Thither*, trans. and ed., Sir Henry Yule, new edition H. Cordier, Hakluyt Society, ser. II, Vol. 37(London, 1913), pp. 217-218.

66 *Ibid.*, p. 216.

67 *The Commentaries of the Great Afonso Dalboquerque*, trans. and ed., W.de Gray Birch (London, MDCCCLXXV), Vol. I, p. 15,

"When all these things had been settled, the native Christians came to Afonso Dalboquerque and told him that, as he was desirous of confirming to them their ancient customs, they

A full examination of the copper plates of Sthāṇu Ravi permit us to draw some tentative conclusions. We may infer that Mar Sapīr before he came to India had some experience as a merchant, and that it was not unusual for the East Syrian church in India in this period to acquire revenue from trade. The Maṇigrāmam association was probably in existence before the church fathers arrived. The duties assigned to them suggest that they had prior experience of the handling of commerce.The same name Maṇigrāmam it may be noted, may have been used by an association in the early centuries A.D.at Kaveripattinam when the city was well-known for its trade.[68] An area of the recently excavated site of the city known to be occupied in that period is called the Maṇigrāmam by local people even today. In the ninth or tenth century when the Maṇigrāmam emerged as an association in Quilon, it appeared to consist of a group chiefly concerned with foreign trade but the copper plates give the impression that they were overshadowed by the East Syrian church. This was not the case at Takuapa on the Thai-Malaysian peninsula where a fragmentary Tamil inscription of the ninth century was found which Nilakanta Sastri believes belonged to the reign of Pallava Nandivarman III (A.D. 826-50).[69] It referred to a tank protected by the Maṇigrāmam, and to a group of armed warriors, probably militia associated in medieval times with the protection of trade.

E. *The Maṇigrāmam at Takuapa, Thailand*

The establishment of a base of the Maṇigrāmam at Takuapa may be seen as a continuation of old historical links of the Indian subcontinent with Southeast Asia and also as a further indication of the Indian role in maritime trade. Sailors from India appear to have visited from very early times, the isthmus of Kra, the narrow neck of land linking present-day Thailand with Malaysia. The earliest Indian literary allusions to this area of Southeast Asia appear in the *Mahā-niddesa* which refers to a place called Tamali.[70] Tambralinga was a place name used in medieval times to denote a state bordering the Bay of Bandon and it is believed that both Tambralinga and Tamali refer to the same geographical area. The location of the isthmus made it

---

begged him that he would graciously preserve for them another custom, to wit, that the Christians who had management of the church, also should have in their keeping the seal and the standard weight of the city, which privilege the King of Coulão had taken from them for the fault and negligence of one of their number."

68 R. Champakalakshmi, "Archaeology and Tamil Literary Tradition", *Purātattva*, 2 (1975-76), 114.

69 K.A.N. Sastri, "Takuapa and its Tamil Inscription", *JMBRAS*, 22, pt. i (1949), 25-30.

70 Sylvain Lévi, "Ptolémée, le Niddesa et la Bṛhatkathā", *EA*, 2 (1925), 1-2 cited in P. Wheatley, *The Golden Khersonese* (Kuala Lumpur, 1966), p. 181.

important both for seamen from India and for traders coming from the far east. Ships crossing the Gulf of Siam used the northeast monsoon to cross the bay. From India the southwest monsoon was normally used by sailing vessels approaching Southeast Asia. The isthmus provided a halting place for traders from both directions. Goods for exchange could have been off-loaded, stored, or transported across the isthmus. A particularly well-known land route linked Takuapa to the Bay of Bandon.[71] From Ko Kao island, a few miles away from Takuapa, it was possible to travel down the Takuapa river for some distance. Then following a slight elevation the traveller approached the Khirirat river which flowed towards the Bay of Bandon. In this coastal area was located the state of Tambralinga which was probably synonymous with Madamalingam of the Tanjore inscription of Rājēndra Cōḷa I.[72] The Kedah to Patani route was frequently used across the Malaysian peninsula.[73] From present-day lower Burma there seem to have been at least two well-known routes in use in early times connecting Burma with Thailand.

The state of Tambralinga has been defined by Wolters as "associated with the coastal lands around the Bay of Bandon in the narrowing waist of the Malay peninsula."[74] Tambralinga had an early association with Tamil traders and with Takuapa on the opposite coast. We may quote Wolter's definition in full.

> Sometimes it is referred to as the State in the Ligor area. Little is known of its extent north or south. To the south it may have reached towards the State of Langkasuka which scholars tend to locate in the Patani area. To the north it may have extended as far as Jaiya and probably further.[75]

Wolters further notes that in the late medieval period it was known as Nagara Sri Dharmaraja thereby underlying no doubt the importance of the town of this name in the state.[76] Nagar~ Sri Dharmaraja may have been linked with the opposite coast by a route running through the valley of the Trang

71 Wheatley, *op. cit.*, pp. 195-196. S.J. O'Connor, *Hindu Gods of Peninsular Siam* (Ascona, MCMLXXII), pp. 15, 60-62 shows that at Vieng Sra two Cōḷa period statues have been found and that at Jaiya a Cōḷa style Sūrya was found. These constitute some evidence of Tamil penetration of the Takuapa to Bay of Bandon route in the early Cōḷa period as also the Cōḷa period Tamil inscription at Nagara Sri Dharmaraja (G. Coedès, *Recueil des Inscriptions du Siam*, deuxième partie, Bangkok, 1961, pp. 38-40).

72 K.A.N.Sastri, *The Cōḷas*, 2nd rev. ed. rpt. (Madras, 1975), p. 217 and p. 242, f.n. 126; Wheatley, *op. cit.*, p. 201.

73 Wheatley, *op. cit.*, p. 195; A.W. Hamilton, "The Old Kedah-Pattani Trade Route", *JSBRAS*, 86 (1922), 389-392; W.E. Maxwell, "Journey on Foot to the Patani Frontier in 1876", *JSBRAS*, 9 (1882), 1-67.

74 O.W. Wolters, "Tāmbraliṅga", *BSOAS*, 21, pt. iii (1958), 587.

75 *Ibid.*

76 *Ibid.*, p. 588.

river. There is early evidence of Hindu influence in Nagara Sri Dharmaraja and in Jaiya. A Viṣṇu image from Jaiya has been dated "not later than 400 A.D."[77] Two Viṣṇu images from Nagara Sri Dharmaraja with close affinities both to the Jaiya image and with an image from Oc-Eo have been dated the fifth century.[78] Stylistically it is believed these images derive from the Kuṣāna style of Mathura as transmitted through the sculptural tradition of Nagarjunakonda.[79] An inscription from the Malaysian peninsula further south of Nagara Sri Dharmaraja which may be of the fourth or fifth century further confirms the spread of Indian influence in this area in this period, probably as the result of trading contacts.[80] A single line inscription from Nagara Sri Dharmaraja of the sixth century or earlier has been noted by Lamb and de Casparis. The latter read in it a reference to Siva.[81] A tentative but more complete reading of the inscription offered by K.G. Krishnan is

Tamarāyā / da / gēsvarah,

or the Siva of Tamarāyā.[82] The reading confirms de Casparis' suggestion and also links Saivite worship with Nagara Sri Dharmaraja in the fifth to the sixth century.

The Takuapa inscription of the Maṇigrāmam was found east of the town in association with a group of stone sculptures commonly called the Pra Narai group. It is held that both the statues and the inscription probably were located earlier in a shrine across the river. The inscription it has already been pointed out belongs to the ninth century. The Pra Narai group, it is most likely, belongs to the same or a slightly earlier period and may have been transported from India or made locally by Indian sculptors.[83] Convincing analysis has shown that it was not the work of local artists. Both the statues and the inscription point to the existence of a Hindu colony at Takuapa. The Tamil traders who came to Takuapa in Pallava times included some armed soldiers since the inscription speaks of protection extended to a tank. The colony may have been founded by this group, or may have been in existence earlier.

At Ko Kao island at the mouth of the Takuapa river sizeable ceramic and glass desposits and beads have been found. Some of them may have come from West Asia and the rest from China and possibly some from India.[84]

77 O'Connor, *Hindu Gods*, p. 39.

78 *Ibid.*

79 *Ibid.*

80 B.Ch. Chhabra, "Expansion of Indo-Aryan Culture During Pallava Rule as Evidenced by Inscriptions", *JASB*, Letters, 1 (1935), 16-20.

81 A. Lamb, "Kedah and Takuapa: Some Tentative Historical Conclusions", *FMJ*,6 (1961), 70.

82 K.G. Krishnan, personal communication, 11 March 1983. Tamarāyā = Dharmaraja.

83 O'Connor, *Hindu Gods*, p. 54.

84 A. Lamb, "Takuapa: The Probable Site of a Pre-Malaccan Entrepôt in the Malay Peninsula", *Malayan and Indonesian Studies*, John Bastin and R.Roolvink, eds. (Oxford, 1964), p. 82.

Many of the sherds of Chinese origin belong, it is believed, to the period of the T'ang dynasty.[85] Undoubtedly these finds indicate that the Takuapa area was used by the traders dealing in merchandise from both ends of the maritime route, China and West Asia. In the ninth century both Ko Kao island and the port of Mantai (Mannar) in northern Sri Lanka were in use for similar entrepôt trade.[86] The Quilon inscription of the Maṇigrāmam may be about the same date as the Takuapa inscription or may belong to the second half of the ninth or at the latest the early tenth century. The Quilon inscription and the Takuapa inscription show that the Maṇigrāmam traders had a specific interest in overseas trade.

At Quilon, based on the information given in the inscription, a well defined local infrastructure existed capable of dealing with overseas trade. Warehousing, protection, and the regulation of levies and taxes was prescribed in an agreement made between the foreign traders and the Maṇigrāmam and the king. The role of the Maṇigrāmam in this respect was clearly demarcated. At Quilon the Maṇigrāmam received their mandate from the king. There is nothing in the Takuapa inscription to suggest a similar relationship between the Maṇigrāmam and local authority at the isthmus of Kra. At Takuapa on the other hand the inscription with its invocation of the Pallava king's title suggests the Maṇigrāmam functioned here independently of local authority. There is no indication of sanction from local chiefs. The Takuapa Maṇigrāmam base probably was an autonomous coastal settlement.[87] It is possible that the isthmian area at that time did not support organised local authority capable of negotiating with a group of foreign traders. J.C. Van Leur has postulated that many of the traders from the Indian subcontinent in Southeast Asia were *populo minuto*, pedlars carrying wares with them.[88] This assessment does not suggest the existence of organised trade and the Quilon and the Takuapa inscriptions clearly indicate that the conduct of trade was effectively organised. At Takuapa the Maṇigrāmam provided their own militia for protection. While it is possible to envisage that local distribution of wares was effected by itinerant salesmen, and at Quilon,

85 H.G. Quaritch Wales, "A Newly Explored Route of Indian Cultural Expansion", *IAL*, 9, No. 1 (1935), 10. R.L. Hobson identified the pieces for Quaritch Wales as belonging to the T'ang dynasty though one piece, he believed, was earlier. Lamb, *ibid.*, had the sherds examined by Basil Grey and Pinder Wilson who identified them as belonging to the period of the T'ang. The West Asian sherds they believed might belong to the eighth or ninth century. O'Connor, *Hindu Gods*, p. 50, seems to accept Tom Harrisson's identification of sherds from the same site as being partly T'ang and partly Sung but Harrisson possessed no special expertise on the subject.

86 Excavations at Mantai, 1980, Preliminary Report of the Field Director, Martha Prickett, unpublished.

87 F.H. Van Naerssen, *Orientalia Neerlandica* (Leiden, 1948), cited in Wheatley, *The Golden Khersonese*, p. 187.

88 See J.C. van Leur, *Indonesian Trade and Society, Essays in Asian Social and Economic History* (The Hague, 1955), pp. 133, 135-7, 197-200.

there is some suggestion that imported wares were locally distributed, there is no indication that this was so at Takuapa. The role of the Maṇigrāmam at Takuapa may have consisted partly of exchanges with foreign traders and partly of the collection of local produce, aromatics perhaps which moved into the region to meet the demands of traders. The area was known for its production of tin and Wong Lin Ken believes that as early as the fifth century, there is evidence that Indians working in the region exported this tin.[89] Based on the evidence of the Quilon inscription we may speculate that the regulation of the exchange of wares, payment for local produce, and the onward consignment of goods may have been handled for the Indian trader by groups such as the Maṇigrāmam.

F. *The Maṇigrāmam in South India: The Tenth, Eleventh and Twelfth Centuries*

Tracing the history of the Maṇigrāmam association further it may be noticed that in the South Indian peninsula four brief tenth century inscriptions of the Maṇigrāmam have been found. These are located at Ramantali in the Chirakkal taluk of the former Malabar District, at Kuttallam in the Tenkasi taluk of Tirunelveli District, at Srinivasanallur in the Musiri taluk of Tiruchchirappalli District and Tiruvellarai in the Tiruchchirappalli taluk of the same district.[90] Of these the Ramantali and Kuttalam inscriptions belong to the early tenth century. The others are probably later. The location of the inscriptions shows that the members of the Maṇigrāmam did not function exclusively at coastal sites such as Quilon or Takuapa but also at townships in the interior of the peninsula. The recording of endowments to temples was the purpose of these inscriptions and there is otherwise little to be gleaned from them.

At Talakkad in the Mukundapuram taluk of the former Cochin State (present-day Kerala) a long inscription was found in which the Maṇigrāmam was mentioned.[91] The inscription consists of two sections which may have been inscribed at different times. The first portion of the inscription could belong to the ninth or early tenth century on paleographic grounds but the contents suggest an eleventh century date. The second half of the inscription was inscribed in the first half of the eleventh century. Section one of the inscription describes the founding of a market. The *ūrār* or responsible citizens of the village defined the boundary of the market area: "...west of the

89 Wong Lin Ken, "The Malayan Tin Industry", in K.B. Tregonning ed., *Papers on Malayan History* (Singapore, 1962), p. 10.

90 *ARE* 474 of 1926; *ARE* 439 of 1917 (*SII*, XIX, 417); *ARE* 597 of 1904 (*SII*, XIII, 26); *ARE* 519 of 1905 (*SII*, XIII, 28).

91 *ARE* 358 of 1927. I am grateful to Dr. K.V. Ramesh, Mysore for his assistance in the translation of the inscription from the estampage.

boundary of Sirupalli to the north of the big banyan tree to the east of Kalapalli and to the south of the lands belonging to the *dēvar* of Kilattirukoyil". Within this area the merchants were permitted to put up shops. The *ūrār* who may also have been members of the assembly of the village levied tax in kind on the stalls, but gave the merchants a free hand in running the market. The second portion of the inscription mentions two members of the Maṇigrāmam, who were given the right to set up shops in the market and were exempted from certain specific taxes. The taxes which irrespective all the merchants had to pay include *ulgu*, the tax on goods coming in by sea. It was also stated in the inscription that local people were free to buy in the market. Some conclusions of interest may be drawn from this inscription. The Maṇigrāmam merchants enjoyed a special position as compared to the other merchants. Goods from outside came into the locality and there was a local demand for these goods. There is no hint here in the eleventh century of self-sufficient isolated village communities and of a subsistence economy. On the other hand the movement of trade is indicated as well as the opening up of village communities to itinerant traders. There was buying capacity and a market in rural areas for goods other than those produced locally including overseas wares. The Talakkad inscription provides a useful insight into the relationships established between a village community and local and itinerant merchants on the west coast of South India in the eleventh century.

Another eleventh century inscription in which the Maṇigrāmam is mentioned describes the donation made to a temple by a merchant who belonged to the Maṇigrāmam of Kodumbalur.[92] The word Maṇigrāmam in this inscription is used to describe a locality within the famous medieval town of Kodumbalur which was called Maṇigrāmam. Kodumbalur is located in the Pudukkottai tracts about equidistant between Madurai and Thanjavur, the Pāṇḍyan and Cōḷa capitals. This particular inscription is found at the entrance of the Sukhavanesvara temple, Salem and it was this temple which was the recipient of the donation. In chronological order the next inscription to be found in which the Maṇigrāmam is mentioned is a twelfth century inscription from Thanjavur district in which a member of the Maṇigrāmam from the Pāṇḍyan area gave a donation to a temple near Kumbakoṇam.[93] One other inscription from the Tamil country may be noted. It is a twelfth century inscription found in Tiruchchirappalli District in which there is a reference again to the Maṇigrāmam of Kodumbalur.[94]

F. *The Thirteenth Century: Overseas Trade again Important*

We may consider next the well-known copper plate inscription in the

92 *SII*, IV, 147.

93 *ARE* 46 of 1930-31.

94 *ARE* 288 of 1964-65.

possession of the Syrian Christian church at Kottayam, the Kottayam plate of Vīra-Rāghava which is now considered, based on the contents of the inscription, to belong to the thirteenth century.[95] Both earlier and later dates have been assigned to it by epigraphists but the thirteenth century date suggested by the latest scholar to study the grant seems the most sober assessment of its age.[96] It is an inscription describing rights granted to the merchant, Ravikoṟṟan of Maṇigrāmam. Ravikoṟṟan was given rights in the port of Kodungallur (Cranganore) on the west coast of the peninsula. Kodungallur is generally identified with Muziris which was an important port in the early centuries A.D. at the time of the Roman trade. The port had a long association with traders coming from across the Arabian Sea. In the twelfth century, the letters of Jewish merchants refer to the export from two other ports on the west coast, Mangalore and a port south of Cannanore, of iron, cardamom, pepper, betel nuts, ginger, cubebs, coir, coconut and aloeswood.[97] The trade referred to in the Jewish letters was handled by the Jews, but on two specific occasions the letters also referred to ships owned by Indians from the west coast.[98] A similar trade may have been conducted from Cranganore in the thirteenth century when the charter was granted to Ravikoṟṟan. There is no indication that Ravikoṟṟan was a Jew. The inscription described him as "lord of the city". There is one phrase in the inscription which may be interpreted as the grant of certain export rights to the Maṇigrāmam. Monopoly rights were granted as well as a commission on many commodities including musk, salt and sugar. Unfortunately, the other commodities are not named. The Maṇigrāmam was also given the right to the customs which could be levied on goods which arrived at the mouth of the river and were then transported to the interior. If one puts together all the inscriptions from the west coast of South India on the Maṇigrāmam and overseas trade then the inscriptions of Sthāṇu Ravi of the ninth to tenth century come first followed by the eleventh century Talakkad inscription of the former Cochin State in which there is a definite reference to goods coming by sea, and to this we may add the Kottayam plate of Vīra-Rāghava of the thirteenth century, the inscription just examined which deals with trade at the port of Kodungallur. In the Sthāṇu Ravi inscription and the Vīra-Rāghava inscription the right to handle foreign trade was formally granted by the king. At Talakkad, the arrangements were worked out betwen the *ūrār* and the Maṇigrāmam traders. At both Quilon and Kodungallur the

95 *EI*, IV, 41. Also Gundert, "Ancient Documents", p. 118.

96 Elamkulam Kunjan Pillai, *Studies in Kerala History* (Kottayam, 1970), p. 391. The date suggested is c. A.D. 1225.

97 S.D. Gotein, *Letters of Medieval Jewish Traders* (Princeton, 1973), p. 188, and "From Aden to India", Specimens of the Correspondence of India Traders in the Twelfth Century", *JESHO*, 23, pt. i and ii (April, 1980), 43-66.

98 *Ibid*.

incoming foreign trade was considered to have brought great prosperity to the city.

In the context of west coast overseas trade the Cochin plates of Bhāskara Ravivarman may next be briefly examined since in them we find the grant of trading rights to the Añjuvaṇṇam at Kodungallur in the eleventh century most probably around A.D. 1016.[99] The copper plate grant is now in the possession of the Jews of Cochin and the donee named Issuppu Irappān may have been a Jew. The Hebrew signatures to the Sthāṇu Ravi plates showed, as stated earlier, that Arab Jews may have been among the trading groups at Quilon in the ninth to tenth centuries. This would explain why the script used for some of the signatures in the Quilon inscriptions was Hebrew while the names were largely those used today exclusively by Muslims. All other references to the Añjuvaṇṇam merchants elsewhere in India indicate that they were Arab Muslim traders. The Quilon inscription shows that the foreigners involved were a mixed group of Christians, Arab Muslims possibly Arab Jews and Zoroastrians. It is likely that the foreigners to whom the Cochin grant was made may also have been of mixed origin and we may speculate further that the group included a large number of Jews led by the Jew Issuppu Irappān. The grant given to Issuppu Irappān included certain personal honours which were largely identical with those granted to Ravikoṛṛan in the thirteenth century. In the trading rights given to Issuppu Irappān or Joseph Rabbān may be noted a possible grant of tolls on elephants and horses. The inscription is not quite clear on this point but if this interpretation is correct, then at Kodungallur the Añjuvaṇṇam may have had something to do with the incoming horse trade. Among those ratifying the grant were the chieftains of Ērānāḍu and Vaḷḷuvanāḍu whose descendants also ratified the grant made to the Maṇigrāmam in Vīra-Rāghava's time.

In the Tamil country in the thirteenth century, and the first decade of the fourteenth century, the Maṇigrāmam was associated with the distribution of commodities of internal and overseas trade. Their base, judging by the content of the inscriptions in which they are mentioned, was at Kodumbalur in the present District of Pudukkoṭṭai. Dated the early thirteenth century an inscription found in the Rajarajacolisvaramudaiyar temple at Koilpatti, Kulittalai taluk, Tiruchchirappalli District mentioned the Maṇigrāmam of Kodumbalur.[100] Earlier inscriptions, one of the eleventh and the other of the twelfth centuries also contained references to the Maṇigrāmam of Kodumbalur.[101] A major inscription of the thirteenth century found at Piranmalai on the borders of the present Pudukkottai District was issued by the

99 *EI*, III, 11. See also Gundert, "Ancient Documents".

100 *ARE* 283 of 1964-65.

101 *SII*, IV, 147; *ARE* 288 of 1964-65.

Ayyāvoḷe guild and the *citramēḷi* association and in this also the Maṇigrāmam of Kodumbalur was mentioned.[102] The Piranmalai inscription shows the merchants of the Maṇigrāmam of Kodumbalur as one of the many groups which met to discuss the taxes to be levied on the goods passing through the area, for the benefit of temples. In the long list of commodities enumerated the commodities of overseas trade, both exports and imports, were significantly present. These included pepper, myrobalans, iron, cotton, cotton yarn, thick and fine cotton fabric, wax, honey, sandalwood, aloeswood, silk, rose water, yak's tail, civet, horses and elephants.[103] The inscription was composed by a member of the association identified as *kudirai-ceṭṭi* or horse trader.

Another important inscription of the thirteenth century A.D. 1269 was found at Tittandatanapuram, Tiruvadanai taluk, former Ramanathapuram District. Here the members of the Maṇigrāmam were found in collaboration with the Kaikkōḷas who in the thirteenth century had much to do with cotton weaving, the Valañjiyar (or merchants) of southern Sri Lanka, and the Añjuvaṇṇam.[104] It is possible that one of the commodities they exported from this town was cotton fabric. The text of the inscription indicates this possibility. Tittandatanapuram was not far from the port of Tondi. Finally one notes the early fourteenth century inscription found in the Rajarajacolisvaramudaiyar temple, Koilpatti.[105] Here again the Maṇigrāmam of Kodumbalur is mentioned with the Ayyāvoḷe and the *citramēḷi*. The estampage of the inscription enumerates all the commodities of overseas trade which passed through this little town and on which taxes were levied for the benefit of a temple. Kodumbalur was obviously in the thirteenth and early fourteenth centuries a major centre of the Maṇigrāmam.

Archaeological search for evidence of foreign trade, of export and import in medieval times in South India has so far yielded very few results. One reason for this may be that Chinese ceramics and West Asian ware were not imported in large quantities into South India. The household use of china is associated in India more with the Muslims in the North than with the Hindus in the South.[106] Therefore sherds of these easily identifiable wares are few in

102 *SII*, VIII, 442.

103 See Abraham, "A Medieval Merchant Guild". These commodities may be compared with those listed in O. Wheatley, "Geographical Notes on some Commodities involved in Sung Maritime Trade", *JMBRAS*, 32, pt. ii (June, 1959), 5-140.

104 *ARE* 598 of 1926-27.

105 *ARE* 286 of 1964-65. *ARE* 285 of 1964-65 also probably of about the same date mentions the Maṇigrāmam of Kodumbalur.

106 Basil Gray, "The Export of Chinese Porcelain to India", *TOCS*, 36 (1964-65, 65-66), 31. On the export of porcelain to India he remarks," It seems likely that the Chinese trade with India catered for the Moslem ruling class in spite of the fact that the political control of the ports on the Malabar coast was in Hindu hands".

South India, whereas they are found in sizeable quantities in the Maldives and in northern Sri Lanka.[107] At Takuapa and at Mantai it is the presence of these sherds which enables one to draw conclusions about the entrepôt functions of these coastal sites. Structural evidence of port facilities do not exist at Takuapa and one awaits the results of the Mantai (Mannar) excavations. The excavation at Kaveripattinam is only a small beginning in South India and much yet remains to be done at coastal sites. The commodities of maritime trade in this period other than ceramic ware were perishable of which one does not expect to find traces. Foreign coins constitute evidence of the presence of foreign goods and of foreigners, but these disappear fast on monsoon-swept beaches though some have been found on the Coromandel coast.[108] The real unshakeable evidence of foreign trade though is the inscriptions on stone which lists the taxes on foreign goods and mentions the merchant associations which handle this trade. This reconstruction of the history of the Maṇigrāmam, and the evidence which points to the role of Indian merchants in medieval Asian maritime commerce becomes then part of the growing body of research on this wide-ranging trade. By the thirteenth century, as just shown, many important commodities were included in this trade. In the two most important inscriptions of the Maṇigrāmam in the thirteenth and early fourteenth centuries, there is also indication of a growing internal trade in basic commodities including agricultural produce.[109]

At Quilon, there is clear evidence of a religious group directing commercial enterprise. From the Sthāṇu Ravi inscription one deduces that the lands adjacent to the church were being used partly as a trading settlement, for which purpose a contract was made with the rulers of this coastal area. Both at Quilon and at Kodungallur, the inscriptions show that in the popular mind urban growth was linked to the growth of commerce. Maruvāṇ Sapīr Īśō was said to have "founded the city of Kollam." The so called "Kollam era," it is very likely, dates from the time of the arrival of this immigrant group. Maruvāṇ Sapīr Īśō was also granted great personal honours. These appear to have been granted to him for his services to the urban settlement of Kollam (Quilon).[110] In the thirteenth century at Kodungallur the head of the Maṇigrāmam was described as "lord of the city", again popular recognition of the importance of commerce to urban development.[111] A. Appadorai, using as Prof. Burton Stein has pointed out, evidence of the twelfth and thirteenth centuries and some foreign descriptions of Vijayanagar times has

107 J. Carswell, "China and Islam, A Survey of the Coast of India and Ceylon"; *TOCS*, 42 (1977-78), 25-68, and J. Carswell, "China and Islam in the Maldive Islands", *TOCS*, 41 (1975-76, 1976-77), 121-198.

108 Sir W. Elliot, *Coins of Southern India* (Varanasi, 1970 rpt.), p. 35.

109 *SII*, VII, 442; *ARE* 286 of 1964-65 (based on estampage).

110 *TAS*, II, pp. 64, 76.

111 *EI*, IV, 41.

said; "... a temple has often been made the nucleus around which a town in course of time grew."[112] Stein connects urban growth in the same period in Tamil areas both with increased trade and the "increased tempo of temple building."[113] The evidence for Quilon differs in that it comes from the west coast and belongs to the ninth or early tenth century. One notes also that it was primarily the commercial importance of the location of Quilon which made it possible for the Christian church and associated groups to develop trade. At Kodungallur in the thirteenth century and also on the west coast incoming overseas trade and exports appear to have been of importance and possibly contributed decisively to urban growth.

There are some scattered indications of the social groups from which these traders were drawn. The Sthāṇu Ravi plates suggest that in the ninth or tenth century, the Maṇigrāmam was associated with an elite ruling urban group at Quilon. The service castes in the trading colony at Quilon, the Iḷavar, the washermen, the carpenters, even the cultivating Veḷḷāḷars, appear in the inscription to have been of lower status than the members of the Maṇigrāmam and the Añjuvannam.[114] The thirteenth century Kottayam plate of Vīra-Rāghava clearly ascribed the status of a merchant prince to Ravikoṟṟan.[115] Other inscriptions such as the eleventh century Talakkad inscription showed members of the Maṇigrāmam to have been just shopkeepers, owners of booths in a market place, and also itinerant traders.[116] The thirteenth century east coast Tamil language inscriptions depicted the members of the Maṇigrāmam as traders transporting merchandise along major trade highways and in definite subordination to their patrons at that time, the Ayyāvoḷe *aiññūṟṟuvar* merchants.[117] It would appear then that traders belonging to widely disparate social groups had the right to describe themselves as members of the Maṇigrāmam. We may refer once more to the observation already made that in the early twentieth century the descendants of members of the Maṇigrāmam in Kerala were *śūdra* Hindus but had later become Nayars, evidence that in modern times certainly the social and ritual status of these traders was in a state of flux and that social mobility was possible.[118]

112 A. Appadorai, *Economic Conditions in Southern India, 1000-1500 A.D.*, Vol. 1 (Madras, 1936), pp. 338 ff, cited in Burton Stein, *Peasant State and Society in Medieval South India* (Delhi, 1980), p. 248.

113 Stein, *PSSMSI*, p. 252.

114 *TAS*, II, 9.

115 *EI*, IV, 41.

116 *ARE* 358 of 1927.

117 *SII*, VIII, 442; *ARE* 286 of 1964-65.

118 See supra f.n. 62.

Chapter II

The History of the Ayyāvoḷe Association

A. *The Origin and Early Beginnings*

While the first and many subsequent inscriptional notices of the Maṇigrāmam guild were located at coastal sites, the earliest inscription referring to the merchant guild of the five hundred *svāmis* of Ayyāvoḷe is found in the central Deccan plateau at Aihole which is in the present-day Hungund taluk of Bijapur District. Aihole is situated in the *doāb* formed by the Krishna and the Tungabhadra, on the banks of the Malprabha river which is itself a tributary of the Krishna. Manyakheda (Malkhed) associated with the Rāṣṭrakūṭas lay to the north of Aihole as also Kalyana, capital of the later Caḷukyas. The early Caḷukyan sites of Badami, Vikramapura and Patadkal were close by. It has been pointed out that Aihole, Badami and Patadkal formed a "triangular area" and that it was within this territory, the heartland of the early Caḷukyas that "the temples of the Caḷukyas were built in the sixth, seventh and eight centuries."[1] The Aihole inscriptions which refer to the merchant guild Ayyāvoḷe, range chronologically from the eighth century to the early twelfth century.[2] They first appear therefore in about the same period as the early Maṇigrāmam inscriptions. Within the geographical area in which Aihole is situated, the Raichur *doāb*, there are many other known inscriptions referring to the activity of the guild. These inscriptions begin about the early eleventh century and continue till the mid-thirteenth century.[3]

[1] R.S. Gupte, *The Art and Architecture of Aihole* (Bombay, 1967), p.2.

[2] *IA*, VIII, LIX, p. 287, 8th or 9th century A.D;
KR 94 of 1941-42, c. 8th century;
KR 24 of 1952-53, A.D. 1102-3;
KR 97 of 1941-42, A.D. 1120.

In Appendix A many of the other inscriptions relating to Ayyāvoḷe are listed, with approximate dating where possible and the location of the inscriptions. Over 150 inscriptions have been included, and the conclusions drawn in this study are based primarily on epigraphic sources. It is believed there are no Kannada literary references to this guild. I am indebted to Prof. S. Settar for this opinion.

[3] Some of these are: A.D. 1000, Chikodi taluk, Belgaum District, *KI*, IV, 55;
A.D. 1074, Hadagalli taluk, Bellary District, *SII*, IX, 139;
A.D. 1096-7, Badami taluk, Kaladgi District, *IA*, VI, XXXII;

Aihole was also known as Ayyāvoḷe, Āryapura and Ahichchatra and these names are frequently used in the guild inscriptions. In one particular inscription of the mid-twelfth century the members of the guild are described as *Ahichchatra vinirggatarum*, i.e. those coming from Ahichchatra.[4] In another inscription of the same period Ahichchatra and Ayyāvoḷe are considered identical.[5] Aihole, in the mystique which came to be associated with the guild was considered the parent city of this corporate association. The members of the guild are described in inscriptions in phrases such as "ornaments on the brow of that great lady, the city of Ahichchatra"[6] or "the Five Hundred Svāmis of the Illustrious town of Ayyāvoḷe,"[7] and so on. There are other and frequent allusions in guild inscriptions of both Kannada and Tamil-speaking areas to the link between the guild and its birthplace, the great town of Aihole.[8]

From a close and meticulous examination of the epigraphs in which the guild is mentioned and which are found in Aihole, one obtains some idea of what the origins of this corporation were. The Aihole Lad Khan temple epigraph of the eighth or ninth century is considered to contain the first mention of this merchant guild. The inscription is a record of a charitable grant and the key phrase in it transliterated reads, "*Āryajana-samudāy ōdita-var Āryapura adisthānada Sri mahāchāturvidya samudāyam ai-nūruvarkam*...."[9] This has been translated, "... the five hundred (who constituted) the great body of Chaturvēdis of the excellent capital of Āryapura which arose from a collection of worthy people."[10] It will be noticed that these phrases give no indication that the Five Hundred *Caturvēdis* formed a merchant guild, but a leading Kannada scholar and historian has pointed out

A.D. 1099, Ron taluk, Dharwad District, Bombay-Karnatak I, pt.ii, 148;
about mid-twelfth century, Gabbur, Raichur District, *ARE* 13 of 1960-61;
A.D. 1181, Jamkhandi taluk, Bijapur District, *KI*, V, 98;
A.D. 1196, Mundargi taluk, Dharwad District, *SII*, XV, 211;
A.D. 1220, Hungund taluk, Bijapur District, *SII*, XV, 164.

[4] *EI*, XIX, 4B, A.D. 1144.

[5] In *EI*, XIX, 4A, A.D. 1135, Ahichchatra and Ayyāvoḷe are deemed to be the same. "*Ahichchatram = enisuv = Ayyāvoḷe.*" P.B. Desai, "Trade Guilds in Karnataka and their Jaina Associations," *Voice of Ahimsa* (1959), has commented on these phrases. The tradition of emigrants from Ahichchatra who are Brahmans is a recurring theme in Karnataka (e.g. *EC*, VI, Sk. 186) and the linking of Ayyāvoḷe with Ahichchatra in guild *praśastis* is therefore a possible indication of the presence of Brahmans in Aivalli associated with this guild.

[6] *EI*, XIX, 3, A.D. 1250, "*Ahichchāl ttrāl-purīlalāna-lalāta-tilakarum.*"

[7] Desai, Adki no. 11.

[8] *EC*, IV(new), Chamrajnagar 146, 11th century;
EI, XIX, 3, A.D. 1250;
SII, VIII, 442, 13th century.

[9] *IA*, VIII, LIX.

[10] *Ibid.*

that an inscription dated A.D. 733-47 also from Aihole, has phrases which show that the *Mahājanas* of Aihole and the *nagara* or commercial guild of the town were connected. Here the phrase used is "*Rāja Srāvitam Mahājanamu Naka (ga) ra Srāvitam.*"[11] The term *Mahājanas* was frequently used to describe Brahmans and in the Aihole epigra[illegible]s appears as a description of a group administering the *agrahāra*. That Aihole already contained an *agrahāra* is clearly suggested in the description in the Lad Khan temple epigraph of the Five Hundred *Caturvēdis* of Āryapura. G.R. Kuppuswamy believes that in joint-tenure *agrahāras* the *Mahājana* group was purely Brahman.[12] K.G. Kundankar points out that *Mahājanas* were not inevitably Brahman since they were also appointed in non-*brahmadeya* villages.[13] But in Aihole, in all probability they were Brahmans since the same numerical group 500 was earlier used to describe the *Caturvēdis*. It is held that collaboration between *Mahājanas* and corporate groups such as the *nagara* as well as others holding official status was common even though the primary responsibility for the administration of the *agrahāra* lay with the *Mahājanas* alone.[14]

The epigraphs have shown so far that a group of *Mahājanas* and a *nagara* or town guild were both contemporaneously contained in Aihole and that Aihole also had an *agrahāra*. Another inscription of the eighth century found on a beam of the Gaudaragudi temple at Aihole, also refers to "The great Chaturvēdis — the 500 *Mahājanas* of Āryapura, the eight *nagara (nakara)s*, and 120 *Ūrāḷis*." joining together to make a grant to the goddess Durgābhagavatī who later emerges as one of the patron deities of the Ayyāvoḷe guild.[15] This is some further evidence of collaboration between *Mahājanas* and local groups in Aihole though as yet no proof has emerged that the 500 *Mahājanas* were identical with the corporate group Ayyāvoḷe. Unmistakeable evidence that the two groups identified with each other appears in an epigraph of the first quarter of the twelfth century located on the walls of the Charantigudi temple at Aihole. This inscription is a record of a donation by

[11] G.S. Dikshit, "The guild of Ayyāvoḷe", unpublished paper, says: "secondly in an inscription assigned to the period 733-47 A.D. we have a reference to the *Nagaras* in the expression *Rāja Srāvitam Mahājanamu Naka(ga)ra Srāvitam*. This is one of the earliest references to the *Mahājanas* as well as to the *Nagara* guild of Aihole". (The inscription number is omitted).

[12] G.R. Kuppuswamy, "The Role of the Mahājanas in Medieval Karnataka," *JKU*, Social Sciences, 6 (1970), 61-66.

[13] K.G. Kundankar, *Inscriptions in Northern Karnataka and Kolhapur* (Kolhapur, 1939), cited by Dr. Kuppuswamy.

[14] S.L. Shanthakumari, "Agrahāras in Ancient Karnataka", Diss. Karnatak Univ., 1970.

[15] Transliteration and translation courtesy, Prof. Ritti, "*Śri-mad-Āryapura-da śri-mahāchaturvidya samudāyav-aynūṟu Mahājanamu entunnagaramu nura ippadinvaru ūrāḷigalu....*" *KR* 94 of 1941-42 c. 8th century. Prof. G.S. Dikshit in "Guild of Ayyāvoḷe", unpublished paper, refers, to the same inscription and points out the connection between Durgābhagavatī and the Ayyāvoḷe group.

the Jaina Kēsavaseṭṭi who was "like the son of the Five Hundred Svāmis of Ayyāvoḷe". The phrase used for describing Aihole and the city and the guild is "*Śriman-mahāgrahārav ayyāvoḷe ayṇūrvvar-svāmigala.*"[16] The Kannada phrases indicate that Aihole was by then a *mahāgrahāra* to which the five hundred *svāmis* belonged. In the Ayyāvoḷe merchant guild inscription the phrase 500 *svāmis* was used frequently and the numerical description was always the same as was used to describe the *Mahājanas.*[17] One concludes that the terms *Mahājanas* of Ayyāvoḷe (Aivalli, Aihole) and the 500 *svāmis* were used in these epigraphs to indicate the same group. A.M. Annigeri arrived at the same conclusion when he said that "Aihole was an *agrahāra* consisting of 500 *Mahājanas* who were also described as 500 *Svāmis*. That constituted the Chaturvēdi Samaya."[18] The Lad Khan inscription goes back to the eighth or ninth century. The Charantigudi inscription was recorded in the early twelfth century. Therefore one deduces further that Aihole remained an *agrahāra* at least throughout this period and that it was most likely that the guild Ayyāvoḷe 500 was founded by a group of Brahman *Mahājanas* from Aihole.

Several *agrahāras* such as Lakkundi and Kodanganur were active commercial centres and the establishment of the corporate, commercial organisation, the 500 *svāmis* of Ayyāvoḷe in an *agrahāra* was not unusual.[19] While medieval *agrahāras* in Karnataka were intended to function as Brahman establishments supporting religious and educational foundations many other groups also lived in the *agrahāra* such as craftsmen, *seṭṭis* and cultivators who may have had land in the *agrahāra* rented out to them.[20] Buddhist and Jaina temples were supported by *agrahāras*, such as for example the Buddhist *vihāra* at Hombal and the Jaina Charantigudi at Aihole.[21] The presence of Jains and Buddhists and the establishment of commerce in an *agrahāra* in Karnataka was not uncommon. One may therefore visualise the founding of the Ayyāvoḷe group as the decision of a group of *Mahājanas* of the *mahāgrahāra* at Aihole, to institutionalise control of existing commerce in that

[16] *KR* 97 of 1941-42, *BK* no. 148 A.D. 1120.

[17] *SII*, XI, pt. ii, *BK* no. 148, A.D. 1099; *EI*, XIX, p. 37, A.D. 1142;
ARE 13 of 1960-61, mid-twelfth century.

[18] *KI*, IV, pp. 122-23.

[19] *EC*, XI, Davangere 149, A.D. 1113;
EI, XV, 24, A.D. 1098.

[20] *SII*, XV, no. 73, Cultivators.
BK, II, no. 137, *Seṭṭis* and *Telligas*.
EC, VII, Sk. 75, Fishermen.
BK, I, II, no. 153, Goldsmiths.
These examples have been cited by D. Shanthakumari, *op. cit.*, pp. 62-63.

[21] e.g. *IA*, X, CXVI, c. A.D. 1096 and *BK*, I, II, 144, Buddhist *vihāra* at Hombal.
KR 97 of 1941-42, A.D. 1120, Charantigudi at Aivalli.

region. If that was so, then the formation of the corporate group Ayyāvoḷe probably took place in the eighth century towards the close of the period of the Cāḷukyas of Badami or in the opening years of the Rāṣṭrakūṭa rule.

In chronological sequence, after the first two Aihole epigraphs in which the Ayyâvoḷe guild is mentioned were recorded, the next known epigraphic mention of this guild appeared in Munasandal, in the Tirumayam taluk of Pudukkottai.[22] This is the area of modern-day Tamil Nadu which is south of the Vellar river and, one notes, far from the Raichur *doāb*. From Munasandal the coast is easily accessible. Present-day Pudukkottai District is bordered by the modern Madurai, Tiruchchirappalli and Ramanathapuram Districts. That epigraphic mention of this guild should appear so far away from its original home in the Raichur *doāb* and so early in the history of the guild is not easy to comprehend and the Munasandal inscription could well be treated almost as a freak occurrence if it were not that in the Tirumayam and Kulattur taluks of Pudukkottai and at Piranmalai on the border of the former Ramanathapuram and Pudukkottai Districts, a dozen other inscriptions have been found which appear to relate to this merchant association.[23] A concentration of Ayyāvoḷe inscriptions in this limited geographical area would suggest that a major base of this guild was located here. However, these inscriptions were recorded in Tamil and appeared in a form different from the Kannada inscriptions. Therefore whether both the Tamil and Kannada inscriptions referred to the same association becomes a debatable point but a closer look at the inscriptions seems to provide the answer.

The early Munasandal inscription is not complete, only fragments of the epigraph have survived. It was issued, it is held, in A.D. 870, that is the end of the ninth century, in the twentieth year of Cōḷa Parakēśarivarman, probably Vijayālaya. The inscription referred to a tank named after this merchant association, the *Aiññūṟṟuvapēr-ēri* (the tank of the 500). The inscription then recorded the name of the donating or ratifying body, the "*śai-āyiranaññūṟuvar Valañjiyar Aiññūṟṟuvar*.[24] The corporate body here mentioned shared the same numerical description 500 or *aiññūṟṟuvar* as the Kannada Ayyāvoḷe merchants. The actual word moreover was the same in both Kannada and Tamil — *aiññūṟṟuvar*. The text of the Munasandal inscription made it clear that this corporate body was probably a merchant association since along with it was mentioned the Valañjiyar a group with known commercial affiliations. In other Tamil inscriptions referring to the same group the fragmentary *śai-āyiranaññūṟṟuvar* appears as

[22] *PSI*, 61, Tirumayam taluk, Pudukkottai. Pudukkottai is used in this study to describe the territory of the former Pudukkottai state, an area roughly corresponding to the present Pudukkottai District.

[23] See Appendix C

[24] *Ibid.*

nānādēśi-tiśai-āyirattaiññūṟṟuvar.[25] K.A. Nilakanta Sastri has translated this as the "Five Hundred of the Thousand directions in all countries."[26] It will be seen that apart from the similarity in the numerical description the Tamil and Kannada associations used different terminology to describe themselves. Based on the Munasandal inscription alone it is not possible to determine whether there was any relationship between the two corporate groups the *tiśai-āyirattaiññūṟṟuvar* and the Five Hundred *Caturvēdis* or *svāmis* of Aihole.

More information on the Tamil association and its relationship with Aihole is however derived from subsequent inscriptions, particularly those recorded in Pudukkoṭṭai. Beginning in the early eleventh century the Kannada Ayyāvoḷe guild inscriptions frequently included an elaborate *praśasti* (i.e. a eulogy as well as description) of the guild. Portions of this *praśasti* became quite standardised and reappeared in many Tamil and Kannada guild inscriptions. Kempanapura in the Chamrajnagar taluk of Mysore has an inscription dated early eleventh century which includes portions of the standard Ayyāvoḷe *praśasti*, including the phrase *pañca śata vīra śāsana*.[27] This phrase in the *praśasti* is a hallmark of the Ayyāvoḷe Kannada inscriptions and is repeated not only at Kempanapura but also in many other Tamil inscriptions and also, since we are here particularly investigating Pudukkottai, in the great Piranmalai inscription.

A portion of this inscription reads:

> *Tribhuvanāśraya Pañca śata Vīra śāsanam*
> *Lakṣana-Lakṣmi-vilāsālankrita Vakṣa-*
> *sthala Bhuvanaparākrama Śri Vāsudēva-*
> *sahāyaka (n) Dēvimūlapatralōpa Śri Aimpoḷir-*
> *Paramēśvarikkum Bhūmidēvikkum makkaḷāgi....*[28]

The concluding portion of the extract quoted above mentions one of the

[25] e.g. *ARE* 601 of 1902;
ARE 131 of 1926.

[26] Sastri, *The Cōḷas*, p. 595.

[27] *EC*, IV (new), Chamrajnagar 146. The same inscription (in Tamil) also refers to the children of Paramēśvari of the town of Ayyāpoḷil (Ayyāvoḷe). The phrase *pañca śata vīra śāsana* has been translated in *Epigraphia Carnatica* as "the great edict of five hundred heroes."

[28] *SII*, VII, 442, Tamil. One may note phrases in two other epigraphs as a matter of comparison. *EI*, XIX, 4B, Miraj, A.D. 1144, Kannada.
"Samasta bhuvana vikhyata pañca śata vīra
śāsana.... lakṣmi nivāsa vakṣa(s) sthala..."

or,

EZ II, pp. 235, 248, 251 of the late twelfth century, Sinhalese script from a village near Polonnaruva, Sri Lanka.

"Śri samaṣtha bhuvanāgra pañca śata vīra śāsanam ali (ngita Lakṣmi) (va) Lakṣana-(vakṣa) sthala bhuvana parākrama...."

Praśastis of this guild in several other inscriptions repeat the same phrases.

deities of Ayyāvoḷe, Aimpoḻir Paramēśvari, the phrase used being "*Aimpoḻir Paramēśvarikkum Bhūmidēvikkum makkaḷāgi...*," which may be translated as the children of Paramēśvari of Ayyāvoḷe and of Bhumidēvi." The members of the association were here claiming ancestry from Paramēśvari of Ayyāpoḻil or Ayyāvoḷe.[29] In two other twelfth century temple inscriptions of Pudukkottai the deity Ayyāpoḻiya Nācciyār is mentioned who is identified with Paramēśvari of Ayyāvoḷe.[30] On these grounds one concludes that the early Munasandal inscription was an indication that a corporate association with very close links with the Kannada group of the five hundred *svāmis* of Ayyāvoḷe had moved into Pudukkottai and remained active in the two present-day taluks of Tirumayam and Kulattur right through almost till the end of the thirteenth century. The members of the Tamil-speaking group identified themselves with the five hundred *svāmis* of Ayyāvoḷe in their use of the same numerical formula in their title, in their use of the same *praśasti*, indicating a very close bond, and in their adherence to the deities of Ayyāvoḷe. As will be made clear subsequently, the social groups who sponsored the founding of the guild in Aihole and those who belonged to the guild in Tamil-speaking areas were different. The analysis contained in the succeeding chapters also shows that the common economic objectives of both Kannada and Tamil-speaking merchants of Ayyāvoḷe included a marked interest in long-distance trade.

That the Ayyāvoḷe or *aiññūṟṟuvar* association of Tamil areas should emerge so soon after the establishment of the Kannada Ayyāvoḷe merchants of Aihole at first sight is difficult to explain. The distance between the two regions was great by medieval standards. The location of Pudukkottai may have made the area suitable for the establishment of a base for long-distance traders. If merchant traffic had been initiated between the Raichur *doāb* and this area of the Tamil-speaking country earlier, then some of these merchants may have carried with them the notion of the value of corporate association and of the advantage to be derived from identification with the trading network that existed in Aihole. The evidence to support this suggestion is hard to locate though, and in any case would not suffice unless one were also to look at some aspects of the movement of Kannada-speaking peoples from the Deccan into Tamil Nadu from early times. These then

[29] *SII*, VIII, 442, which one may compare with *EC*, IV (new), Chamrajnagar 146. "...*Śri Ayyapoḻilpura — paramēśvarikku makkaḷāgi....*" *See also* V. Rangacharya, *A Topographical List of the Inscriptions of Southern India*, Vol. I (Madras, 1919), p. 553 regarding the equation of Ayyāpoḻil and Aivalli (Aihole).

[30] *PSI*, 134, A.D. 1156-57; *PSI*, 148, A.D. 1190-91. K.R. Venkatarama Ayyar, "Medieval Trade, Craft and Merchant Guilds in South India," *JIH*, 25, pt. 1 (1947), 276 suggests Ayyāpoḻil Nācciyār "is also referred to as Kandali (the supreme one according to the Tolkāppiyam)", or Padmāvati or Paramēśvari. Padmāvati is a Jaina deity and figures frequently in the *praśastis* of the Ayyāvoḷe guild, particularly in Kannada areas.

might suggest traditional links between the north Deccan, south Karnataka and the coastal plains of Tamil Nadu. In this category one places the movement of the Kurumbars into the region, or, and here one treads on firmer historical ground, the Jaina tradition of migration from Karnataka into Andhra or into the Madurai District. An overall view appears necessary when watching the topograpical spread of the Ayyāvoḷe association of merchants from Karnataka into Tamil Nadu. In reaching back and enquiring into the movement of peoples, and into the special geographical features of regions which favoured the establishment of commerce, some indications are obtained as to the probable routes linking Kannada and Tamil-speaking areas.

The *Manual of the Pudukkottai State* has a chapter in which is described the "Settlement of Castes and Tribes" in Pudukkottai.[31] In this the Kurumbar migration to Pudukkoṭtai is described. In recorded and in oral tradition the Kurumbars, a pastoral Kannada-speaking people, are considered among the oldest settlers of Pudukkottai.[32] They are also associated with the Palni hills near Madurai and perhaps one might then conceive in general terms of a drifting of Kannada peoples into this area via the region around the Palni hills in very early times. The Kurumbars are also believed to have been the early inhabitants of the Kongu country, represented in modern times roughly by the former Coimbatore District, and part of the neighbouring Salem, Tiruchchirappalli and Madurai Districts. M. Arokiaswami cites references in early literature to the Kurumbar presence and to their defeat by the early Cōḷas.[33] If so, they may not have been completely subjugated by the Cōḷas and Kurumbar power may well have survived in some areas, since epigraphic sources indicate the presence of the Kurumbar in the period of the Gangas.[34] A Cōḷa inscription refers to a division known as *Kurumburnāḍu*,in the mid-tenth century.[35] *The Catalogue Raisonné* refers to a Kurumbar fortress near Kanchi captured in Viyayanagar times.[36] It is believed that as late as the eighteenth century, a principality known as Kurumbenāḍu

[31] K.R. Venkatarama Ayyar ed., *A Manual of the Pudukkottai State*, Vol. II, pt. i (Pudukkottai, 1944), pp. 542-543. The *Vēmbāttūrar Tiruvilaiyāḍal Purāṇam* ch. 58 and 59 is interpreted to indicate the early presence of Kurumbars in the area.

[32] Information on oral traditions regarding the Kurumbars and other aspects of Pudukkottai history has been obtained from P.M. Subramaniam, Pudukkottai. Sellugudi, Vythur, Perambur and Nangupatti in Kulattur taluk are still Kurumbar settlements. The dialect of the Kurumbars is strongly Kannada-based.

[33] M. Arokiaswami, *The Kongu Country*, (Madras, 1956), p. 41, points out that the Kurumbars are refered to in Sangam works such as the *Pattināppalai* and the *Perumbāṇārrupadai*, also in the *Maṇimēkhalai*.

[34] *MAR*, 1933, 1, 38, c. A.D. 801.

[35] *ARE* 20 of 1907, mid-tenth century.

[36] Rev. W. Taylor, *Catalogue Raisonné of Oriental Manuscripts in the Government Library*, Vol. III (Madras, 1862), p. 420, p. 438.

survived in North Malabar.[37] It would not be inconceivable that in the Rāṣṭrakūṭa period when the Ayyāvoḷe guild moved into (modern) south Tamil Nadu, the Kurumbars with their Jaina and Kannada affiliations still held power in isolated, limited areas.

That Kannada influence could have spread to Tamil Nadu quite early is also suggested in the traditional accounts of the Jaina migration. It is believed that Jainism was brought into the Tamil country by the disciples of Bhadrabāhu, and if this tradition has a historical basis then Jainism came from Karnataka into Tamil areas in the third century B.C.[38] Some of the Tamil Brahmi inscriptions in Pudukkottai, Madurai and Tirunelveli Districts are dated between the second century B.C. and the first century A.D. It is just possible that some of these inscriptions tie in with the Bhadrabāhu tradition.

If the hypothesis is acceptable that Jaina settlements were often established in areas of commercial importance then the location of these Brahmi Jaina inscriptions on the east coast may indicate portions of an old trade route.[39] In two areas where early Jaina inscriptions are found the Ayyāvoḷe merchants operated in early medieval times. One such area is the Pudukkottai District and the other is the Tirunelveli taluk of Tirunelveli District.[40] The Ukkirankottai inscription of the Tirunelveli taluk refers to a merchant of the Ayyāvoḷe association, "Ayyapoḷil Aiññūṟṟuva(n)." The inscription was probably recorded in the tenth century. The Tirunelveli taluk is far from the original home of the Ayyāvoḷe merchants in the Raichur *doāb*. But from the taluk the Aryankavu pass through the Western Ghats was close and Quilon where the early ninth century base of the Maṇigrāmam was located was nearby. As already noted Quilon was a centre for maritime export and import in the ninth century, possibly earlier as well. Trans-peninsular trade between Quilon and the east coast probably passed through the taluk. The Tamil merchant of the Ayyāvoḷe group at Ukkirankottai (Ayyāpoḷil Aiññūṟṟuva(n)), was, it is most likely, a long-distance trader.

[37] Sir W. Elliot, *Coins of Southern India* (London, 1886), p. 89, cites extracts from travel accounts referring to the principality of Kurumbenadu in the late eighteenth century.

[38] P.B. Desai, *Jainism in South India and some Jaina Epigraphs* (Sholapur, 1957), p. 2.

[39] I. Mahadevan, "Corpus of the Tamil-Brahmi Inscriptions," in *Seminar on Inscriptions*, ed., R. Nagaswamy (Madras, 1966), pp. 57-68, lists the inscriptions. They are located in Pudukkottai at Sittanavasal. In Madurai District they are found at Thiruparankundram and at Alagarmalai, also at Varichiyur, Kongan Puliyankulam, Mettupatti and Kilavalavu. Further south in Tirunelveli District one is noticed at Marugaltalai. (Kalugumalai near Kovilpatti in the same district has three belonging to the eighth and ninth centuries). Proceeding from north to south in a line parallel to the coast but some distance away from it, one notes that the Tamil-Brahmi Jaina inscriptions are located in the hills of Pudukkottai, in the hills around Madurai, and in some areas of Tirunelveli District where the Deccan plateau merges with the coastal plains.

[40] *EI*, XXIII, 45, about tenth century A.D.

The Pudukkottai tract was probably also connected with the Palghat gap through routes crossing the peninsula from the former Coimbatore District, swinging past Dharapuram, skirting the Palni hills and the area around present-day Dindigul, and then proceeding to Pudukkottai. If the distribution of Roman coins is acceptable as evidence supporting the possibility of such a route then one notes, apart from the finds of single coins, the hoards at Vellalur in Coimbatore district, at Kattangani, Pollachi, Karuvur, the hoard at Pudukkottai, the Kaliyamputtur hoard in Madurai, and the six aurei found at Karivalamvandanallur in the Sankarankovil taluk of Tirunelveli.[41] The last find is close to the Kovilpatti taluk where a Tamil-Brahmi inscription is found in the Jaina caves at Kalugumalai. The conjectural construction of a route such as this remains a tentative hypothesis as the evidence is so tenuous. But topographically it is possible to envisage routes from the Palghat gap and from Shencottah meeting somewhere around Pudukkottai. As earlier pointed out the Manigrāmam guild also functioned in Pudukkottai, at Kodumbalur and possibly at Valaramanikkam, facts which underline the commercial importance of this region in the past.

In seeking an explanation for the early establishment of the Ayyāvole guild in Pudukkottai both its strategic location and some of its links with the Kannada country have been described briefly. It remains to consider which routes were used by traders travelling between Kannada and Tamil areas in the days in which the Ayyāvole guild began moving south. One such route, it is most likely, was that taken by the armies of the Rāṣṭrakūṭa Krisṇa III in the mid-tenth century.

Chronologically, the invasion of the Rāṣṭrakūṭas and the establishment of the Pudukkottai base were fairly close. The armies of Krisṇa III probably moved down the valleys of the Palar and its tributaries. The Karhad plates refer to Melpati which is fourteen miles away from Vellore, on the Palar as it now flows. Here the Rāṣṭrakūṭas struck camp and not far away the decisive battle of Takolam was fought after which Krisṇa III is said to have gained control of Tondaimaṇḍalam.[42] In the mid-fourteenth century Kumāra Kampana similarly moved down the Palar valley. Obviously, this was a well-worn point of entry into Tamil areas. In the *Madhurā-Vijayam* it is stated that

[41] Approximate dating of hoards, Karuvur, Augustus-Claudius (d. A.D. 54) and Augustus-Tiberius (d. A.D. 37); Kattangani, Augustus-Tiberius (d. A.D. 37); Pollachi, Augustus-Tiberius (d. A.D. 37); Vellalur, Augustus (A.D. 14); Pudukkottai (to Vespasian, A.D. 79); Karivalamvandanallur (latest, Hadrian, A.D. 118).

R.E.M. Wheeler, "Arikamedu: An Indo-Roman Trading Station on the East Coast of India," *Ancient India*, No. 2 (July, 1946), 116-118.

[42] *EI*, IV, 40 and *ARE* 428 of 1902.

The entire southern campaign of the Rāṣṭrakūṭas included the capture of Thanjavur and is even said to have included Ramesvaram, but as no inscriptions are found south of Pondicherry the rest of the route remains a matter of pure conjecture. However, that the entry was down the valleys of the Palar and its tributaries is fairly certain.

Kumāra Kampana proceeded from Mulbagal to Virinchinagara, and then on to Kanchi.[43] The Palar valley was then used by invading armies and also probably by traders moving south from Kannada areas in the tenth century, in the days in which the Ayyāvoḷe merchants were first noticed in Pudukkottai.

Traders and caravans may also have moved between Tamil and Kannada areas in the eleventh century, by a route connecting the Kongu country and the Satyamangalam gap with the Ganga capital of Talakad.[44] This was the most likely route followed in the early Cōḷa invasions of South Karnataka and in all probability this route was in use in earlier times as well.

B. *Ayyāvoḷe Tamil Merchants Move into South Karnataka*

From the early eleventh century onwards in both Kannada and Tamil areas, the Ayyāvoḷe association branched out. Inscriptional evidence indicates that these merchants moved out both of the Raichur *doāb* and Pudukkottai and acquired a number of new bases. In Tamil areas, as noted, the Ayyāvoḷe guild first moved into the area now known as the Pudukkottai District, which in early medieval times was the home of the Irukkuvēl chieftains of Kodumbalur. In the eleventh century the Tamil Ayyāvoḷe or *aiññūṟṟuvar* merchants travelled northwards towards the Kannada country probably in the wake of the Cōḷa conquests. The earliest Ayyāvoḷe guild inscription of Pudukkottai, as stated earlier, appeared in A.D. 870 or the first quarter of the tenth century. If the first extant epigraph is dated late ninth or early tenth century, then it is possible the guild came into the region earlier when the Irukkuvēḷ chieftains of Kodumbalur were in power and before Cōḷa hegemony had been extended to the area. Presumably, as ruling chieftains, the Irukkuvēḷs took an interest in commercial transactions within their territory. When Cōḷa overlordship was established over this region and the chieftains were clearly allies of the Cōḷas, the Cōḷas appeared to have extended their protection to the guild. So one must assume, for this appears the only explanation for the community of interest which caused the *aiññūṟṟuvar* merchants to appear in the valleys of the tributaries of the Kaveri, just south of Talakad, after the Cōḷa conquest of the area.

In this connection, the special relationship between the Cōḷas and Irukkuvēḷ chieftains is of much relevance. It is believed that Vikki Aṇṇan, who fought on the side of Cōḷa Āditya I against the Pāṇḍyas was probably a Vēḷir

[43] S. Thiruvenkatachari, trans., *Madhurā-Vijayam of Gaṅga Devī* (Annamalai, 1957), p. 31, Canto IV, *Ślōka* 47.

"King Kampana reached Muluvayipattinam after crossing the Karnata country within five or six days...." (Muluvayipattinam — modern Mulbagal).

Ślōka 50. Then he proceeds along the Palar and reaches Viriñchinagara.

Canto V, Kampana rules from Kanchi.

[44] See following pages, section B.

chieftain of Kodumbalur.[45] In the time of the successors of Āditya, the Irukkuvēḷs were clearly on the side of the Cōḷas against the Pāṇḍyas.[46] There is moreover clear evidence of a dynastic connection between the Vēḷir chieftains of Kodumbālūr and the Cōḷas. The daughter of a Vēḷir chieftain married Arikulakēsari, a son of Parāntaka I.[47] A daughter of either Āditya I or Parāntaka I, Anupamā, may have married a Vēḷir chieftain of Kodumbalur.[48] It is also likely that Bhuti Vikramakēsari of Kodumbalur married Varaguṇa of the Cōḷa family.[49] Both the commercial and political importance of Pudukkottai might explain the many dynastic links that were established between the Irukkuvēḷs and the Cōḷa rulers. The region around Pudukkottai formed a buffer area between the powers controlling the Kaveri delta and the rulers of Madurai.[50] Kodumbalur was the scene of one of the major battles in the Pāṇḍya-Cōḷa war, according to the larger Śinnamanūr plates.[51] In the reign of Sundara Cōḷa Parāntaka II another crucial battle against the Pāṇḍyas was fought at Cevur, just south of Pudukkottai.[52] In this war also an Irukkuvēḷ, Parāntakan Śiṛiyavēḷar of Kodumbalur fought for the Cōḷas.[53]

[45] *ARE* 286 of 1911; *ARE* 1912, II. ii; K.A.N. Sastri, *The Cōḷas*, p. 119, footnote 29 says summarising a report in *ARE* 1912, II, ii; "...we find the suggestion thrown out that Vikki Aṇṇan was like his wife Kadam-ba-mādēvi, of Karṇāṭaka origin and that he was a Vēḷir chieftain of Koḍumbālūr (Pudukkōṭṭah)."

[46] *SII*, III, p. 449, cited K.A.N. Sastri, *op. cit.*, p. 125, "...Parāntaka was aided in his Pāṇḍyan campaign by the Vēḷir chiefs of Koḍumbāḷūr." See also M.S. Govindaswamy, "The Role of Feudatories in Cōḷa History", Diss. Annamalai Univ., 1974.

[47] *SII*, III, 96. M. Arokiaswami, *op. cit.*, pp. 241-242, goes as far as to say that Āditya was himself of Kodumbalur origin. A quotation from Arokiaswami reads "...the *Tiruthondarthokaianthāthi* of Nambiāndar Nambi (A.D. 10th century) describes Āditya I as "Enkad Iraivan Irrukkuvēlūr mannidam..."; "...the imperial Cōḷas ... appear as Vēḷir chieftains in their origin with their centre at Koḍumbālūr." K.A.N. Sastri, *op. cit.*, p. 109, footnote 32, cites Venkayya's opinion from *ASI* 1905-6, pp. 176-7. Venkayya in his account of the Cōḷas claims Iḍangaḷi, a possible ancestor of Áditya I, was *vēḷ* chieftain of Kōṇāḍu, Pudukkottai. Sastri disagrees but does not rule out the possibility of a dynastic alliance much earlier than that of the time of Parāntaka.

[48] K.A.N. Sastri, *op. cit.*, p. 134. M.S. Govindaswamy *op. cit.*, pp. 15-16 holds a slightly different view of this dynastic alliance.

[49] Sastri, *Ibid.*, p. 155. Govindaswamy, pp. 15, 16 and 21 disagrees and feels it was a later chieftain who married Varaguṇa.

[50] M. Arokiaswami, *Early History of the Vellar Basin* (Madras, 1954), p. 122. "It is curious that the state of Pudukottah must have been chosen as the Pāṇḍyan base of attack. The list of Pudukottah inscriptions records many inscriptions of this Māravarman (*PSI*, no. 282, 320) which leave no doubt in our mind that the Pāṇḍyan ruler had made it his stronghold and in course of time as a result of successive invasions the state became an open gateway for the Pāṇḍyan attack of the Cōḷa."

[51] *SII*, III, p. 449.

[52] "The Leiden Grant", *EI*, XXII, 34.

[53] *ARE* 302 of 1908.

The same warrior chief also led an expedition to Sri Lanka (A.D. 965) and there he died.[54] In subsequent invasions of Sri Lanka also, in the time of Rājarāja, the Irukkuvēḷs played a prominent part.

With this close connection between the Irukkuvēḷs and Cōḷas in mind one may then assume that a successful merchant enterprise with a strong base in the Pudukkottai tracts would receive protection from the Cōḷa overlord, either directly, or through the intervention of the interested feudatory. Therefore, it was possible, that with the Cōḷa expansion towards South Karnataka into the strategic areas north of the former Coimbatore District, south of the Kaveri, the *aiññūṟṟuvar* merchants were also encouraged to follow. The particular strip of territory these merchants moved into was close to the Ganga capital of Talakad.

The physical features of this tract of territory explain its importance to some extent. The Kaveri rises in Coorg, flows eastwards, and then swings south between Coimbatore and Salem Districts. South of present-day Mysore, two tributaries join the Kaveri, the Kabbani from the Western Ghats and the Swarnavathi from the hills north of the Nilgiris. The Swarnavathi joins the Kaveri just opposite Talakad. Along the valleys of the Kabbani and the Swarnavathi are found many of the epigraphs relating to the establishment of the *aiññūṟṟuvar* merchants in the early eleventh century. While following the Swarnavathi south from its junction with the Kaveri one arrives close to the Satyamangalam gap leading into the Kongu country. Similarly following the Kabbani to its source one arrives close to Manantavadi on the opposite side of the Western Ghats. From Manantavadi, Cannanore, Mahe, Tellicherry, Quilandi and Kozhikode are accessible. Both the Swarnavathi and Kabbani valleys were suitable for use as trade highways between Keraḷa and South Karnataka and similarly between the former Coimbatore District and Karnataka. The location of the Ganga administrative capital Talakad acquires greater significance when linked with the Kabbani and Swarnavathi river systems and the easy entry from these valleys into Cēra and Kongu country.

The first conquest of Talakad by the Cōḷas may have taken place under Āditya I who, it is believed, conquered Kongu.[55] But the capture of Talakad may not have been permanent and the real attempt to capture the region came only in the time of Rājarāja I. The conquest of Coorg preceded the capture of the Ganga capital.Some time before A.D. 991 the Cōḷa conquest of the regions of Tadigaipadi, Talakad and Nolambapadi took place.[56] The

[54] *ARE* 116 of 1896, *SII*, V, 980, *Cv.*, 54, 12-16, cited by K.A.N. Sastri, *op. cit.*, p. 154.

[55] C.M. Ramachandra Chettiar ed., *Kongadēsa Rājākkaḷ* (Madras, 1950), p. 10. Sastri *op. cit.*, p. 114 feels that in this instance there is no reason to dispute the testimony of the *Kongadēsa Rājākkaḷ*.

[56] *ARE* 67 of 1923; *ARE* 1923, II, p. 27.

route for the invasion was most probably through Kongu and the Satya-mangalam gap.[57]

Shortly thereafter in the eleventh century the Ayyāvoḷe guild inscriptions appeared in the taluks of Heggadadevankote and Nanjangud along the Kabbani river. The inscription from Belathur, Heggadadevankote is dated A.D. 1033, 22nd year of Rajēndra Cōḷa and is in Kannada.[58] Only a portion of the inscription remains but the references both to the Ayyāvoḷe guild and to Rajēndra Cōḷa are unmistakable since there are allusions to his overseas victories in Kadaram and his triumph against the Cēras and Pāṇḍyas. The inscription is clearly issued in territory which was newly conquered by the Cōḷa since it is quite different in content and style from the previous inscriptions of the area, although the language used is still Kannada.

Further up the Kabbani river valley, in the Nanjangud taluk, the first Ayyāvoḷe guild inscription found is in the Tamil and Kannada languages and in the Kannada script.[59] It refers to a land sale for charitable purposes by a Cōḷa official of a *brahmadeya*. The ratifying body included the merchants of Ayyāvoḷe and the *nānādēśis*, also a merchant group. Of interest is the inscription found in Kalale in the same taluk, which on paleographic grounds has been dated between the twelfth and thirteenth centuries.[60] It is fragmentary but portions of the Ayyāvoḷe *praśasti* have survived in it and are followed by references to Talakad and it would appear from the inscription that the Ayyāvoḷe merchants were among the groups established in the town. The conquest of Talakad and its environs has also been described in the seventeenth century *Kongadēsa Rājākkaḷ*. While the chronicle is frequently unreliable there is no need to disbelieve the account it gives of the Cōḷa settlement of a newly-conquered town.[61] The facts chosen as relevant

[57] This conjecture is based on a study of the topography of the region.

[58] *EC*, III (new), Heggadadevankote 59, A.D. 1033.

[59] *EC*, III (new), Nanjangud, 213, A.D. 1015-16.

[60] *EC*, III (new), Nanjangud, 359.

[61] *Kongadēsa Rājākkal*, p. 13 and W. Taylor, trans., "*Conga dēsa Rājākal*" in *MJLS*, 14 (1847), 17. The description in the chronicle is also interesting for the obvious assumption that the Brahman and the trader are part of the necessary establishment and that after the conquest of a town the trader is required to provide the capital necessary for settling the Brahman in his *agrahāra*. The provision of *agrahāras* as one of the first acts of a monarch after the capture of a city is frequently referred to elsewhere in the *Kongadēsa Rājākkaḷ*, e.g. p. 10, para 29.

In Suttur in Nanjangud, in A.D. 1032— "In the 31st regnal year of the capturer of the eastern country and the Ganga, Parakēśarivarman... Rājēndra-cōḷa dēva...." — the *mahājanas* representing the *sabha* and the *agrahāra*, and the merchants, apportioned between themselves the cost of endowments to the temple and maintenance of the tank, by order of Rājēndracōḷa. The impression gained is that these two groups were important elements in the administration of the town. (*EC*, III (new), Nanjangud 215). Rājēndracōḷa asked for the gifts to provide for maintenance of the tank, food for the god and merit for himself. The donations were provided by individual *seṭṭis*, the *nānādeśis*, all oil-mongers, and the "*samaya*".

by the chronicler are thus related. After the conquest Rājarāja gave "the town of Keriyur (which he now named as Rājarājapura) in the Talakad District to the merchants of Dalavanapuram and by their hands made *agrahāras* for the Brahmans and gave these to them, these Vaisyas having always been accustomed to worship the divine Brahman." The merchants of Dalavanapuram described in the chronicle may possibly have been the Ayyāvoḷe group since the Kalale inscription records their presence in Talakad. However, the conquest took place in the eleventh century and the inscription has been dated the twelfth to the thirteenth century, so it is not possible to relate with certainty the Ayyāvoḷe and Dalavanapuram merchants.

Other evidence of the presence of Tamil merchants in Nanjangud is provided in another inscription of either the thirteenth or fourteenth century which refers to merchants and officials and is in Tamil and Grantha.[62] Nanjangud was possibly a merchant centre of some importance judging by another epigraph of the area and the reference to export and import duties and the transport of merchandise.[63] As late as the eighteenth century there is an inscriptional description of the carriage of goods along roadways in this taluk and to the *ubhaya-nānādēśi* merchants who apparently functioned even at that time.[64]

Not far from the Kabbani river, in the valley of the Swarnavathi river lie the modern taluks of Kollegal, Yelandur and Chamrajnagar, and in a neighbouring valley by a tributary of the Kabbani is the taluk of Gundlupet. Kollegal has four Ayyāvoḷe inscriptions of the eleventh century in Tamil and Grantha. Unfortunately only portions of these epigraphs have survived.[65] Opposite Kollegal taluk on the other side of the Kaveri, is the site of the former Talakad. Kollegal continued to be of commercial importance long after the Tamil occupation, since even in 1323 under the Hoysalas, there survives a record of a meeting of merchants of Mudigoṇḍasōḷapuram in Kollegal, which included the merchants of Talakad.[66] The record contains a vivid description of caravan traffic in the area and lists some of the expensive luxuries which arrived in the local market such as silk thread, incense and

[62] *EC*, III (new), Nanjangud 394. Thirteenth to fourteenth century on palaeographic grounds.

[63] In an inscription of the 15th century there is reference to import and export taxes paid on goods taken by road. *EC*, III (new), Nanjangud 181, A.D. 1467.

[64] *EC*, III (new), Nanjangud 237, A.D. 1771, Suttur.

[65] *EC*, IV (new), Kollegal 100, Kollegal 101, Kollegal 104, Kollegal 2 — all estimated to be early eleventh century.

[66] *EC*, IV (new), Kollegal 97, 1323 A.D.

Mudigonda is probably the same as the modern town of the same name Mudigondam in Kollegal taluk. In *EC*, IV (new) Kollegal 97 it is described as Mudikoṇḍasōḷapuram alias Desi-uyya (kkoṇḍa-paṭṭinam) on the south bank of the Kaveri, while 'Talaikkadu' is described as being on the north bank. Mudikoṇḍasōḷapuram is normally taken to be Palaiyaru near Kumbakonam. (K.A.N. Sastri, *op. cit.*, p. 346) but there are also other towns of the same name.

sandal suggesting either the presence of an affluent local clientèle or that the region constituted an important trade and transit area. As late as A.D. 1398, an inscription was recorded by the Ayyāvoḷe merchants at Singanallur in Kollegal.[67] South of Kollegal, Yelandur taluk has an Ayyāvoḷe inscription of the eleventh century in Tamil and Grantha and one of the twelfth century also relating to Ayyāvoḷe. There is also an Ayyāvoḷe inscription in Kannada of Hoysaḷa times.[68]

In the same river valley the Chamrajnagar taluk was a major Ayyāvoḷe centre. There are four Ayyāvoḷe inscriptions in Tamil and Grantha of the eleventh century at Kempanapura, Mangala and Hale Aluru.[69] At Kempanapura the *aiññūṟṟuvar* and *nānādēśi* and other groups ratified a resolution converting an *agrahāra* Velur or Rājadhirāja *caturvēdimangalam*, into an *erivīrapaṭṭinam* which, it is believed, meant a 'fortified mart'.[70] From the description in this inscription the impression gained is that an *erivīrapaṭṭinam* was a merchant settlement protected by militia. The inscription describes the caravans and their guards arriving in the region and records that provision was made by the guild for supplying them with clothes. The Cōḷa administrative units *vaḷanāḍu* and *maṇḍalam* were used indicating that this was Cōḷa territory. The signatories to the inscription bore titles relating to the officialdom of the Tamil country, not of the Kannada-speaking areas. The inscription of Mangala also refers to the arrival of merchant caravans. Eight miles away from present-day Chamrajnagar, Hale Aluru has two Ayyāvoḷe Tamil inscriptions of the eleventh and twelfth centuries. It also has another merchant inscription of the eleventh century referring to a *vyāpārī* of Keralāntaka-vaḷanāḍu.[71] In A.D. 1277, under the Hoysaḷas, Hale Aluru was declared a 'southern Ayyāvoḷe' which may mean that it was then considered a major centre for the organisation.[72] In A.D. 1278 there is again reference to Hale Aluru as a southern Ayyāvoḷe in a Jaina inscription.[73] In A.D. 1294 it was declared an *agrahāra*, Arasaganda -

[67] *EC*, IV (new), Kollegal 55, probably 14th century.

[68] *EC*, IV (new), Yelandur 17, estimated early eleventh century and Yelandur 19, estimated twelfth century (both Tamil). Yelandur 158 of Hoysaḷa Vīra Narasimha's time mentions the street named after the *aiññūṟṟuvar* in Mamballi west of Mudigonda, and a land sale negotiated between the *nānādēśis* and the *aiññūṟṟuvar*. Other inscriptions referring to the *nānādēśis*, Yelandur 159, Yelandur 160, Yelandur 163. Yelandur 156, 210 refer to the *ceṭṭis*.

[69] *EC*, IV (new), A.D. 1018-1054? Chamrajnagar 146, Kempañapura.
EC, IV (new), possibly early eleventh century, Mangala, Chamrajnagar 133.
EC, IV (new), possibly early eleventh century, Hale Aluru, Chamrajnagar 193.
EC, IV (new), eleventh to twelfth centuries, Hale Aluru, Chamrajnagar 353.

[70] Venkatarama Ayyar, "Mediaeval Trade, Craft and Merchant Guilds", p. 277.

[71] *EC*, IV (new),Chamrajnagar 186, A.D. 1058-59.

[72] *EC*, IV (new), Chamrajnagar 188, A.D. 1277.

[73] *EC*, IV (new), Chamrajnagar 195, A.D. 1278.

Rāma-*caturvēdimangalam.*[74] Again under Vijayanagar in A.D. 1403, it was referred to as Alur, the southern Ayyāvoḷe.[75] For close on to four centuries then the Ayyāvoḷe guild functioned in Hale Aluru. Till approximately the fourteenth century there does not seem to have been any major local production centre in the Swarnavathi or Kabbani river valleys, nor is there evidence of the mining of precious metals.[76] One may then suggest, therefore, that the strategic location of this region was largely responsible for the presence of Ayyāvoḷe merchants in the area for some centuries.

Nearby, Gundlupet taluk was also occupied by the Cōḷas and has an Ayyāvoḷe guild inscription of the eleventh century in Tamil and Grantha at Kandagala mentioning the *aiññūṟṟuvar* and the *valaṅgai* or right-hand division of the army.[77] In the same village a portion of another Ayyāvoḷe inscription in twelfth century script was found.[78] In the village of Kelasuru in the same taluk a twelfth century Jaina inscription in Tamil has also been found although it does not relate to any merchant guild.[79] Gundlupet like all the other neighbouring taluks in which the Tamil Ayyāvoḷe inscriptions were found fell within the Cōḷa administrative division of Gangaikondasōḷavalanāḍu and Mudigoṇḍasōḷamaṇḍalam.[80]

Also in the eleventh century, the Tamil Ayyāvoḷe guild inscriptions are noticed in the valleys of the Palar and its tributaries, at Kanchipuram near the delta, in Kolar taluk, and in adjoining Chittoor District. The Palar valley, as already noted, was used by the Rāṣṭrakūṭa armies and by Kumāra Kampana, and may have been used by merchants proceeding either north or south, between Kannada and Tamil areas. By A.D. 1007, at least this region right up to Kolar and beyond formed part of the Cōḷa conquests. In Kanchipuram taluk in A.D. 1050 the Ayyāvoḷe and Valañjiyar merchants supported a *maṭha.*[81] Soon afterwards they were in Kolar taluk north of the upper reaches of the Palar.[82] In both areas the inscriptions are in Tamil and Grantha. Also in Karshanapalle, in adjoining Chittoor District, they were present as early as A.D. 1011.[83] In A.D. 1109, a Kannada inscription notes

[74] *EC*, IV (new) Chamrajnagar 183, A.D. 1294.

[75] *EC*, IV (new), Chamrajnagar 184, A.D. 1403.

[76] This conclusion is based on an examination of epigraphs. From the fourteenth century onwards there is evidence of possible production of silk and cotton yarn in Kollegal taluk. *EC*, IV (new), Kollegal 97.

[77] *EC*, III (new), Gundlupet 154, eleventh century based on paleography.

[78] *EC*, III (new), Gundlupet 114, twelfth century based on paleography.

[79] *EC*, III (new), Gundlupet 102, twelfth century based on paleography.

[80] Gangaikondasōḷavalanāḍu and Mudikoṇḍasōḷamaṇḍalam probably included the whole of present-day southern Karnataka. This would include of Kannada territorial division, Gangāvadi 96,000.

[81] *ARE* 264 of 1955-56, about 11th century based on script (Tamil).

[82] *EC*, X, Kolar 19, A.D. 1051? Tamil and Grantha.

[83] *ARE* 321 of 1912. Karshanapalle, Chittoor District.

their presence in Mulbagal near the upper Palar.[84] The Ayyāvoḷe guild then, it is most probable, moved into these areas soon after the Cōḷa occupation. Their continued presence in many of these regions long after the invading armies left suggests that in this period the Tamil Ayyāvoḷe guild was interested in control of major highways and in some form of long-distance trade. In Kolar taluk the second range of Tamil inscriptions in the late twelfth century may perhaps be linked with the revival of Cōḷa fortunes under Vikramacōḷa II.

C. *Overseas Interests of the Aiññūṟṟuvar in the Eleventh Century. The Tamils in Sri Lanka*

In the eleventh century may be noticed further the movement of the *aiññūṟṟuvar* merchants into Sri Lanka. The penetration of Sri Lanka by the *aiññūṟṟuvar* is of great interest because the sources for historical study are rich compared to those available in India. The chronicles, the *Mahāvaṃsa* and *Cūlavaṃsa* and literary sources, used in conjunction with epigraphical evidence, make it possible to invest skeletal outlines with flesh and blood. Substantive and contextual analysis take on new dimensions. The movement of the *aiññūṟṟuvar* merchants into Sri Lanka may be correlated to the Cōḷa invasions and the so called Cōḷa "occupation" of the island. The invasions of Sri Lanka in the time of Rājarāja I and Rājēndra I were almost contemporaneous with the Cōḷa invasions of South Karnataka examined earlier in the chapter. Both the South Karnataka and the Sri Lankan wars were followed by an increased merchant presence and in particular one notices the activities of Tamil *aiññūṟṟuvar* merchants. It is also possible to show specifically that the Irukkuvēḷs of Pudukkottai took a special interest in the Cōḷa-Sri Lanka wars. It is understandable that, as in South Karnataka, Irukkuvēḷ and Cōḷa interest and the interests of the *aiññūṟṟuvar* with their base in Pudukkottai coincided and that these merchants could and did appear in northern Sri Lanka after the conquest.

Examination of the Cōḷa-Sri Lankan wars is possible in far greater detail than of the South Karnataka wars. This close examination is justified for not merely does it add to our knowledge of the history of the Tamil *aiññūṟṟuvar* merchants but also the nature of the relationship of merchants with ruling powers becomes clearer. Many scholars have analysed these wars, but there has been little agreement as to the motives for war.[85] While the Sri Lanka

[84] *EC*, X, pt. 1, Mulbagal 247.

[85] K.A.N. Sastri, "Cōla invasions: Downfall of Anuradhapura," in University of Ceylon, *History of Ceylon*, Vol. I, Book III (Colombo, 1959), Chapter 5; G.W. Spencer, "The Politics of Plunder: The Cholas in Eleventh Century Ceylon," *JAS*, 35, No. 3 (1976), 405-419; W.M.K. Wijetunga, "Some aspects of Cōḷa Administration of Ceylon in the Eleventh Century," *UCR*, 23, Nos. 1-2 (1965), 67-81; S. Pathmanathan, "Cōḷa rule in Sri Lanka; circa 993-1070," in *Proceedings of the Fourth International Conference Seminar of Tamil Studies*, Vol. II (Jaffna, 1980), pp. 19-35; S.Pathmanathan, *The Kingdom of Jaffna* (Colombo, 1978).

war has earlier been seen in the wider context of other Cōḷa military and naval invasions, the South Karnataka war has never been taken into account as a point of comparison.

In order to understand better the Indo-Sri Lankan wars in the time of Rājarāja I and Rajēndra I some salient points on the South India — Sri Lanka conflicts in the years preceding their reigns may be noted. For this purpose one follows largely the *Cūlavaṃsa* and the reconstruction of events by K.A.N. Sastri with the addition of new material derived from the epigraphic studies of K. Indrapala.[86] In the mid-ninth century the armies of the Sinhalese king Sena II invaded Pāṇḍyan territory, laid siege to Madurai and placed the Sinhalese candidate Vāraguṇavarman on the throne. But in the early tenth century Sinhalese and Pāṇḍyan armies joined to face a Cōḷa attack and were defeated at the battle of Vellur. The Cōḷas had earlier subdued the Pallavas and staved off an incursion from the north by the Rāṣṭrakūṭas. The victory at Vellur then came for the Cōḷas after a series of minor successes. The Pāṇḍyan king fled the mainland taking with him his crown and regalia and was received, according to the *Cūlavaṃsa*, with honour by Dappula IV of Sri Lanka.[87] But quarrels within the Sinhalese court and intrigues against the Pāṇḍyan forced him to flee to Kerala leaving behind his crown and other symbols of sovereignty. Parantaka meanwhile consolidated his hold in the Pāṇḍyan kingdom and then desiring the Pāṇḍyan crown for himself — this is the motive ascribed to him in the *Cūlavaṃsa* — crossed the straits.[88] He seems to have overrun some part of the northern plains and may even have occupied Anuradhapura. But Parāntaka did not succeed in capturing the crown jewels and retreated to the mainland fairly early. Parāntaka's ally and leader of his armies in the campaign was the Vēḷir chieftain Vīrasōḷan Ilangovēlan, an Irukkuvēḷ chieftain of Pudukkottai.[89] As earlier noted the Irukkuvēḷs were allies of the Cōḷas. The fact of his participation in the Sri Lankan war is recorded at Kudumiamalai in the Kulattur taluk of Pudukkottai. Whether Parāntaka's temporary successes in Sri Lanka led to the occupation of any part of the Rājaraṭṭha, the northern plain of the island is not clear. The *Cūlavaṃsa* account would suggest that if that was the case it was a tenuous occupation and short-lived.[90] With the Pāṇḍyan recovery after the Rāṣṭrakūṭa invasion the balance was again reversed and Sinhalese and Pāṇḍyan troops fought the Cōḷas once more. After initial Pāṇḍyan success, at the decisive battle of Cevur south of Pudukkottai, the Pāṇḍyan power was overthrown by the Cōḷas. Soon after

[86] K. Indrapala ed., *ET*, I, II (1971).

[87] *Cv.*, 53, 6-7.

[88] *Cv.*, 53, 41-43.

[89] *ET*, I, i, No. 5, p. 19.

[90] *Cv.*, 53, 45-47.

an Irukkuvēḷ leader from Kodumbalur, which is located in the Kulattur taluk of Pudukkoṭṭai invaded Sri Lanka but was killed in battle.[91] According to the *Cūlavaṃsa* the Cōḷas were defeated, and retreated after making a pact with the kings of Anuradhapura. In both these invasions the Cōḷa forces included Irukkuvēḷ army leaders. If one conceives of Cōḷa control of the army as somewhat personalised then this coincidence may be of significance as also the fact of merchant activity in Pudukkottai.

Subsequently, in the reign of Rājarāja Cōḷa and later in the reign of Rājēndra Cōḷa the Tamils established themselves in some parts of northern Sri Lanka and they held these areas for some years. Within this period of Cōḷa occupation of the north the *aiññūṟṟuvar* merchants moved into Polonnaruva and the *nānādēśi,* an affiliate of the *aiññūṟṟuvar* established themselves in Padaviya. One assumes some connection between their arrival and the establishment of control of these areas by Tamils from the mainland.[92]

The naval foray of the Cōḷas aimed against ports and trading centres on the Malaysian peninsula and in Sumatra took place around A.D. 1025 during the period of Cōḷa occupation of Sri Lanka. This feat was paralleled approximately one century later in the naval raid led by the Sinhalese against Burma. Both ventures had economic objectives but these are given closer attention in the section of the work dealing with maritime trade and imports and exports. An Ayyāvole guild inscription of A.D. 1088 has been found in Loboe Toewa, Barus, Sumatra.[93] This inscription was recorded sixty-three years after the naval raid. It is not possible to say that the presence of the *aiññūṟṟuvar* in Sumatra in A.D. 1088 was a direct benefit obtained as a result of the Cōḷa raid in A.D. 1025. The inscription confirms though that the *aiññūṟṟuvar* had direct links with Southeast Asia, in this case with the camphor-growing area of Sumatra, camphor being a prized commodity of medieval trade. If there is evidence that the *aiññūṟṟuvar* were in Sumatra in A.D. 1088 it is possible and likey that they came into the area earlier. Around the time that this guild inscription appeared in Sumatra we notice the activities of Tamil merchants and the guild on the Andhra coast and particularly at important ports like Vishakhapatnam. (See Section E of this chapter.)

D. *Ayyāvoḷe Merchants in the Eleventh and Twelfth Centuries in Kannada-speaking areas*

Meanwhile in Karnataka from the Raichur *doāb*, the original home of the

[91] *ARE* 116 of 1896; Sastri, *The Cōḷas*, p. 154. He was Parāntakan Siriyavelar of Kodumbalur.

[92] See Chapter V on international trade and the guilds where these points are dealt with in much detail.

[93] K.A. Nilakanta Sastri, "A Tamil Merchant-guild in Sumatra", *TBG*, deel lxxii (1932), 314-27.

guild, the Ayyāvoḷe merchants were regularly expanding the area of their operations. By A.D.1000 they were in force in the Chikodi taluk of Belgaum district in the foothills of the Western Ghats. The tributaries feeding the Krishna river flow down into the plains from this section of the Ghats and on the other side lie the coastal plains. According to the inscription from Chikodi the Ayyāvoḷe merchants exercised their punitive power and killed thirteen people in retaliation for the murder of a travelling merchant. The *seṭṭis* who gathered to reward the executioner came from "round about Uchchangi (Bellary District), Raichur *doāb*, in Nizamabad District and Mysore, respectively."[94] This covered a wide area and illustrates that from the find-spot of an inscription alone it is not possible to assess the area of operations of the guild. The absence of merchants from the coastal plains is to be noted. The *praśasti* of the guild in this inscription merits attention because it was long and elaborate, giving in detail the full genealogy of the guild and describing their attributes. In the inscriptional history of the guild in Karnataka this was possibly the first *praśasti* that was so detailed. A certain flamboyant self-confidence is noticed in this inscription which possibly was a sign of their growing commercial power.

From an analysis of inscriptions of Karnataka in the eleventh century the location of other centres of guild operations appear to be the Shimoga, Dharwad, Belgaum and Kaladgi Districts.[95] These inscriptions were issued in the reign of Caḷukya Vikramāditya VI. In the early twelfth century, also in the region of Vikramāditya VI inscriptions appear again in Dharwad District, in the Davangere taluk of Chitradurga District, in Bijapur District and at Mulbagal in Kolar District.[96] In the twelfth century the Ayyāvoḷe guild was noticed functioning at many locations north of the Krishna river, some of these being Miraj, Managoli, Agarkhed, Hire-Bavanur, Nimbal and Adki.[97]

Within this group of inscriptions of the early twelfth century there are references for the first time to the establishment of 'southern Ayyāvoḷes'. Thus Piriyakereyur, modern Hirekerur in Dharwad, Mulbagal and Kodanganur in Davangere taluk (Chitradurga), all *agrahāras* were designated

[94] *KI*, IV, p. 121.

[95] *IA*, V. XIX, Belgaum District A.D. 1093-94;
EC, VII, Shikarpur 94, Shimoga District, A.D. 1094;
IA, X, CXVI, Dharwad District, A.D. 1095-96;
IA, VI, XXXII, Kaladgi District, A.D. 1096-7;
BK I, pt. II, 148, Dharwad District, A.D. 1099.

[96] *KI*, IV, 34, Dharwad District, A.D. 1109;
EC, XI, Davangere 149, Chitradurga District, A.D. 1113;
BK I, pt. ii, 168, Bijapur District, A.D. 1119;
EC, X, pt. I, Mulbagal 247, A.D. 1109.

[97] *EI*, XIX, 4; *EI*, V, 3; *SII*, XX, 71; *SII*, XX, 85; *ARE*, A2 of 1958-59; *ARE* 135 of 1976-77.

Ayyāvoḷes.[98]. Of Mulbagal it was said, 'The Five Hundred made the Mahēndrachaturvēdimangala an Ayyāvoḷe.' The Chitradurga inscription referred to 'The immemorial *agrahāra*, the southern Ayyāvoḷe, Kodanganur.'

An analysis of the term 'southern Ayyāvoḷe' has been attempted in Chapter IV. It may have been that the townships so singled out had by then become commercially prominent and centres of local trade networks. Perhaps also, one may speculate that some sort of decision-making authority may have been vested in the prominent traders of these towns. The early 'southern Ayyāvoḷes' were generally established, as Aihole was, in *agrahāras* suggesting continued Brahman participation in the guild. The use of the term 'southern Ayyāvoḷe' is noted mainly in Kannada-speaking territory.

In the latter half of the twelfth century, the territorial expansion of the guild in the Deccan continued and inscriptional notices are found as already stated north of the river Krishna in the Bijapur and Gulbarga Districts, and also in some areas of interior Karnataka and again in the Kolar District.[99]

In the last two decades of the twelfth century, the Ayyāvoḷe notices were issued in Kolar A.D. 1180 in Kannada and in A.D. 1198 in Tamil.[100] The Kannada and Tamil inscriptions of Kolar may represent periods in which eastern Gangāvadi was alternatively under Caḷukya and Cōḷa influences. The Kolar area as already noted had access to the Palar valley and thence to Kanchi and the coastal plains.

E. *Tamil Merchants Along the Andhra Coast*

Meanwhile it is possible to trace the expansion of Tamil mercantile interest along the Andhra coast. In A.D. 1090 a Telugu inscription found at Vishakhapatnam mentioned a donation to an *aiññūṟṟuva perumpaḷḷi* which was possibly a Jain temple sponsored by the *aiññūṟṟuvar*.[101] A group called the *añjuvaṇṇatu-vyāpāri,* who were probably Arab Muslim traders were mentioned in the inscription.[102] The collaboration between these merchants and the Ayyāvoḷe merchants at the port of Vishakhapatnam confirms that the *aiññūṟṟuvar* were interested in overseas trade. The inscription gives no indication of the commodities exchanged. Although the inscription at Vishakhapatnam is recorded in Telugu, it seems reasonable to look at the

[98] *KI*, IV, 84; *EC*, X, pt. 1, Mulbagal 247;
EC, XI, Davangere 149.

[99] For example, *EC*, X. pt. 1, Kolar 170, Kolar 131, A.D. 1180, A.D. 1198;
ARE 478 of 1914, Bellary District, A.D. 1178;
EC, VIII, Sorab 328; *SII*, XV, 106;
EC, V, pt. 1, Belur 177; *KI*, V, 37; *ARE* 216 of 1918.

[100] *EC*, X, pt. 1, Kolar 170, A.D. 1180; Kolar 131, A.D. 1198.

[101] *SII*, X, 651, A.D. 1090.

[102] See Chapter I on *Añjuvaṇṇam*.

presence of *aiññūṟṟuvar* merchants in Vishakhapatnam as part of the general movement of Tamil merchants into Andhra. Tamil merchants were at this time in many of the coastal towns of Andhra and as far north as Draksharama in the Ganjam district of Orissa.[103] A.D. 1076 marks the union of the Cōḷa and Vengi kingdoms and in Kulōttunga I's time his sons were deputised to rule over Vengi. The first invasion of Kalinga may have taken place as early as A.D. 1077.[104] From the time of Kulōttunga I continuing through the time of the second Pāṇḍyan empire, Tamil influence is noted in administration, and in the use of the Tamil language for many inscriptions and in the renaming of several ports.[105] Vishakhapatnam became Kulōttungacōḷapaṭṭinam.[106] Ghantasala in the Divi taluk of Krishna District was Cōlapāṇḍyapuram.[107] In interior Andhra on the other hand there are only stray references to *Cōḷamaṇḍalamunavyāpārī*.[108]

F. *The Twelfth and Thirteenth Centuries, Sri Lanka*

In the late twelfth century there is evidence of the Ayyāvoḷe merchants functioning near Polonnaruva in Sri Lanka.[109] Possibly as late as the latter half of the thirteenth century the Ayyāvoḷe merchants were also well established in townships south of the northern plains of Sri Lanka.[110] The movement of these merchants southward is quite clearly associated with the movement of Sinhalese people away from the Rājaraṭṭha or the northern plains towards the "wet zone" of the island.

G. *Under the Hoysaḷas and the Pāṇḍyas*

The thirteenth century marked the beginnings of shifts in power in the Deccan and in Tamil areas. In the Kannada speaking region the Caḷukyas of Kalyan were replaced by the Hoysaḷas their former feudatories. The Hoysaḷas to begin with exercised their power in the "modern Hassan, Chikmagalur, parts of the Shimoga, Tumkur, Mysore and Mandya districts watered by the Tunga, Bhadra, Vedavati, Yagachi, Hemavati and Simsa rivers."[111] This was Hoysaḷa country and it is in some of these new areas that the

[103] *ARE* 1935-36, Part II, para. 16.

[104] *EI*, XXII, 23, p. 141.

[105] K. Sundaram, *Studies in Economic and Social Conditions in Medieval Andhra* (Madras, 1968), pp. 95-96.

[106] *ARE* 99 of 1909, Rangacharya, III, p. 1663.

[107] *SII*, X, 114.

[108] Sundaram, *op. cit.*, p. 92; *SII*, IV, 1306, A.D. 1107. Vyāpāri — trader.

[109] *EZ*, II, pp. 235, 248, 251.

[110] *CTI*, I, p. 55; *CTI*, II, p. 15; *CTI*, I, p. 74. See Sri Lanka map.

[111] S.Settar, *Hoysala Sculptures* (Copenhagen, 1975), pp. 15-16.

Ayyāvoḷe guild is noticed functioning in the thirteenth century.[112] New 'southern' Ayyāvoḷes were constituted in this period in the Hassan, Tumkur, Chitradurga and Shimoga Districts.[113] There does not appear to have been though any formal relationship between the Hoysaḷa dynasty and the Ayyāvoḷe merchants to explain their presence in the Hoysaḷa *nāḍ*. On the other hand, in an elaborate Hoysaḷa inscription of A.D. 1267 found in Dod-Ballapur, the Ayyāvoḷe merchants claimed descent from Cōḷa and Caḷukya houses in the words of the epigraph "connected with the Cōḷa *kula*, of Chāḷukya descent... or "*Chōḷa kulanvitarum Chālukyānvayarum*"[114] These remarks may have been formalised expression of the existence of royal patronage from these houses but one is not able to infer any similar Hoysaḷa sponsorship of the guild. It has earlier been suggested that Ayyāvoḷe enjoyed the patronage of the Cōḷas, and the Hoysaḷa inscription of the thirteenth century of Dod-Ballapur just quoted, seems to refer to this connection.[115] The inscription was issued in the territory around modern Bangalore which was close to the Cōḷa country.

In the Hoysaḷa *nāḍ* proper it is possible to suggest that the Ayyāvoḷe merchants came in as a result of an increase in commercial activity and urban development in many areas of the central Deccan. One notices in this period a definite interest in long-distance trade especially in its relationship to overseas imports. Thus the import of horses, elephants and pearls received inscriptional mention and there was a very marked reference to transport of goods from the east to the west, the 'west to the east' and the 'south to the north'.[116] And both in the Kolar District and around Bangalore one comes across allusions in Ayyāvoḷe epigraphs to the power of the *seṭṭis* in relationship to the growth of towns. In A.D. 1267 a member of the Ayyāvoḷe guild is described as a "maker of towns".[117] The Kolar Ayyāvoḷe inscription of A.D. 1198 describes a *seṭṭi* who was *ādi-vanikēśan*, chief merchant who 'settled people in the great city of Kuvalālam' (Kolar) and who owned the 'city of Alagai'.[118] Also in Hoysāḷa times the Ayyāvoḷe guild was in the Chamrajnagar taluk, an earlier-established centre of trade.[119] They were in the

[112] See appended inscriptional table 'A'.

[113] *EC*, V, Arsikere 77; *EC*, XII, Gubbi 11;
EC, XI, Holalkere 121; *EC*, VIII, Sorab 268;
SII, IX, pt. 1, 372.

[114] *EC*, IX, Dod-Ballapur 31.

[115] The links which probably existed between the early Cōḷas and these merchants have been referred to earlier.

[116] *EC*, V, Arsikere 22.

[117] *EC*, IX, Dod-Ballapur 31.

[118] *EC*, X, Kolar 131.

[119] *EC*, IV (new), Chamrajnagar 188, 195.

Raichur *doāb* as well in the first quarter of the thirteenth century but do not seem to appear in that region thereafter.[120]

The major political change in Tamil areas in the thirteenth century was the beginning of the Pāṇḍyan resurgence after a period of Cōḷa domination. Most of the territory of the former Pudukkottai state was absorbed into the Pāṇḍyan kingdom quite early, possibly in the reign of Māṟavarman Sundara Pāṇḍya, and to the same ruler is ascribed two successive conquests of Cōḷa areas in the first three decades of the thirteenth century. Ayyāvoḷe merchants continued in these times to occupy their traditional base, the region around Pudukkottai and in addition were in the neighbouring Madurai and Tirunelveli Districts and Ramanathapuram (former) District. These regions formed part of the core of the Pāṇḍyan kingdom.

The presence of the Ayyāvoḷe guild in Ramanathapuram District is noted as early as the reign of Māṟavarman Sundara Pāṇḍya. An inscription of Pillaiyarpatti in the Tiruppattur taluk of the same district mentions the *nagarattār* who lived in the street named after the *aiññūṟṟuvar* in Enkarikkudi. The purchase of land at Marudangudi for the founding of a new colony to be called Rajanarayanapuram is also recorded.[121] The word *nagarattār* possibly refers to the Nattukottai Chettiars of modern times since the term *nagarattār* is now used extensively by this community. The arrival of the *nagarattār* at Enkarikkudi was according to Chettiar oral tradition the result of a Pāṇḍyan request to the Cōḷas that this group be permitted to migrate from Kaveripattinam and settle in their territory.[122] One other inscription also at Pillaiyarpatti notes the founding of the Rajanarayanapuram colony but may be of a latter date, possibly the reign of Māṟavarman Kulaśēkhara Pāṇḍya.[123] The two inscriptions corroborate oral accounts still current, and even the name of the new colony Rajanarayanapuram remains alive today in the folk-memory of this community. Tradition however ascribes a dating of about the eighth century to this migration from Kaveripattinam. The epigraphs belong to the thirteenth century. Even though the dates do not tally if oral tradition and the inscriptions are accepted as recording an actual transfer of residence of a *vaiśya* community in Pāṇḍya times, one has then an instance of a ruling

[120] See Appendices.

[121] *ARE* 1935-36, 150, thirteenth century. 11th year of Tribhuvanacakravartin Kōnērinmaikoṇḍān, probably identical with Māṟavarman Sundara Pāṇḍya.

[122] Weerasooria, W.S., *The Nattukottai Chettiar Merchant Bankers in Ceylon* (Dehiwala, 1973), p. 3.
N.VR.N.M. Subbiah Chettiar, in conversation, July 13, 1977.
Thurston E., *Castes and Tribes of Southern India,* rpt. (Delhi, 1975), Vol. V, p. 260.
Also *ARE* 1935-36, p. 80: "It is of interest to note that Rajanarayanapuram is the name of one of the nine places wnere the present Nattukottai Chettiars colonised in the Pāṇḍya country...."

[123] *ARE* 147 of 1935-36 (Tribhūvanacakravartin Kulaśēkharadēva who was pleased to take all countries, 18th year).

power inviting a commercial group to settle in their kingdom for the purpose presumably of fostering commerce. The *nagarattār* occupied an *aiññūṟṟuvap-perunteruvu* or "street of the *aiññūṟṟuvar*," from which one may deduce their connection with the Ayyāvoḷe guild. It would seem then that the Pāṇḍyas at the time of the second empire were especially interested in obtaining the services of this commercial guild. One may then also argue a measure of state sponsorship for Ayyāvoḷe merchants under the Pāṇḍyas.

Probably to the thirteenth century belongs one of the most impressive epigraphs issued by the Ayyāvoḷe guild. The inscription was found in the Sokkanatha temple at Piranmalai in the Tirupattur taluk of former Ramanathapuram District.[124] The Piranmalai hill borders the neighbouring Tirumayam taluk of Pudukkottai. The inscription is in Tamil and is remarkable for its literary quality. It was issued jointly with the *citramēḷi* a powerful agricultural organisation and registered the levy of toils on commodities passing through the region.[125] In it were also noted in detail the many organisations, towns, *nāḍu, vaḷanāḍu* and the eleven groups of *nagarattār* who subscribed to the edict. Five groups of *Disai Āyirattaiññūṟṟuvar* were also mentioned.

The eleven groups of *nagarattār* who attended the meeting were identified by the townships from which they came. Based on the translation of K.V. Subrahmanya Aiyer these were:

"The *nagarattār* of Aruvimānagaram *alias* Kulaśēkhara-Paṭṭiṇam in Kēraḷasiṅga-vaḷanāḍu.

The *nagarattār* of Eripaḍainallūr-Vaḍamaṭṭai in Tuvarāpatināḍu.

The *nagarattār* of Pudutteru, *alias* Śēranārāyaṇapuram in Puramalai-nāḍu.

The *nagarattār* of Kodumbāḷur - maṇigrāmam of Kaḍalaḍaiyādilaṅgai-koṇḍa-sōḷa-vaḷanāḍu in Urattūr.

The *nagarattār* of Maṇiyambalam in Tirukkōttiyūr.

The *nagarattār* of Aḷagāpuram *alias* Śēliyanārāyaṇapuram in Kēraḷasiṅga-vaḷanāḍu.

The *nagarattār* of Sundarapāṇḍiyapuram in Ayyapoḷil-vaḷanāḍu.

The *nagarattār* of Alagaimānagaram *alias* Jayaṅgoṇḍaśōḷapperunteru in Kaḷavaḷi-nāḍu.

The *nagarattār* of Maṇḍaligan - Gambīrapperunteru.

The *nagarattār* of twelve *nagarams* including Jayangoṅdaśōḷapuram.

The *nagarattār* of Karuvūr, Kaṇṇapuram, Paṭṭōḷi, Talaiyūr, Rājarājapuram, Kiranūr, and other cities."[126]

[124] *SII*, VIII, 442.

[125] Some of these commodities were imports such as horses, rose water, and probably *aghil* (aloeswood). These were all commodities current in the overseas commerce of the region in the thirteenth century and could have arrived in Piranmalai from the ports of Tondi and Kayal.

[126] K.V. Subrahmanya Aiyer, "Largest Provincial Organisations in Ancient India", *QJMS*, 45, No. 4 (1955), 272.

Subrahmanya Aiyer noted that the first ten groups came from the Pāṇḍya territory and the last from Kongu country. Of particular interest is Sundarapāṇḍiyapuram in Ayyapoḻil-vaḷanāḍu. Sundarapāṇḍiyapuram is probably Pillamangalam in the present Pudukkottai District. Ayyapoḻil-vaḷanāḍu was probably a term used by the merchants of the association to describe the central core of their territory. In the map Pudukkottai I on page 70 many of the places named above are identified and marked. Geographically the places from which the *nagarattār* came covered a large area of the peninsula and illustrates the wide range of long-distance trade. The *nagarattār* in this inscription refers to merchants who were probably part of the organisation and, as subsequent analysis shows, could also have included members of the Nattukottai Chettiar group.

The importance given to the guild at the time of the second Pāṇḍyan empire gains significance if linked with the foreign accounts of the commerce of this region in this period. According to Marco Polo, at the Pāṇḍyan port of Kayal, 'all the ships touch that came from the west, as from Hormos, and from Kis and from Aden and all Arabia...."[127] For the Arabs the Pāṇḍyan coast was Ma'bar which Wassaf described as 'the Key of Hind.'[128] The Pāṇḍyan country was also a focus for the Maṇigrāmam guild which, as described in the first chapter, apart from Kodumbalur in Pudukkottai had an effective organisation in Tittandatanapuram not far from the Pāṇḍyan port of Tondi. Here it will be recalled the Maṇigrāmam met with the Añjuvaṇṇam, the *ten-ilangai valañjiyar*, the merchants of (South) Ceylon, to ratify a charitable donation in A.D. 1269. It seems clear that both the Maṇigrāmam and the Ayyāvoḷe guild in these areas were involved in the distribution of commodities of overseas trade arriving at Pāṇḍya ports in the thirteenth century. The thirteenth century also marked the peak period of the Ayyāvoḷe guild in the Pāṇḍyan kingdom. By the early fourteenth century as the Pāṇḍyan state began to disintegrate the Ayyāvoḷe guild also disappeared from Tamil areas. In Karnataka the activity of this association noticeably diminished in the first quarter of the fourteenth century, but by the end of the same century the prospects of the Ayyāvoḷe guild again appeared to revive.

H. *Changing Fortunes under Vijayanagar*

Under the early Vijayanagar rulers an Ayyāvoḷe guild inscription of A.D. 1382 in Belur shows that at that time these merchants may have again exercised commercial power. The Belur inscription listed townships in an area of possible commercial influence which included inland areas as well as the

[127] Cited in K.A.N. Sastri, *The Pāṇḍyan Kingdom* (Madras, 1972), p. 169.
[128] *Ibid.*

South Kanara coastal towns, and Mulbagal and Kanchi.[129] Both east and west coast trade was thus involved, and this was no doubt a result of the political control by Vijayanagar over both coasts of the peninsula. The new political and economic dimensions ushered in with the Vijayanagar empire and the consequent effect on commercial organisations such as the Ayyāvoḷe guild however, are not here examined. The Chamrajnagar and Kollegal taluks, long an area of commercial activity continued to be important in the reign of Harihara. Later, as an examination of the list of inscriptions in the appendix shows, the Telugu districts of Guntur and Anantapur may have been a new focus for merchants who used the name Ayyāvoḷe and invoked the deities of Ayyāvoḷe in their inscriptions. But in all probability they were a new group of merchants, based in Telugu-speaking areas, with little or no links with the old Kannada and Tamil Ayyāvoḷe. The last available inscription describing an organisation of merchants of "Ayyāvoḷe" is probably that of Lepakshi in Anantapur District dated A.D. 1680, which is also listed in the appendix. This township was in the centre of the cotton textile weaving area and these merchants may have provided the finance and marketing facilities for the great Andhra cotton fabric manufacture of the late seventeenth century.

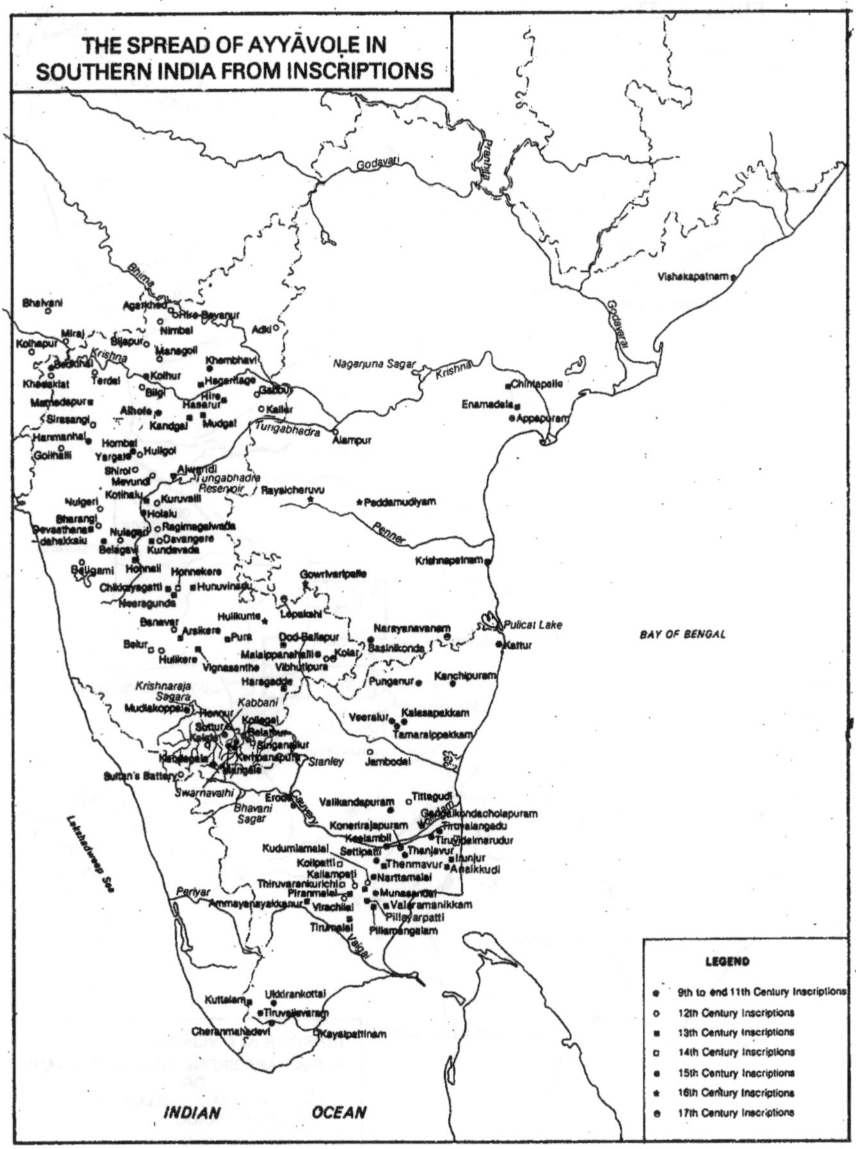
THE SPREAD OF AYYĀVOLE IN SOUTHERN INDIA FROM INSCRIPTIONS
BAY OF BENGAL
INDIAN OCEAN
LEGEND
9th to end 11th Century Inscriptions
12th Century Inscriptions
13th Century Inscriptions
14th Century Inscriptions
15th Century Inscriptions
16th Century Inscriptions
17th Century Inscriptions

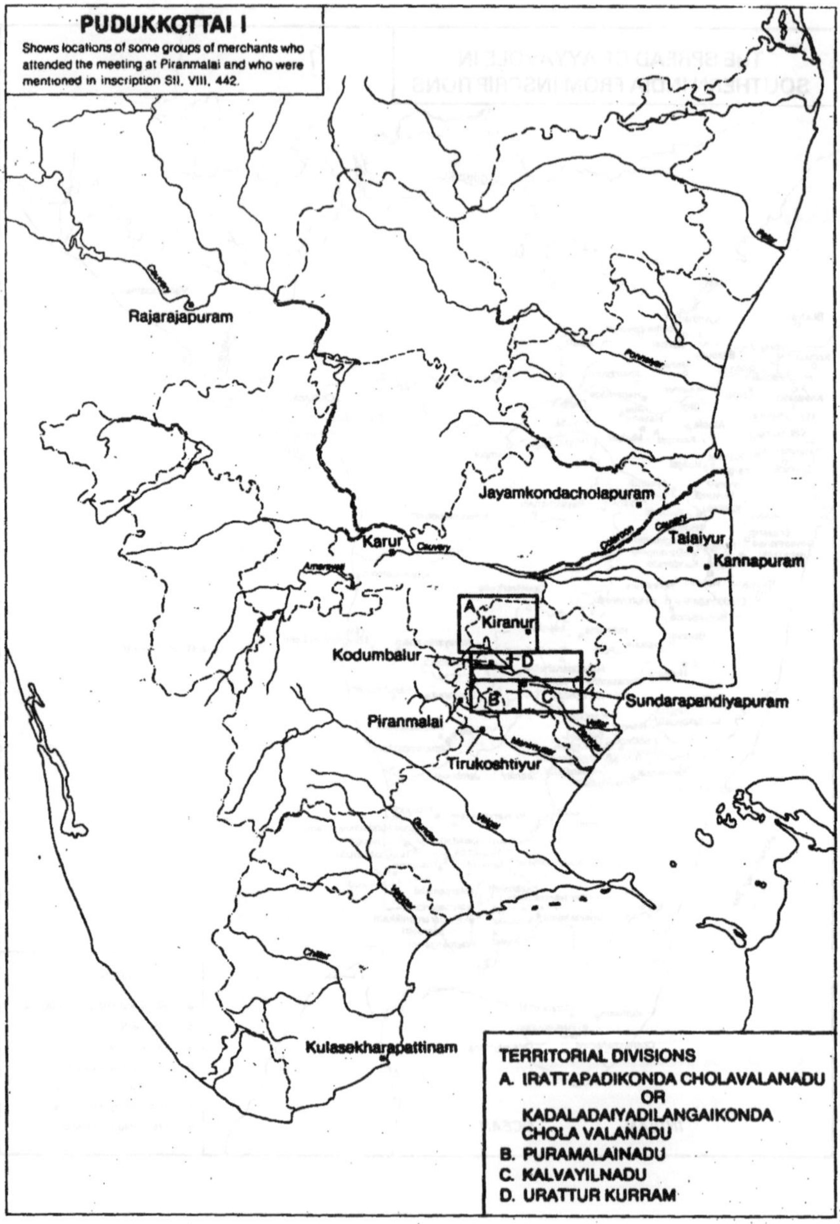
PUDUKKOTTAI I
Shows locations of some groups of merchants who attended the meeting at Piranmalai and who were mentioned in inscription SII, VIII, 442.
Rajarajapuram
Jayamkondacholapuram
Talaiyur
Kannapuram
Karur
Kiranur
Kodumbalur
Sundarapandiyapuram
Piranmalai
Tirukoshtiyur
Kulasekharapattinam
A
B
C
D
TERRITORIAL DIVISIONS
A. IRATTAPADIKONDA CHOLAVALANADU OR KADALADAIYADILANGAIKONDA CHOLA VALANADU
B. PURAMALAINADU
C. KALVAYILNADU
D. URATTUR KURRAM

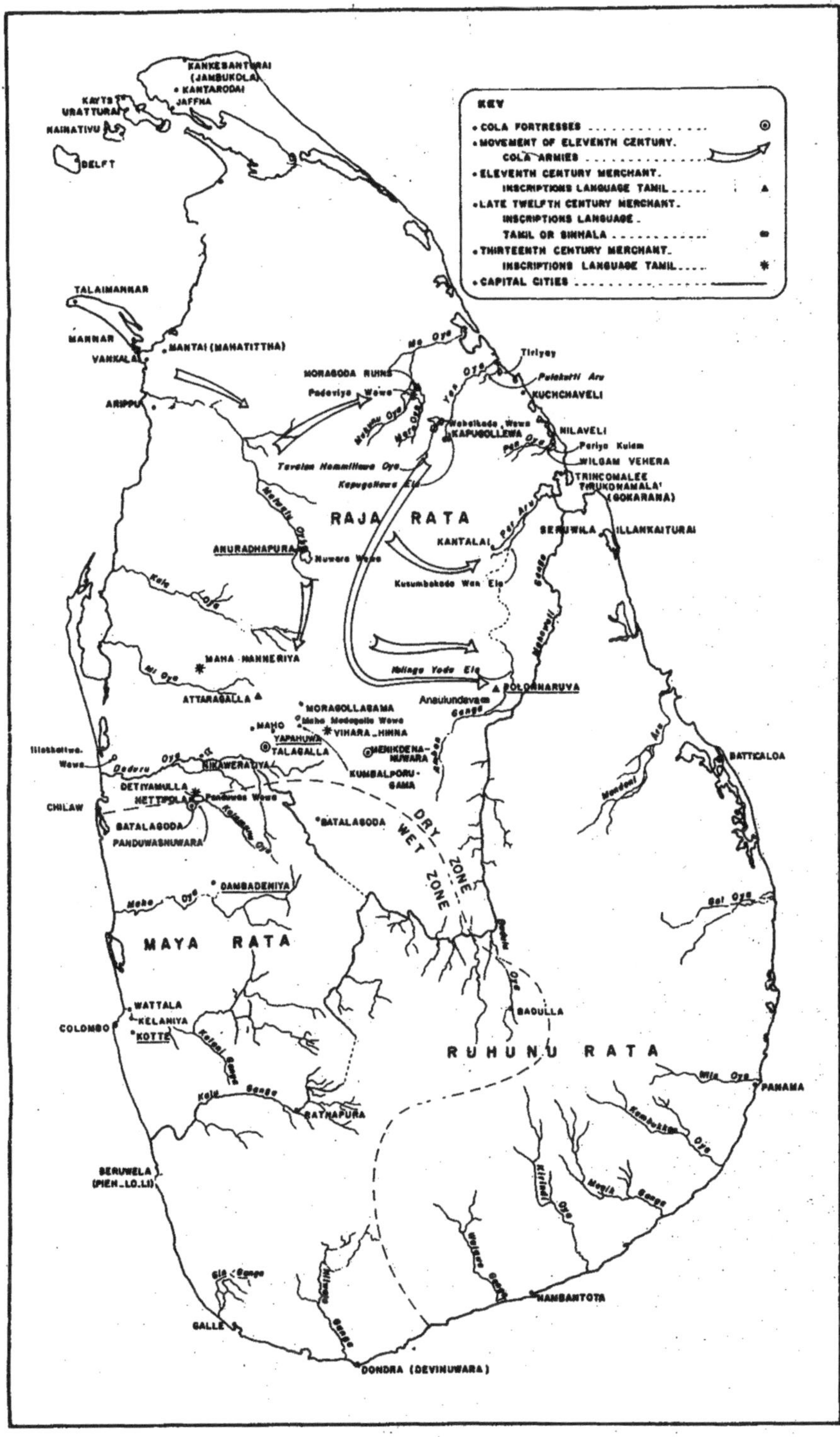
KEY
COLA FORTRESSES
MOVEMENT OF ELEVENTH CENTURY COLA ARMIES
ELEVENTH CENTURY MERCHANT INSCRIPTIONS LANGUAGE TAMIL
LATE TWELFTH CENTURY MERCHANT INSCRIPTIONS LANGUAGE TAMIL OR SINHALA
THIRTEENTH CENTURY MERCHANT INSCRIPTIONS LANGUAGE TAMIL
CAPITAL CITIES
KANKESANTURAI (JAMBUKOLA)
KANTARODAI
JAFFNA
KAYTS
URATTURAI
NAINATIVU
DELFT
TALAIMANNAR
MANNAR
VANKALAI
MANTAI (MAHATITTHA)
ARIPPU
MORAGODA RUINS
Padaviya Wewa
Tiriyay
Pulakutti Aru
KUCHCHAVELI
KAPUGOLLEWA
NILAVELI
Periya Kulam
WILGAM VEHERA
TRINCOMALEE
TIRUKONAMALAI (GOKARANA)
Kapugollewa Ela
RAJA RATA
KANTALAI
SERUWILA
ILLANKAITURAI
ANURADHAPURA
Nuwara Wewa
Kala Oya
Kusumbokada Wen Ela
MAHA NANNERIYA
Mi Oya
ATTARAGALLA
POLONNARUVA
Anaulundeva
MORAGOLLAGAMA
MAHO
YAPAHUWA
VIHARA_HINNA
TALAGALLA
MENIKDENA-NUWARA
KUMBALPORU-GAMA
NIKAWERATIYA
Deduru Oya
DETIYAMULLA
HETTIPOLA
Panduwas Wewa
CHILAW
BATALAGODA
PANDUWASNUWARA
BATALAGODA
DRY ZONE
WET ZONE
DAMBADENIYA
Maha Oya
MAYA RATA
BATTICALOA
Gal Oya
WATTALA
KELANIYA
COLOMBO
KOTTE
Kelani Ganga
BADULLA
RUHUNU RATA
Kalu Ganga
RATNAPURA
PANAMA
Kumbukkan Oya
BERUWELA (PIEH_LO_LI)
Menik Ganga
Kirindi Oya
Walawe Ganga
HAMBANTOTA
Gin Ganga
Nilwala Ganga
GALLE
DONDRA (DEVINUWARA)

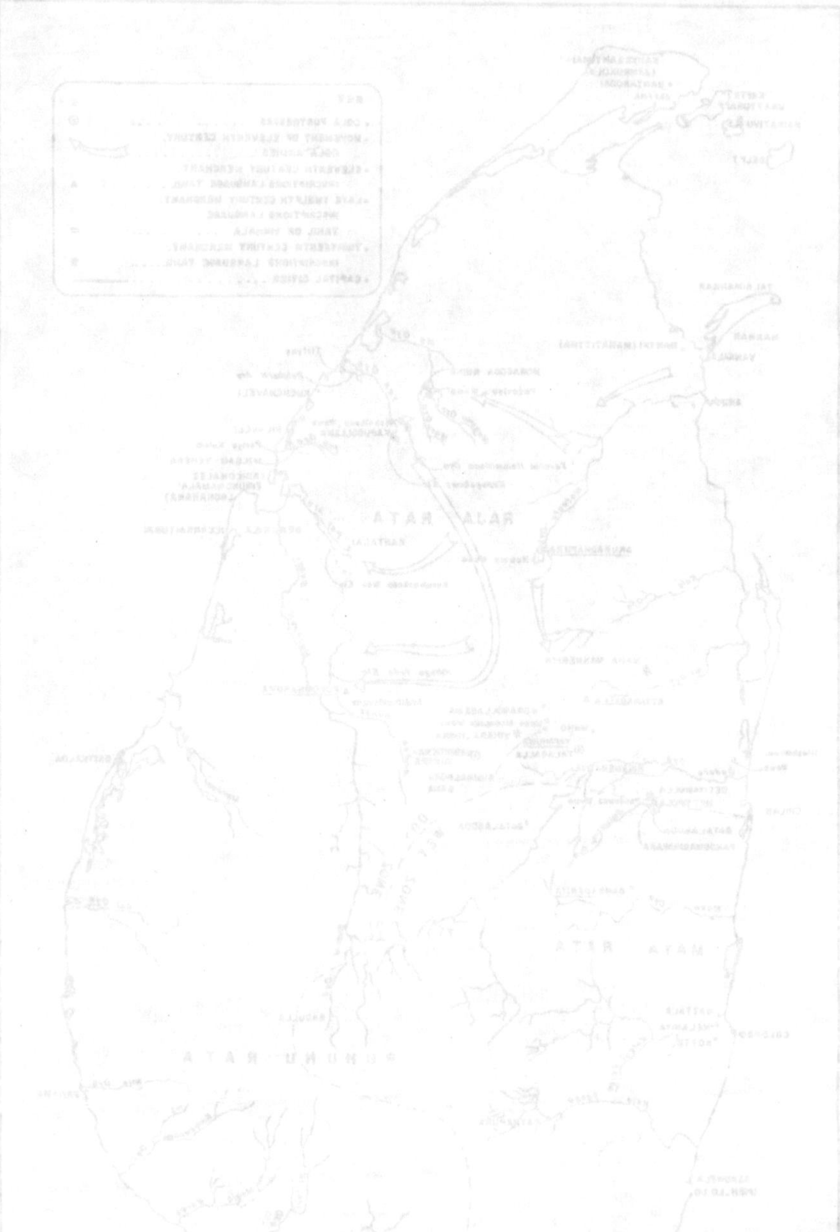

Chapter III

Some Aspects of the Structure and Functioning of the Ayyāvoḷe Association

A description of the Ayyāvoḷe association is incomplete without taking into account the many affiliate groups with which the association was linked and in this chapter, as far as possible, these groups are identified. An attempt is also made to analyse the position of the merchant vis à vis other elements in the social and political milieu of medieval times, for it is within this context that the functioning of the Ayyāvoḷe association is best comprehended.

The Ayyāvoḷe epigraphs seem to indicate considerable economic expansion in the latter half of the twelfth century, including a marked increase in both overseas trade and the development of urban settlements. Appendix A has a table of Ayyāvoḷe epigraphs, which include comments on the contents of the inscriptions. A study of these comments helps to illustrate these points. There is increasing mention of trade in grain and basic agricultural commodities as well as of trade in goods intended for export and import. There is also increasing reference to urban settlements.

Along with changes in the economy one notes shifts in the social order, and changes in the relationship of traders with the state, with the *agrahāra* Brahman and with peasant cultivators and landowners. Against the backdrop of these changes we may look at other aspects such as the composition of this important merchant guild. Although there are undoubtedly limitations to the extent of enquiry possible since one relies primarily on the inscriptions, nevertheless it is possible to examine the association in terms of the caste, kinship and religious affiliation of its members. The question of the financing of trade and the important question of whether markets were self-regulating or administered are reserved for subsequent portions of this study. While much work has been done on medieval South Indian marketing and on medieval trade, there is room for a re-appraisal in the light of what has emerged from this study of these two merchant guilds.[1] The role of these merchants in overseas trade receives attention in a separate chapter.

A combination of inscriptions of the Tamil, Kannada and Telugu-speaking areas relating to the merchant group known collectively as the Ayyāvoḷe

[1] Kenneth R. Hall, "The '*Nagaram*' as a Marketing Center in Early Medieval South India", Diss. Michigan Univ., 1975, contains a useful description and analysis of South Indian marketing. See also K.R. Hall, *Trade and Statecraft in the Age of the Cōḷas* (New Delhi, 1980).

association, when assembled in a time sequence, begin in the eighth or ninth century and continue almost till the end of the seventeenth century. This is a long life span if one conceives of the association as a monolithic corporation with a common purpose and a common direction. Most historians of medieval South India, while agreeing on the importance of the association, differ on the question of whether or not there was in fact a central "bureau" directing its affairs in both Kannada and Tamil areas. A. Appadorai, T.V. Mahalingam and L.D. Barnett have assumed that there was something like an apex group of five hundred controlling the organisation.[2] This view was obviously not held by K.A.N. Sastri who speaking of merchant guilds in Cōḷa times has said, "Trade was carried on by merchants banded together in guilds and corporations." Of these the "*aiññūṟṟuvar* were the most "celebrated". He believed they had a long history and were probably established in the Tamil country before the "rise of the Imperial Cōḷas." He suggested that they continued to function in the twelfth century but does not trace their history further. He believed they played a part in the overseas trade of their times and also seemed to suggest that the Kannada and Tamil inscriptions referred to the same organisation.[3] Kenneth Hall described them as "the elite among South Indian itinerant merchant organisations."[4] K. Indrapala believed they were "primarily traders in various types of merchandise" and that they were "a loosely organized body" but not a "corporation or trading guild," and discounted the idea that they were a "single unified corporation of merchants."[5]

G.S. Dikshit who has analysed the working of the Kannada Ayyāvoḷe association more closely than others believes the association formed "small and workable federations extending over a district or two."[6] In effect this means that he does not believe in a mammoth single corporation covering Tamil and Kannada areas. Analysis of specific inscriptions such as an eleventh century Kannada inscription and the thirteenth century Tamil Piranmalai inscription supports Dikshit's idea but suggests that the unit of commercial operations was much larger than envisaged by him. The eleventh century Kannada inscription shows that an area covering at least four modern districts was treated as a commercial unit.[7] The thirteenth century Tamil Piranmalai inscription covers an even larger area.[8] Eleven

[2] A. Appadorai, *Economic Conditions*, Vol. II, p. 394; B.A. Saletore, *Social and Political Life in the Vijayanagara Empire (A.D. 1346-1646)*, Vol.II (Madras, 1934), p. 98 citing T.V. Mahalingam, *South Indian Polity* (Madras, 1955), p. 392.

[3] Sastri, *The Cōḷas*, pp. 595-597.

[4] Hall, "The *Nagaram*", p. 187.

[5] K. Indrapala, "Some Medieval Mercantile Communities of South India and Ceylon," *JTS*, 2, No. 2, pt. 1 (1970), 5-6.

[6] G. S. Dikshit, "Constitution of the Trade Guilds in Medieval Karnataka", *JKUH*, 3 (1959), 53.

[7] *KI*, IV, p. 121.

[8] *SII* VIII, 442.

groups of *nagarattār* (in this case, merchants) were mentioned among those who met at Piranmalai and they included merchants who came from Kulasekharapattinam on the coast, merchants within and close to modern Pudukkottai District and merchants from towns in the Kongu country such as Karuvur, and perhaps even Talakad. The map Pudukkottai I, on page 70 illustrates this point very well.

In both the Kannada and Tamil regional kingdoms the association formed close links with royal houses. A personal relationship between the *aiññūṟṟūvar* merchants and the Cōḷas has been earlier suggested in view of the dynastic connection between the Cōḷas and the Irukkuvēḷs in the eleventh century. The argument has been put forward that as a consequence of these dynastic links the Cōḷas sought to foster the interests of this association established in the region of Pudukkottai and that with the Cōḷa advance into the strategic tract of territory south of Talakad the Ayyāvoḷe guild followed.[9] Similarly, merchants moved into the Telugu country soon after the union of the Cōḷa and Vengi kingdoms. A further indication of the personal nature of the link between ruler and merchant is the traditional account of the Pāṇḍyan invitation to the Nattukottai Chettiars, members of this guild, to migrate to their territory from Kaveripattinam. If this was so it was based on knowledge of the commercial services rendered by the Chettiar community to the Cōḷa monarchy, or else it is hardly likely that the group would have been encouraged to move into the Pāṇḍyan kingdom. No evidence of a similar personal bond between the association as a whole and the ruler is forthcoming from Kannada sources although in the twelfth and thirteenth centuries individual merchant princes in Kannada areas obviously enjoyed direct royal patronage. In both areas the association had strong regional links. Since the Tamil and Kannada kingdoms were frequently in rivalry with each other it is difficult to visualise that the Ayyāvoḷe association, covering a territory stretching from the Raichur *dōāb* to Sri Lanka, ever had central coordinating direction.

One envisages though that when trans-peninsular or intra-regional movement of commodities was required the Ayyāvoḷe infrastructure in both the northern and southern Deccan served a common purpose. Unrecorded agreements between Kannada and Tamil *aiññūṟṟuvar* merchants probably facilitated the passage of goods from one region to the other. Inscriptions show, for example, that commodities of overseas trade, some of them of Southeast Asian origin, arrived in interior Karnataka. It is unlikely that the Southeast Asian products came in through ports on the west coast of India but rather through the Coromandel ports in Andhra and Tamil areas. The distribution of these commodities in Karnataka areas was undoubtedly facilitated by cooperation between Tamil and Kannada *aiññūṟṟuvar* merchants since it

[9] These points are all elaborated in the earlier reconstruction of the history of the association.

was the Tamil groups who were most active in the coastal areas where these goods first entered the South Indian market.

A. *Affiliate Organizations*

The vast trading network established by the Ayyāvoḷe merchants was in part dependent on cooperation from other less important but nevertheless active corporate bodies. Many of these were listed in the inscriptions of the *aiññūṟṟuvar* but were mentioned as if in a subordinate relationship to them. The Valañjīyar, most probably a group of merchants, were mentioned separately as early as the ninth century in Tamil inscriptions and were linked with the *aiññūṟṟūvar* in the Munasandal inscription recorded on a slab by the side of the Munasandal tank in which rights were granted to the *"sai-āyiranaññūṟṟūvar Valañjiyar Aiññūṟṟūvar."*[10] They figured quite frequently in the tenth century Ayyāvoḷe inscriptions and they were mentioned in the twelfth century in Sri Lanka.[11] This group was probably already in existence when the first *aiññūṟṟūvar* centres were established in Tamil-speaking areas. An epigraph linking the Valañjiyar and the *aiññūṟṟuvar* ascribed, on paleographic grounds, to the tenth century shows that the *aiññūṟṟūvar* gave a gift of 15 *kaḻañju* of gold for two lamps in memory of a Valañjiyar who was killed in what may have been a quarrel between two merchants.[12] The Maṇigrāmattār were also associated with this donation. In the eleventh century at Kanchipuram, *aiññūṟṟūvar* and Valañjiyar apparently jointly maintained a *maṭha*.[13]

The *nānādēśis* are sometimes equated with *aiññūṟṟuvar* or Ayyāvoḷe, but there is evidence that they were distinct entities since there exist records of land sales between *nānādēśis* and *aiññūṟṟuvar* which would hardly have taken place if they had not been separate organisations.[14] The *ubhayanānādēśi* mentioned so frequently in the Kannada inscriptions were probably

[10] *ARE* 101 of 1973-74 unpublished, and *PSI*, 61.

[11] *ARE* 622 of 1909; *ARE* 131 of 1926; *EZ*, 11, 1928/b.

[12] *ARE* 308 of 1964-65.

[13] *ARE* 264 of 1955-56.

[14] Sastri, *The Cōḷas*, p. 596 believed the *nānādēśis* were to be equated with the *aiññūṟṟuvar*. The land sales referred to between *nānādēśi* and *aiññūṟṟuvar* took place in Hoysaḷa times; "...the officer in charge of lease of lands of Mudigonda, *sēnapati* Vāsudēvaperumāl, Alvan Tiruvandai, Vīran Chokkanayan...dannāyaka...manichcham...issued a sale-deed charter to all the *nānādēśis* of Māmpalli fixing the value thus.... In the month of Vaikasi, in the year Pramōduta, the *aiññūṟṟuvar* receiving the land value from the *nānādēśis* gave the land (which was made) tax-free for as long as sun and moon endure...," *EC*, IV (new), Yelandur, 158. There are many epigraphs in which the *nānādēśi* were mentioned independently of the *aiññūṟṟuvar*, as for example *ARE* 17 of 1960-61, *ARE* 576 of 1961-62, also the *nānādēśi* inscription of the thirteenth century found at Pagan, *EI*, VII, pp. 197-198. These are only a few of the many records of their activity.

a group which traded both within the country and outside, *svadēsi* and *paradēśi*.[15]

An eleventh century Tamil inscription mentions groups such as the *seṭṭis, seṭṭiputras, kavares, kaṇḍalis, bhadrakas, gāvuṇḍa-svāmis, śingam, śirupuli,* and *valattukai*.[16]Some of these categories are identifiable. For example, the *seṭṭis* and *seṭṭiputras* were merchants. The *gāvuṇḍa-svāmis* may have been agriculturists.[17] The *kavares* are not easy to place but the *gavares* who were mentioned frequently in the Kannada inscriptions were, it is believed, basket makers, or corn merchants.[18] The *valattukai* may be a reference to mercenary groups associated with the Right Hand Division, of which more will be said later. In many of the inscriptions of merchants in Kannada and in Tamil areas, the number eighteen is frequently attached to the terminology used to describe merchant groups. The *padineṇ-bhūmi* so frequently referred to could have been the name of a merchant group or a semi-mythical eighteen districts on either side of the Kaveri. The Valañjiyar occasionally used this number. So did a group known as the *vāniya-nagarattār*.[19] A late Tamil inscription of the sixteenth century referred to the *padineṭṭu-nāḍu*.[20] The *padineṇ-viṣaiyattōm* in the thirteenth century were active in the Pāṇḍya country and we find them mentioned like the *citramēḷi* in major inscriptional records.[21]

Kannada inscriptions referred to the *sēnabōva*, a village accountant, who was quite often mentioned in the Ayyāvoḷe inscriptions.[22] The *seṭṭiguṭṭas* who figured often in the Kannada records were either leaders of *seṭṭis* or '*vaiśya seṭṭis*'; the word *guṭṭa*, it has been suggested could mean *gupta* —a *vaiśya*.[23] The *birudas* frequently mentioned could have been officials with local titles. The *gātrigas* were a particularly ubiquitous group judging by the many references in Kannada Ayyāvoḷe inscriptions. The *gātrigas* were betel leaf sellers and betel leaf and areca were in universal demand. The Terdal inscription of A.D. 1123 for example describes a donation given by them: "The *gātrigas* trading on the great road to the Haḷasige Twelve Thousand

[15] K. R. Venkatarama Ayyar, "Medieval Trade, Craft and Merchant Guilds", p. 276. There are several inscriptions which mention the *ubhaya- nānādēśi* both in Kannada-and Telugu-speaking areas. To cite a few example, *EC*, IX, Kankanhalli 77 and 78; *EC*, VII, pt. 1, Shikarpur 313; *SII*, X, 567; *SII*, X, 495.

[16] *ARE* 256 of 1912.

[17] G. S. Dikshit, *Local Self-Government in Medieval Karnataka* (Dharwad, 1964), pp. 62-63.

[18] *Ibid.*, p. 30.

[19] *ARE* 337 of 1960-61, and p. 23. Also *EC*, 1,20, Palur, Mercara taluk, where an undated endowment is guaranteed by the Śrivaiṣṇavas of the Eighteen countries, the Valañjiyar of the Eighteen countries, and the Brahmaṇas of the Eighteen *nāḍus*.

[20] *ARE* 98 of 1973-74, unpublished, found near Kozhikode.

[21] *SII*, VI, 40; *SII*, VI, 41; *SII*, VI, 47.

[22] Dikshit, *Local Self-Government*, pp. 65-66.

[23] Suggested by G. S. Dikshit in conversation, December 10, 1977

gave 100 leaves on one load...."[24] Clearly the description shows that these were not traders of high local status or influence. These were wayside sellers of a perishable commodity in constant demand in rural and urban areas.

Among the most important of all the groups associated with the *aiññūṟṟuvar* or Ayyāvoḷe merchants were the semi-military groups, armed guards, swordsmen, mercenaries of whom many probably received a share of the profits of trade. These groups may have been hired by the traders to ensure protection for itinerant groups and for caravans, and also to guarantee the safety of trading settlements. It is also possible that groups originally hired for protection later diversified and engaged in various forms of trade themselves. A classic example were the *mummuridaṇḍas* of Kannada areas. The word *mummuridaṇḍa* probably meant advance guards.[25] They were mentioned independently of the five hundred *svāmis* or any other major trading group in the early eleventh century in the Dharwad district.[26] By the late eleventh and in the twelfth century they were mentioned frequently along with the 500 *svāmis* of Ayyāvoḷe, but in a subordinate relationship to them.[27] The *mummuridaṇḍa* in this period also were seen collaborating with other merchant groups such as the *ubhaya-nānādēśi*.[28] In the second half of the twelfth century there is a record of their special *praśasti* in which they claimed to have been of the same lineage as the 500 *svāmis*.[29] The present-day districts of Gulbarga, Bellary and Dharwad were areas in which the *mummuridaṇḍas* were quite prominent. In the early thirteenth century they were trading independently in commodities of importance such as paddy, black pepper, asafoetida, green ginger, turmeric, oil, areca nuts, betel leaves, sugar and horses.[30]

Other groups mentioned with the *aiññūṟṟuvar* who were obviously groups hired for the protection of trade included the *bīravanigas* in Kannada inscriptions.[31]. In Tamil language Ayyāvoḷe inscriptions are mentioned the *erivīras, munaivīras, and, koṇgavālas.*[32] Of these, the *kongavalar* were mentioned in the inscriptions of Sri Lanka. It is held that mercenary groups were brought in large numbers by merchants such as the *aiññūṟṟuvar* into Sri Lanka in the eleventh century and that they remained in the island and later

[24] *IA*, XIV, p. 14.

[25] Dikshit, "Constitution of the Trade Guilds", p. 57.

[26] *ARE* 46 of 1972-73.

[27] For example, *EI*, V, 3; *SII*, XV, 106; *SII*, IX, pt. 1, 139.

[28] *ARE* 173 of 1971-72.

[29] S. Gururajachar, *Some Aspects of Economic and Social Life in Karnataka* (A.D. 1000—A.D. 1300) (Mysore, 1974), p. 119.

[30] *EI*, XIII, 3a.

[31] *EC*, III, Nanjangud 359.

[32] *ARE* 1912-13, p. 100,also *ARE* 342 of 1912-13. See also Indrapala, "Some Medieval Mercantile Communities".

served under Sinhalese princes.[33] An eleventh century *aiññūṟṟuvar* inscription from the border area between Tamil and Kannada country described a protected merchant settlement and mentioned provision made for the hired guards during a caravan halt. The preparations included "clothes for a swordsman, oil for the lamp of the good Kavarai-Iśvaram-uḍaiyār, food for the merchant bodyguards and a pig for feeding in memory of the deceased heroes".[34]

B. *Some Social Groups Associated with Ayyāvoḷe*

Mercenaries both in Kannada and Tamil areas were drawn from social groups quite different from the groups prominent in the early history of the association in Kannada territory. It will be recalled that the Ayyāvoḷe association in Kannada areas, from its inception in Aihole, till about the mid-twelfth century was closely associated with the *agrahāra* and *agrahāra* Brahmans.[35] Kannada Ayyāvoḷe settlements or markets were frequently located in *agrahāras* and, as will be shown subsequently, there is frequent evidence of the actual participation of Brahmans in trading ventures. One concludes that the controlling interest in much of the trade handled by the *aiññūṟṟuvar* merchants in what is now modern Karnataka was drawn from Brahman groups. These included elite members of the sedentary society which flourished in the Raichur *doāb* close to the royal establishments of the Rāṣṭrakūṭas and Caḷukyas. Brahman interest is also to be noticed in Dharwad. In Gadag taluk a mid-twelfth century inscription noted the Ayyāvoḷe traders were present at a district assembly, a *mahānāḍu*, at Hugligola, an *agrahāra* and "the foremost trading centre of the south."[36] At Davangere, in Chitradurga District an inscription of the early twelfth century mentioned an Ayyāvoḷe market centre which was located in an *agrahāra*.[37] Mudnur in Shorapur taluk, Gulbarga District, was known to be a trading centre and an *agrahāra* from A.D. 1100 and by the first quarter of the thirteenth century one notices that the Ayyāvoḷe organisation was established there.[38]

[33] Indrapala, *op. cit.*, and Indrapala, "South Indian Mercantile Communities in Ceylon, circa 950-1250", *CJHSS*, n.s., Nos. 1, 2 (1971), 101-13.

[34] *EC*, IV (new) Chamrajnagar 146, may be of the time of Rājādhirāja I.

[35] Some of these inscriptions linking the *agrahāra* with the trade of this association are, 8th or 9th century *IA*, LIX, Aivalli, Bijapur District; A.D. 1113, *EC*, IX, Davangere 149, Chitradurga District; A.D. 1142, *EC*, V, pt. 1, Arsikere 110, Hassan District; A.D. 1167, *SII*, XV, 106, Huilgol, Dharwad District; A.D. 1185, *EC*, VII, Honnali 91, Shimoga District; A.D. 1185, *SII*, XV, 65, Konnur, Bijapur District; A.D. 1203, *ARE* 419 of 1964-65, Koppal, Raichur District; A.D. 1218, *ARE* 519 of 1960-61, Mudnur, Gulbarga District; A.D. 1245, *EC*, VIII, Sorab 268, Shimoga District.

[36] *SII*, XV, 106.

[37] *EC*, XI, Davangere 149.

[38] In A.D. 1100, Mudnur, Shorapur taluk, Gulbarga District was already an *agrahāra* with

The *agrahāra* was not closely linked with the *aiññūṟṟuvar* in the late tenth and the eleventh centuries in Tamil-speaking areas. At that time as shown earlier the Irukkuvēḷ chieftains probably had a considerable say in the long-distance trade of the *aiññūṟṟuvar*. The Irukkuvēḷ homeland in and around modern Pudukkottai was thickly forested and even today forest dwellers, and people who live by hunting and fishing are still found in the area.[39] One speculates that in the early eleventh century many of these people may have profited from the trade passing along the trade routes which went through the Pudukkottai tracts for it is possible that it was these and similar people who were recruited as mercenaries by trading associations in medieval times. The protection of itinerant trade and perhaps participation in the transportation of merchandise would have been occupations suited to people living on the fringes of settled society. On two occasions in the mid and late twelfth century Niṣādarājan chiefs made grants to a temple dedicated to Ayyapoḷiya Nācciyar in Tirumayam taluk, Pudukkottai.[40] The Niṣādarājan chiefs were, it is claimed, Valaiyars, hunters and forest dwellers.[41] While there are also instances of Brahman participation in the trade of the *aiññūṟṟūvar* in Tamil areas, these links were not many and not as visible as they were north of Tamil areas.[42]

C. *Local Institutions and Their Relationship with Ayyāvoḷe*

The most significant groups with which the *aiññūṟṟuvar* were increasingly associated from the twelfth century onwards were the *okkalu* or *aruvattokkalu* in Kannada areas and the *citramēḷi* in Tamil-speaking areas. Both these organisations were composed primarily of agriculturists and they were increasingly mentioned from the mid-twelfth century onwards in Ayyāvole

---

mahājanas and separately, 500 *banajigas*. The *mahājanas* were Brahmans but not yet referred to as 500 *svāmis*. (*ARE* 520 of 1960-61). By A.D. 1129, the *mahājanas* of Mudnur were already referred to as 500 *mahājanas*. They were therefore employing the classic number associated with trade and assuming that the *mahājanas* were Brahmans, we probably have here an instance of Brahmans claiming a share in the commercial enterprise of the *agrahāra*. (*ARE* 526 of 1960-61). Evidence of the growing commercial importance of Mudnur is the *mahānaḍu* held in A.D. 1182 with *mummuridaṇḍa, ubhaya-nānādēśi* and *36 bidu* present. (*ARE* 524 of 1960-61). By A.D. 1218 the trading enterprise of this *agrahāra* came under the umbrella of the Ayyāvoḷe. (*ARE* 519 of 1960-61). (The development of commerce in Mudnur and finally the link established with the 500 *svāmis* has been traced in this footnote from a reading of the transcripts of the inscriptions.)

[39] A fuller analysis of Pudukkottai is contained in a later chapter.

[40] *PSI* 134; *PSI* 148.

[41] P.M. Subramaniam, 4 Nov. 1981, in course of oral analysis of Pudukkottai District. P.M. Subramaniam believes they were the original inhabitants of the area.

[42] See subsequent pages for instances of Brahmans engaged in trade in Tamil-speaking country.

inscriptions. The alliance between agriculturist and trader is deduced from the many references to the *okkalu* in the Kannada Ayyāvoḷe inscriptions and from the important joint inscriptions issued by the *citramēḷi* and the *aiññūṟṟuvar* in Tamil. In these same inscriptions may be noticed also the increasing mention of the cess levied on a wide range of agricultural commodities. This may be noticed as early as the twelfth century but becomes very marked in the second half of the twelfth century and in the early thirteenth century in both Tamil and Kannada country.

The *okkalu* never became as important as the *citramēḷi* but the relationship of both these groups with the *aiññūṟṟūvar* was an important feature of medieval South Indian economic history. The *citramēḷi* association was composed largely it is believed, of people who belonged to a caste group, similar to, if not identical with, that of the present-day Veḷḷāḷas. Several local institutions of medieval South India remain ossified and intact in the Jaffna peninsula today and the *citramēḷi* as it still survives there is composed of persons known as *citramēḷi* Veḷḷāḷas with group traditions of coming from India.[43] That the *okkalu* and *citramēḷi* were organisations particularly linked with the farming interests is now well established.[44] In Tamil usage and in Kannada the word "*mēḷi*" means a plough, though M.D. Sampath has pointed out that earlier the word *mēḷi* or *mēṭi* meant "a pillar in the middle of the threshing floor to which oxen are bound".[45] It is claimed that a Tamil *citramēḷi* inscription recorded as early as the eleventh century has been found.[46] An association known as *meḷi-sāsiravu* was in existence in Caḷukyan times.[47] The *okkalu* was mentioned in Kannada inscriptions as early as the late tenth century. But as earlier pointed out these agricultural organisations became increasingly prominent from the second half of the twelfth century onwards.[48]

In present-day Andhra the *citramēḷi* became important in the same period and it is surely not without economic significance that in so many areas of the South Indian peninsula these changes in the social structure should have taken place around the same time.[49] One notes also the contemporaneous

[43] June, 1981, interview with Vidvan Chelliah, Sittirameli, Jaffna.

[44] Stein, *PSSMSI*, p. 221.

[45] M.D. Sampath, "The Chitramēḷi", *Studies in Indian History and Culture* (Dharwad, 1971), p. 315, cited M. Abraham, "The Ayyāvoḷe Guild of Early Medieval South India", M. Phil. Diss. Jawaharlal Nehru Univ., 1978, p. 95.

[46] R. Nagaswamy, *Studies in Ancient Tamil Law and Society* (Madras, 1978), pp. 75, ff.

[47] Sampath, *op. cit.*, p. 315. See also Stein *op. cit.*, p. 221, f.n. 18.

[48] As noted for example in *KI*, I, 25; *KI*, V, 64; *SII*, VIII, 442.

[49] The *citramēḷi* inscriptions of Andhra are generally inscribed in Tamil or Kannada, as for example, *ARE* 70 of 1963-64 (Tamil), Nellore District;
ARE 23 of 1968-69 (Tamil), Cuddapah District;
ARE 18 of 1953-54 (Kannada), Anantapur District;
ARE 15 of 1953-54 (Kannada), Anantapur District;
ARE 6 of 1953-54 (Tamil), Anantapur District;
ARE 70 of 1963-64 (Tamil), Nellore District.

development in neighbouring Sri Lanka of the growth in power of the land-owning classes. In the late twelfth and early thirteenth centuries in Sri Lanka the same phenomenon was to be noticed. Niśśanka Malla was forced to issue a proclamation condemning the ambitions of the Govi or land-owning classes. "People of the Govi caste should not aspire to the dignity of kingship for (this should be) like the crow apeing the swan....However powerful the people of the Govi caste may be, they should not be elected (to rule) the kingdom."[50]

The growing importance of the farming interests and the rise in the status of peasant cultivators in South India was accompanied by changes in local administration. These have been described as "the emergence of assemblies called the *periyanāḍu* acting over an enlarged locality and signalling diminished isolation among previous nuclear regions, or *nāḍus* and at the same time, augmenting power in the hands of supra-level leaders of the enlarged locality...." [51] Several inscriptions describe donations made jointly by the *aiññūṟṟuvar* and the *citramēḷi periyanāṭṭār*.[52] In some of these the *aiññūṟṟuvar* appear in a subordinate relationship to the *citramēḷi periyanāṭṭār* which is a change of some consequence since in all other inscriptions mentioning the *aiññūṟṟuvar* with their affiliate bodies the *aiññūṟṟuvar* were clearly the most important. For example, at Managoli, Bijapur District, in A.D. 1161, it is recorded that the proceedings at a *mahanāḍu* were 'headed' by the five hundred *svamis* of Ayyavoḷe. After them were listed the *gavares*, *mummuridaṇḍas*, the *nakaras*, the *gātrigas* and others.[53] In A.D. 1186 at Sirasangi, Belgaum District, again another Kannada inscription mentioned the five hundred *svāmis* and, after them, the *seṭṭis*, *seṭṭiguṭṭas* , *mummuridaṇḍas, ubhaya nanadēśigal*, the *birudas*, the *bīravanigas*, the *gavares*, *gātrigas*, the fifty *okkals* and the *nakaras*.[54] In the eleventh century in a Tamil inscription the *aiññūṟṟuvar* were shown ahead of the *seṭṭis*, *seṭṭiputras*, *kavares, kaṇḍalis, bhadrakas, gāvuṇḍa-svāmis, śingam, śirupuli, valattukai* and others.[55]

In contrast at Tittagudi, South Arcot, in A.D. 1168, the representatives of the *citramēḷi periyanāḍu* preceded the *aiññūṟṟuvar*.[56] In the formal phrases used in the *praśastis* of the inscriptions jointly issued by the *citramēḷi* and the *aiññūṟṟuvar* ritual objects were mentioned, the *cenkōl*, symbol of royal authority, the plough, the symbol of the *citramēḷi*, and the *cempon pasumpai*,

[50] *EZ*, II, p. 164.

[51] Stein, *PSSMSI*, p. 216.

[52] *SII*, VIII, 291; *SII*, VIII, 442; *ARE* 286 of 1964-65; *ARE* 285 of 1964-65; *ARE* 296 of 1964-65.

[53] *EI*, V, p. 23.

[54] *KI*, I, 25.

[55] *ARE* 256 of 1912.

[56] *SII*, VIII, 291.

the trader's symbol of the pouch. Where the plough preceded the pouch it is held, this was a further indication of the dominance of the *citramēḷi*.[57] At Piranmalai in the former Ramanathapuram District, the trader's pouch came first and the plough followed, which was indication of the pre-eminance of the trader in that locality.[58] The fact that the *cenkōl,* the sceptre, was always mentioned before the plough and the pouch would indicate royal approval of the *citramēḷi*. The opening phrases of the *citramēḷi* inscription of Nellore, *tiru vāyk kelvi munnaga* has been described as a phrase connoting 'cognition by the king'.[59]

Where did the *citramēḷi periyanāṭṭār* and the *aiññūṟṟuvar* convene their assemblies when they met for the purposes of determining donations to temples? *SII,* VIII, 291 records that the *citramēḷi periyanāṭṭār* and the *aiññūṟṟuvar* met in a *maṇḍapa* in a courtyard of the Viṣṇu temple where they set up the shrine of Sri Bhumippirattiyar, surmounted by a plough. Vaisnavite and Saivite shrines were named after the *citramēḷi* in areas where they were powerful and it is possible that in these temples, or close to them, these particular assemblies of the *periyanāṭṭār* were held. Some temples had *maṇḍapas* named after the *citramēḷi* – *citramēḷi maṇḍapa*, and these were probably used as meeting places. The greatest of the combined *citramēḷi* and *aiññūṟṟuvar* inscriptions is that of Piranmalai.[60] As recorded the assembly described in the inscription is noteworthy for the wide geographical range from which its membership was drawn, and for the remarkable and comprehensive list of trade goods enumerated. The meeting was undoubtedly large in terms of numbers and it was probably held in the open at the foot of the Piranmalai hill just off the highway linking the Pudukkottai tracts with Madurai and Tiruchchirappalli, since the Sokkanatha temple on the outer wall of which the inscription is inscribed was far too small to accommodate a large gathering.

In Karnataka an important assembly which was frequently mentioned in connection with the Ayyāvoḷe merchants was the *mahanāḍu.* The *mahanāḍu* was an assembly convened on occasion to decide donations to temples but almost certainly other matters of commercial importance were decided at these meetings, though of these there is no inscriptional mention. At a twelfth century assembly at Sedambal were included Prithvi Seṭṭi and Boppanaya, both merchants, the *rāja-srēṣṭi*, a royal merchant, other traders mentioned by name such as Vespayya Seṭṭi and Sovanna Seṭṭi. Shopkeepers and towns people were included as well as members of craft associations — goldsmiths, leather workers, basket makers, potters. Also included was the

[57] The significance of the order in which the trader's pouch and the plough were mentioned was first pointed out to me by Dr. R. Nagaswamy in June 1979, Madras.

[58] *SII*, VIII, 442.

[59] K.V. Subrahmanya Aiyer, "Largest Provincial Organisations", p. 283; *SII,* V, 496.

[60] *SII*, VIII, 442.

nāḍ-pergade who was probably an official in charge of several villages.[61] The *mahanāḍu* resembled the assembly of the *citramēḷi* in that it cut across narrow, locality affiliations, though unlike the *periyanāḍu,* the *mahanāḍu* , it is likely, dealt primarily with commercial matters.[62] The *mahanāḍu* met largely on fair days. It is also likely that at the *mahanāḍu* matters which were never the subject of epigraphic record were discussed such as pricing or the enforcement of district monopolies.

It is possible that many of the decisions affecting merchant guilds which were discussed at the *mahanāḍu* in Kannada areas, were in the Tamil country settled in the *nagaram* assemblies. The *nagaram* assemblies pre-dated the Cōḷas.[63] It has been pointed out that there were several in existence in Pallava times and that by "the end of the twelfth century Cōḷa epigraphy designated almost one hundred *nagaram.*"[64] Stein describes a *nagaram* as a "trade settlement", "under the control of merchant groups."[65] Hall describes the *nagaram* as "primarily a commercial district inhabited by merchants and others who earned their living from commercial activities." He also refers to it as "an assembly".[66] Nilakanta Sastri describes the *nagaram* as "in all probability a primary assembly of merchants, which was organised as one of the local assemblies in important trade centres and was the only assembly in places where the mercantile interest overshadowed all the rest."[67] Nilakanta Sastri's observation is in part borne out by the tradition of the Chettiar community of merchants. In this group the *nagaram* is an assembly which still functions, meeting mainly in temples. Membership of the *nagaram* is now confined to the elders of the community and disputes in the group are settled by the *nagaram* which still also levies contributions for religious foundations.[68] But the word *nagaram* appears to have meant more than an assembly of merchants. The *nagaram* was also a settlement containing within it both artisans and merchants.[69] The *nagarattār* were members of the *nagaram* and this again would refer either to their location within the spatial confines

[61] *EI*, XIX, 4.

[62] At Hirsingi, in the twelfth century, representatives of twelve towns were present at a *mahanāḍu* (*KI*, 1, 25). G.S. Dikshit believes the *mahanāḍu* did not have "any specific functions" and did not form "part of the administrative machinery as the *nāḍu* and village assemblies did", *Local Self-Government,* p. 34.

[63] Hall, "The *Nagaram*", p. 65.

[64] *Ibid.*

[65] Stein, *PSSMSI*, p. 282.

[66] Hall, *op. cit.*, p. 67

[67] Sastri, *The Cōḷas*, p. 503.

[68] N.S. Pichappan, 30 June, 1977 and N.Vr.N.M. Subbiah Chettiar, 13 July, 1977, in an interview. The *nagaram* meets today in each of the nine temples of the Nattukottai Chettiars. Representatives of the Chettiar villages are members of the *nagaram*.

[69] Hall, "The *Nagaram*", pp. 66-67.

of the *nagaram* or to their membership of the *nagaram* assembly. The present-day Nattukottai Chettiars refer to themselves as *nagarattār* and in the case of this community the word is used also to denote membership in a kinship group.

Based on Hall's list of known *nagaram* in Cōḷa times only one or two of the eleven groups of *nagarattār* mentioned in the thirteenth century Piranmalai inscription, as having attended the joint meeting of *citramēḷi* and *aiññuṟṟuvar*, were members of the *nagaram* in the spatial sense.[70] The term *nagarattār* in the inscription could well have been used in this case to indicate the Nattukottai Chettiars since many of the places of origin of the *nagarattār* groups, as mentioned, were located within the traditional homeland of the community.[71]

If the Piranmalai *nagarattār* in this instance may be equated with the Chettiars, then these *nagarattār* were obviously itinerant traders and members of the Ayyāvoḷe association. According to the Nattukottai Chettiar tradition the *nagarattār* were ancestors of the modern Nattukottai Chettiars. Among the *nāḍus* and villages whose representatives ratified the decision of the Piranmalai assembly was the village of Mattur. Mattur is today one of the places where an important Chettiar temple is located, the present-day community being distributed among nine temple circles, membership of which is determined by patrilineal descent. All members of a temple circles claim a common ancestor. The Mattur temple still maintains worship of the deity of the Ayyāvoḷe guild, *aiññuṟṟīsvarar*.[72] Tradition has it that five hundred related families founded this temple group. Pillaiyarpatti very close by has another Nattukottai Chettiar temple around which a temple circle group is maintained. An epigraph relating to the Ayyāvoḷe guild and this community has been found there.[73]

The members of a Chettiar temple circle have a common ancestor and they form kinship groups with a definite regional base which in Pāṇḍyan times was rural, although in Cōḷa times tradition has it that they were linked with the port town of Kaveripattinam. Their relationship with the *citramēḷi* as evidenced by the Piranmalai inscription finds a curious, perhaps allegorical, parallel in their traditions where it is said that after their migration from the Cōḷa country to the Pāṇḍyan kingdom, young males in the community were all married to Veḷḷāḷa women, the Veḷḷāḷas being the agricultural community closely associated with the *citramēḷi* assemblies.[74] Other inscriptions which mention the *nagarattār* and the Ayyāvoḷe but do not relate to this area

[70] Based on comparison of *SII*, VIII, 442 and Hall *op. cit.*, pp. 274-281.

[71] Their traditional locus under the Pāṇḍyas was north of the river Vaigai, west of the sea (Bay of Bengal), east of Piranmalai hill and south of the Vellar river. E. Thurston, *Castes and Tribes of Southern India*, Vol. V (Delhi, 1975), p. 260.

[72] Mattur is mentioned in the Piranmalai inscription *SII*, VIII, 442.

[73] *ARE* 150 of.1935-36.

[74] Thurston, *Castes and Tribes*, p. 260.

of the Pāṇḍyan kingdom do not necessarily refer to the Nattukottai Chettiars. In these cases the *nagarattār* may be taken to mean the members of a merchant assembly, the *nagaram*.

The *nagaram*, it is said, was a meeting ground for "commercial contact between local and itinerant traders". The same scholar states that, "Itinerant trade during Cōḷa times thus seems to have been conducted under partnership agreements betrween local trade centres – usually a *nagaram* and the external market."[75] These comments were formulated prior to the publication of work relating to the *aiññuṟṟuvar.*[76] In subsequent portions of this study which relate to urban settlements and markets this statement is further examined. In this section is also dealt the question of the relationship between the *nakara* assembly of Karnataka and the Ayyāvoḷe traders. The *nakaras* were merchants as is clear in the Managoli inscription where it is recorded that "the *Nakaras* gave half a *viśa* per *honnu* on each bale of the things they bought including rubies and all the stocks of cotton and the twelve kinds of grain...."[77] Many other Kannada inscriptions record collaboration between the *nakaras* and Ayyāvoḷe merchants.

Less conspicious but of much earlier origin than the *citramēḷi periyanāḍu*, was the *nāḍu*, an agrarian territorial unit and an assembly in both Kannada and Tamil areas. The territorial unit the *nāḍu,* also existed in Karnataka. No specific commercial functions were attached to the *nāḍu* although there were many instances of the assembly of the *nāḍu* cooperating with merchants in Kannada territory.[78] Villages were contained within the *nāḍu* as well as the *nagaram* and the *agrahāra*. In Tamil areas, *nāḍu* units were in the time of Rājarāja I, subsumed within the *vaḷanāḍu*[79] and in the twelfth century were among the constitutent units of the *periyanāḍu*.

D. *The Ruler and the Association*

There is nowhere Tamil or Kannada inscriptional evidence or any indication that these itinerant merchants were a neutral factor either in their relationship with the apparatus of local adminsitration, or in their relationship with ruling chieftains, princes and kings.[80] In the late tenth century and in the first half of the eleventh century there is a strong possibility that the *aiññuṟṟuvar* traders in Tamil areas had personal links with tribal chieftains, the Irukkuvēḷs,

[75] Hall, "The *Nagaram*", p. 182.

[76] See Abraham, "A Medieval Merchant Guild".

[77] *EI*, V, 3.

[78] *ARE* 476 of 1959-60, and *EC*, XI, Davangere 105 are two of the many examples of cooperation between members of the *nāḍu* assembly in Kannada areas with merchants.

[79] Y. Subbarayalu, *Political Geography of the Chola Country* (Madras, 1973), p. 67.

[80] Spencer, "Politics of Plunder", p. 414 is in disagreement with this view.

and with the Cōḷas. This point has been elaborated earlier. One assumes Irukkuvēḷ sponsorship since after their dynastic links with the Cōḷas had been established came the Cōḷa advance into South Karnataka and northern Sri Lanka, both areas where the *aiññuṟṟuvar* seem to have followed in the wake of the armies. It is useful to look at the Pudukkottai base of the *aiññūṟṟuvar* in the light of Karl Polanyi's description of ancient trade. Polanyi claimed some traders may have belonged to the king's own family or entourage or were employed by him.[81] It is unlikely that any of the Pudukkottai-based merchants were "employed" by the Cōḷas but they could have belonged to the same kin group as the Irukkuvēḷs. The *aiññuṟṟuvar* were in the Pudukkottai region before the Cōḷa alliances with the Irukkuvēḷs. And if our analysis is correct they were an offshoot of the Aihole association with commitments to maintain and service itinerant trade networks. It is not probably correct to describe them as having been "employed" by the ruler either Cōḷa or Irukkuvēḷ. One may argue though that they were under obligation to him for his sponsorship of their trading aims. On occasion the ruler derived support from them. The already quoted inscription of Rājēndra I's time in newly conquered territory illustrates this point.[82] The king consolidated his hold through the trader and the *agrahāra* Brahman. This may well have been a concept that fitted in with Tamil perception of the functioning of the monarch in the eleventh century and possibly in later times as well. The extract from the *Kongadēsa Rājākkaḷ* already quoted seems to indicate this possibility. The chronicle, written in the seventeenth century, endorses these same ideas in its reconstruction of Cōḷa history.

The chronicle says that after conquest the Cōḷa king gave the town of Keriyur (which he now named Rājarajapura) in the Talakad District to the merchants of Dalavanapuram and by their hands made *agrahāras* for the Brahmans.."[83] Rājēndra's inscription recorded in A.D.1032 in a neighbouring settlement shows the king ordering the trader and the *agrahāra* Brahman to arrange endowments to the temple and to maintain the village tank.[84] Here one sees some of the vital elements in the Cōḷa state synthesis of the eleventh century, trader, Brahman and temple. The early relationship between the Ayyāvoḷe merchant and the ruler is to be comprehended within this framework.

It is possible that certain other payments were expected from the trader by the ruler in the form of gifts and percentages of rare commodities imported. These aspects remain veiled. In the Carolingian period in medieval Europe professional itinerant merchants were required to supply goods, particularly

[81] Karl Polanyi, "Traders and Trade", in *Ancient Civilisation and Trade*, eds., J.A. Sabloff and C.C.Lamberg – Karlovsky (Albuquerque, 1975), p. 138.

[82] *EC*, III (new), Nanjangud 215, A.D. 1032.

[83] *Kongadēsa Rājākkaḷ*, p. 13. See previous chapter.

[84] *EC*, III (new), Nanjangud 215. See also previous chapter.

luxuries, to the court every year, or once in two years.[85] Similar practices, it is more than likely, were also followed in medieval South India. Apart from the south Karnataka wars, the Cōḷa naval foray into Southeast Asian waters may have been undertaken to ensure profits to the Cōḷa state from medieval maritime trade. This war again then, if this view is accepted, was fought to further trade. In the section of this work that follows dealing with maritime trade and the guilds, the naval war is analysed again in terms of its importance in maintaining the flow of overseas commodities into South India and in permitting the South Indian merchant to lay claim to a share in the trade with Southeast Asia and with China.

The complex inter-relationship just described between tribal chief, Cōḷa monarch and the merchant did not last beyond the twelfth century. However, under the new dispensation that followed the relationship between the trader and the ruler although altered remained important. The Pāṇḍyan rulers saw the advantages of obtaining the services of a highly organised merchant association capable of handling the transfer and distribution of commodities of internal and external origin. Hence the invitation issued to them to migrate to Pāṇḍyan territory.[86]

A relationship with the monarch is also implied in the stylized, opening phrases of the *praśasti* of the *citramēli*. This instance has been noted earlier but is repeated as it gains added point in the context of this discussion. Among the ritual symbols mentioned in the *citramēḷi praśasti* was the *cenkōl* symbol of royal authority.[87] The inclusion of the *cenkōl* was not, it is held, meaningless. T.N. Subramaniam has said that the *citramēḷi* "was spread all over the Chola empire with a network of local branches during the reign of Kulōttunga III...." He also says that the "*meykkīrtti* of the Sittiramēḷi organisation fairly echoes the *praśasti* of Kulōttunga III."[88] From this it is argued that there may have been royal patronage to expalin the expansion of the *citramēḷi* in the reign of Kulōttunga III, Stein has also quoted Nilakanta Sastri and T.N. Subramaniam who claimed further:

> The organisation of the Śittirmēḷi-Periyanāṭṭavar which came into existence about this time (the fourth regnal year of Rājādhirājachōla II, c. A.D. 1172) very soon obtained a firm footing in the Tamil country and was very influential throughout the reign of Kulōttunga III. We may not therefore be wrong in surmising that this organisation paved the way for the ultimate success of Kulōttunga in getting the Chōḷa throne.[89]

[85] M. Postan and E.E. Rich eds., *The Cambridge Economic History*, Vol. III (Cambridge, 1963), p. 10.

[86] See previous chapter.

[87] See pp. 82, 83.

[88] T.N. Subramaniam ed., *SITI*, Vol. III, pt. ii (Madras, 1957), p. 100.

[89] *EI*, XXXI, 37, pp. 274-5, K.A. Nilakanta Sastri and T.N. Subramaniam, "Hemavati Pillar Inscription of Kulōttungachōḷa (III), year 21." Stein, *PSSMSI*, p. 253.

If this interpretation is correct then the association of peasant farmers with which the *aiññuṟṟuvar* were linked, maintained a close relationship with the ruler. The association, it is claimed, was so powerful that the ruler may have depended on it for support in securing his throne.

Much scholarship has been expended on the nature of the Cōḷa state and on kingship. The several instances listed in this chapter describing the ruler in relation to the *aiññūṟṟuvar* and the *citramēḷi* may throw some more light on the subject. The eleventh century manipulation of the trader, the Brahman and the temple was an important aspect of kingly rule. From the twelfth century onwards with shifts in social configuration and with increased urbanisation and trade and increased food prodution, sections of the population, hitherto quiescent, the peasant landowners, emerged as a group which had to evolve new relationships with the ruler. The exact role of the ruler vis à vis the merchant in the new economic order of the late twelfth and thirteenth centuries is more difficult to determine. But the Pāṇḍyan invitation to the Nattukottai Chettiars indicates that the merchant continued to function with the active support of the monarch.

Under the Western Caḷukyas, particularly in the reign of Vikramāditya VI, judging by the number of extant epigraphs, the Ayyāvoḷe merchants were very active. The only evidence to date of a personal bond between the Caḷukyas and this association of merchants is an epigraph of Hoysaḷa times, already quoted, which seems to suggest the merchants were claiming connections with the Caḷukyas. The relevant phrase is "Cōḷa kūlanvitarum, Caḷukyānvayarum" – "Of the Cōḷa family and of the lineage of the Caḷukyas."[90]

In Hoysaḷa times in Kannada areas we note the rise of individual Ayyāvoḷe merchants to positions of great power and influence with the court. Thus Chaṭṭi-Seṭṭi, a Brahman, caused to be engraved at Arsikere an elaborate inscription detailing the splendid lineage of the Hoysaḷas followed by the virtues of his own family, after which he detailed his commercial and charitable achievements before including the *praśasti* of the Ayyāvoḷe group – an indication that he belonged to this organisation. The commodities he traded in were luxuries suitable for royal establishments. As he himself said he "sold them to kings with pleasure...", he was purveyor to the court and himself a merchant prince.[91] An A.D. 1198 Tamil inscription from Kolar (when under the Hoysaḷas) speaks of an *ādi-vanikēsan* who may have been the father of a merchant who was *trailōkyapaṭṭanasvāmi*. The *ādi-vanikēsan*, chief merchant, it is said, "settled people in the great city of Kuvalalam of spotless fame" and he "owned the city of Alagai".[92] There are no comparable instances in the Tamil kingdoms of individual merchants as powerful in

[90] *EC*, IX, Dod-Ballapur 31.

[91] *EC*, V, Arsikere 22.

[92] *EC*, X, Kolar 131.

this period, the late twelfth century. Contemporaneous Ayyāvoḷe epigraphs of the Tamil kingdom reveal the power of the *citramēḷi periyanāṭṭār* and of the peasant-trader combination, not the influence of individual traders. The translation of a portion of the inscription recorded by Chaṭṭi-seṭṭi in A.D. 1187 follows. From it both the links between merchants and the court and the importance of powerful merchants in urban areas is apparent.[93] Of interest also is the record of urban improvement undertaken by this merchant.

> Be it well. Obtainer of the band of five great instruments... lord of the excellent city of Dvārāvatī, a submarine fire to... the ocean the Tuḷuva force, the forest fire to kinsmen, an elephant to the lotus-garden the Pāṇḍya-race... a delighter to the multitude of all panegyrists and a rejoicer in gifting to the competent, obtainer of boon from the goddess Vāsantikā... fierce in battle, a champion over the Maḷepas (hill chiefs) – including such epithets... capturer of Talakādu, Koṅgu, Naṅgali, Gaṅgavāḍi, Noṇambavāḍi, Banavaśe and Hānungal, the mighty – armed... unassisted hero... a Rāma of firm character, *niśśanka-pratāpa* Hoysaḷa Vīraballāḷadēva was ruling Gaṅgavādi Ninety Six Thousand from his capital at Dōrasamudra, in peace, wisdom and happiness punishing the wicked and upholding the good.
>
> To describe the lineage of the dweller at his lotus feet...Chaṭṭi-seṭṭi of the mint: a treasure of humility, a bee at the lotus feet of lord Śiva, commended as virtuous, possessed of good qualities, adorned with virtues, compassionate, a manifestation of the treasure of dignity-thus people on earth praise well Machideva with affection. The loving woman i.e., wife of that Brāhmana Māchidēva, endowed with good qualities, beautiful, chaste, an ornament to the earth, Dugale...begot Māreya, a treasure of true knowledge, with affection. O private man earning your bread by true or genuine means continually, say that Māra a great resolute, possessed of all virtues, having duty, wealth and desire with humble supplication, earning wealth with pleasure by trade, associating himself in all pious acts and pleasures, – shines (on earth) exceedingly. Like ocean, a treasure that is not seen by six eyes, like the son of the moon, lord of the earth, like the lord of the lotus (Viṣṇu), follower of virtuous path and honoured by the virtuous people – is Māri-Seṭṭi of the good (Brāhmaṇa) family. She is (said to be) the wife of Cupid i.e., Rati in shape, in unequalled manifestation and in honest qualities; to the resolute Pōchale, to the supporter of virtues and to the lady of good fortune-well, truth is the strength. In magnificence of liberality she puts into commotion the celestial tree, in greatness she is greater than the glory of the mountain Mēru, in purity she is the daughter of the Earth i.e., Sita and iṇ her knowledge she is (equal to) the wife of the lotus-born (Brahma) i.e., Sarasvati—thus shone on earth the matchless Pōchiyakka in great magnificence.To the lotus-eyed Pōchale and to Māra who is a match to the Flower-arrowed (i.e., Cupid) were born

[93] Translation of *EC*, V, Arsikere 22, courtesy of The Institute of Kannada Studies, Mysore.

Chaṭṭi-seṭṭi of the mint (*kammaṭada* Chaṭṭi-seṭṭi) and noble Dāsi-seṭṭi to gain happiness. Praised by the entire illustrious world, a delighter (in giving) shelter (houses) to the learned, a friend to the dear friend of Sōmakaḷadhāra (i.e., Kubera), a follower of right path, a great celestial tree on earth to his dependents—thus became famous Chaṭṭi-seṭṭi who viewed from any aspect, was a Dhanada to the earth in the growth of wealth. *Kammaṭada...* Chaṭṭapa-seṭṭi having brought in ships (by sea), a multitude of horses which were ornaments to the horse of Hari, elephants which were equal to the elephant of Indra (i.e., Airāvata) and pearls comparable to the pearls of raindrops (of Svāti) from the sky and sold them to kings with pleasure. Possessed of wisdom, endowed with virtue, beauty and compassion, a rejoicer in giving, knower of all religions, devoted to her husband, stainless, associated with good fortune-Nange, wife of Chaṭṭi-seṭṭi, shines constantly. He transported the collection of goods from the eastern quarters to the west; increased the goods of the west in the eastern quarter abundantly; see, he brought suitable goods of wealth from the north to the southern quarter; and sent the brilliant valuables from the south to the northern corner—see, the matchless trader Dāseya, far from sins. Worshipper of the feet of the supreme substance śri Kaḷidēva, of stainless good character, of firm mind, a rutting elephant to his elder brother, was the illustrious Dāsi-seṭṭi, a rejoicer in giving. The lotus-faced, the lotus-eyed, (equal to) the lotus-seated (i.e., Lakṣmi). Chaste, possessed of all virtues, a lady of beauty, a great donatrix, respectable, Pōchale the wife of chief Dāsi-seṭṭi shines. Who is equal on the earth to this stainless Kannale, wife of virtuous Dāsi-seṭṭi, shining with the manifestation of very charming beauty and with great and eminent virtues? His lord Giriśa, his mother Pōchale, his father Māreya, his wealthy brother Dāsi-seṭṭi, his daughters virtuous Jakkale, Chikkale, Pōchalānke, Basavaive and Naṅgale excellent on earth, his son Kaḷidēva of excellent virtues, his wife Naṅge—how fortunate was Chaṭṭapa-seṭṭi on the earth! Chaṭṭa-seṭṭi having caused to be enlarged two tanks close to Muttana Hosavūr and a marvellous new tank, became famous and fortunate. On the north-eastern direction of Dōrasamudra an ornament of the earth, virtuous Chaṭṭi-seṭṭi got built a great tank which became famous for ever like truth. Chaṭṭa of proper intellect caused to be enlarged the too small tank of praise-worthy Bānavūr into a larger one and to be built a sluice to it with affection. *Kammaṭada* Chaṭṭi-seṭṭi caused to be enlarged the small Bammachiyakaṭṭa (which became) famous on earth; his virtue shone at Bāṇavūr as incomparable virtue. For the merit of his son (he)caused to be built Kallanakeṛe and the famous Māvinakere completely—how fortunate was the wise *Kammaṭada* Chaṭṭi-seṭṭi. With paddy plants grown and bent down, with flocks of parrots, gardens along with the groups of bees, Bānavūr, covered by the groups of full tanks shines on earth.

While it is said that there is no one in the possession of all virtues, in the knowledge of *dharma* and in speaking the truth like these (two), Muddagāuṇḍa chief of Bāṇavūr and Chikkasa-gāuṇḍa shone on this renowned world ... gentle ... Chaṭṭa, with love, enlarged the *maṇṭapa* of Kalidēva (temple) .... The trader Chaṭṭama, ... caused to be erected the shining abode for god Chaṭṭēśa and ... many tanks in the famous Bāṇavūr. *Kammaṭada* Chaṭṭi-seṭṭi knower of all virtues caused to be erected the abode of Chaṭṭēśa with the mind daily engaged in (the deeds of) merit which is said to be peerless.

Be it well. Possessed of all virtues, a delighter to good people, of world-wide renown, having acquired five hundred charters (vīr-aśāsanas), adorned with many good qualities, truth, purity, conduct and character, justice, modesty and knowledge, protector of the righteous path of the merchant class (*vīra-Banañja-dharma)* longing for the lotus feet of the teacher, a bee at the lotus feet of god Hara, of pure heart, of character pleasing to the minds of all people, purifier of his family—the renowned *Kammaṭada* Chaṭṭi-seṭṭi caused to be erected the temple of god Chattēśvara and for the daily offerings, decorations, festivals and services, temple-repairs, perpetual lamps and for the feeding of ... priest and servants, having obtained lands from the hands of the village chiefs and the villagers citizens of Bāṇavūr, on the day of *vyatīpāta-saṅkramana*, the 15th of the dark fortnight of Paushya, in the cyclic year Plavanga, of the Śaka year 1110; be it well; laving the feet of Achalēś-varapaṇḍita, disciple of Bhūpajīya distinguished for self-restraint, discipline, study of scriptures, meditation ... concentration, silent prayer, performance of religious rites, repetition of sacred formulae, absorption of the mind in god, virtue, and good qualities and pouring libation water, granted ... wet land ... dry field ... and 1 oil-mill by hand granted to the flower-garden by Muddagāuṇḍa....

E. *Caste in the Association*

The membership of the association of *aiññūṟṟuvar*, merchants in both Kannada and Tamil areas can be broken down to define caste, religion and locality affiliations. The origin of the association in an *agrahāra* has already now been reiterated several times. But we may note that long after the association moved away from the *agrahāra* of Aihole the Kannada merchants hearkened back to their caste origin in the repetition of the phrase, the 500 *svāmis* of Aihole. *Svāmis* in common usage denoted the Brahman. The stress on the common origin was repeated and the caste group linked with the city of Aihole.[94] In some of the Kannada inscriptions of the eleventh and twelfth centuries the *svāmis* were said to have come out of Ahichchatra, a place origin that was frequently ascribed to Brahmans in Karnataka.[95] The occasional identification of Ahichchatra with Aihole has already been noted. In approximately the same period the members of the guild also

[94] See Chapter II.

[95] See Chapter II.

acquired a lineage, they were said to be descendants of *Vāsudēva, Khaṇḍali, Mūlabhadra—Vāsudēva, Khaṇḍali, Mūlabhadra Vamsōdbhavarum*—and they were lords of Ayyāvoḷe—*Ayyāvoḷe pura paramēśvararum*. The statement of their lineage was thereby linked with the city of Aihole which was their locality focus. These were of course only concepts but appeared in some of the *praśastis* in Kannada and Tamil and Telugu areas and even in Sri Lanka. It formed a part of their self-image regarding their group origins and perhaps also indicated that the guild was acquiring a corporate personality. We may compare two extracts. In A.D. 1033 a portion of a Kannada inscription read

> ...famous in all lands, having obtained five hundred vīra-śāsanas, adorned with many good qualities, of virtuous and pure conduct, just, modest and wise, of the Virabalañja dharma, shining with the gudda flag, possessing undiminished prowess, broad in the chest, courageous in the world, born of Khaṇḍali—Vāsudēva and Mūlabhadra....[96]

Around the end of the twelfth century, a Sinhalese language inscription found at Anaulundava, north of Polonnaruva in Sri Lanka contained the fragmentary phrases repeating the same characteristic lineage formula.

1. *Śri Samastha bhuvanagra pañca śata vīra śāsanam ali (ngita Lakṣmi)*
2. *(–ya) lakṣana—(vaksa) sthala bhūvana-parākrama Sri Vasudēva—Kaṇḍali Mūla (purtti -bha–)*
3. *..Khaṇḍali, Mūla-purtti bhadra....*"[97]

After the association had expanded to centres other than Aihole the frequent location of operations in other *agrahāras* suggests continued Brahman participation. An *agrahāra* was frequently an inhabited village handed over to a Brahman donee from which he and other Brahmans who joined in the administration of the *agrahāra* received the revenue.[98] It is likely that *agrahāra* status was often conferred on already flourishing trade centres and this might in part explain the coincidence of trade guilds being located in *agrahāras*. One could then further argue that the founding and location of the guild in an *agrahāra* meant perhaps only Brahman supervisory interest in the guild in return possibly for a share of revenue, and did not necessarily mean actual participation along with *vaiśya* groups. But there are other pointers indicating the actual inclusion of more than one caste in the Ayyāvoḷe group in some regions, as well as the inclusion of Brahmans, not merely in the early stages, but also subsequently.

[96] *EC*, III (new) Heggadadevankote 59.
See also *EI*, XIX, Miraj, p. 39; *EC*,V, pt. 1, Belur 177; *EC*, IX, Dod Ballapur 31. These are only a few representative instances.

[97] *EZ*, II, ii, p. 235 *et. seq.*, twelfth to thirteenth century.

[98] Dikshit, *Local Self Government*, p. 103. "When an inhabited village was given to the *mahājanas* of an *agrahāra*, what was actually given was the revenue which the government required from the village but not all of it. The *agrahāra* paid to the government a small quit-rent."

One may note, for example, the *aiññūṟṟuva bhaṭṭan* of Pudukkottai,[99] or the *seṭṭis* who were Brahmans in the Ayyāvoḷe Hoysaḷa inscription earlier quoted in full,[100] or as late as the seventeenth century, Prithviseṭṭi Rayanamantri Bhāskaran, a Brahman minister and merchant, and 'Lord of Ayyāvoḷe.'[101] One may note also that the *aiññūṟṟuva bhaṭṭan* of Pudukkottai used his guild membership to identify himself almost as if it were a badge denoting a *jāti* or sub-caste. A *nagarattār* from present-day Tirunelveli District, in an early inscription, used his guild membership in the same way but as a prefix to his name. He was Aiññūṟṟuvan Inban Dēvancheṭṭy.[102] The use of the term *Brahmaseṭṭi* by participants in trading ventues in north Tamil Nadu, and in Telugu country perhaps also indicates the inclusion of Brahmans in trading ventures, if the word denotes, as it suggests, an amalgam of Brahman and trading status.[103] *Brahmaseṭṭis* are noted in the Ayyāvoḷe association in the eleventh century. If we are to analyse the term further it would appear that a Brahman by birth and ritual status had in this instance adopted the profession of a *seṭṭi* i.e., trade. He was a professional trader by choice, not by descent. Moreover, his announcement of his profession in the adoption of this new caste denomination apparently did not affect his ritual standing. Evidence of Brahmans engaged in trade in general, and in other occupations is not hard to find, for example Brahmans and Valañjīyar traded together in the South bazaar at Ennayiram.[104] Vijnanēśvara's *Mitakṣara* has been cited to show that apart from trade, Brahmans may also

[99] *PSI*, 621 or *ARE* 437 of 1917. Bhaṭṭan is a term used to describe a Brahman.

[100] *EC*, V, Arsikere 22.

[101] *ARE* 377 of 1911.

[102] *EI*, XXIII, 45 D. R. Narasimha Rao, *Corporate Life in Medieval Andhra Desa* (Hyderabad, 1967), p. 30, makes a similar point. Analysing an epigraph he says it "registers a gift to the local temple by the people of the 18 *Jāti* of that place including the *Balamji seṭṭi kamdru.* If the word *Jāti* is taken to mean an endogamous sect, it would be rather intriguing that the Pekkamdru which was a socially mixed up group should be described as a distinct *Jāti.* For this there can be only one explanation. And that is that the Pekkamdru whose members were originally drawn from many of the then existing different social groups evolved, in course of time, into a separate and distinct social group with all the characteristics of an endogamous sect. Members of the sect began to distinguish themselves by adding to their names such suffixes or prefixes as a Banamja, or Balañja, Vīrabalanija etc."

[103] *EC*, III (new) Nanjangud, 213, Tamil and Kannada language, Kannada script, perhaps early eleventh century. "Aychamayya, a Brahman, *odeya* of Kereyur in Kadambaligenad, the *nānādēśis* of the *nāḍ,* and the *Brahmaseṭṭis* of Ayyāpoḷal were to protect these gifts. The five hundred". As suggested in the text, the word *Brahmaseṭṭi* may have been a new term coined to describe the Brahman who took to trade. S.H. Ritti, University of Karnataka disagrees with this interpretation and believes *Brahmaseṭṭi* is a surname. He believes that in this epigraph the honorific plural is used. Telugu references to the *Brammiseṭṭi, SII,* VI, 136, cited in Narasimha Rao, *Corporate Life,* pp. 21-23, pp. 43-44.

[104] *ARE* 343 of 1917 cited in Sastri, *The Cōḷas,* p. 598.

have taken part in such unlikely occupations as that of cowherds.[105] One notes further that evidence so far uncovered of Brahmans engaging in trade, both in a supervisory capacity, and as actual participants, suggests that acquisition of wealth through commerce was not considered derogatory, as in the Arsikere inscription where the wealth of the Brahman Chaṭṭi-seṭṭi was extolled.[106] Vijñānēśvara's *Mitakṣara* has also been cited to show that the word for guild, *srēni*, meant a group of people who followed the same profession but were not necessarily of the same caste.[107] The presence of several castes in associations such as the *citramēḷi* has been inferred from the phrase in their *praśasti* "*Śāsanam Bhūmi putrānam catu(r) varna, kulōdbhavam*".[108] This could be interpreted to mean '(comprised of) the four classes', though it has also been translated to mean 'sprung from the fourth class'.[109] If the former meaning is tenable then one notes that it probably represented an aspect of the social ferment of the late twelfth and thirteenth centuries. In Karnataka in the mid-thirteenth century an inscription at Sorab refers to Sorab as a southern Ayyāvoḷe, an *agrahāra* and a *banañju paṭṭinam* or trader's town. Both the term *agrahāra* and the term *banañju paṭṭinam* were stated in equal terms in the epigraph indicating that equal weight was given to both aspects of the functioning of this southern Ayyāvoḷe.[110] Within this epigraph is also contained what appears a quite unequivocal statement that the protection of the Ayyāvoḷe guild, and the four *nāḍus* and other commercial organisations in the region, were being extended to all four castes, Brāhman, Kṣatriya, Vaiśya, Śūdra. The same epigraph condemns excessive stress on caste distinctions. The Sorab inscription is a record of charity of Kotīśvara, a Saivite deity. The emphasis on the need to discount the importance of caste distinction suggests the possibility of Veerasaivite influence in Sorab.

In the early thirteenth century in Anekal, in present-day Bangalore District a Tamil epigraph was recorded in which the *aiññūṛṛuvar* and the *vīrakoḍiyar*, a group probably of mercenaries cooperating with the *aiññūṛṛuvar* identified themselves with the right hand or *Valaṅgai* division of medieval South Indian society. The inscription says,

> We—the merchants and those of the heroic flag (...) in the Eighteen country (*sic.*)—constructed this? (building) in Parangalani and gave it to

[105] Appadorai, *Economic Conditions*, pp. 357-63.

[106] We may contrast this with the early hierarchical division of society in China where scholars were placed first followed by farmers, then by artisans and finally by merchants.

[107] Appadorai, *loc. cit.*

[108] *SII*, VI, 129.

[109] K.V. Subrahmanya Aiyer, "Largest Provincial Assemblies," pp. 45-46. "comprised" of all four classes; NDI, II, pp. 824 *et. seq.* "sprung from the fourth class".

[110] *EC*, VIII, Sorab 268. A.D. 1245.

Samayamantri. We swear by the country, we swear by the Five-hundred, if any one enter this veranda and the village and injure them, he shall be a traitor to the army (?) of the Right-hand class.[111]

Nilakanta Sastri has said that, "No picture of the social divisions in South India under the Cōḷas will be complete without a reference to the broad divisions of the industrial population of the country into the Right-hand and Left-hand, *Valaṅgai* and *Idaṅgai* divisions." He has also associated these divisions with many of the regiments of the army in the time of Rājarāja I.[112] Burton Stein has recently reiterated this point as did V. Venkayya earlier.[113] Stein has suggested that *Valaṅgai vēlaikkārar* were used in those special units of the Cōḷa forces which were closely associated with Rājarāja I and Rajēndra I.[114] Whether these warriors were in permanent service or hired when occasion arose is not clear. *Valaṅgai* and *Idaṅgai vēlaikkārar* were also mentioned in the mid-twelfth century inscription of Polonnaruva and here they were referred to as *Valaṅgai vēlaikkārar* who were probably under the leadership of the *nānādēśi* and *valañjīyar* merchants.[115] Indrapala says, "In the case of the *Valangkai*, the Nānādēsi and Valanciyar were among the leaders, while the *Idangkai* had the Nakarattār as one of their leaders...."[116]

Stein suggests that the *vēlaikkārar* were drawn from the Right Hand Division and were largely composed of members of the "dominant peasantry of the Chola heartland or Cholamandalam and Tondaimandalam."[117] If that is accepted then it is possible the *Idaṅgai* or Left hand *vēlaikkārar* who accompanied Tamil merchants in Sri Lanka were drawn from groups below the status of Veḷḷāḷa, perhaps from warrior and tribal groups living in parts of the South Indian peninsula unsuited for permanent cultivation such as forested or arid country. The *Valaṅgai* and *Idaṅgai* divisions have ben described as categories of classification extending beyond the spatial confines of village and *nāḍu*, categorisation which permitted the absorption of new artisan and merchant groups.[118] There is little inscriptional evidence of these divisions impinging on the activities of the major merchant guilds except where mercenaries or some of the associations who cooperated with the *aiññūṟṟuvar* were concerned. For example, in the eleventh century, an inscription found on a slab in Basinikonda, Chittoor District, describes the

[111] *EC*, IX, Anekal, 67.

[112] Sastri, *The Cōḷas*, p. 550.

[113] *SII*, II p. 10; Stein, *PSSMSI*, pp. 188-189.

[114] Stein *loc. cit.*

[115] *EZ, IV*, 20.

[116] Indrapala, "Some Medieval Mercantile Communities", p. 10, who cites in support of this view *EC*, XI, p. 61 and *The Imperial Gazetteer of India*, Vol. XVIII, pp. 198-199.

[117] Stein, *loc. cit.*

[118] Stein, *PSSMSI*, pp. 176-180.

establishment of an *erivīrapaṭṭinam*, a fortified merchant settlement, and the decision was ratified by a group consisting of townspeople (*nagara*), the *nāḍu*, the *nānādēśis* and mercenary bodies, as well as a group described as *Valaṅgai* weavers.[119]

In contrast to these divisions which cut across locality barriers there were also encapsulated within the Ayyāvoḷe association, groups with a definite locality base. A locality group is indicated in some of the inscriptions of Karnataka in the late eleventh and early half of the twelfth century in present-day Shimoga and Dharwad Districts, in the Kaladgi District and at Miraj and Kolhapur, and at Managoli in the Bijapur District.[120] These inscriptions were surmounted by sculptured representations of a *liṅga*, a man, a curved sword, the moon and a cow and a calf. There were variations, such as the addition occasionally of a bull, and the omission of the cow and calf, or the omission of one or two of the other motifs. But in general the devices were very similar. On occasions they were varied with the addition of a representation of a Tara, when the inscription related to a Buddhist charity, or a Jinēndra when the inscription described a donation to a Jain temple. The devices also appeared in other inscriptions in the region.[121] Therefore, they were not related to the guild alone but were probably symbols used by a regional group, of whom some members may have been associated with the Ayyāvoḷe group of traders.

F. *Jainism in the Association*

In Tamil areas, prior to the twelfth century, there is epigraphic evidence of Jain participation in the association. An inscription of Pudukkottai, possibly of the eleventh century, speaks of the maintenance of a Jain temple in Kulattur taluk, an *aiññūṟṟuvar perumpaḷḷi*, which obviously was a Jain religious foundation sponsored by the *aiññūṟṟuvar*.[122] In approximately A.D. 1090 a donation to an *aiññūṟṟuvar perumpaḷḷi* in Vishakhapatnam was recorded at a time when Tamil commercial influence had percolated into the territories now known as Andhra Pradesh.[123]

In Kannada areas Jain influence is noticed from many epigraphs of the Ayyāvoḷe traders located in or near Jain temples which relate to charities to

[119] *ARE* 342 of 1912.

[120] *IA*, V, XIX, A.D. 1094, Belagavi, Shikarpur, Shimoga District.
IA, X, CXVI, A.D. 1095, Hombal, Gadag taluk, Dharwad District.
IA, VI, XXXII, A.D. 1096, Kattageri, Badami taluk, Kaladgi District.
EI, XIX, 4, A.D. 1144, Miraj.
EI, V, 3, A.D. 1161, Managoli, Bijapur District.

[121] *IA*, VI, XXXIII.

[122] *PSI*, 1283.

[123] *SII*, X, 651.

Jain foundations. These inscriptions were recorded in the twelth and in the first half of the thirteenth century. Of these we notice the inscriptions at the Charantigudi in Aihole, at Terdal and Kandgal in Bijapur District, at Shravan Belgola, Kolhapur, Holalkere in Chitradurga District, and Mamadapur in Belgaum District.[124] We may notice in particular an inscription at Sorab in Shimoga District in A.D. 1159 which began "with the terms of the Jain cosmogony, 'How beautiful, it says are the three transitory worlds without the illusion of a creator....'"[125] Sorab was an important commercial centre by the mid-thirteenth century, and as earlier noted, it was designated a southern Ayyāvoḷe, it contained an *agrahāra,* and was described as a "*banañju paṭṭinam*". It also showed by then traces possibly of Veera Saivite influence. The Jain aspects of commerce in Sorab obviously preceded this period. Specific invocations to Jain deities occurred in some other epigraphs such as that of Mamadapur which described the guild members as "constant in the worship of Hari, Brahma, Siva and the great Jinas." The same *prásasti* referred to the goddess Padmāvati as "*Padmāvati dēvi labdha vara prasādarum*," which may be translated as 'recipients of the grace of boons from the goddess Padmāvati'.[126] Padmāvati was considered "*śāsana dēvata* of the twenty-third Tirthankara Pārsvanatha."[127] She is mentioned in other inscriptions as well as also is Bhagavati who figured in a very early Aihole inscription, and in other inscriptions of Karnataka and Tamil Nadu.[128] These are some instances of Jain influence in the association. They form only a part of the total picture of Jain influence in trade and merchant associations in medieval Karnataka, a subject which in itself deserves separate and detailed inquiry.

[124] Charantigudi, Aivalli, Hungund taluk, Bijapur District, A.D. 1119 (*KR* 97 of 1941-42);
Terdal, Jamkhandi taluk, Bijapur District, A.D. 1123
(*IA*, XIV, p. 11, and *KI*, V, 98, A.D. 1181);
Shravan Belgola, A.D. 1130
(*EC*, II, 208);
Kolhapur, A.D. 1135
(*EI*, XIX, 4);
Kandgal, Hungund taluk, Bijapur District, A.D. 1220 (*SII*, XV, 164);
Holalkere taluk, Chitradurga District, A.D. 1228 (*EC*, XI, Holalkere 104);
Mamadapur, Belgaum District, A.D. 1250
(*EI*, XIV, 3).

[125] *EC*, VIII, Sorab 328, A.D. 1159; *EC*, VIII, p.9.

[126] *EI*, XIX, 3, A.D. 1250.

[127] P.B. Desai, "Trade Guilds in Karnataka and their Jaina Associations," *Voice of Ahimsa,* 1959.

[128] For example, Padmāvathi, *IA*, XIV, p. 11;
Bhagavati, *KR* 94 of 1941-42, p. 2;
EC, VIII, Sorab 268; *SII*, VIII, 442.
While Padmāvati is clearly a Jaina deity, K.R. Venkatarama Ayyar in "Medieval, Trade, Craft and Merchant Guilds", p. 276 equates Padmāvati with Bhagavati, who,he says is "called in the Tamil inscriptions Aimpoḻil Paramēsvari or Aiyapoḻil Nācciyār, also referred to in the *Tolkāppiyam,* Padmāvati or Paramēsvari."

Chapter IV

Trading Settlements, Towns and Markets

A. *Trading Settlement. The Pudukottai Tracts*

Analysis of the working of the guild based on phrases in the *praśastis* and the text, and on the location of medieval inscriptions can be supplemented by an examination of an area in the former Pudukkottai State which was an actual locale of operations of the *aiññūṟṟuvar*. For this purpose oral and written accounts are used along with available figures on the caste composition of the population of Pudukkottai obtained from the census of 1931. An early nineteenth century source is used for descriptions of agricultural practice, the location of markets and of roads and tracks, natural resources and the existence of crafts and other forms of specialization. Matching medieval information with early nineteenth century information, as well as through the use of present-day sources a picture is formed which may help to provide tentative answers as to why this area became a base for the *aiññūṟṟuvar* in Cōḷa and Pāṇḍya times.

The early nineteenth century source referred to is popularly known as the *Statistical Account* of 1813 and was prepared by the Darbar of Pudukkottai for the East India Company. It consists of approximately 1,000 pages of palm leaf.[1] It furnishes statistics of the state under the following heads: taluks and their boundaries and area, revenue divisions with lists of villages in each division, lists of towns, villages and forts, rivers and channels, irrigation tanks, springs, rocks, temples and charitable establishments, palaces, lists of looms used for weaving, description of *topes* and forests, enumeration of roads, pathways and passes through hilly areas, description of mineral wealth, soil classification and lists of markets with an account of the commodities traded. The *Statistical Account* describes the territory of the former Pudukkottai State, an area of 1179 square miles within which many of the medieval inscriptions of the *aiññūṟṟuvar* are found. Actually within

[1] This is described in the catalogue of the Government Museum, Pudukkottai, p. 21, as the *Palm-Leaf Gazetteer of the Pudukkottai State.* The catalogue also says it was "compiled in 1813 A.D. under the orders of the Raja Vijaya Ragunatha Raya Tondaiman (1807-25). It is written in Tamil on *cadjan.* It gives a complete account of physical features, irrigation channels, temples, roads, imports, exports, etc. of the erstwhile Pudukkottai State." P.M. Subramaniam of Pudukkottai gave valuable assistance in hand-copying, on paper, relevant portions, a task which made use of the *Palm Leaf Gazetteer* immeasurably easier. P.M. Subramaniam's detailed knowledge of Pudukkottai has been of great help throughout the preparation of this chapter.

the state it is an even smaller area in which these inscriptions are located, the two present-day taluks of Tirumayam and Kulattur. The taluk, Alangudi has no *aiññūṟṟuvar* inscriptions.

Pudukkottai State was once thickly forested except for the west and south-west borders of the state which are hilly with prominent rock formations. Four rivers flow through the state, the Vellar, Pambar, Agniar and Ambuliyar, of which the Vellar is the largest. The waters of the Vellar are used for irrigation. The other main source of water for irrigation was the irrigation tanks which were rainfed or supplied with water diverted from the rivers. There are several irrigation tanks which had the capacity to irrigate over five hundred acres each.[2] The average rainfall is low, only 35 inches per year.[3]

According to tradition the original inhabitants of the area were Veduvars, or hunters who survived by hunting wild pigs and other animals. Veduvars are still found in the tracts adjoining Piranmalai near the southwest boundary of the state. The state histories name the Kurumbars as the next group to migrate to the state and they are still to be seen in the state mainly in parts of Kulattur taluk.[4] Till recently most of them were shepherds and were well known also as producers of coarse blankets woven of sheep's wool.

The next stream of immigrants according to oral and written tradition were the Veḷḷāḷas from Tondaimandalam near Kanchipuram.[5] They cleared the forests and brought land under cultivation. They were agriculturists who dug tanks to store rain water and constructed channels leading from adjoining jungle streams and rivers to provide extra water for the tanks.[6] With their expert knowledge of subsoil water they are said to have dug several irrigation wells near tanks. These were perennial wells and these are even now referred to as Kārālan wells after the Kāṛālan Veḷḷāḷas who moved into the area. The remains of Kārālan wells, it is believed, are still to be seen in the villages of Annavasal, Madia Nallur, Kunnandar Coil located in Kulattur taluk and at Virachilai, Karaiyur, and Pillamangalam in Tirumayam taluk.[7] Wells, tanks and irrigation facilities were important in the arid areas of Pudukkottai.

In the Pudukkottai region the settlement areas of the Vellālas were known as Kōnāḍu and Kānāḍu. Kōnāḍu consisted of the villages which were under the rule of the Cōḷas and Kānāḍu of the villages which were considered to be

[2] Venkatarama Ayyar, *Manual,* Vol. I, p. 173.

[3] *Ibid.*, p. 15.

[4] See Chapter II.

[5] S. Radhakrishna Aiyar, *A General History of the Pudukkottai State* (Pudukkottai, 1916), pp. 55-56, based on manuscripts in the possession of the Tekkatūr Vēḷar family.

[6] Venkatarama Ayyar, *Manual,* Vol. II, pt. i, p. 547.

[7] P.M. Subramaniam, personal communication, 5 March 1980. Also based on traditional oral accounts collected by P.M. Subramaniam.

in the Pāṇḍyan area. Roughly Kōnāḍu corresponds to the area west of the present Tiruchchirapalli – Madurai road which runs through the state. Or alternatively, the river Vellar may be considered the boundary between the divisions.[8] A palm leaf manuscript in the possession of the Tekkatur Vēḷār family states the Veḷḷāḷas were brought firstly from Kanchipuram into the Cōḷa territory and later 48,000 families from east Kanchipuram were brought to Pāṇḍyan territory known as Kānāḍu – forest land. Radhakrishna Aiyar points out that Kōnāḍu extended beyond the confines of the former state. "The former (Kōnāḍu) extended from Uraiyur near Trichinopoly to Solavandan in the Madura district, and included Pirānmalai, Ponnamaravati, Karaiyur, Oliamangalam, Annavasal and Vayalokam."[9]. Urattur *kūṟṟam,* Ollaiyur *kūṟṟam* and Uraiyur *kūṟṟam* were part of Kōnāḍu. Kānāḍu stretched "as far south as Tondi and Kalaiyarkovil and included the whole of the Alangudi taluk and the eastern portion of the Tirumayyam taluk from Viracchalai."[10] The *aiññūṟṟuvar* inscriptions are about evenly distributed between Kōnāḍu and Kānāḍu. The Veḷḷāḷa divisions of the territory were apparently not relevant to their operations.

The Veḷḷāḷas are supposed to have brought with them eighteen sub-castes. These were barbers, potters, *dhobis,* accountants, goldsmiths, blacksmiths, brass workers, carpenters, oil pressers, betel leaf growers, flower vendors, garland makers, tailors, watchmen, fishermen, shepherds, minstrels and poets.[11] With the arrival of the Veḷḷāḷas it is likely that social stratification increased and the Veḷḷāḷas were obviously the dominant group. Of the so-called "service castes" many, as for example the fishermen and the shepherds may have been there before the Veḷḷāḷas came. Others may have moved in as the areas of cultivation expanded and settlements were established.

Folk tradition, still current, is that the Veḷḷāḷas arrived some time before the seventh or eighth century.[12] The belief that the main Veḷḷāḷa immigration into the area and increase in cultivation took place some time before the eighth or ninth century A.D. receives some support from the inscriptions on irrigation tanks. The construction of these irrigation tanks is in the popular mind attributed to the Veḷḷāḷas. The construction of sluices to the tanks known as Arumaikulam at Narttamalai and Pappankulam at Rasalipatti relate to the reign of Pallava Nandivarman.[13] (The *Statistical Account* of

[8] Radhakrishna Aiyar, *General History,* p. 2. In the rest of this paragraph the synthesis contained in pp. 54-58 of the *General History* is used.

[9] *Ibid.,* p. 56.

[10] *Ibid.*

[11] Based on traditional accounts colected by P.M. Subramaniam, June 1980.

[12] Radhakrishna Aiyar, *General History,* p. 56 dates the main Veḷḷāḷa influx to the seventh or eight century. Sadasivan, 19 August 1981, in conversation at the Residency, Pudukkottai, believes the Veḷḷāḷas came some time between the eighth and ninth centuries. His opinion is based on oral accounts.

[13] *PSI,* 11, 16.

1813 states that there were 2550 tanks and natural lakes). The allocation of cash for the maintenance of the Munasandal tank took place in the reign of Parāntaka I.[14] An endowment of land for the maintenance of Kavinad Eri, a large tank, took place in the reign of Āditya I.[15] A tank at Kunnandar Coil was excavated in the time of Pallava Dantivarman.[16] Therefore, we may assume that some of the tanks were constructed earlier than the eight century and some in the two centuries after. If the Veḷḷāḷas were responsible or associated with their construction then they may have come into the area about that time. Many irrigation tanks were constructed elsewhere in the Tamil areas in the eighth, ninth and tenth centuries.[17]

The Veḷḷāḷas were then, most probably, one of the groups *in situ* when the first *aiññūṟṟuvar* merchants were in the area. The Kārālan Veḷḷāḷas are associated especially with Kodumbalur. The Vallamban, a group who claims Veḷḷāḷa origin, are listed separately in the census of 1931. The present-day Vallamban belt stretches from Tirumayam to Piranmalai. Traditional accounts lay stress on Veḷḷāḷa agricultural enterprise. Some other aspects of Veḷḷāḷa immigration into this area have received less prominence but are nevertheless important. The Veḷḷāḷas played some part in reducing Jain influence. Jainism may have come into Pudukkottai as early as the second century B.C. The Tamil Brahmi inscriptions at Sittanavasal and Narttamalai have been noted earlier. Jainism remained a force in several areas of the state. At Settipatti in Kulattur taluk a Jain religious foundation was supported by the *aiññūṟṟuvar* in the late tenth or early eleventh century.[18] There are though less well known Jain sites in Tirumayam taluk where Jain shrines existed and several of these were appropriated by Veḷḷāḷas who removed traces of Jain occupation and installed Saivite deities in them.[19]

In 1931 the largest caste group in the state were the Valaiyan and related groups such as Muttiriyan, Valuvadi and Akamutaiyar.[20] At the present moment the Valaiyan population is largely concentrated in Tirumayam taluk, though they are also found in considerable numbers in the other two taluks of the state. The Valaiyan are also now called *ambalakārar, kāvalakārar* and *pujari*. There are records suggesting either that they were

[14] *PSI*, 61.

[15] *PSI*, 28.

[16] *PSI*, 17.

[17] T.M. Srinivasan, "Irrigation and Water Supply in South India upto 1300 A.D.", M.Phil. Diss. Madras Univ. 1968.

[18] *PSI*, 1083.

[19] One of the sites, within a short distance of Tirumayam town was inspected by me, 20 August, 1981. Regarding the existence of other sites, I have accepted the statements of P.M. Subramaniam, Sadasivan, and members of the former ruling family of Pudukkottai.

[20] See Venkatarama Ayyar, *Manual*, Vol. I, pp. 102-137, where the statistics of the census of 1931 are quoted.

immigrants into the region, or that like the Veduvars, they were "original" inhabitants. All oral accounts stress that the Valaiyan were hunters and fishermen, expert at laying traps in the forest and at spreading nets to catch river fish.[21] They were employed till recently by the rulers of the state as beaters in the forest during the royal hunt.[22] They were skilful at tracking animals and some of them have been granted *inam* lands on the borders of reserve forests as remuneration. They were also employed as watchmen – *kāvalakāran* – by the villagers in return for protection of property. The temples also employed them as watchmen. Villages temples dedicated to Karuppan, Aiyanar and Kali occasionally appointed priests from among the Valaiyan. It is likely that the Valaiyan were a strong component of the population of the state in medieval times.

The Maravars are mentioned in the inscriptions of the Pudukkottai state in which they are called the Maramudalis. In the palm leaf manuscripts describing the Veḷḷāḷas of Pudukkottai it is stated that the Maravars were invited into the area to fight for factions of the Veḷḷāḷas community when disputes arose on matters of temple worship and the sharing of river water. The manuscripts say that five hundred families of Maravars came from Rajendramangalam and three hundred from Unjanur and Sembamarinadu as well as seven hundred from Mangalanadu.[23] The Maravars were in Sangam literature known as warriors and hunters. At the present they are located in Pudukkottai largely in Tirumayam taluk. Ponnamaravathi, Sundaram, Sevalur, Kuliparai, Athur, Rangiam, Kattur, Virachilai, Lembalakudi and Melapayanur contain a large proportion of Maravars.[24] Most of the them now cultivate the land and a few are traders.

The Akamutaiyar, a group similar to the Maravars, were personal servants of the ruler in modern times and members of the royal household. They received land grants in return for services and many of this group have become agriculturists.

The Kallars, another warrior group, it is believed, came from around Tirupati and the area between Tirupati and Kanchipuram. In the history of the lineage of the former rulers of Pudukkottai it is said that their particular clan of Kallars came into the region in Vijayanagar times.[25] But if the migration of the entire body of Kallars in the state took place in Vijayanagar times the Kallars were not in Pudukkottai in the period under consideration in this

[21] Based on extensive local enquiry.

[22] This paragraph is based on a synthesis of accounts in Venkatarama Ayyar, *Manual*, the 1931 census figures, and oral interviews conducted in August, 1981.

[23] Radhakrishna Aiyar, *General History*, pp. 62-66.

[24] Personal communication, P.M. Subramaniam.

[25] N.B. Dirks, "The Structure and Meaning of Political Relations in a South Indian Little Kingdom," Humanities Working Paper No.14, California Institute of Technology (October, 1978), p. 10.

study. They were supposed to have come into the state from the northeast and then to have settled in the area now known as Alangudi taluk, eventually extending themselves into Kulattur taluk. The rulers of the state called on them for military services. Land grants were made to select members of the Kallar group and these were known as *amaram*. In the *Rules for the Settlement of Inams* formulated towards the end of the nineteenth century, but based on earlier practices, "amarams were held, for military service by men, who are in the remnants of the old militia of the country...."[26] *Amaram* tenures which involved military service were a feature of the Vijayanagar state.

It was estimated in 1867 that a great deal of the land in Pudukkottai was held under this form of tenure. "The largest portion of the (alienated) land was held by individuals on the condition of leading into the field when called upon a certain number of peons and supporting all their expenses during their service...."[27] Dirks has pointed out that "From the names in the records it appears that most of the *amarakārars* were of the Kallar, Valaiyan, Maravar and Akamutaiyār castes...."[28] The tradition that still earlier, in medieval times, the bulk of the Maravar and Akamutaiyar were warriors is probably quite accurate, as also the tradition that the Valaiyan were hunters and "watchmen" who offered protection on payment to villages and temples.[29]

From the population figures of 1931 it is seen that Valaiyan, Valuvadi, Muttiriyan, Akamutaiyar and Maravar when combined formed the largest single grouping in the state. The traditional agriculturists, the Veḷḷāḷas and Vallamban together were just about equal in numbers to the shepherd community, the Idaiyar.[30] If the Kurumbars are also treated as shepherds then the pastoral group is larger than that of the agriculturists. Nomads with flocks of sheep are still to be seen in the state territory. The Nattukottai Chettiars were in 1931 largely in Tirumayam taluk. The largest Valaiyan concentration was also to be found in the same taluk. Sociologists warn against using modern caste figures as an index for medieval times. In this case, however, the physical geography of the state, and the rainfall pattern suggest that the 1931 figures probably reflect at least broadly, medieval realities. Burton Stein has said that in "arid, ecotypic contexts",

[26] *Ibid.*, p. 18 citing from the *Report on the Administration of Pudukkottai for the Year 1881-82*, Pudukkottai Darbar Record Office.

[27] *Ibid.*, p. 22 quoting from *Madras Political Consultations*, 199 (17 October, 1854).

[28] *Ibid.*, p. 23.

[29] *PSI*, 439 refers to a contract in which payment is specified to a Valaiyar in return for protection.

[30] Venkatarama Ayyar, *Manual*, Vol. I, pp. 102-137.

> "Social realities were influenced by the fact of very low population densities; there was no surplus for the support of brahmanical institutions of learning or religion. There were continual chances of attack from the more powerful peasant neighbours as well as from non-peasant folk of the hills and forests both of which peoples the arid zone peasants occasionally joined. The situation seems to cover the Maravar and Kallar people of Ramnad, Madurai and Pudukkottai at times....[31]

Paddy is grown today in the wet lands near tanks. The important crops raised in the dry lands include maize, red gram, lentils, horse gram and chillies. Cotton is grown in part of Kulattur taluk near Viralimalai. Groundnut and cashewnut which are also grown are probably very recent additions.[32] In the *Statistical Account* of 1813 it is claimed that there were seven forts, 1301 inhabited villages and 1288 uninhabited villages. The last two figures, if accurate, may suggest a shifting population. The total number of sheep in the state at that time were about equal to the total number of cattle and buffaloes put together. The *Statistical Account* does not suggest that there was a heavy urban concentration of population anywhere. There were 33 handlooms for silk and 1045 for cotton, 314 for wool. There were seven iron ore "mines" in 1813, but iron ore was not moved out of the state according to the 1813 record.

In 1910, twenty-three weekly fairs were held at different localities within the state and of these the largest and most important fairs were those held at Konnaiyur (near Piranmalai) and Viralimalai in Kulattur taluk.[33] In 1813, chillies, pepper, mustard seed, cummin seed, areca nuts, garlic and onion, food grains and pulses were brought in for sale at the fairs from Tiruchchirappalli, Vallanad and Madurai. Textiles such as saris, cotton cloth locally woven and blankets were also sold in the local markets. Some coloured saris and woollen blankets were taken out of the state and sold in Madurai, and parts of present Thanjavur District.[34] These commodities may be compared to the long list given in the Piranmalai inscription of commodities in the area on which cess was levied for the benefit of the temple. The Piranmalai inscription was probably recorded in the second half of the thirteenth century.[35] The commodities then mentioned were salt, paddy, rice, lentils, castor seed, areca nuts, pepper, turmeric, dry ginger, onion, mustard seed, cummin seed, chebulic myrobalans, embellic myrobalans, beleric myrobalans, iron, cotton, yarn, thick cloth, thin cloth, thread, wax,

[31] Burton Stein, "Historical Ecotypes in South India", in *Proceedings of the Second International Conference Seminar of Tamil Studies*. January, 1968, Vol. II (Madras, 1971, p. 287.

[32] Based on local modern accounts obtained from government administrators. The rest of this paragraph is based on the *Statistical Account*.

[33] *Revenue Settlement Report for Pudukkottai* (Pudukkottai, 1910), p. 50.

[34] *Statistical Account*, section 13 on trades and fairs.

[35] *SII*, VIII, 442.

honey, sesamum, gunny, sandalwood, *aghil* or aloeswood, silk, rose water, yak's tail, camphor, civet, horses, elephants and other aromatics. The cotton textiles, and the mustard seed, cummin seed, pepper, areca nuts and onions figure in both the lists. The medieval list is far longer and the major difference is the presence of overseas imports, sandalwood, aloeswood, silk, rose water, camphor, civet, horses, elephants. Iron also travelled along the medieval trade route and this was probably not an import,but may have been exported. It does not figure in the modern local market list. The Piranmalai inscription, as earlier stated, was a joint inscription issued by the *citramēḷi* and the *aiññūṟṟuvar*. In Pāṇḍyan times the commodities of overseas trade flowed through the area. In 1813, in British times, overseas trade no longer came into this region.

Piranmalai lies just outside the borders of the former state. From Pudukkottai the road proceeds to Konnaiyur before approaching Piranmalai. Konnaiyur marks the boundary of Kōnāḍu, and the end of Veḷḷāḷa territory. Piranmalai is still largely populated by the Valaiyan. The existing large temple at Piranmalai was built in Nayak times. Behind it stands the Sokkanatha temple on which the *aiññūṟṟuvar* inscription just referred to is recorded. The large temple is built like a fortress with its own internal supply of water. It has high fortress walls surrounding it with slits through which defence is possible either through the use of fireams or with bows and arrows. Built securely against the rocky face of the Piranmalai hill the temple commands the countryside. The local village nearby today is poor and populated by the Valaiyan and Harijans. There are a few *agrahāras* in the vicinity. The only rationale for a temple as splendid as this in this relatively, unpopulated area was its strategic importance. Major routes passed by the hill. Madurai was only forty miles away and the road called in recent times the Mangammai Salai linking Madurai and Tiruchchirappalli passed by Piranmalai. This particular route may have existed in far earlier times. One conjectures that the trade passing along the routes near Piranmalai required protection and safeguards from the Valaiyan surrounding the hill. This region is by and large still Valaiyan territory. The map Pudukkottai II shows the routes within the state and the main road linking Tiruchchirappalli and Madurai in relationship to Piranmalai, as well as the roads linking Thanjavur with Madurai which also touched the Piranmalai hill. The reconstruction of these routes is based on information contained in the *Statistical Account* on roads, passes and cart tracks in each of the five divisions of the state in 1813, Vedamugham, Melmugham, Kilmugham, Tenmugham, Keelanilai.[36] The roads connecting Tiruchchirappalli with Madurai existed from early times. Piranmalai also connected with the Chettiar port of Adirampatnam. Sailing from Adirampatnam to Jaffna was possible during the southwest

[36]See map, Pudukkottai II on page 126.

monsoon.[37] Sailing from Adirampatnam to the Burma coast and the Straits of Malacca was also possible during the southwest monsoon. The imports of Southeast Asia as noted in the Piranmalai list may possibly have come through this port. The West Asian products, horses, rose water, civet, may have come in through Kulasekharapattinam since the *nagarattār* of Kulasekharapattinam were among the specific groups present at the Piranmalai convention of the *citramēḷi* and the *aiññūṟṟuvar*. Some of the commodities mentioned in the inscription such as the areca, iron and perhaps the cotton yarn and woven cloth could also have been intended for export.

The Piranmalai hill is in the present-day Tiruppattur taluk of the former Ramanathapuram District, which borders the Tirumayam taluk of Pudukkottai. From Tirumayam Piranmalạị is visible and dominates this taluk. Tirumayam and Kulattur taluks retain traces of the *aiññūṟṟuvar* occupation. In Tirumayam taluk the village of Kallampatti has a temple dedicated to a patron goddess of the *aiññūṟṟuvar*, Ayyapoḷil Nācciyār. About A.D. 1157 a Niṣādarājan chief gave a gift to the temple. A further grant was made in A.D. 1190-91.[38] The Niṣādarājan was probably a Valaiyar and he obviously benefited from the activities of the *aiññūṟṟuvar* merchants, hence his propitiation of their deity. In the village of Virachilai in the same taluk members of the *aiññūṟṟuvar* association lived and their names appeared in the land sales recorded in the late thirteenth century.[39] Pillamangalam, also in the same taluk had an *aiññūṟṟuvar* tank mentioned in an inscription of A.D. 1250.[40] In the Piranmalai inscription, Pillamangalam (Sundarapandyapuram)is described as being in Kalvayil *nāḍu* which is further described as being in Ayyapoḷil *vaḷanāḍu*.[41] This area was obviously a core region for the *aiññūṟṟuvar* merchants of Tamil-speaking areas in Pāṇḍyan times. The village of Valaramanikkam, with a strong Chettiar concentration, was once an *aiññūṟṟuvannallūr*, an *aiññūṟṟuvar* village.[42] Many Nattukkottai Chettiars still lived in this taluk in 1931. The period in which, according to the inscriptions, the *aiññūṟṟuvar* were most active in the taluk was in the second half of the twelfth century and in the thirteenth century. The earliest inscription of the *aiññūṟṟuvar* in the taluk, is, as already noted,the Munasandal inscription estimated to be of the late ninth century.[43]

In the hilly areas of Kulattur taluk Kurumbar settlements are still to be seen. Two villages in the taluk, Annavasal and Sittanavasal, have Jain

[37] Interview with Edward Poobalarayan, Capatain, S.S. Ramanujam, May, 1979.

[38] *PSI*, 134, 148.

[39] *PSI*, 421, 393.

[40] *PSI*, 363.

[41] *SII*, VIII, 442. See *PSI* 390 for identification of Sundarapandyapuram.

[42] *PSI*, 1022.

[43] *PSI*, 61.

antiquities. In Settipatti, another village, the Jain *aiññūṟṟuvar perumpaḷḷi* was located as noted in an inscription of Rājarāja's time.[44] Narttamalai has two *aiññūṟṟuvar* inscriptions, one of which was probably recorded in the year A.D. 1055.[45] The inscription refers to a gift of gold by merchants for the setting up of *sandhi* lamps in the temple. There is also mention of the installation of an image of Sangu Paramēśvari. An early Tamil Brahmi inscription was located in Narttamalai. The most important town in this area in early medieval times was undoubtedly Kodumbalur. It was associated with the Irukkuvēḷs and was considered the capital of Bhuti Vikaramakēsari Irukkuvēḷ. It is believed that Kodumbalur once supported one hundred and eight temples. Three of the Kodumbalur temples are particularly well known, the Muvarkoil, the Muchukundesvaram and the Aintali. Kodumbalur was also a centre for the Maṇigrāmam.[46] Nearby is Kudumiamalai where an *aiññūṟṟuvar* settlement was located.[47] The total area of this taluk is only 464.82 square miles. Kulattur taluk is south of Tiruchchirappalli and roughly parallel but also intersecting part of the northern area of the taluk was the Mangammai Salai linking Tiruchchirappalli with Madurai. Kulattur and Tirumayam taluks were under Cōḷa suzerainty and then later under the Pāṇḍyas. After the twelfth century the Irukkuvēḷ chieftains were not heard of in this particular region. The Irukkuvēḷ and Cōḷa alliance and its possible effect on commercial enterprise and on traders in the region have been commented on. Both in Cōḷa and in Pāṇḍya times, the *aiññūṟṟuvar* flourished in this part of the South Indian peninsula. After the early fourteenth century records of the *aiññūṟṟuvar* in this area ceased.

Speculating on the reasons for Pudukkottai being an area of commercial importance under both the Cōḷas and Pāṇḍyas, one returns to the suggestions already expressed that one of the causes could have been that the routes crossing the peninsula from the Malabar coast through the Palghat gap, or from the extreme south, the Aryankavu pass near Shencottah, would pass by the Pudukkottai tracts. This was largely long-distance trade and some of the commodities could have come from as far off as the west coast of India. As the map Pudukkottai II shows from Pudukkottai, Madurai, Tiruchchirappalli and Thanjavur were easily accessible. Long-distance trade required safeguards and if Pudukkottai served as an "entrepôt" area from which consignments were distributed either to Cōḷa or to Pāṇḍya country, then one surmises that the large population of Valaiyan and other warrior people would have assumed the duties of protection of trade. Both the arid land and the forested land in Pudukkottai, with a population in which

[44] *PSI*, 1083.

[45] *ARE* 359 of 1904.

[46] See Chapter I.

[47] *PSI*, 125.

pastoral people and warriors predominated, was suited for this purpose. Some arrangement, linking the warrior group with trade is suggested in two inscriptions in which the Niṣādarājan chiefs, the Valaiyars, made donations to Ayyapoḷiya Nācciyār. Both incoming and outgoing goods would have required protection and the Valaiyan and other warrior castes may have provided this security.

As the lists of commodities have shown, the trade passing through did not depend, except marginally, on local production centres. The dispatch of locally made textiles to Madurai and Thanjavur is noted in the early nineteenth century and would have taken place earlier. It is unlikely that textiles of quality suitable for the overseas market were produced. There is no evidence that this region was used in Cōḷa times as a port of entry for imported goods, although by the mid-twelfth century these imports were arriving in interior Karnataka. In Cōḷa times the port of Nagapattinam was probably the main centre of exchange for imported goods. But in Pāṇḍyan times the most important aspect of the trade passing through Pudukkottai was the incoming overseas trade. In the Piranmalai inscription there is reference to a category of *Diś'ai Āyirattaiññūṟṟvar* of *Ēru-śāttu* and *Iṟangu-śāttu.* K.V. Subrahmanya Aiyer has pointed out that this category might refer to assemblies having supervision over or regulating the conduct of traders engaged in exports and imports, settled principally in coastal towns with royal emporiums (*sic*)...."[48] This interpretation, if correct, supports the hypothesis that exports and imports were redistributed by the *aiññūṟṟuvar* at or near Piranmalai. The actual exchange of goods may well have taken place at the market place of Konnaiyur near Piranmalai. Both Cōḷa and Pāṇḍya capitals were accessible from this point. Protection at the place of exchange and on the routes to the interior could have been guaranteed by the Valaiyar. One notes also that not merely overseas goods but also local goods destined for local markets could have been easily re-routed from some central point in Pudukkottai territory to Cōḷa and Pāṇḍya dominated areas.[49] The map Pudukkottai II illustrates this point, as well as the map Pudukkottai I, on pages 126 and 70 respectively.

B. *Trading Settlement: The Agrahāra*

We move now to a consideration of trading settlements which were

[48] K.V. Subrahmanya Aiyer, "Largest Provincial Organisations", April, 1955, p. 271.

[49] I am gratefulk to Prof. L.W. Gunawardena for suggesting that it was useful to compare Pudukkottai to a "port of trade". Pudukkottai had access to a vast and important hinterland and several locations on the coast provided points of entry from which imports could enter easily. Protection for trade was probably offered by Valaiyan or other warrior groups. However, there is no hint that Pudukkottai actually was a meeting ground for negotiations between foreign traders and local merchants as Revere suggests. These meetings took place probably at points on the coast. Pudukkottai was not neutral, as many parts of the territory were under Cōḷa and later Pāṇḍya control. See Robert B. Revere, "Ports of Trade in the Eastern Mediterranean", in *Trade and Market in the Early Empires,* Karl Polanyi *et. al.* (Glencoe, 1957), pp. 38-63.

located in *agrahāras,* in fortresses and in staging posts on trans-peninsular routes. It is known that the nucleus of the trading group, the *aiññūṟṟuvar* in Kannada-speaking territory was located in the *agrahāra* of Aihole.[50] It is likely that the merchants occupied a street or a location in the *agrahāra.* Since the early founders of the *aiññūṟṟuvar* association were the group of *Mahājanas* of Aihole we may assume that they were by right of birth part of the *agrahāra.* Itinerant *seṭṭis,* long distance traders associated with them but not necessarily of the same ritual status may have had special areas in the *agrahāra* alloted to them. In Tamil-speaking area, in contrast, Munasandal, where the early Pudukkottai traders were located, was probably a village not distinguishable from other villages in the area.[51]

C. *Trading Settlement: The Fortress*

In the ninth century the copper plates of Sthāṇu Ravi, as described in Chapter I, located the market in a fortified settlement at the port of Quilon, while the church, also actively interested in trade, was located outside the fortified area. A tenth century Tamil inscription located the *aiññūṟṟuvar* in the fortress of Ukkirankottai (Karavandapuram) in Tirunelveli District.[52] Ukkirankottai was a military stronghold and also a trading outpost. The entire settlement at Karavandapuram appears to have been enclosed within the high walls of the fort. The epigraph relating to the *aiññūṟṟuvar* within the fort has been dated to the reign of Rājasimha III and described a shrine named after the trading community of the *nagarattār* one of whose members at least was also a member of the Ayyāvoḷe association. He was Ayyapoḷil Aiññūṟṟuva(n) Inban – Devanchetty. Other contemporary epigraphs at the same spot recorded the founding of an *ambalam* named after the *nagarattār* by the local feudatory. The maintenance of the *ambalam* was in part dependant on the *nagarattār* and in part on Tennavan Pallavadiaraiyan the local chief. Another charity in the same fort, in the same period, was placed under the protection of the *nagarattār* and the soldiers guarding the fort.[53] The weightage given to the *nagarattār* in those inscriptions of Ukkirankottai is an indication of the importance of the trading functions of this fortress. Other inscriptions suggest that fortresses continued to be used for trade by other merchant groups. One of these inscriptions is as late as the thirteenth century.[54]

[50] Based on reconstruction of the history of the association in Chapter II.

[51] *Ibid.*

[52] *EI,* XXIII, 45.

[53] *Ibid.*

[54] The tradition of the use of fortresses for trade is quite persistent. The trading community of the Nattukottai Chettiar explains the term Nattukottai as the *Kottai* (fort)in the *nāḍu* and claims that the Chettiars were always called upon to contribute to the building of the fort. See also *SII,* VI, 47; *SII,* VI, 41 – Thanjavur District.

The epigraphs referred to above all suggest that the sale or the exchange of goods took place within the fortified precincts. There is no suggestion that goods were being manufactured within these trading settlements. Using the information contained in the Karavandapuram and Quilon inscriptions we notice that the population of these settlements consisted of the following component groups: the king or his representatives in the form of local ruler and officials, those whose duty was defence or the protection of the settlement, local merchants, foreign merchants (at Quilon), those connected with religious establishments and service groups such as sweepers, washermen, toddy tappers, carpenters and others not specified. Trading groups and religious groups were closely connected in Quilon. Similar in principle, but smaller in area, was the protected market described by the author of the *Yaśastilaka* composed in the mid-tenth century, probably reflecting actual conditions in the Dharwad or Raichur areas at the time of the Rāṣṭrakūṭas. The market owned by the priest Sribhuti was

> furnished with tents containing many compartments and large stores of merchandise, with stalls for cattle nearby. Water, fodder and firewood were easily available, and the establishment covered an area of about four miles. It was closely guarded by troops, and protected by moats, gates, walls and ramparts.... Here merchants from many countries were allowed to carry on their business, the rates of toll and rent being extremely moderate.[55]

It is probable that both at Ukkirankottai and in interior Karnataka at that time, prices of commodities, tolls and rents were fixed. At Quilon, on the other hand, where some international trade took place, it is possible that prices fluctuated depending on the demand for the commodities exchanged.

D. *Trading Settlement: The Erivirapaṭṭinam*

Trading settlements were also consciously created or converted into protected trading bases by the Ayyāvoḷe guild. These were referred to in the eleventh century Tamil inscriptions of the Ayyāvoḷe as *erivīrapaṭṭinam.*[56]

[55] *K.K. Handiqui, trans. and ed., Yasastilaka and Indian Culture* (Sholapur, 1949), p. 120.

[56] e.g. *ARE* 321 of 1912; *ARE* 342 of 1912; *EC,* IV (new), Chamrajnagar 146.
The term *erivīrapaṭṭinam* is taken to refer to a 'mercantile town' (T.N. Subramaniam, *SITI,* III, pt. 2 Annexure, p. XV). But K.R. Venkatarama Ayyar (See Chapter II, f.n. 70), considers it a "fortified mart". Indrapala, "South Indian Mercantile Communities", points out that "Erivīrar (lit. warriors who throw, i.e. those who are adept in the art of throwing javelins etc.) refers to a class of warriors who were associated with the mercantile communities". He also says of the *erivīrapaṭṭinam* that from "the context there is little doubt that these were market-towns probably protected by the Erivīrar. But it must be admitted that there is a lack of clarity as to the nature of these towns". The extract cited in this study (*EC,* IV (*new*) Chamrajnagar 146) describing the establishment of an *erivīrapaṭṭinam* bears out Indrapala's interpretation.

The following extract from an inscription, already once quoted in another context, is here re—quoted as it is the only inscription which describes the founding of an *erivīrapaṭṭinam* so vividly. The merchants were said to have

> made a resolution (and converted) the village (called) Vēlūr alias Rājādhirāja—chaturvēdimangalam in Padināḍ in Gaṅgaikoṇḍasōḷavaḷanād in Mudigoṇḍasōḷa-maṇḍalam into an *erivīrapaṭṭinam* (by the mercantile organisation, the tiśai-āyirattaiññūṟṟuvar of Ayyapoḷil) and (this organisation) supplied clothes to the members of higher and lower ranks of the merchant caravans, clothes for a swordsman, oil for the lamps of the god Kavarai-Īśvaram-uḍaiyār, food for the merchant bodyguards... during their stay and a pig for feeding in memory of the deceased heroes.

The provision made for the merchant bodyguards indicates the presence of militia employed by the guild. The signatories to the inscription included a member of the *aiññūṟṟuvar,* of the *nānādēśis,* of a trading group referred to as from the eighteen countries and other *seṭṭis.* Some of these merchants may have been persons of some local status since terms such as *araiyan* and *peraraiyan* were appended to their names, titles which were used by "persons distinguished in civil occupations" in the Cōḷa period.[57] In a similar fashion the *nānādēsis* met at Mylapore and converted Ayyapulal-Kattūr into an *erivīrapaṭṭinam.* They also stipulated that "communal contributions" need not be paid by the residents of the township, and that reasonable law and order should prevail. Merchants who did not conform were to be expelled.[58] Similar resolutions were passed at Basinikonda.[59] An inscription from Karshanapalle also refers to an *erivīrapaṭṭinam* at Muttukur.[60] These *erivīrapaṭṭinam* appear to have been townships where guild custom prevailed. Officialdom in the *erivīrapaṭṭinam* may have been appointed from the merchant community. Merchants to some extent administered the town and had the privilege of abolishing some contributions or taxes. The eulogy of the king which is included in the Basinikonda inscription indicates that the Ayyāvoḷe merchants sought and probably received the approval of the monarch for their exercise of authority in the *erivīrapaṭṭinam.* While it was normal for a lengthy eulogy of the king to precede a royal grant or a donation by a high state official, or for a brief eulogy with the regnal year of the king to be included for purposes of dating, the impression given in this inscription is one of royal sanction of a trade charter.

57 Sastri, *The Cōḷas*, p. 462.

58 *ARE* 1912-13, pp. 99-100. Vahalkada in Sri Lanka was a "Vīrapaṭṭinam", Indrapala, *op. cit.*, p. 107.

59 *ARE* 342 of 1912.

60 *ARE* 321 of 1912.

E. *Trading Settlement: The Camp*

Trading settlements of a different sort appear to be indicated in the phrase "*kadigai-tāvaḷam*" used frequently in Tamil inscriptions of Ayyāvoḷe. The phrase forms part of the praśasti where it has been reduced to a ritual formula, the sixty-four *kadigai-tāvaḷam* which is one of the corporate groups mentioned along with groups such as the eighteen *paṭṭinam* and the thirty-two *velarpuram.*[61] The number may be mythical but it has been pointed out that *tāvaḷakkārar* means in Tamil "traders from distant parts". [62] *Tāvaḷam* also seems to mean a camp. The word then has connotations either suggestive of itinerant trading groups or of trading stations which were not necessarily part of urban settlements. It has also been pointed out that the *tāvaḷakkārar* are referred to in other inscriptions relating to professional guilds, for example the *Vāṇiya-nagarattār* at Tirumanmedu, Tiruchchirappalli District. The inscriptions speaks of the deity Danmadāvalan-tambirān.[63] A group known as Danmadavalavar is also noted in another inscription from Tirumalai in the former Ramanathapuram District.[64] It is believed that the Danmadavalavar were a merchant group 'an associate body of *tiśai-āyirattaiññūṟṟuvar*' and that Tirumanalmedu where the deity Danmadavalar-tambirān was housed could have been one of the sixty-four *kadigai tāvaḷam.*[65]

F. *Merchants and their Location in Urban and Rural Settlements*

There are also instances on record of trading areas demarcated in established settlements expressly for the Ayyāvoḷe guild and occupied by them. In Mamballi, Yelandur taluk under Hoysaḷa Vīra Narasingha it is noted that a street *aiññūṟṟuva-perunteruvu* was occupied by the *aiññūṟṟuvar*. Land and property in the street appear to have been owned by them.[66] In the thirteenth century at Pillaiyarpatti in Ramanathapuram District an inscription mentions the *nagarattār* who were settled in the *aiññūṟṟuvap-perunteruvu* at Enkarikuddi.[67] It is also recorded that they bought land at Marudangudi for founding a new colony. The *aiññūṟṟuvap-perunteruvu* or *aiññūṟṟuvar* street may have been constructed on land owned by them. One conjectures that in these streets occupied by the guild business transactions were concluded and that some facilities existed for warehousing.

[61] e.g. *SII*, VIII, 442.

[62] Indrapala, *op. cit.*, p. 108.

[63] *ARE* 337 of 1960-61.

[64] *ARE* 20 of 1924.

[65] *ARE*, 1960-61, p .23.

[66] *EC*, IV (new), Yelandur 158.

[67] *ARE* 150 of 1935-36.

There probably were other instances in the twelfth and thirteenth centuries, when the association was established in urban-type settlements, of the occupation by this guild of a particular street or location in the town. Our records give us only two definite instances, but in contrasting and comparing this association with the *hang* in China some light is thrown on the problem. In the T'ang and Sung periods in China "the merchants' associations were known by the name of "hang" but the term "hang" was also used in the sense of a street or street block consisting of shops dealing in the same goods or engaged in the same trade".[68] It has been argued in Shigeshi Katô's classic study that the association *hang* developed in the "street of shops of the same trade".[69] Thus, if this argument is accepted, the *hang* of early medieval China grew out of the combination of groups of people engaged in retail trade of particular commodities, and these were located in urban areas, very often in walled cities. The fortress locations of South Indian traders is comparable in some respects to the location of the *hang* in the walled urban settlement, in the period of the early T'ang. There is no evidence in China in the ninth and tenth centuries of merchant autonomy such as exercised by the Nestorian church and the Maṇigrāmam in Quilon. Nor are there parallels to the *'erivīrapaṭṭinam'* - townships where to a large extent merchant custom prevailed and merchant administration was accepted.

G. *The Market: The Southern Ayyāvoḷe*

We may notice also in Kannada areas the towns and villages which were often *agrahāras* and which were given the title Ayyāvoḷe or southern Ayyāvoḷe. Thus it was recorded in the twelfth century at Mulbagal in Kolar District that the "Five-Hundred made the Mahēndracaturvēdimangala into an Ayyāvoḷe".[70] Or in the twelfth century in Davangere taluk, Chitradurga District, one notes the "immemorial *agrahāra* the Southern Ayyāvoḷe, Kodanganur".[71] In A.D. 1294 Hale Aluru, declared a southern Ayyāvoḷe, was formed with two other villages into an *agrahāra,* Arasaganda-Rāmacaturvēdimangalam.[72] Many southern Ayyāvoḷes were constituted in Kannada-speaking areas and one speculates that some form of tax concession may have been made in these centres to merchants.[73] Warehousing facilities may

[68] Shigeshi Katô, "On the Hang or the Associations of Merchants in China, With Especial Reference to the Institution in the T'ang and Sung periods", *MTB,* 8 (1936), 45-83, especially p. 46.

[69] *Ibid.*

[70] *EC,* X, pt. 1, Mulbagal 247.

[71] *EC,* XI, Davangere 149.

[72] *EC,* IV (new), Chamrajnagar 183.

[73] e.g. *KI,* IV, 34; *EC,* X, pt.1, Mulbagal 247;
EC, XI, Davanagere 149; *EC,* VII, Sorab 328;
ARE 478 of 1914; *EC,* V, Arsikere 71; *EC,* XI, Holalkere 121;

have existed. It is also possible that the southern Ayyāvoḷeṣ functioned as marketing centres in the region. The southern Ayyāvoḷes were a feature of Kannada areas in the twelfth and thirteenth centuries while the *erivīrapaṭṭinam* were establishments peculiar to Tamil areas in the eleventh century.

The markets of the southern Ayyāvoḷe in medieval times were probably similar and could even well have been near identical to the market at Gubi as described by Buchanan in the early nineteenth century.[74] An inscription of A.D. 1226 on a temple stone in Gubi, Tumkur District, locates a southern Ayyāvoḷe in the township.[75] In A.D. 1807 Buchanan described commerce at Gubi and we may repeat here his meticulous careful observations. He says:[76]

> At *Gubi* is one of the greatest weekly fairs in the country, and it is frequented by merchants from great distances. The country, for ten or twelve cosses round, produces for sale coarse cotton cloth both white and coloured, blankets, sackcloth, *betel-nut* of the kind called *wallagram*, or neighbouring, coco-nuts, *jagory*, tamarinds, capsicum, wheat, rice, *ragy* and other grains, *lac*, steel and iron. Besides the sale of these articles and of those imported for the consumption of the neighbourhood, this is also an intermediate mart for the goods passing through the peninsula.
>
> From *Mudo-Biddery*, and *Subrahamani*, two places in the country we call Canara; and from *Codagu-Bogundi*, some place in what we call *Coorg*; and from a place in Malayala called Calesa, are brought black pepper, cardamoms, *rol*, the gum and *dupa*, the wood of the*Chloroxylon Dupada*, Buch; MSS, ginger, *betel-nut* of Bengal, cinnamon, *Cabob-China*, or cassia-buds, *casturi-china*, or wild tumeric, *capili* flour, and a sweet smelling root called *cachora*. These people take away *jirigay*, one of the carminative seeds, blankets, sackcloths of many kinds, but chiefly coarse; sugar-candy, sugar, the pulse called *tovary*, tamarinds and cash.
>
> From *Tellichery* (a port) are brought dates, raisins, nutmegs, saffron, borax, pepper and *terra japonica*. The returns are the same as those above mentioned.
>
> The merchants of *Gubi* frequent a weekly fair, at a place called *Biruru*, which is east from thence 24 cosses. This is a great resort of the merchants of *Nagara*, and of *Malayala*, who sell to those of *Gubi* black pepper, Deshavara *betel-nut, terra japonica*, dates, ginger, *danya*, an umbilliferous seed, garlic, *fenugreek*, wheat, the pulse called hessaru, and

---

EC, VIII, Sorab 268; *SII*, IX, pt. 1, 372;
EC, IV (new), Chamrajnagar 188.

[74] F. Buchanan, *A Journey from Madras through the Countries of Mysore, Canara and Malabar* (London, 1807), Vol. II, pp. 31-32.

[75] *EC*, XII, Gubi 11.

[76] Buchanan, *ibid.*

> capsicum. They buy sugar and sugar-candy, *lac*, coarse cotton cloth, sack-cloth and *bagy*, or *calamus aromaticus* and receive a large balance in money.

Continuing to describe the fair at *Biruru*, he says,

> From Seringapatam is brought money to puchase *betel-nut*, sugar-candy, sugar, *jirigay-seed, Madras* goods and blankets.
>
> The merchants of *Bangalore, Colar,* and other adjacent places, bring cotton cloths, and a few of silk, and take away *betel-nut* both *Deshavara* and *Wallagram,* black pepper, coco-nuts, cinnamon, ginger, *terra japonica, capili* flour, and *carthamus,* or *cossumba.* If the demand be sudden they bring ready money: but commonly they bring as much cloth, as when sold, procures their investment backwards; and sometimes even more.

Gubi also had its access to overseas imports at the Coromandel coast. Buchanan notes: "Merchants from *Gubi* and its neighbourhood, go to *Wallaja Petta,* near Arcot, with *Deshavara betel-nut,* and black pepper; and bring back cloth and all kinds of goods imported by sea at Madras."[77] From the descriptions it is clear that Gubi was an important node of trade in the Deccan, with routes passing across the peninsula and connecting with the coast passing through Gubi. This entrepôt aspect may have been one of the primary attributes of a 'southern Ayyāvoḷe'. One notes also that Gubi was itself a production centre of important commodities, such as textiles required for daily use, betel nut, articles of food, steel, iron and lac. The production of these goods took place in the country surrounding Gubi. As just noted, "The country for ten or twelve cosses round, produces for sale coarse cotton cloth..." and so on. Therefore Gubi in many ways approximated to what in European terminology would be called a town. Production, entrepôt trade, "redistribution", and the market were all here concentrated; but there was no suggestion that in appearance it resembled the walled townships of medieval Europe. At Gubi it appears that the countryside merged with the 'urban' aspects of the settlement. One judges also by Gubi as it is today. The weekly market at Gubi served a host of related markets and production centres. In medieval times protection for traders who came to the market was probably guranteed by the Ayyāvoḷe. Buchanan describes both the use of barter and money sales at Gubi. In the early nineteenth century the impression gained from Buchanan's account is that money prices and rates of barter fluctuated with supply and demand. In the early thirteenth century it is possible that the production of commodities, the links with other markets, and perhaps even the system of pricing resembled the early nineteenth century descriptions given by Buchanan.

[77] "Wallaja Petta" is located in the Palar valley linking Kannada areas with the coast. Buchanan, *ibid.*, p. 32.

H. *Guild Merchants and Towns*

So far we have noted examples of the relationships of the guilds with urban areas in the ninth, eleventh and thirteenth centuries. Speaking of the South Indian medieval township Stein points out that

> Terms such as *nagaram, puram, paṭṭinam* may be seen to be attached to certain settlements in recognition of their market functions and possibly their somewhat more diverse (though not necessarily greater) populations. However, such settlements may be seen as but minor variations within the complex structure of essentially rural localities in South India before A.D. 1100.[78]

He believes that Thanjavur and Kanchipuram were exceptions. By the twelfth and thirteenth centuries though, he recognizes that many more settlements with distinctly urban characteristics developed.[79] Analysis of Ayyāvoḷe and Maṇigrāmam inscriptions show that the twelfth century marked a turning point, a period in which we notice the emergence of many urban centres with a population requiring the supply of food grains from rural areas. This deduction is based on the many guild inscriptions in this period in which the tie-up between agricultural and trading interests is noticed, a feature common to Tamil and Kannada areas. The influx of a non-agricultural population into urban areas may have been caused by increased long-distance trade, the development of crafts such as weaving and increased local trade, all of which would predispose towards the development of urban commercial nuclei.[80] In addition one notes that sectarian movements and the growth of temple complexes and *maṭhas* also created a non-food-producing population whose needs had to be met from rural areas, and for whose use, as well as for the use of pilgrims, market facilities had to be provided.[81] Religious and economic developments in the twelfth and thirteenth centuries created conditions favourable to the development of towns.

The alliance between the *okkalu* and *citramēḷi* and the trader as has already been pointed out meant that the trader and agriculturist combined to control the supply of food grains to urban markets.[82] However, it must be

[78] Stein, *PSSMSI*, pp. 242-243.

[79] Stein, *PSSMSI*, p. 216. Stein speaking of the late twelfth century and the thirteenth century describes "the emergence of a new tier of centres of civilization – towns – which served to integrate the enlarged localities of the period...."

[80] The location of some weaving groups close to, or in urban settlements is likely. The Basinikonda inscription as early as A.D. 1050 associates *valaṅgai* weavers with an *erivīrapaṭṭinam* (*ARE* 342 of 1912). The thirteenth century Maṇigrāmam inscription (*ARE* 598 of 1926-27) associates the weaving community Kaikkōḷas with traders and exporters. The impression is that the Kaikkōḷas belonged to the township.

[81] See subsequent pages.

[82] In medieval South India whether it was the landowning *agrahāra* Brahman or the peasant

pointed out that the urban settler in medieval South India may have been a food producer himself since it is likely that towns were semi-rural, affording opportunities for the town inhabitant to engage in some form of agriculture. There is evidence that food grains were grown in the vicinity of towns but it may not have been sufficient to meet the city's needs at a time of urban growth and therefore grain was brought in from outside. An inscription of A.D. 1168 speaks of "the twelve kinds of grain which they imported from outside... and the paddy which they brought and loaded in the locality itself."[83]

Other basic factors may have brought the farmer and trader together. The participation of the peasant farmer in trade has been noticed in earlier phases of Indian history. R. Thapar speaking of the post-Mauryan period has said,

> The investment required for an elaborate trade can only be provided by a well-endowed social group which can invest its surplus in risk-taking ventures. The obvious category was the *gahapati* who could fall back on the land if the venture failed. That it turned out to be highly successful is clear from the fact that only did the *seṭthis* emerge from the ranks of the *gahapatis*, but by the post-Mauryan period, had an independent identity as financiers and gradually superseded the *gahapatis*.[84]

In medieval times the increased participation of the South Indian peninsula in overseas trade coincided with urban growth and with the alliance between peasant farmer and trader already noted. Imported goods and other commodities of long-distance trade as well as bulk consignments of paddy, sugar and a variety of grains and spices, came into the towns under the aegis of both these groups.[85] High profits appear to have been associated with this trade and a wealthy Ayyāvoḷe trader of Hoysaḷa times dealing in overseas commodities was able to pour money into urban settlements.[86] These were all surely interdependent phenomena, the lucrative overseas trade, the trader and agriculturist alliance and the development of towns. The provision of agricultural capital for trade, and the influx of gold and copper from overseas trade probably contributed to the establishment and growth of trading interests in already existing towns, particularly the ports, and also contributed to the development of many of the minor redistributing centres

---

Veḷḷāḷa landowner some basic support for Ayyāvoḷe trade came from landowning people. The "trading Veḷḷāḷa" referred to in the eighteenth century Dutch account of customary laws among the Veḷḷāḷas personifies this concept. See Ludo Rocher, "Jacob Mossel's Treatise on the Customary Laws of the Vellalar Chettiyars," *JAOS*, 89 (1969), 27-50. I am very grateful to Prof. Burton Stein for drawing my attention to this article.

[83] *EI*, V, p. 223. See also *KI*, II, p. 79.

[84] R. Thapar, "Continuous beginnings", *Seminar* (Jan. 1984), 29.

[85] Abraham, Diss., Chapter IV.

[86] *EC*, V. pt. 1, Arsikere 22.

throughout the peninsula, as for example the "southern Ayyāvoḷe" of Karnataka.[87] In Karṇataka certainly all these centres did not fade out in Vijayanagar or post-Vijayanagar times. One finds them functioning as flourishing market towns and entrepôts even in the early nineteenth century. This is evident from Buchanan's descriptions. In the nineteenth century these centres were used for the exchange and sale of local as well as imported goods.[88]

I. *Temples and the Trader*

The relationship between sectarian movements and the development of commerce in this period is illustrated by an examination of the township of Belagavi in Shikarpur taluk, Shimoga District, which was in medieval times an important centre for the Saivite Kālāmukhas and also for Ayyāvoḷe merchants. The best known of the Ayyāvoḷe epigraphs, *EC*, VII, Shikarpur 118, was recorded in the Somesvara temple which was probably a Kālāmukha establishment. This inscription described both long-distance trade encompassing several parts of the subcontinent as well as a thriving local trade. Evidence of the link between the Ayyāvoḷe merchants and the Kālāmukhas appears also in an inscription of A.D. 1094 also at Belagavi, which recorded a donation made by several people including Ayyāvoḷe merchants to a Kālāmukha *ācāryā* at the temple of Nakaresvara.[89] The donation was intended to cover the costs of temple ritual, food for the students attached to the temple, and for the ascetics'. Other inscriptions which link the Kālāmukhas firmly with Belagavi are Shikarpur 98 of A.D. 1103 which referred to the important Kālāmukha Dakṣina Kedaresvara temple and Shikarpur 123 of A.D. 1159 which referred to the Pañcakriya Kālāmukha temple in Belagavi and the college or Kodiya-*maṭha* of the Kālāmukhas also in Belagavi. There existed also in the twelfth century and perhaps earlier, a Pañca-*maṭha* in Belagavi, an amalgam of five *maṭhas* of which three were Hindu, one Jain and one Buddhist. The existence of these establishments meant that large numbers of non-agricultural people were in Belagavi. Belagavi was urban. The *maṭhas* and the temples undoubtedly generated much commerce. The food needs of these establishments, as well as those of pilgrims had to be met. Ritual in the temples necessitated the use of oil or *ghi*, as well as aromatics and flowers. Textiles and clothing were required. The position of the Shimoga District favoured urban growth. It was equidistant

[87] See Section G of this Chapter.

[88] See f.n. 76.

[89] *EC*, VII, Shikarpur 94. The rest of this paragraph is based on descriptions of Belagavi taken from D.N. Lorenzen, *The Kāpālikas and the Kālāmukhas* (New Delhi, 1972), p. 113. Stein, *PSSMSI*, p. 246 describing medieval Tamil areas says, "Sizeable urban settlements became an adjunct of great temples..."

from the ports of Mangalore and Karwar, on the west coast and favourably located for trans-peninsular trade. Temple-oriented Belagavi contrasted with the southern Ayyāvoḷe which were primarily market centres, serving a series of other neighbouring market towns, as well as functioning as staging posts on long-distance trade routes. Two important Kālāmukha priests at Belagavi met in A.D.1150 at the meeting of Ayyāvoḷe merchants whose proceedings are recorded in Shikarpur 118. They were the priest of the Pañca Linga and the priest of the Tripurāntaka temple.[90] A portion of the inscription is here reproduced as it illustrates very clearly the great interest of Ayyāvoḷe merchants in long-distance trade, and also conveys vividly some of the flavour of commercial life in Belagavi in the mid-twelfth century.[91]

> Be it well. Famed throughout the world; having acquired five hundred *vīra-śāsanas;* adorned with many good qualities, truth, purity, good conduct, policy, condescension, and prudence...conspicuous with the flag of the holy hill; their breasts embraced by the Lakṣmi of unfailing energy; great in the earth through bravery; born in the race of Vāsudēva, Khaṇḍali and Mūlabhadra; obtainers of a boon from the goddess Bhagavati... of the sect of Brahma, Viṣṇu and Mahēśvara. The earth as their sack; the eight regents at the points of the compass as the corner tassels; Vāsuki as the girth; the serpent race as the cords; the betel pouch as a secret pocket; the horizon as their light; a sharp sword as their wood knife; the invaluable articles in their bags as their wealth; visiting the Chēra, Chōḷa, Pāṇḍya, Maleya, Magadha, Kauśala, Saurāshtra, Dhanushtra, Kurumbha, Kāmbhōja, Gaulla, Lāla, Barvvara, Pārasa, Nēpāla, Ēkapāda, Lambakarṇṇa, Strī-rājya, Ghōlāmukha, and many other countries... and by land routes and water routes penetrating into the regions of the six continents; with superior elephants, well bred horses, large sapphires, moonstones, pearls, rubies, diamonds, lapis lazuli, onyx, topaz, carbuncles, coral, emeralds... and various such articles; cardamoms, cloves, bdellium, sandal, camphor, musk, saffron... and other perfumes and drugs; by selling which wholesale, or hawking about on their shoulders, preventing the loss by customs duties, they fill up the emperor's treasury of gold, his treasury of jewels, and his armoury of weapons; and from the rest they daily bestow gifts... enjoying in great comfort, merit, wealth, pleasure and property (the four objects of human desire); carriers with asses and buffaloes, adorned with red trappings; the sixteen of the eight *nāḍs, gavaregas, gātrigas, seṭṭis, seṭṭiguṭṭas, ankakāras, bīras, bīravanigas, gandigas, gavundaś, gavuṇḍa-svāmis*, thus with... white umbrellas as their canopy, the mighty oceans as their moat, Indra as the hand-guard, Varuna as the standard-bearer, Kubera as the treasurer, the nine planets as a belt, Rahu as a tassel, Ketu as a dagger, Kulika as the fight, the sun and moon

[90] *EC*, VII, Shikarpur 118.
[91] *Ibid.*

as the backers, the thirty-three gods as the spectators; they draw forth the sword *kṣame* (patience), and with it piercing the enemy named *krōdha* (anger)... Five hundred *svāmis* of the auspicious Aiyyāvoḷe, the best among their people, of unsullied fame, of lofty and brilliant glory, in truthfulness like Gāngēya, in firmness like Duryyōdhana, in might like Bhīmasha; like the elephant, they attack and kill; like the cow, they stand and kill; like the serpent, they kill with poison; like the lion, they spring and kill; wise as Brihaspati; fertile in expedients as Narayana; perfect in disputes as Nārada-rishi; raising a fire, they seize like death... the tiger with a collar on they irritate; on the moving cart they place their feet; clay they set fire to: of sand they make ropes; the thunderbolt they catch and exibit; the sun and moon they draw down to earth.... In the case of a sack which bursts from the contents collected from the points of the compass, an ass which runs away (laden) with grain, a wounded and fallen body, a cart that has been robbed, a blood load that has been lifted, a bar of gold that has been seized, a tax that has been evaded, a cry of looting, an assembly connected with caste customs, a bargain that has been made, ... they are not ones to fail; taking the head of an intruder as the tassel, they bind the enemy's hand as a badge (on a pole), and parade about; gambling they will not allow; to a dead body they are good.

Be it well. To the Five hundred *svāmis* of Ayyāvoḷe, possessed of all titles, having made prostration with the six members, salute with joined hands raised to the head, pull out that sack, and present offerings of food, O Seṭṭi! To the Five hundred *svāmis* of Ayyāvoḷe present the *tāmbūla* in a tray, wishing them all good fortune.

Be it well. The ever supremely happy Five hundred, with the *pattanasāvi* Mechi-Seṭṭi, Kirtti-Seṭṭi and all the townspeople, for the decorations of the god Gavarēśvara, and repairs of the temple, granted the following dues:- The shops of the *nagaras,* 10 *visa* a year for each; the gold merchants, 10 *visa* a year for each; the local *gavares*, 1 *pana* a year per sack; the *gavares* of other countries, 1 *haga* a year per sack; for camphor., musk, saffron, sandal, pearls and all such commodities sold by weight, 2 *kāni* per *pon;* local cloth merchants and foreign cloth merchants, 2 *kani* per *pon;* for black pepper, cummin seed, mustard... bishops's weed and coriander, 1 *visa* per *pon;* for sugar, asafoetida, dry ginger, long pepper, cardamoms, green ginger, turmeric, and all drugs and roots sold by weight, 1 *visa* per *pon.*

J. *The Nagaram. The Market*

The southern Ayyāvoḷe of Kannada areas may be compared to the marketing centre, the *nagaram* in Tamil areas. Kenneth Hall has shown that each administrative unit or *nāḍu* in Tamil areas had its own *nagaram* where commercial negotiations were transacted.[92] Hall has suggested that "in the

[92] Hall, the *Nagaram*, p. 117.

early Pallava-Chola period a *nagaram* was created after a series of negotiations between representatives of a political unit and a group of merchants."[93] A *nagaram*, he believed, was sometimes confined to a particular clearly-defined part of a town, and on occasion was also located outside the town walls.[94] In some areas epigraphic mention was made, he points out, only of a *nagaram*, not of an ancillary town.[95] A *nagaram*, he believed, held land of its own, administered land for private individuals as well as temples, collected state taxes, and was responsible for administration within the spatial confines of the nagaram.[96] Finally, and this is Hall's most important conclusion, he believed that the "*nagaram* was an important marketing institution which not only established the rules and regulations for its market place but also dominated trade within a series of lesser and subordinate markets."[97] Hall suggested that the *nagaram* exercised some monopoly rights in the locality and that itinerant merchants dealt directly with the *nagaram* and not with local markets.[98] This study has shown that while there were many instances of cooperation between the *nagarattār* and the *aiññūṟṟuvar*, there is no specific indication that the *aiññūṟṟuvar* dealt directly only with the *nagaram* and not with the local markets. The difference between the *nagaram* and the Karnatak southern Ayyāvoḷe appears to have been that the southern Ayyāvoḷe were created or controlled completely by Ayyāvoḷe merchants while the *nagaram* was a separate independent entity.

K. *Commodities. Markets. Prices.*

In both the inscriptions of the *aiññūṟṟuvar* and in *nagaram* inscriptions there is some suggestion that both institutions had direct connections with artisans.[99] There are many inscriptions which suggest a link between weaving communities and the *nagaram*.[100] There are also some *aiññūṟṟuvar* inscriptions which reveal close links between *aiññūṟṟuvar* merchants and weavers.[101] Textiles were one of the commodities handled by the *aiññūṟṟuvar*, judging by the levy of cess on cotton fabric mentioned in some of their inscriptions in the twelfth and thirteenth centuries. Some of the commodities of external trade handled by the *aiññūṟṟuvar* have already been

[93] *Ibid.*, p. 74.

[94] Ibid., pp. 67, 68.

[95] *Ibid.* The value of Hall's analysis of the spatial structure of a *nagaram* would have been enhanced if the chronology of the inscriptions cited had been taken into consideration.

[96] *Ibid.*, Chapter 3.

[97] *Ibid.*, p. 91.

[98] *Ibid.*, p. 109.

[99] *Ibid.*, p. 160.

[100] See inscriptional tables, Appendix A.

[101] *Ibid.*

identified. Based on a reading of the transcripts and estampages of inscriptions which give lists of commodities on which cess was granted to temples, the commodities of internal trade dealt with in the eleventh century were betel leaf, paddy, pepper, oil, and areca nuts. In the twelfth century, salt, wheat, other grains, groundnut, sesamum, elephants, jewels, jaggery, sugar, pulses, cotton, cummin, coriander, mustard, ginger and turmeric were included.[102] The mid-twelfth century Shikarpur inscription gives an impressive list of commodities imported and those of local origin. Some of these, including the luxuries, were sold in the local shops as the inscription quoted earlier clearly shows. There was then internal consumption of these luxury articles in Belagavi. If one relates the importance of markets to the value and quantity of commodities sold one sees that by the mid-twelfth century bulk trade in articles of food as well as luxury articles, spices, and other articles of great value was apparently handled by these merchants and these commodities were available for local consumption. There is not much change in the thirteenth century in commodities of internal exchange except that there appears to be a greater emphasis on the sale of textiles, dyes and iron and steel.[103] These commodities were transported to and from markets by porters and on the back of asses, buffaloes, in carts and on rafts when river passage was required.[104]

The retail sale of these commodities took place in shops in the town or at the weekly fairs. In Kannada areas the weekly markets were conducted often by the *paṭṭanasvāmi*, "lord of the town", who probably received in return certain perquisites and income from tolls.[105] The *nakara* or town assembly of Belagavi in A.D. 1094 was convened apparently by the members of the Ayyāvoḷe association and included the *paṭṭanasvāmi*, an accountant, a "manager", representatives of guilds, and some very prominent merchants who were mentioned by name. The assembly was considered competent to make decisions for the "whole city" regarding the levy of a contribution for charity which took the form of payment in cash and kind from shops, from some householders and from those who held "rent-free" land.[106] In Tamil areas weekly fairs may have been conducted by the *nagaram*. Weekly fairs are still held in Kannada and Tamil areas.

Barter may have been practised at these fairs. Equivalences for exchange of commodities may have been established and in some areas these may have functioned in lieu of money prices. Hall has pointed out that equivalences

[102] The evidence on commodities of internal trade is based upon careful examination of the transcripts and estampages of many inscriptions – for information on the levy of cess on goods in transit, see also inscriptional tables Appendix A.

[103] See Chapter Five.

[104] Conclusions derived from Ayyāvole inscriptions.

[105] Dikshit, *Local Self-Government*, p. 158.

[106] *EC*, VII, Shikarpur 94.

in paddy were established in some parts of the Chengalpattu District in the late eleventh and early twelfth centuries and these were not altered for many years.[107] Hall also notes some aspects of a regulated market in Chidambaram in the early eleventh century.[108] On the other hand he also points out that cash prices for paddy fell steadily in the eleventh century in another locality in Chengalpattu District.[109] In Belagavi in Shimoga District in the the mid-twelfth century retail prices of luxuries were calculated in gold as were the prices of cardamom, camphor and other aromatics in the early eleventh century in Thanjavur District.[110] Evidence that in the twelfth and thirteenth centuries the prices of overseas imported goods was calculated in money appears in the Motupalli inscription of the Andhra coast and the Nainativu inscription of northern Sri Lanka.[111] The taxes on imported goods are specified in these inscriptions and were, both in India and Sri Lanka "fixed". The inscription clearly suggests this. If taxes were "fixed" and recorded on stone we may assume that these taxes were based on a price structure which probably did not alter for some time.There is no indication, however that prices were fixed by the king or his administrative agent. It is not unlikely that the foreign seller, or a cartel of sellers, fixed prices, based on what the market would bear. This is the suggestion implicit in the letter of a Jewish merchant involved in the "India trade" in the mid-twelfth century writing from Aden to his counterpart in Cairo and it illustrates that in Cairo traders in imported commodities accepted the principle of a self-regulating market. The trader writes,

> I am asking you now, relying on your favours, when this shipment, God willing, safely arrives, to kindly take delivery of one-half of the aforementioned bales and sell them for me whatever price God will apportion and grant. After the price is agreed upon, turn everything into gold and silver—nothing else—and distribute it among various merchants, coreligionists, or others if they are known as reliable and send it on.[112]

Surely, however delicately phrased, the principle here accepted is that a hard bargain had to be driven based on demand and on buying capacity. It is possible that in South India similarly prices of imports were negotiable and depended on local demand. There is some evidence of monopolies exercised by traders in Cranganore in the thirteenth century.[113] This would have meant

[107] Hall, "The *Nagaram*", p. 102.

[108] *Ibid.*

[109] *Ibid.*, p. 104.

[110] *Ibid.*, p. 103 and *EC*, VII, Shikarpur, 118.

[111] See Chapter Five.

[112] Gotein, *Letters*, p. 184.

[113] See Kottayam Plate of Vīra-Rāghava, *EI*, IV, 41. K.R. Venkatarama Ayyar sees evidence of exclusive trading rights exercised by the Valañjiyar – *Valañjiyattil tanic-cettum* – "Medieval Trade, Craft and Merchant Guilds in South India", p. 269.

that a group of merchants could maintain a price level artificially. However, in addition, demand for the commodity undoubtedly affected the retail price within "commercial zones". These zones, one imagines, were not circumscribed by the boundaries of kingdoms but may, for example, have linked ports on the African and Arabian littoral with the west coast of India and Sri Lanka. This form of commercial interdependence and the political rivalries of Asian kingdoms involved in maritime trade receives fuller attention in the following chapter.

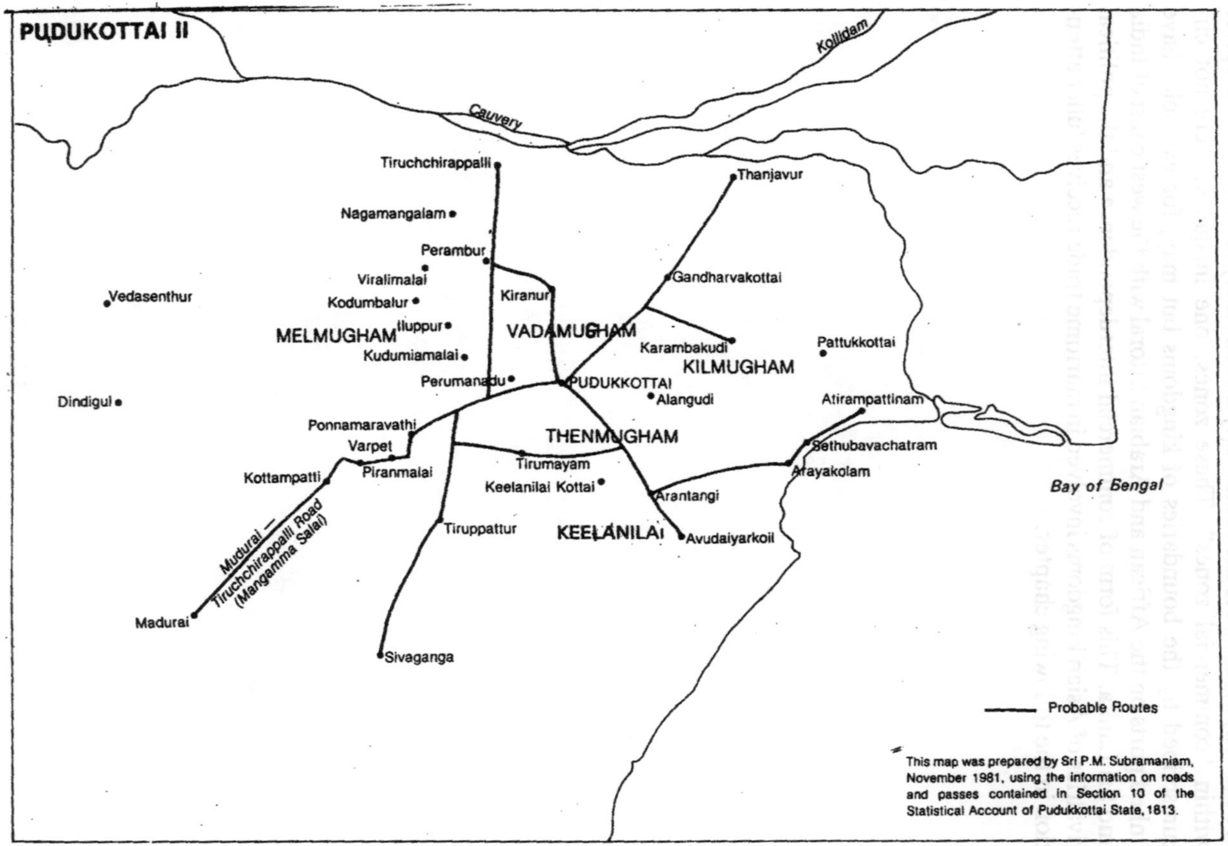

PUDUKOTTAI II
Kollidam
Cauvery
Tiruchchirappalli
Thanjavur
Nagamangalam
Perambur
Viralimalai
Gandharvakottai
Vedasenthur
Kodumbalur
Kiranur
MELMUGHAM
Iluppur
VADAMUGHAM
Karambakudi
Pattukkottai
Kudumiamalai
KILMUGHAM
Perumanadu
PUDUKKOTTAI
Dindigul
Alangudi
Atirampattinam
Ponnamaravathi
THENMUGHAM
Varpet
Sethubavachatram
Kottampatti
Piranmalai
Tirumayam
Arayakolam
Keelanilai Kottai
Bay of Bengal
Arantangi
Mudurai — Tiruchchirappalli Road (Mangamma Salai)
Tiruppattur
KEELANILAI
Avudaiyarkoil
Madurai
Sivaganga
Probable Routes
This map was prepared by Sri P.M. Subramaniam, November 1981, using the information on roads and passes contained in Section 10 of the Statistical Account of Pudukkottai State, 1813.

Chapter V

SECTION ONE

Some Aspects of International Trade and Medieval South Indian External Commerce

At various stages in the preceding four chapters there have been references to the overseas interests of the two major South Indian merchant guilds. South Indian interest in many parts of Asia in the ninth and tenth centuries has been noted in Chapter I in the history of the Maṇigrāmam association of traders. The Quilon (Kerala) and the Takuapa (Thailand) inscriptions of the Maṇigrāmam which have been referred to earlier both belong to the same period and are in themselves proof of the existence of long-distance foreign trade in which the South Indian merchant took part. In the late tenth and early eleventh centuries the Cōḷas and Tamil merchants were actively engaged in foreign maritime trade. The Chinese dynastic histories bear testimony to this fact. Some of the international tensions of medieval times in Asia may be related to the tussle for the benefits of long-distance trade.

In this chapter an attempt is made to explain some selected aspects of medieval international affairs in Asia, and this explanation, it is hoped, will in turn form a background, against which we may look at economic rivalries between South India, Sri Lanka and some areas of Southeast Asia. The special role of the Ayyāvoḷe and Maṇigrāmam should be seen in relation to this political and economic background. To date the South Indian participation in medieval, maritime trade has never been explored fully and this chapter provides more information on this point than any of the previous histories. But the picture is by no means complete. There is far more work to be done on this aspect of South Indian economic history. Nevertheless, a beginning has been made here. In addition some aspects of Cōḷa and Pāṇḍya foreign relations which bear on the question of maritime trade are investigated.

To buttress the conclusions arrived at on foreign trade a detailed analysis of the commodities of international trade handled specifically by the Maṇigrāmam and the Ayyāvoḷe is provided in the second half of this chapter. All this information put together provides a solid basis for the assertion that the South Indian peninsula was influenced deeply by the sea and by overseas interests. The Coromandel faced the east and early Cōḷa expansion may be noted in Sri Lanka and Southeast Asia. From the mid-twelfth century onwards there are definite indications of participation in foreign trade judging by the overseas imports on sale in South India.[1] Towards the end of the thirteenth century, and in the early years of the fourteenth century the trade of the guilds with Southeast Asia was significant. The Pāṇḍyan coast was a focus for the Southeast Asian trade. From the mid-fourteenth century onwards with the growing European demand for spices from India, the west coast of India, the pepper-growing coast, became very important commercially. The purchase of pepper by Venice at the entrepôts of Alexandria and Beirut grew dramatically at this time and later reached a peak at the end of the fifteenth century. The pepper trade is described in the subsequent portion of this chapter dealing with commodities of maritime import and export handled by the Maṇigrāmam and Ayyāvoḷe merchants.

But to start with we go back to the eleventh century and look again at the Cōḷa invasions of Sri Lanka bearing in mind the commercial compulsions of the times. No textbook on South Indian or Sri Lankan history gives all the information that is provided here on these wars. Research on this phase of political history has been worthwhile because from it emerges a new appraisal of the Cōḷa invasions and a better understanding of the overseas expansion of the trading interests of the Ayyāvoḷe. This exercise is followed by a fresh look at the Cōḷa naval raid on Southeast Asia during the reign of Rājēndra Cōḷa, and by a synthesis of the evidence available on Cōḷa trade overtures to China. A resumé of some aspects of the overseas interests of the South Indian mainland, Sri Lanka, and Burma, in the twelfth century is included. Further, the trade coming in to the Pāṇḍyan homeland and to the Andhra coast in the thirteenth century is described, and on this subject there is very accurate inscriptional evidence available. The Chinese trade missions to South India under the Yüan are mentioned in the Chinese dynastic histories and they underline the importance of South India and its overseas trade in that period.

Changes in the commodities of maritime trade may also be noticed at this time. Luxuries became less important and basic necessities such as dyes, yarn, textiles, processed iron, pepper, and horses figured more prominently in the Ayyāvoḷe inscriptions. These changes may be seen quite clearly in the section on commodities in the second half of this chapter and may also be studied in the table of inscriptions provided in Appendix A where the taxes on commodities of overseas trade distributed by the guilds within the South Indian peninsula are noted. In some specific inscriptions it is stated quite explicitly that the Ayyāvoḷe merchants were importers of foreign goods.[2]

What we do not know is how these goods came into the South Indian market, which of these were intended for onward trans-shipment, and who the

[1] *EC*, VII, Shikarpur 118; *EC*, V, pt.1, Belur 177; *EC*, V, pt.1, Arsikere 22. See also Appendix A.

[2] *Ibid.*

shippers and carriers were. There is sixteenth century evidence of regular routes employed by Tamil sailors who went to Southeast Asia and these same routes may have been in use much earlier.[3] But the goods could well have also been brought into India by Southeast Asian and West Asian carriers. Three overseas inscriptions of the ninth, eleventh and thirteenth centuries, suggest that the guilds sent their agents quite far abroad and established trading stations. These inscriptions are the Takuapa Maṇigrāmam inscription already discussed at length in Chapter I, the Ayyāvoḷe Barus inscription discussed later in this chapter and the *nānādēśi* inscription of Pagan.[4] The establishment of trading stations may have been a common practice, though there is no hard evidence for such an inference. Closer home some of the Ayyāvoḷe inscriptions of Sri Lanka may also indicate the establishment of trade and collection bases.[5]

A. *Invasions of Sri Lanka*

We proceed now with an examination of the Cōḷa invasions of Sri Lanka in the late tenth and early eleventh centuries and first we look at the religious chronicle of Sri Lanka, the *Cūlavaṃsa*, and its account of the events preceding the invasions of Rājarāja I in the late tenth century. The chronicler comments on the anarchy in the Sinhalese kingdom and the weak administration of the Sinhalese king Mahinda who was unable to raise sufficient revenue and therefore could not pay his South Indian mercenary troops. The news that the times favoured Rājarāja's venture was brought to him by a merchant. "But a horse-dealer, who had come hither from the opposite coast, told the Cōḷa king on his return about conditions in Lanka. On hearing this, the powerful (prince) with the purpose of taking possession of Lanka, sent off a strong body of troops."[6] If this extract from the *Cūlavaṃsa* represents the actual sequence of events then merchants had access to Cōḷa kings and were in a position to advise on matters which were vital to the interest of the ruler. One may then pursue the argument further and suggest that possibly the trader also stood to gain from a Cōḷa invasion. The furthering of trading

[3] In the sixteenth century the Turkish sea captain Sidi Ali Celebi spent some years in Gujarat and wrote a sailing guide based on Arab navigational guides of the previous centuries. See for example the "27th voyage from Diu to Malacca" with its description of Tamil divergent routes (distinct from the Arab and Gujarati routes) contained in G.Ferrand, *Relations de voyages et textes géographiques arabes, persans et turks relatifs à 1 Extreme – Orient du VIIIe au XVIIe siècles,* Vol. II (Paris, 1913-14),p. 465.

[4] Takuapa – See Chapter I, f.n. 71.
Barus – See subsequent pages of this chapter.
Pagan – *EI,* VII, pp. 197-8.

[5] e.g. *ET,* I, i; *EZ,* I, p. 181 and *CTI,* pt.II, pp. 23-24.

[6] *Cv.,* 55, 13-15.

interests could well have been one of the motives for the invasion of Sri Lanka under Rājarāja I and Rājēndra I.

This appears to be the view taken by K.A.N. Sastri, who says of the wars of Rājarāja I:

> He pursued an active, maritime policy calculated to extend the commerce of his country and convert the Bay of Bengal into a Cōḷa lake, and the possession of Ceylon was no longer merely a buttress to his continental empire on the mainland, but an integral part of the plan of building up sea power.[7]

While Sastri's description of the Cōḷa state may not be acceptable, nevertheless his thesis merits attention. This thesis could be expanded to include the idea that at a time of the general revival of Asian trade, the external policy of the Cōḷas was designed to favour the expansion of overseas interests from which both the Cōḷa ruler and the merchant guild derived benefit. A diametrically opposite view is put forward in a recent analysis of the Cōḷa-Sri Lankan wars in which the invasions of Sri Lanka under Rājarāja I and Rājēndra I were said to have been "based upon more ruthless plunder and destruction of major political and religions centres in northern Ceylon, followed by the establishment of semi-permanent, fortified encampments from which wide-ranging raids could be carried out in other parts of the island".[8] The prime motive for war was seen to be the acquisition of quick, liquid capital from plundering raids necessary, it is held, in view of the uneasy hold of the Cōḷas over their own home territory. The Cōḷa state is here viewed as an overlordship extending over areas of settled agriculture as well as areas of forest peopled by "un-assimilated or semi-assimilated tribal peoples.' Governance, it is believed, came largely from 'local chiefs' and 'peasant assemblies' who were not completely amenable to the Cōḷa demand for taxes. Hence the need for extra resources which were in part met by plundering raids. Merchant alliances established trade 'networks' but were not 'the creatures of any dynastic regime.' They functioned with a great deal of independence and the Cōḷas accepted the 'political neutrality of trade.' In contrast, the thesis upheld in this work is that trade was an important factor in framing Cōḷa policy and that Cōḷa rulers had links with the merchant community, and that some degree of mutual benefit was derived,both by the ruler and the merchant, from an external policy which supported the trader.

The plundering aspects of Rājarāja's invasion are described vividly in the *Cūlavaṃsa*. The invasions are represented as acts of pillage as well as assaults on the established religion of Sri Lanka.

[7] K.A.N. Sastri, "Cōḷa invasions: Downfall of Anuradhapura", pp. 347-48.

[8] Spencer, "Politics of Plunder", p. 409. Spencer's views on the Cōḷa state and on merchant associations which are summarised in the rest of this paragraph are quoted from the same article.

> In the three fraternities and in all Lanka (breaking open) the relic chambers (they carried away) many costly images of gold, etc. and while they violently destroyed here and there all the monasteries, like blood sucking yakkhas they took all the treasures of Lanka for themselves.[9]

The *Cūlavaṃsa* description of the Cōḷa invasions may have been telescoped to include both Rājarāja's incursion and the subsequent invasion of Rājēndra in one account. If so, one assumes that this description of the invasion represents a general view, and not necessarily an account of one specific incursion. It was probably of Rājēndra's invasion that the *Cūlavaṃsa* said: "the Cōḷas seized the Mahēsi, the jewels, the diadem that he had inherited, the whole of the (royal) ornaments, the priceless diamond bracelet, a gift of the gods, the unbreakable sword and relic of the torn strip of cloth."[10] The *Cūlavaṃsa* also said the Sinhalese capital of Anuradhapura was "utterly destroyed in every way by the Cōḷa army...."[11]

After the raid on Anuradhapura, Rājarāja's forces may have moved to Padaviya and it has been suggested, may even have established a camp city there before the Cōḷas moved to Polonnaruva. Padaviya was located in the centre of the northern plains of Sri Lanka and Polonnaruva lay southeast of Anuradhapura in the valley of the river Mahavali which leads straight down to the harbour of Trincomalee on the east coast of Sri Lanka. In Padaviya the ruins of Hindu shrines have been found as also an epigraph of Rājarāja's time in Tamil and Grantha of the eleventh century.[12] In this inscription for the first time the *nānādēśi* merchants are mentioned in Sri Lanka. The *nānādēśi* merchants were an affiliate group of the *aiññūṛṛuvar* and are named in subsequent inscriptions in Sri Lanka.[13] There is no earlier record of their functioning in Sri Lanka and one has then perforce to give some credence to the idea that this merchant corporation may have come in the wake of the armies. It has been pointed out that prior to the Cōḷa invasions some Sinhalese merchants were organised in associations similar to the Tamil guilds.[14] The existence of an infrastructure of trade networks and markets appears all the more reason for the mainland merchants to have attempted to obtain a foothold for themselves. Apart from merchants who were part of recognised associations, there are records of influential merchants at Matottam, a commercial centre of Cōḷa times.[15]

Evidence of the Cōḷa move to the eastern seaboard of Sri Lanka appears

[9] *Cv.*, 55, 20-22.

[10] *Cv.*, 55, 16-17.

[11] *Cv.*, 74, 1.

[12] *ET*, I, i, p. 33.

[13] *EZ*, I, p. 181 and *CTI*, pt. II, pp. 23-24.

[14] Spencer, "Politics of Plunder", pp. 49, 415.

[15] S. Pathamanathan, *The Kingdom of Jaffna*, pp. 49-50.

in the eighteen odd inscriptions of the Cōḷa period found in Trincomalee and its environs. These particular inscriptions have not been mentioned in standard textbooks of Sri Lankan history so far. Of these inscriptions fourteen were found in the Buddhist Velgam *vihāra* at Periyakulam nearby, and there were others within the precincts of the present town of Trincomalee and on the outskirts of the town.[16] One other mentioning the former *agrahāra* of Kantalai nearby may also be of Cōḷa times.[17] Several of the inscriptions were probably inscribed in the reign of Rājēndra I.

This is the largest concentration of Cōḷa epigraphs of the early period within a limited area of Sri Lanka. The extensive Tamil patronage extended to the Velgam *vihāra* of Periyakulam somewhat contradicts the *Cūlavaṃsa* emphasis on the anti–Buddhist nature of the Cōḷa occupation. Trincomalee then also emerges, as one of the early areas of settlement and one to which the Tamils attached much importance. In Trincomalee in addition there are traditions of migrant communities and of a prince of Cōḷa descent who ruled this important area.[18] Two inscriptions refer to a Cōḷa Iḷankēśvaradēva who may have been appointed in the reign of Rājēndra I, or later in Rājādhirāja's time.[19] There is some scholastic controversy on the exact period of his rule. But epigraphic evidence and local tradition combine to suggest the importance to the Cōḷas of control of this crucial area of the eastern coast of Sri Lanka. Polonnaruva which became the capital city of the Cōḷas had easy access to Trincomalee since Polonnaruva was located on a tributary of the Gal Oya, itself a tributary of the Mahavali Ganga which leads right down to Trincomalee and the sea. In this period the Cōḷas re-named Polonnaruva Jananathamangalam after a title of Rājarāja I. The Cōḷa occupation of northern Sri Lanka lasted approximately eight decades and specifically, within the early period of this occupation, the Ayyāvoḷe guild is noticed functioning at Polonnaruva.[20] In all probability, the *aiññūṟṟuvar* merchants came with the armies, or a short while later as a result of Tamil occupation of the area.

The Cōḷas after establishing their hold on Polonnaruva appeared to have attempted to push further south into Rohana. This attempt may have taken place around A.D. 1017-18. The Cōḷas claimed that after conquering the area they were in control of the 'whole Iḷamaṇḍalam on the transparent

[16] *ET*, I, i, No. 9, "Fourteen Cōḷa inscriptions from the Ancient Rājarāja – perumpaḷḷi (Velgam Vehera/Natanar Kovil) at Periyakulam"; *Trincomalee Inscriptions*, Series No.2, "Three Cōḷa Inscriptions from Trincomalee"; S. Gunasingham, "A Tamil Slab Inscription at Nilāveli," *SLJH*, I, No.1 (1975), 61-71.

[17] *Trincomalee Inscriptions*, Series No.1, "Two Inscriptions of Cōḷa Iḷankēśvara Dēva". See Sri Lanka map on p. 71.

[18] Canmukarattina Aiyar ed., *Konecar Kalveṭṭu* (Jaffna, 1909).

[19] *Trincomalee Inscriptions*, Series No.1, *Iḷankēśvaradēva* may be translated "Lord of Lanka".

[20] *CTI*, pt. II, 9-12.

sea.'[21] They also claimed to have seized the Pāṇḍyan crown and the crown of the king of Sri Lanka and his queen, in addition to much other wealth. The king, Mahinda was taken prisoner to India. There is little documentation on how far the Cōḷas succeeded in penetrating into Rohana or whether they were able to establish any permanent bases there. Opposition to the Cōḷas in Rohaṇa first crystallised around the person of the son of Mahinda. But he died early according to the *Cūlavaṃsa,* and it was some years later that young prince Kitti, son of a chieftain of Rohana, succeeded in suppressng local opposition to his leadership. Kitti, the future king Vijayabāhu, then laid plans for war against the Cōḷas who meanwhile it is said were "ravaging Rājaraṭṭha."[22] He appears to have sent a tribute mission to Rāmanna (kingdom of Pegu) and the king of Pegu either sent gifts in return or a trade mission, the *Cūlavaṃsa* description leaves room for doubt. "Then arrived in the harbour many ships laden with various stuffs, camphor, sandalwood and other goods."[23] The camphor and sandalwood were articles in high demand in the Indian Ocean trade of this period. The arrival of this cargo, a source of rich revenue for the prince helped to consolidate his position. He was able to set up a large encampment at Tambalagama which may have been in the present Galle district.[24] The port at which the ships arrived could have been either Galle or Weligama.[25] As described in the *Cūlavaṃsa* it would appear that from then on the Cōḷa position weakened. "All the inhabitants of Rājaraṭṭha grew hostile to one another and paid no further tribute. The adversaries of the Cōḷa King full of arrogance, left his commands unheeded, ill-treated the appointed officials and did what they pleased."[26] If one examines the event which the chronicler of the *Cūlavaṃsa* sees as relevant to a narration of the war, one has here an account of what is either a trade mission, or costly foreign gifts arriving at Sinhalese controlled ports, after which the Cōḷas found it difficult to maintain their position of supremacy.

The gifts sent by the Burmese were obviously highly prized in Sri Lanka. It is likely that these goods were once available in Sri Lanka, but that the

[21] *SII,* III, p. 28. Iḷamaṇḍalam refers to Sri Lanka.

[22] *Cv.*, 58, 3.

[23] *Cv.*, 58, 9-10.

[24] *Cv.*, 58, 10.

[25] B.J. Perera, "The Foreign Trade and Commerce of Ancient Ceylon," 1, "The Ports of Ancient Ceylon," *CHJ,* 1 (2 October, 1951) 115 cites the eleventh century testimony of Masudi who claimed that "there was no longer a direct connection between India and China in his time, but that ships from either side of India came to Galle which was a halfway point from which Chinese vessels sailed to Khanfu."

Ibid., p. 118, B.J. Perera points out that Weligama was mentioned in the time of Parākramabāhu I, *Cv.*, 75, 45. "It was at this port that the Burmese ambassador Ramadutin was brought ashore by the storms when he was on his way to Ceylon from Burma in the latter half of the 15th century."

[26] *Cv.*, 58, 11-12.

Cōḷa occupation of Sri Lanka had cut off the normal Sinhalese access to Southeast Asian ports. If this reconstruction is acceptable it reinforces the theory that a prime motive for the Cōḷa invasion was a desire to control the trade of Sri Lanka east coast ports. This would then explain the logistics of the Cōḷa military thrust which was directed towards the eastern seaboard. Anuradhapura once conquered was of no great importance to them, but Polonnaruva, the lower reaches of the Mahavali and the harbours of the east coast were. That Burma was able to send goods such as camphor and sandalwood to Vijayabāhu also meant that Burma was a participant in Southeast Asian trade. These products were not native to Burma, and may have been obtained from traders arriving in Burma or at their places of origin, or even at the entrepôt markets of the area at the isthmus of Kra or the Kedah coast where "Kadaram" of the Cōḷa raid may have been located.[27] The sandalwood and camphor were used mainly in religious services. Vijayabāhu it is noted, after the Cōḷas were expelled, arranged "many offerings (religious) of sweet smelling savours," whereas his successor Vikramabāhu who was no friend of the religious establishment took away "the sandalwood, the aloes, the camphor" presented to the Temple of the Tooth Relic.[28]

In the second half of the eleventh century the prince Kitti launched a series of attacks on the Cōḷas. The Sinhalese thrusts were followed by counter-thrusts from the Cōḷas. Polonnaruva was captured by the Sinhalese but they were then forced to retreat when fresh armies came from the mainland. Finally a skillfully planned Sinhalese attack on both Anuradhapura and Polonnaruva was successful. Polonnaruva fell first, and then Anuradhapura. Fresh armies were sent across the Palk Straits by Vīrarājēndra Cōḷa but ultimately the Cōḷas either fled after a defeat or withdrew around A.D. 1070.

Evidence of the island of Sri Lanka being part of a maritime trading world in which China, Southeast and South Asia and West Asia were linked comes from a wide range of sources. The well-known sixth century description of the Nestorian monk Cosmas of trade at Malabar ports and in Sri Lanka has been quoted in Chapter I.[29] In the sixth century it is believed that a corporate group of bankers existed in Anuradhapura who especially venerated the Buddha Dipamkara, patron of all sailors.[30] There are several well-known statues of the Buddha Dipamkara in Southeast Asia, and it is held that this group in Anuradhapura probably had connections with traders proceeding

[27] See Chapter I on Tamil trading interests at the Isthmus of Kra and in Kedah.

[28] *Cv.*, 60, 18-19; *Cv.*, 61, 57-58.

[29] See Chapter I, f.n. 22.

[30] P. Wheatley, "Satyānṛta in Suvarnadvīpa From Reciprocity to Redistribution in Ancient Southeast Asia," in *Ancient Civilisation and Trade,* eds. J.A. Sabloff and C.C. Lamberg-Karlovsky (Albuquerque, 1975), p. 261, f.n. 14, 15, 16. Wheatley also cites S. Paranavitana, *Ceylon and Malaysia* (Colombo, 1966), p. 176 as evidence of the existence of this group.

to Southeast Asia.[31] There is some evidence of missions sent from Sri Lanka to China, in the sixth, seventh and eighth centuries, and also of the visit of pilgrims in the fourth, fifth, sixth and seventh centuries.[32] Nearer home it is believed that Sinhalese monks travelled to the Indonesian islands and established a monastic settlement there. A portion of a late eighth century inscription from Central Java reads thus: "This Abhayagiri Vihāra here of the Sinhalese ascetics trained in the sayings of discipline of the best of the Jinas was established."[33] The opening lines of the inscription are said to be clearly Mahayanist. De Casparis deduces from this inscription that Indonesian traders visited South India and Sri Lanka. As he says, "... early trade carried on by Indonesian shippers created a necessary condition without which it would be difficult to understand cultural contacts in later centuries."[34]

Wheatley in his article cited earlier, "Satyānṛta in Suvarnadvīpa" cites inscriptional evidence of the early tenth century which mentions Sinhalese in Kaladi, East Java.[35] He also cites another inscription which mentions Sinhalese as tax collectors in Palebuhan, East Java in A.D. 927.[36] Wheatley also cites inscriptions which mention the *vāṇigrāma,* which he defines as an association of merchants in East Java and in Bali also in the tenth century.[37] An inscription of the tenth century from Sri Lanka mentions an association of merchants known as the *vāṇigrāma.*[38] Gopinatha Rao speaking of the South Indian use of the word *vāṇigagrāmattār* believed it denoted a community.[39] One may infer that the Sinhalese links with Java and Bali in the tenth century, and the existence of association of merchants, could well have facilitated trade between these areas.

[31] See P. Dupont, "*Les Buddhas dit d'Amarāvati en Asie du Sud-Est,*" *BEFEO*, 49 (1954), 631-36. Wheatley notes that Buddha statues of this genre have been found in Thailand, Vietnam, Sumatra, eastern Java and Sulawesi. Wheatley *ibid.*, p. 235 believes that Sri Lanka was "the style center for at least three of the erroneously ascribed Amaravati Buddhas that constituted the earliest South Asian archaeological finds in Southeast Asia." Wheatley also cites M. Levi d' Ancona, "Amaravati, Ceylon and the Three 'Imported Bronzes'" *The Art Bulletin,* 34 (1952), 1-17 and A. Foucher, *Etude sur l'iconographie bouddhique de l'Inde, d'après des documents nouveaux,* Vol.I (Paris, 1900-05), pp. 189-209. The connection between the Anuradhapura group and Southeast Asia is based on Paranavitana *ibid.*

[32] B.J. Perera, "The Foreign Trade and Commerce of Ancient Ceylon, III," "Ancient Ceylon's Trade with the Empires of the Eastern and Western Worlds," *CHJ*, I, No.4 (1952), 301-320 especially p. 307.

[33] J.G. de Casparis, "New evidence on cultural relations between Java and Ceylon in ancient times," *Artibus Asiae*, 24 (1961), 241-248.

[34] *Ibid.*

[35] Wheatley, "Satyānṛta", p. 267.

[36] *Ibid.*

[37] Cited *ibid.*, p. 268.

[38] *EZ*, V, p. 182, Badulla Pillar Inscription.

[39] Gopinatha Rao, "A Note on Maṇigrāmmattār", p. 70.

If one enquires further as to which commodities were traded, then almost certainly the aromatics, camphor and sandalwood were the most important. Both the camphor and sandalwood were products of Southeast Asia used primarily for ritual purposes. These were the products the Burmese sent to Vijayabāhu during the Cōḷa wars in the eleventh century. The prestige and economic value attached to these commodities in pre-modern times is not to be underestimated. R.McC. Adams quotes Ford's comment on the importance of "the constant demand for expendable, sacred items," which is what these commodities were in the trading world of South and Southeast Asia.[40] Java was known for its sandalwood and to a lesser extent camphor. (See sections on camphor and sandalwood in "Commodities".)

The anonymous Arab work the *'Aḥbār as Sīn wa'l-Hind,* a collection of travel stories of the ninth century although of somewhat dubious value as a source, nonetheless has a description of Sri Lanka which is interesting. The island, it says, is rich in precious stones, rubies, topaz and sapphire, aloes, gold and pearls.[41] If we are to attach credence to this description it would mean that some Southeast Asian produce, aloes and gold, came into Sri Lanka in this period. A more reliable source is the mid-ninth century account of Ibn Khurdadhbih. Ibn Khurdadhbih states that Sri Lanka had aloes, pepper, many aromatics, perfumes, musk, diamonds and precious stones, coconut, emery, rock crystal and pearls.[42] If one looks at this list critically it is obvious that the aloes, musk, gold, the many aromatics, diamonds and rock crystal were not Sri Lankan produce. If Ibn Khurdadhbih was right it means that these products were imported into Sri Lanka and then re-exported. The aloes, gold and aromatics were probably Southeast Asian imports. All the evidence put together suggests that Sri Lanka in the tenth century was known to the Arabs as a place where valuable commodities were available, some of Southeast Asian provenance. The inscriptional evidence earlier cited shows the Sinhalese had definite links with the Indonesian islands.

The coastal site of Tiriyayi on the east coast of Sri Lanka has a well-known inscription in Pallava Grantha script of the seventh century which refers both to seafaring and to commerce.[43] In the eleventh century there is again evidence of Sinhalese traders in Java in the inscriptions of the time of Airlangga.[44] It has been pointed out that in the *Kathāsaritsāgara* composed in

[40] R.I. Ford, "Barter, gift or violence: An analysis of Tewa Intertribal exchange," in E.N. Wilmsen ed., *Social exchange and interaction,* Museum of Anthropology, University of Michigan, Anthropological Papers 46 (1972), p. 45, cited in R. McC. Adams, "Anthropological Perspectives on Ancient Trade", *Current Anthropology,* 15, No.3 (1974), 242.

[41] Ferrand, *Relations de voyages*, Vol.I, pp. 31-3.

[42] C. Barbier de Meynard, "Le livre des routes et des provinces", *JA,* sixième serie, 5 (1865), 283-6.

[43] *EZ*, IV, pp. 151-160, 312-319.

[44] G. Coedès, *The Indianized States of Southeast Asia,* ed., W.F. Vella and trans., S.B. Cowing (Kuala Lumpur, 1968), p. 146.

about A.D. 1070 there appears the story of a Brahman who sailed from India to Southeast Asia looking for his son. The sea route he followed on his return took in Simhaladvīpa.[45] This was probably a normal route for merchant vessels at that time. Sri Lanka was normally within the orbit of medieval maritime trade.

Tangible evidence of trade between Sri Lanka and the east are the Chinese coin hoards at Polonnaruva and the finds of Chinese ceramics at Polonnaruva and in the Jaffna peninsula.[46] A survey of the coast has however shown that there is little or no trace of medieval port sites on the east coast. It is believed though that in the period A.D. 600-1000 a large scale colonisation of the "coastal regions of eastern Ceylon" may have taken place and this conclusion is based on sites examined, not on the coast, but "in the hinterland."[47] The sites with "their physical association with numerous artificial reservoirs suggests that their occupants subsisted by reservoir irrigated rice cultivation."[48] However, S. Deriyanagala who has formulated this hypothesis also cautions that his arguments are "based on insecurely dated pottery."[49] The sites he mentions specifically are at Chembi Male near the Kokkilai lagoon, a site near Kuchchaveli and another near the temple complex of Seruvila close to Trincomalee.[50]

Absence of port sites on the east coast is not in itself a proof of lack of trading contact. Carswell in his search for medieval South Asian ports notes that "the violence of the twice-yearly monsoon is such that the ground is scoured right down to the surface of the laterite, and any trace of occupation is thereby washed away."[51] He also writes that every storm turns the sand dunes "upside down."[52] On the east coast of Sri Lanka both the frequent cyclones and the British naval build-up at Trincomalee could well have obliterated possible evidence. At many port sites clearly identified tangible evidence of medieval commerce is scanty. Except at some sheltered locations such as Mantai (near Mannar), which was not merely a port but an important medieval city, archaelogical evidence of overseas commerce is hard to find. Besides, most important, as Carswell notes, "The ports need to be studied in the context of their hinterlands, for they were often no more than

[45] N.M. Penzer, *The ocean of story: being C.H. Tawney's translation of Somadeva's Katha Sarit Sāgara* (London, 1924), *taranga* 56, verses 56-64.

[46] Polonnaruva, Archaeological Survey of Ceylon, 1911-12, X, p. 56.

[47] S. Deriyanagala, "Archaeological Survey to Investigate Southeast Asian Prehistoric Presence in Ceylon", *Ancient Ceylon,* Occasional Paper No.1, pt. II (August, 1972) 38.

[48] *Ibid.*

[49] *Ibid.*

[50] Deriyanagala, "Archaeological Survey", pp. 18-21.

[51] Carswell, "China and Islam, A Study of the Coast of India and Ceylon," p. 35.

[52] *Ibid.*

immediate stages in the transmission of goods."[53] The connecting links between Polonnaruvạ and the coast are of relevance. The river Mahavali was navigable as far north as the island once known as Kalinga-nuwara from which goods could be offloaded and taken up to Polonnaruva.[54] Some of the canal systems leading off from the Mahavali and the Amban-ganga eventually led to Tambalagam bay and the sea.[55] While many of the canal systems owe their origin or improvement to Parākramabāhu I in the twelfth century some may well have been in use when the Cōḷas invaded.[56] Apart from the lower reaches of the Mahavali other waterways, man-made, connected the Trincomalee coast with its hinterland. Those canals, which were navigable, and in existence when the Cōḷas invaded, could have been used for transporting goods arriving by sea.

B. *The Cōḷas, Southeast Asia and China*

The Cōḷa interest in foreign trade at the time of the invasion of Sri Lanka may be deduced primarily from a series of inscriptions and from the descriptions of the missions to China. In the inscription known as the larger Leiden Grant it is mentioned that the king of Srivijaya and Kadaram supported the construction of a *vihāra* in Nagapattinam. Rājarāja in his 21st year, approximately the early eleventh century, gave a liberal grant of land for the upkeep of the *vihāra*.[57] The construction of the *vihāra* one assumes was linked with Srivijayan commercial interest in the port. In A.D. 1014-15 a gift was presented to the deity of a temple in Nagapattinam on behalf of the king of Srivijaya.[58] Another gift was also made, again possibly on behalf of Srivijaya, in Rājēndra's time.[59] A third gift was made in c.A.D. 1018. This time the king of Kadaram is mentioned and the gift also to a temple in Nagapattinam included *Chīnakkanakam,* Chinese gold.[60] A Cōḷa inscription refers to a gift

[53] *Ibid.*, p. 28.

[54] R.L. Brohier, *Ancient Irrigation Works in Ceylon* (Colombo, 1934), pt. I, p. 12.

[55] Sir Henry Ward's Collected Minutes and Papers, Brohier *op. cit.*, p. 9.

[56] The Kalinga-ela scheme one branch of which is delineated on the map may have been rebuilt or repaired in the time of Parākramabāhu the Great in the twelfth century. The left branch of the canal extended in the direction of Trincomalee. An experienced surveyor believes the canal was obviously designed to take boat traffic as well as serve as an irrigation canal. (U.P. Ratnatunga, personal communication, Colombo, June 1980). Traditionally the construction of the Kalinga-ela is ascribed to the reign of Dhatusēna (A.D. 459). See Sri Lanka map appended to Chapter II.

[57] The Leiden Grants, *EI*, XXII, pp. 213-81. In A.D. 1090 Kulōttunga I renewed the grant to the *vihāra*.

[58] *ARE* 164 of 1956-57.

[59] *ARE* 161 of 1956-57.

[60] *ARE* 166 of 1956-57.

sent by the Khmer king to Rājēndra I. In a later inscription of Kulōttunga's time another gift was given by the king of "Kamboja". Both gifts may have been intended as gestures preliminary to arriving at agreements on commercial exchanges.,[61]

One has to guess the exact nature of the commercial links one imagines underlay these donations to religious foundations. It is possible that Srivijaya was offering the sale of products of the Indonesian archipelago (see section on commodities) and other Southeast Asian and Chinese products. We do not know whether an exchange between these commodities and those of the Cōḷa kingdom was being negotiated or whether Nagapattinam was being used as a 'port of trade' where Srivijayan agents and traders could negotiate sales, purchase and exchange of their products, of other eastern and Far Eastern products and those of South Asian and West Asian origin. There is evidence that medieval maritime trade was not confined to the simple exchange of the native products of one country for the produce of the other trade partner. Foreign commodities were bought at rates fixed, one is led to believe, by the exigencies of supply and demand.[62] The payments may have been in other commodities considered to be of adequate value at the time of sale, or in coined gold, or bullion, or in other acceptable coinage. Some proportion of the foreign commodities after purchase may have found their way into the local markets but some of it was probably transported along with other 'native' products to other overseas markets for re-sale.[63]

The description of the trade mission of Rājarāja I to China which arrived in 1015 is instructive in this respect. The mission, it appears, spent over three years, en route, one way. One envisages that it was a coasting voyage. The sea route of the Cōḷa mission may have included a halt at a Sri Lankan port. The articles of tribute included pearls which may have been from the pearl fisheries of Mannar. (See section on commodities). From the *Sung Shih* and Ma Tuan-lin one obtains the information that 21,000 ounces of pearls were sent, 60 elephant tusks and 60 *catties* (1 catty = 1¼ lbs) of frankincense.[64]

[61] Sastri, *The Cōḷas,* p. 220, p. 317, and K.R. Hall, "Khmer Commercial Development and Foreign Contacts under Sūryavarman I," *JESHO*, 18, No.3 (1975), 318-336.

[62] See previous Chapter.

[63] *EC*, VII, Shikarpur 118 refers to sales within the town of camphor, sandal, pearls, foreign cloth. All these were imports.

[64] *Chau Ju-kua, His Work on the Chinese and Arab Trade in the twelfth and thirteeenth centuries, entitled Chu-fan-chï,* trans., F. Hirth and W.W. Rockhill (St. Petersburg, 1911, rpt. New York, 1966), pp. 100-101, f.n. 11. Rockhill points out that Chau Ju-kua, Ma Tuan-lin, Chou K'u-fei and the *Sung Shih* all obtained the information from the earlier *Ling-wai-tai-ta.* The *Sung Shih,* 489, 20-22, says that the envoy from the Cōḷa country was So-li San-won and that en route they passed the island of Ceylon(?). In the description of Ma Tuan-lin in Hervey St. Denys, *Ethnographie des peuples etrangers à la Chine,* Vol. II (Geneva, 1883), pp. 573-575 it is said that Rājarāja conveyed to the Sung emperor that he had heard of him from "...un vaisseau marchand qui visitait mon royaume." Ma Tuan-lin believed that the products of the Cōḷa kingdom included pearls, coral, crystal, areca nuts, and cotton.

The gifts of the envoys to the Emperor included pearls (6,600 ounces) and 3,300 *catties* of perfumes (aromatic substances). The frankincense could only have come from West Asia. The bulk of the aromatics may have been Southeast Asian. There is little of Indian origin, and cotton textiles are not mentioned. If this mission was sent to solicit trade then obviously it was not the produce of the Cōḷa kingdom which was being offered. The Cōḷa kings were then seeking to establish trade exchanges mainly with imported goods obtained at source, or these were brought to Cōḷa ports by other carriers and then re-exported and the Cōḷa envoys were indicating that, directly or indirectly, the Chinese could obtain these goods from them. They were seeking also, one assumes, acceptance for their traders and agents arriving at Chinese ports. The 1015 mission was sent before the naval raid. A mission sent in 1033 in Rājēndra I's time took with it gifts of a 'pearl coat and hat', 105 ounces of pearls, 100 ivory tusks and a letter written on gold foil.[65]

The Cōḷa missions to China show that the Cōḷa rulers themselves were personally interested in acquiring a share of the profits of maritime trade. Seen in this context, it appears very likely that the invasions of Sri Lanka were partly attempts to corner the overseas trade that came into Sri Lankan ports. In the Sri Lankan war there was also the added specific motive of the capture of the pearl fisheries of Mannar. One of the most desired commodities exchanged in long-distance maritime trade at this time and indeed throughout the period under review were pearls. The considerable quantity of pearls carried as "tribute" to China soon after the conquest have been described. The pearl fisheries off Mannar were well-known in the Tamil-speaking world and with the Cōḷa occupation of Mannar these fisheries were brought securely under their control for the duration of the occupation. Excavations at nearby Mantai off the coast of the Gulf of Mannar show that it was occupied from the second century B.C. and probably was a major port from about the mid-eighth to the mid-eleventh century. Mantai or Mahatittha was a point of ingress for the Cōḷas. Chinese and Islamic ceramic ware have been found at 'upper levels of the site' as well as sherds attributed to the mid/late eleventh century. Carswell believes that the mixture of Chinese and Islamic ware at Mantai "suggests this was one of the great emporiums of the early medieval period, comparable in importance to Siraf on the Persian side of the Gulf."[66]

[65] Courtesy, Chinese scholars, Beijing, these extracts from the *Sung Shih,* "The Section of the Foreign countries," were supplied describing the Cōḷa missions. A mission sent by Rājēndra I in A.D. 1020 was abortive because the envoy died after arrival. The second (the A.D. 1033 mission), is the one here referred to.

[66] J. Carswell, "China and Islam in the Maldive Islands", p.124. Also interview, June 1980 and *Excavations at Mantai, 1980; Preliminary Report of the Field Director,* Martha Prickett, unpublished. Chinese sherds were also found at Vankalai on the other side of the Mannar peninsula.

In A.D. 1025, during the period of occupation of the north of Sri Lanka, the Cōḷa naval raid on ports in the Malaysian peninsula and in the Indonesian islands took place. There are conflicting views on the motives for the raid. Spencer who has made a detailed study of the raid believes the raid was a plundering expedition and the object of the raid was to enhance the prestige of the Cōḷas and to capture booty in order to supplement royal revenues and offset the internal weaknesses within the Cōḷa kingdom and he believes that these were the same motives which prompted the invasions of Sri Lanka.[67] The view others hold is that the raid was undertaken to "protect Indian commercial interests from interference" by Srivijaya.[68]

> Ships passed the seas held by the kingdom of Shrivijaya (the Southern Malay peninsula and Sumatra) and the latter realized that it would be more lucrative for local traders if the China-India trade could be made to terminate in Shrivijaya with local middle-men taking the goods to their eventual destination.[69]

Wheatley believes Rājēndra I either believed Srivijaya was "restricting Indian communication with the Archipelago and China," or the raid was in the form of a *digvijaya yātra*.[70] R.C. Majumdar believes there were two raids, an earlier one he believes took place in 1017,[71] but this is an interpretation that has not received much support. It is generally accepted on the basis of K.A.N. Sastri's analysis that there was only one raid.[72] The sole source for the description of the expedition is the Thanjavur inscription. Therefore, unlike the Sri Lankan expedition which is richly documented a study of the raid is limited in scope. Most of the place names listed in the inscription including Kadaram have been identified and they are located in the Malaysian peninsula and in Sumatra. Spencer points out that in the inscription Srivijaya is assumed to be in some special relationship with Kadaram but that the other places are not specifically linked with Srivijaya.[73] In particular, he believes that Madamalingam—Tambralinga

[67] G. W. Spencer, "Royal Leadership and Imperial Conquest in Medieval South India: The Naval Expedition of Rajendra Chola I c. 1025 A.D.", Diss. California Univ., 1967, p. 35. Spencer says, "The fundamental thesis of this study is that the naval expedition into Southeast Asia under Rajendra I represents the maximum extension of the pattern of plundering raids, and hence also the largest possible inflation of the Chola imperial bubble." Also, G.W. Spencer, "The Politics of Plunder," p. 405.

[68] R. Thapar, *A History of India*, Vol. 1 (Harmondsworth, 1966), p. 196.

[69] *Ibid.*

[70] Wheatley, *The Golden Khersonese*, p. 199.

[71] R.C. Majumdar, *Ancient Indian colonies in the Far East;* Vol. ii *Suvaranadvipa, pt. 1, Political history* (Dacca, 1937), p. 179.

[72] Sastri, *The Cōḷas*, pp. 254-5.

[73] Spencer, *Royal Leadership*, p. 198.

could at that time have been an independent principality.[74] Some places mentioned in the raid are Mappapalam, possibly in lower Burma, and Mayirudingam, Ilangasoka, Talaittakkolam, Madamalingam, Kadaram in the Malaysian peninsula and the isthmus of Kra. Ilamuridesam, Malaiyur, Pannai and Srivijaya were in Sumatra. The Nicobars were en route. Two place names remain unidentified.

In his study, Spencer concludes that it was unlikely that the relationship between the Cōḷas and merchants were close enough for the Cōḷas to act on their behalf. He doubts that "international trade and particularly the China trade was so important that Cōḷa interests were involved in any threat to that trade."[75] The preceding chapters have demonstrated the interdependence between the Cōḷas in the early eleventh century and the merchant guild Ayyāvoḷe. In this chapter, it is attempted to present in detail aspects of the overseas trade of the Asian world, and in particular of the Cōḷas of the eleventh century which make it clear that in common with Sung emperors or the rulers of Srivijaya, the Cōḷas both solicited and sought to foster foreign trade. Our belief is that the raid was undertaken partly at least to establish trading rights for Tamil-speaking merchants in those areas, a trade from which the ruler, the merchant and the Cōḷa bureaucracy could expect sizable profits. Hall and Whitmore believe that the raid had a permanent destabilizing effect on Srivijaya. To the effects of the raid they ascribe the growth of important ports in East Java. They claim that lesser ports in north Sumatra after the attack began to assert their independence, and in the Malaysian peninsula they believe that, "By removing Srivijaya's presence in the ports of the upper Malay Peninsula, the Cōḷas cleared the way for the expanding mainland states to fill the resulting power vacuum."[76]

[74] *Ibid.*, p. 170.

[75] *Ibid.*, p. 199.

[76] K.R. Hall and J.K. Whitmore, "Southeast Asian Trade and the Isthmian Struggle, 1000-1200 A.D." in their eds., *Exploration in Early Southeast Asian History: The Origins of Southeast Asian Statecraft* (Ann Arbor, 1976), pp. 306-307. Hall and Whitmore have accepted the conventional idea that at this time Srivijaya exercised some form of control on both sides of the Straits of Malacca. Bronson and Spencer challenge the conventional view. Spencer points out that there is no evidence that Srivijaya controlled" "all or more of the major entrepôts in Malaya and Sumatra..." (Spencer *op. cit.*, p. 164). Bronson believes that there is a need for a reassessment of the identity and the nature of Srivijaya. Bronson shows that prior to the seventh century there is little evidence of foreign contacts or of any major settlement sites in Sumatra. He says six seventh century inscriptions exist in which Srivijaya is mentioned of which three are located near Palembang. No inscriptions of the eighth and ninth centuries have been found at all in Sumatra. The tenth century inscriptions of Sumatra do not mention Srivijaya. But the eighth century Ligor inscription mentions Srivijaya and so does the eleventh century Cōḷa inscription. Bronson points out that "We can readily imagine that the same name might have been borne by one or two later and equally short-lived Srivijayas which need not have had a significantly close connection with the seventh to eighth century kingdom whose remains are concentrated around

In A.D. 1077, almost fifty years after the naval foray, the Cōḷa monarch Kulōttunga I sent a trade mission to China which took with it among other things, pearls of various sizes, an opaque glass bowl, "plum blossom" camphor, rhinoceros horns, frankincense, rose water, putchuk, asafoetida, borax, cloves and textiles. Few of these products, if any, were native products of the Cōḷa country.[77] The Cōḷas were not offering the sale of their produce but one infers seeking to act as carriers. In A.D. 1079, was issued the so-called "Sri Vijayan Inscription of Canton" which is interpreted as the record of donations made on behalf of Kulōttunga to a Taoist monastery in Canton in return for which one assumes he hoped that Cōḷa commercial ventures proceeding to Canton were ensured success.[78] If the epigraph is not spurious and has been interpreted correctly it gives one an unusual inside look at the sub-surface diplomacy that preceded the commercial moves of the Cōḷas at Canton. By A.D. 1088 as earlier mentioned, the Ayyāvoḷe guild was established near Barus in Sumatra, for which there is inscriptional evidence. The functioning of the guild in the area may have started some years earlier, which means that in this period Tamil merchants had direct access to the famous Barus camphor.[79]

C. *In the Twelfth and Thirteenth Centuries*

It was not till the mid-twelfth century though that the inscriptions of the Ayyāvoḷe guild in India began to record the presence of imported commodities from Southeast Asia, West Asia and China in sizeable quantities in South India. It is possible that prior to this growth of a market within India for imported goods, Tamil merchants had acted as agents and carriers of these goods on sections of the east Asian maritime route. The accounts of the Cōḷa missions to China in the eleventh century would suggest that this was so. By the thirteenth century an impressionistic view of the guild inscriptions is that the volume of overseas imports in South India had increased considerably. Precious stones, pearls, aromatics, perfumes, myrobalans,

Palembang." B. Bronson, "The Archaeology of Sumatra and the Problem of Srivijaya," in *Early South East Asia*, R.B. Smith and W.Watson, eds. (Kuala Lumpur, 1979), pp. 395-405. One notes that Wolters believes Jambi was the new capital of Srivijaya in the eleventh century. "A note on the Capital of Srivijaya during the Eleventh Century," *Artibus Asiae Supplementum 23* (Felicitation Volume Presented to Professor G.H. Luce) (Ascona, 1966), Vol.1, pp. 225-239. Hall claims evidence of eleventh century trade in the north and on the west coast of Sumatra in the form of deposits of Sung porcelain, some of it specifically near Barus. Hall and Whitmore, "Isthmian Struggle", f.n. 12.

[77] *Sung Shih*, 489, 22. Courtesy Chinese scholars, Beijing. See notes on pearls and cotton in "Commodities."

[78] Tan Yeok Seng, "The Sri Vijayan Inscription of Canton (A.D. 1079)". *JSEAH*, 5, No. 2 (1964), 17-24.

[79] See note on camphor in "Commodities," in Section Two of this chapter.

wax, honey, some spices, some textiles including silk, horses and elephants were imported, and the exports consisted of cotton textiles, iron, spices, such as pepper, dyes, ivory, areca and putchuk. The items of export contained little in the way of preciosities. The textiles required technical skill for their manufacture. The iron was either an import or an export. If it was an import then we may perhaps relate this to the well-known import of iron from East Africa which was later processed by unique methods in India and used for the production of the famous Damascus sword for example.[80] Merchants of the Ayyāvoḷe guild who dealt in these commodities were powerful, wealthy and influential. The guild at this time was at the height of its power in urban areas and in trade and transit areas where disbursement of consignments of these goods took place.[81]

Some proportion of these imported goods may have been despatched to India by representatives of the guilds from overseas. In the thirteenth century a *nānādēśi* merchant was in Pagan and the inscriptional record of his visit makes it clear that a Hindu shrine and an emigrant community functioned at the Burmese capital.[82] The earlier Ayyāvoḷe inscription of Sumatra has been noted. But the guilds had no monopoly on the imports brought to Indian ports. The transport by sea of these commodities was in the hands of merchants of all nationalities. The eleventh century *Kathāsaritsāgara* describes the visit of merchants from present-day Malaysia to India.[83] Horses were brought in specifically by Arabs and traders from the Persian Gulf. The thirteenth century Motupalli inscription inviting overseas trade is directed at foreign merchants coming into Andhra ports.[84] The Ayyāvoḷe inscriptions indicate though that within South India, the distribution of imported commodities and re-sale or onward despatch was largely in the hands of the Ayyāvoḷe guild. The Ayyāvoḷe guild also most probably handled the carriage of textiles, iron and steel, spices, dyes areca and some Indian aromatics and perfumes to coastal areas for purposes of export.

The same period, the twelfth and thirteenth centuries, saw the active participation of Sri Lanka in medieval, international trade. In the mid-twelfth century Sri Lanka embarked on a Cōḷa-type naval raid against Burma as a protest both against a Burmese attempt to monopolize the sale of elephants and the Burmese blockade of the passage of the Sinhalese princess and her retinue across the isthmus of Kra to Angkor.[85] The marriage planned for a Sinhalese princess in Cambodia may have had strong commercial overtones.

[80] See note on iron in "Commodities".

[81] See Chapter IV.

[82] *EI*, VII, pp. 197-8.

[83] Tawney, *Kathā Sarit Sāgara*, I, pp. 156 ff.

[84] *EI*, XII, 22.

[85] *Cv.*, 76, 10-15; 17-19; 20-25; 28-36; 39-58.

Sūryavarman II of Cambodia in the first half of the twelfth century was personally interested in trade with China, and in the second half of the twelfth century also evidence of Cambodian participation in overseas trade appears.[86] One cannot ignore the economic aspects of the Burmese war. Economically at stake for Sri Lanka was the right to passage across the isthmus of Kra and the import of elephants on their own terms. Elephants were important to the island kingdom. The Nainativu inscription of the second half of the twelfth century inviting traders to bring in horses and elephants to the island ports off the Jaffna peninsula is some indication of the points of ingress from which elephants and horses were taken into the interior of the island.[87] The Chinese porcelain finds at Allaippidy on the island of Kayts tentatively dated the eleventh century confirm that Kayts was a trading centre and that other commodities such as Chinese porcelain also came in.[88]

In the first half of the thirteenth century, there was no visible change in the pattern of overseas trade of South India. But in Sri Lanka after the invasions of Magha and the invasions of Candrabhanu one sees the close of the trading patterns established between the north and northeast coasts of Sri Lanka and the trading world of Southeast Asia. In South India by the mid-thirteenth century and in the early fourteenth century on the basis of inscriptional evidence, overseas trade, both imports and exports, were received and despatched from points on the Coromandel coast, the delta of the Penner, the delta of the Krishna and the stretch of coast in the Pāṇḍya country between Kulasekharapattinam and Nagapattinam. At this time the Ayyāvoḷe guild in Sri Lanka had pushed down into the wet zone of the island. Their inscriptions are found close to the pepper-growing areas and it is likely that pepper was a commodity of importance to them. Pepper was highly prized in China and in the West and the demand had grown in the thirteenth century. In the Tamil areas where the Ayyāvoḷe guild operated no pepper was grown. The Sri Lankan pepper would have been a convenient source for them.[89]

If one is to list in detail the commodities handled by these merchants which came in from overseas or were exported then the information is found in some of the inscriptions located at sites on or not far from the coast in Tamil

[86] Hall and Whitmore, *Isthmian Struggle*, p. 317. Evidence has been drawn of Cambodian-Sri Lanka relations in the twelfth century from *EZ*, II, 17; *EZ*, II, p.74. Cambodia was an important source of aloeswood.

[87] K. Indrapala, "The Nainativu Tamil Inscription of Parākramabāhu I," *UCR*, 21 (April, 1963), 63-70. A portion of the inscription reads: " ...that foreigners should come and stay at Urraturai, that they should be protected, and that foreigners from many ports should come and gather in our ports; as we like elephants and horses...."

[88] Carswell,"China and Islam, A Survey of the Coast of India and Ceylon", p. 37.

[89] *CTI*, I, p. 55; II, 4.

and in Telugu-speaking areas. These inscriptions are Piranmalai, *SII*, VIII, 442 of the thirteenth century (probably the latter half), *ARE* 286 of 1964-65 located at Koilpatti, Kulittalai taluk, Tiruchchirappalli District, A.D. 1305, and *ARE* 296 of 1964-65 located at Thiruvarankurichi, in the same taluk and the same district. These three inscriptions form a group because foreign goods are mentioned in them, they are near contemporaneous, and because a glance at the map Pudukkottai II shows that Kulittalai taluk is close to the highway linking Madurai and Tiruchchirappalli, to which highway Piranmalai was also connected. On the basis of the location of these inscriptions, it is reasonable to visualise some foreign commodities being taken past Piranmalai towards Tiruchchirappalli in the interior; this was possibly a well recognised route.

The Piranmalai commodities of overseas foreign trade, both imports and possible exports were, areca nuts, pepper, myrobalans, iron, cotton (raw), thick cloth, thin cloth, thread, wax, honey, sandalwood, aloeswood, silk, rose water, yak's tail, camphor oil, civet, horses, elephants. In the inscription of Kulittalai taluk, the transcript of the inscription shows the foreign commodities included pepper, areca, horses, camels, aloeswood, yak's tail, sandalwood, camphor, clothing, wire (or steel?). The *nagarattār* of Kodumbalur Maṇigrāmam and of Narttamalai were also present when the taxes on these commodities were prescribed at Koilpatti, Kulittalai for the benefit of the temple. In the inscription of Thiruvarankurichi, of the fourteenth century the transcript shows, pepper, clothing (?), cotton, iron or steel, yak's tail, sandalwood, elephants, horses, camels, honey and wax, were probably among the imports and exports that passed by the village in the early fourteenth century. In the accepted list of commodities of Sung maritime trade were cloves, frankincense, dried galingale, abaca cloth, umbrellas, swords, bottle-gourd, edible date, medicinal rhubarb, slaves, peafowl, benzoin, cotton cloth, bezoars, putchuck, margosa bark, melons, gardenia flowers, coconut, pandanus mats, sandalwood, areca, aloeswood, oak galls, myrrh, jack-fruit, fermented liquor, lacquer ware, asbestos cloth, ebony, limonite, rhinoceros horn, coral, glass, amber, tortoise-shell, porcelain, sugar-cane, orris-root, cardamom, alum, pearls, arsenic, cinnabar, sulphur, giant clam, dammar, safflower, carnelian, lac, madder, silks, rugs, kingfisher feathers, nutmeg, pepper, camphor, civet, myrobalans, aniseed, ginger peel, cubebs, bananas, rose water, rattan, sappanwood, liquid storax, aloes, dragon's blood resin, ivory, cat's eyes, diamonds, lead, silver, copper, tin, iron, asafoetida, lakawood, mica, indigo, camel-hair cloth, byssus, borax, parrots, salt, muskwood, bees wax, ambergris.[90] The common commodities in the Chinese and South Indian lists are easily identified.

The previous three inscriptions were inscribed in Tamil. The inscription

[90] Wheatley, "Commodities", pp. 5-140.

issued in the territory controlled by the Chagi chiefs at Chintapalle, Sattenapalle taluk, Guntur District (present day), is inscribed in Telugu and in Kannada, Kannada being used largely for the portion of the inscription in which the trade guilds were enumerated.[91] The *ubhayc-nānādēsis, gavares* and Mummuridaṇḍas were also present when the donation was prescribed at a *mahānāḍu*. The commodities of foreign trade, based on reading of the transcript included cotton, cotton yarn, clothing, areca nuts, pepper, sandalwood, camphor, musk, civet. The inscription is dated Saka 1162. Not much is known about the Chagi chiefs except that they claimed that they received authority to rule from Rājēndra Cōḷa. They ruled in the twelfth and thirteenth centuries and their capital was Gudimetta. Their relationship with the Kākatīyas is not clear. In the second half of the thirteenth century the Kākatīyas may have succeeded in undermining the authority of the chiefs and probably eventually took over the area. The Chintapalle inscription may be linked to the Motupalli inscription of the Kākatīya monarch Ganapati in Śaka 1166.[92] Both inscriptions were issued almost at the same time. A portion of the latter inscription reads.

> By this glorious Mahārāja Ganapatidēva the following edict (assuring) safety has been granted to traders by sea starting for and arriving from all continents, islands, foreign countries and cities.
>
> Formerly kings used to take away by force the whole cargo, viz., gold, elephants, horses, gems, etc., carried by ships and vessels, which, after they had started from one country for another, were attacked by storms, wrecked and thrown on shore.
>
> But, we out of mercy for the sake of glory and merit, are granting everything besides the fixed duty to those who have incurred the great risk of sea-voyage with the thought that wealth is more valuable than even life.
>
> The rate of this duty (is) one in thirty on (all) exports and imports,
> One *tulam* of sandal, 1 pagoda, 1/4 *fanam*.
> On one pagoda's value of (country) camphor, Chinese
> camphor, and pearls, 3/4 and 3/8 *fanam*.
>
> On one pagoda's value of rose water, ivory, civet, camphor oil, copper, zinc...lead, silk threads, corals and perfumes, 1 1/4 and 1/8 *fanam*. On all silks, 5 1/2 *fanams* per bale (? *svarupa*). On every lakh of areca nuts, 1 pagoda, 3 1/4 *fanams*.

Both inscriptions refer to the same regional inflow and outflow of commodities of maritime trade, Motupalli was located in the deltaic area of the Krishna river. An inscription of A.D. 1279 in Tamil found at Krishnapatnam in Nellore District records the levies on goods imported and exported through the port,

[91] *ARE* 277 of 1934-35.

[92] *EI*, XII, pp. 188 ff.

and decisions were taken at a meeting at which the *añjuvaṇṇa-vāṇigar*, the *nānādēśi-padineṇ-bhūmi-samasta paradēśigal* as well as *nāḍu* and *nagara* were present. The meeting was held in the *aiññūṟṟuvan – tirukkāvanam.*[93] The *padineṇ-bhūmi-samasta paradēśigal* were there earlier at Krishnapatnam in A.D. 1256. The area remained important for Tamil merchants for a long time. A *nānādēśi* inscription of the fifteenth century has also been found there. The identity of the *añjuvaṇṇavāṇigar* has already been discussed. Apart from the *paradēśigal,* there were also other merchants who traded in overseas commodities and who were not part of the Ayyāvoḷe organisation. Many of them were dealers in specific commodities, such as pearls or horses. There may have been others who participated in the trade at the level of itinerant hawkers and these may have been too unimportant to have received epigraphic mention. In interior Karnataka as the inscriptional tables show, overseas commodities circulated in specific areas such as the Shimoga District in the mid-twelfth century, or South Karnataka in the valleys of the Swarnavathi and Kabbani linking Kongu country with Talakad and with the west coast near Kozhikode (Calicut). There is also evidence of foreign commodities circulating in the area near the capital cities of the Hoysaḷas and in Bijapur and Dharwad districts. Tangible evidence of foreign trade which came into Tamil areas probably in the eleventh century and twelfth century are the fragments of Chinese pottery and porcelain identified at Gangaikondacolapuram. These included a portion of a storage jar, classified as green ware, Liao. The parallel to this jar is said to have been found in Jaffna. Fragments of Chinese white ware, proto-porcelain of the eleventh to twelfth centuries were also found, also pieces of Sung *ch'ing pai* ware, exactly the same, according to Carswell as that found on Kayts island near Jaffna. Some sherds were found at Palayakayal, near Kayal, and these included a portion of a celadon bowl of the fourteenth century.[94]

There is rare inscriptional evidence of the presence of Ayyāvoḷe traders at sites at ports, one of them is the twelfth century inscription from Sultan's Battery which is near Kozhikode (Calicut), a great port.[95] There is also a fourteenth century inscription from Kayalpattinam.[96] One may contrast this with the many Maṇigrāmam inscriptions from coastal towns on the west coast and the inscription from Tittandatanapuram on the east coast, not far from Tondi. A possible explanation for this may be that at east coast points of ingress, when foreign goods entered the South Indian market, Cōḷa and

[93] *ARE* 78 of 1963-64, A.D. 1279. The *padineṇ-bhūmi paradēśigal* were there earlier in A.D. 1256, *ARE* 79 of 1963-64.

[94] These sherds were examined by me at the office of the Tamil Nadu Department of Archaeology, Madras. Prof. J. Carswell identified the sherds earlier.

[95] *ARE* 134 of 1961-62, paleography of about the twelfth century.

[96] I am grateful to the Chief Epigraphist, Government of India, Mysore, for permission to consult this unpublished inscription.

Pāṇḍya practice probably was for royal revenues to be exacted before the commodities were handed over to other agents such as the Ayyāvoḷe for sale or onward consignment. Hence the high visibility of the Ayyāvoḷe traders in the interior as contrasted with their low profile or absence at the ports.

D. *China and South India*

By the late thirteenth century several political changes had taken place on the international scene. The Yüan dynastry had replaced the Sung in China and with the establishment of the Mongols the tempo of trade quickened along the east-west land routes linking China proper with Central Asia and the West. At the end of the thirteeenth century a Papal embargo against trade with Egypt caused some decline in the trade via Alexandria. Lopez points out that Italian colonies were being developed in the Crimea, South Russia, Iran and these were linked with routes crossing Central Asia.[97] Hormuz in its turn was linked with some of the South Russian stations. A regular sea traffic connected Gujarat with Hormuz. Samarkand, Bokhara, Kashgar, Khotan and north China were also linked by established routes.

Both land and sea trade were encouraged by the Yüan. In 1277-78, "the first maritime trade bureau of the Yüan dynasty was established at Ch'üan-chou".[98] This was followed by the establishment of bureaus at Shanghai, Ch'ing-Yuan (Ning-po or Ming-chou), and Kan-fu (on Che-chiang coast).[99] By the year 1293-94, there were in all seven maritime trade bureaus.[100] At Ch'üan-chou a mixed Tamil and Chinese inscription has been found of the thirteenth century probably issued by a group of resident traders.[101] Ch'üan-chou in Fukien province is said to have received its first trading ship's office under the Northern Sung. It grew steadily in importance under the Southern Sung who established a capital near the port. In A.D. 1086-7, the office of Superintendent of trading ships of the port was instituted at Ch'üan-chou.[102] Ch'üan-chou soon became the premier port for overseas trade eclipsing Canton. Marco Polo says the India trade was important to China, particularly the trade in pepper, precious stones and pearls. "And I assure you that for one shipload of pepper that goes to Alexandria or elsewhere, destined for Christendom, there came a hundred such, aye and more too, to

[97] R.S. Lopez, "European Merchants in the Medieval Indies: The evidence of Commercial Documents," *The Journal of Economic History*, I (1943), 171.

[98] H.F. Schurmann, *Economic Structure of the Yüan Dynasty* (Cambridge, Mass. 1967), p. 223.

[99] *Ibid.*

[100] *Ibid.* p. 224.

[101] T.N. Subramaniam in *Handbook*, World Tamil Conference (Madras, 1968), p. 181.

[102] J. Kuwabara, "On P'u Shou-keng", *MTB*, No. 2 (1928), 19.

this Haven of Zayton: for it is one of the greatest havens in the world for commerce."[103] Most of the pepper came from the Malabar coast.

In 1279 Ma'bar – i.e. the Pāṇḍyan kingdom reputedly sent envoys to the Chinese court.[104] Soon after apparently an envoy from the Chinese court was sent to Kullam (Quilon in Malabar) to induce them to send a mission to China.[105] In 1280 a second mission from Ma'bar again accompanied by a mission from Annam may have arrived in China. The Chinese emperor then again sent a mission to Kullam in 1280. After delays on route, primarily in Ma'bar, which kingdom was not anxious that the Chinese mission should reach (Quilon), in 1282 the Chinese envoy finally arrived in Kullam (Quilon). The Syrian Christian community in Quilon at that time still had trading interests. The head of the Christians accompanied the return mission from Quilon, as well as a representative of a neighbouring principality, perhaps Mangalore, another centre reputed for its fine pepper, as was Quilon.

In 1283 and 1284 envoys from Ma'bar came to China, the second mission, with gifts of pearls, rare jewels and light silks.[106] Meanwhile a mission was sent to Sri Lanka in 1282 to procure the alms bowl and corporal relics of the Buddha. In 1285 Kublai Khan sent another emissary to Ma'bar to fetch 'rare and precious things.' In 1287 another mission was sent to Ma'bar to fetch Buddhist relics but brought back instead medicines, aromatic woods and other presents. In 1286, a mission from Kullam arrived in China. In 1286 reputedly another mission came from Ma'bar and in 1289 apparently Ma'bar made a gift to the Emperor, followed in 1290 by another mission from Ma'bar. In 1290 and 1291 apparently missions were sent again by the Yüan to Kollam and Ma'bar. In 1296 a mission to Ma'bar was sent, in 1297 a mission was sent from Ma'bar and in 1314 a mission arrived from Ma'bar (*Yüan Shih*, 19, 6[a], 14[a], 25, 2[b]). Then again after a break of some years, the Yüan sent another mission to Kollam in 1344. (*Yüan Shih*, 41, 5[a]). The Ayyāvoḷe guild inscriptions of the second half of the thirteenth century already mentioned, reveal that a vast range of commodities were exported and imported from the Pāṇḍyan kingdom, and the impression gained from the tone and substance of the inscriptions is that this was a valuable and important trade. The frequent Yüan missions to Ma'bar confirm this impression.

103 H. Yule, trans., *The Book of Ser Marco Polo, the Venetian Concerning the Kingdoms and Marvels of the East*, 3rd ed. revised H. Cordier (London, 1903), Book II, pp. 234-235.

104 Kuwabara, "On P'u Shou-keng", *MTB*, No.7 (1935), 82. *Yüan Shih*, 10, 20b, 26a.

105 This citation from the *Yüan Shih* and the following citations in this paragraph are from W.W. Rockhill, "Notes on the Relations and Trade of China with the Eastern Archipelago and the Coast of the Indian Ocean during the Fourteenth Century," *Toung Pao*, 15, (1914), 430-437. *Yüan Shih*, 210, 16b.

106 *Ibid.* pp. 438-443 in which all the citations from the *Yüan Shih* contained in this paragraph are listed.

E. *Overseas Commerce and the West Coast*

The Yüan missions to Kollam on the west coast of India reveal that a change in commodity demand had taken place and that new trade realities had emerged which made the west coast of South India, as also of Sri Lanka increasingly important commercially from the thirteenth century onwards. The west coast of India was being drawn into more important trade relationships with West Asia and Egypt but primarily Egypt and through these regions with the European West. This trade was not entirely new. The trade between the west coast of South India and the Persian Gulf, Yemenite coast and the Red Sea ports commenced much earlier, as may be deduced from Islamic sources, but precise information on one sector of the trade and on one trading group comes from the documents of the Cairo Geniza. The letters of Jewish traders permit an unusually close look at the commerce between South India, the Red Sea ports and Egypt in the eleventh century and first half of the twelfth century. In this period iron and steel, classified as the most important item of exchange, Indian cotton textiles and silk, pearls, beads, cowries, ambergris, brass and bronze vessels, Chinese porcelain, African ivory, coconuts, timber, spices, dyes, medicines, aromatics, and leather goods were included in the commodities imported by Jewish merchants from India.[107] Sri Lanka also figured in this trade. It is on record that cinnamon from Sri Lanka was imported regularly at Aden and sent to Fustat (Old Cairo) in the first half of the twelfth century. This trade may have started earlier. A particular trader was consigned 6,000 lbs of cinnamon in one shipment in 1130 A.D., a not inconsiderable amount.[108] The Jewish traders and their partners exchanged or sold these Eastern goods in Tunisia, Morocco and Sicily along the Lebanese coast and in Syria.[109] The business dealings handled personally by Jewish merchants of the 'India' trade in Christian Europe were marginal.

In the twelfth century, the Italian city of Pisa was granted trading privileges in both Alexandria and Cairo.[110] The European merchants largely from the cities of South Italy had made their way to Egypt earlier, perhaps even as early as the ninth century, and certainly by the tenth.[111]

Towards the end of the twelfth century, European merchants were prohibited entry into the Red Sea. This protectionist move favoured the rapid development of the Egyptian corporate association of traders known as the

[107] S.D. Gotein, "Letters and Documents on the India Trade in Medieval Times", *Islamic Culture*, 37 (Jan. 1963), 196.

[108] S.D. Gotein, *Letters of Medieval Jewish Traders* (Princeton, 1973), p.185.

[109] *Ibid.* and pp. 7-8.

[110] S.Labib, "Egyptian Commercial Policy in the Middle Ages," *Studies in the Economic History of the Middle East*, ed. M.A. Cook (London, 1970), p. 66.

[111] *Ibid.*

Kārimī.[112] The main commodity of trade that the Kārimī dealt in were pepper and other spices. But they also dealt in "agricultural products", textiles, silk, wood, wheat, flour, sugar, rice, weapons, armour..."[113] Subhi Labib believes that pepper was the most important of their imports and that this was sold to the Venetians at Alexandria.[114] By the thirteenth century the volume and importance of this trade was not to be underestimated. The Kārimī merchants obtained their eastern commodities from Indian merchants – either from Gujarat or the west coast of South India – who brought them to Aden. It was the desire to cut in on this trade that prompted the trade mission of the Sinhalese king Bhuveneikabahu to the Egyptian court in A.D. 1283.[115] The commodities he offered were pearls, precious stones, elephants, textiles, sappanwood, cinnamon and other unlisted goods. He wished to establish trading rights in Aden for his kingdom. The letter suggests clearly that these goods were already coming in to Aden brought by middlemen, probably Arabs as well as the Gujarati *bania*. This then was an attempt at direct Sinhalese participation in the trade with the West, an attempt to break the Gujarati hold on the entrepôt trade at Aden.

F. *State Interest in Foreign Trade*

A proportion of state revenues in medieval Asia appears to have been derived from the taxes and percentages levied, and the monopolies fixed, on incoming and outgoing foreign goods. This was undoubtedly the reason for the great interest shown by medieval rulers in international maritime trade. Bhuveneikabahu the Sinhalese king was acting in the medieval Asian tradition in seeking to initiate foreign trade. Cōḷas, Pāṇḍyas, the Sinhalese kings, kings of Srivijaya, the Burmese and Cambodians rulers, and the Sung and the Yüan solicited foreign trade exchanges, although there were periods when the Sung state deplored the drain of specie from their territory in payment for luxury articles from abroad. Chinese sources are the most explicit on the advantages accruing to the state from foreign trade. In A.D. 1028 the Northern Sung emperor commanded that as foreign trade was decreasing plans should be made to encourage foreign merchants.[116] An imperial ordinance issued in A.D. 1137 in the time of the Southern Sung says "The profit derived from foreign trade is most great. When the management was proper, the income was sometimes counted by millions (of cash). Is this not

[112] *Ibid*, and W.J. Fischel, "The Spice Trade in Mamluk Egypt, A Contribution to the Economic History of Medieval Islam", *JESHO*, 1 (1958), 160.

[113] Fischel, "The Spice Trade", p. 161.

[114] Labib, "Egyptian Commercial Policy," p. 73.

[115] S.M. Yusuf, "Ceylon and the Arab Trade," University of Ceylon, *History of Ceylon*, Vol. I, pt. 2 (Colombo, 1960), p. 707

[116] Kuwabara, "On P'u Shou-keng" (1928), 42.

far better than taxing the people? It is why we pay much attention to it. We could be lenient to the people and let them be a little more prosperous."[117] Under the Sung, duties on custom goods were levied, originally at the rate of ten per cent on pearls, camphor and fine quality goods and at thirty per cent on other goods.[118] In A.D. 1144, the duty on all aromatics was raised to forty per cent.[119] The state also reserved the right to monopolise certain imported goods, and had the right to buy a certain proportion, if required, of other goods.[120] Kuwabara points out that in the middle of the twelfth century "the income of the merchant shipping offices, two millions in the middle of the twelfth century, was nearly one-twelfth of the whole revenue, a very important item in the national budget."[121] However, as a result of increasing foreign trade, cash outflows from China were considerable, and attempts to restrict it failed as smuggled goods were paid for either in copper cash, iron or gold or silver.[122] Under the Yüan,

> the government extended its control over foreign trade in still another way – by lending funds to private traders to engage in foreign commerce and also by actually providing ships and capital for selected merchants who were sent abroad to trade; for their services the traders received thirty per cent of the cargo.[123]

No records comparable to the Chinese histories, topographies and officials records are available for a study of the revenue from maritime trade in the Cōḷa and Pāṇḍya kingdoms. The bulk of South Indian records are in the form of inscriptions which are issued for specific purposes and are of necessity brief. The Kākatīya monarch Ganapatidēva in the Motupalli edict of A.D. 1244 in his attempt to invite overseas merchants decreed that whereas previous monarchs had appropriated the entire cargo of vessels shipwrecked on his shore, he was willing to return the cargo but expected the fixed duties to be paid. In the mid-thirteenth century duties at the Kākatīya port could not have exceeded duties at Nagapattinam or the Pāṇḍya ports, as in that case the object of the edict which was to attract foreign trade would have

[117] *Ibid.*, p. 24. The Nainativu inscription and the Motupalli inscription give clear indication of advantages obtained by the ruler from foreign trade. See pp. 278-279, Motupalli inscription. The Nainativu inscription says: "... if the vessels which bring elephants and horses unto us get wrecked, a fourth (share of the cargo) should be taken by the Treasury and (the other) three parts should be left to the owner; and, if vessels (laden) with merchandise get wrecked an exact half should be taken by the Treasury and (the other) exact half should be left to the owner."

[118] Hirth and Rochkhill, *Chau Ju-kua*, p. 21.

[119] Kuwabara, "On P'u Shou-keng" (1935), 71.

[120] *Ibid.*, pp. 74-75.

[121] *Ibid.*, p. 79.

[122] Wheatley, "Commodities", p. 37

[123] Schurmann, *Economic Structure*, p. 222.

been defeated. The edicts mention a duty of one in thirty as well as specific duties on each commodity.[124] In the inscription, these levies appear to belong either to the ruler or to the 'state'. The Kākatīyas undoubtedly derived benefit from duties levied at ports. Cōḷa and Pāṇḍya rulers probably derived similar benefits but no inscriptional record has survived of the establishment of royal monopolies. In the hinterland of Motupalli, at Chintapalle, exports and imports were handled by the Ayyāvoḷe guild and they levied cess on them for the benefit of the temple, but this was unrelated to government or royal revenues. There are many comparable records of the cess levied on imports and exports by the guild and other powerful local bodies in locations away from the ports in Pāṇḍya and Cōḷa times.

The payments for international exchanges were in kind, or in gold, silver or copper and occasionally iron. Thus payment in kind was advocated in Sung China in 1219 when it was suggested that silks, porcelain, brocades, and lacquerware be offered in exchange for aromatics in order to reduce the outflow of precious metals.[125] Kuwabara records gold, silver and copper cash among the main exports of the Sung period.[126] Chinese copper cash and other coins have been found widely distributed in many places including the Coromandel coast, and Sri Lanka.[127] Numismatists believe that one of the causes of significant metal outflows of this nature could be an unfavourable balance of trade.[128] Chinese imports included pearls, dyes, pepper, aromatics and some drugs which may have come from South Asia and these may well have necessitated considerable cash outflows.

The Indian subcontinent drew in gold, silver and copper in payment for many of its exports. Watson refers to 'the strange power of India' in this respect.[129] In the eleventh and early twelfth centuries the Geniza documents show repeatedly that Jewish merchants trading with South India had to

[124] *EI*, XII, 22.

[125] Wheatley, "Commodities", p. 37.

[126] Kuwabara, "On P'u Shou-keng" (1928), 25.

[127] Perforated copper coins were to be found on Coromandel beaches n 1884, Elliot, *Coins of Southern India*, p. 35. B. Chattopadhyaya, *Coins and Currency Systems in South India c.A.D. 950-1300* (Delhi, 1977), p. 145, refers to three hoards of Chinese copper cash in Tamil Nadu but these were probably deposited after the mid-thireenth century. Yapahuva has coins dating from 996-1225 A.D., W.P.M. Fernando, *Yapahuva*, (Ceylon, 1969) pp. 3, 13. Polonnaruva, *Archaeological Survey of Ceylon*, 1911-12, Vol.X, p. 56. See also M. Abraham, "The Currency System and Monetisation in Karnataka in Vijayanagar Times", *QJMS*, 69 (Jan-June 1978), 12-30. At the end of the thirteenth century the export of metals from China was forbidden and Ma'bar (South Coromandel), Kullam (Quilon) and Fandarina (a port north of Quilon) were specifically mentioned. Rockhill, "Relations", p. 425.

[128] A.M. Watson, "Back to Gold-and Silver", *The Economic History Review*, Second Series, 20, No. 1 (1967), 21.

[129] Watson, *op.cit.*, p. 34. Watson also says gold came into China in the same fashion.

make payment in gold to offset their unfavourable trade balances.[130] R.S. Lopez says that in the early fifteenth century, Egypt acted as a middleman selling spices (largely from India) and aromatics to Europe. At the end of the fifteenth century, it is estimated that 1,150,000 lbs of pepper were purchased annually by Venetians at Alexandria.[131] It is believed that as a result of the sale of spices through Egypt a constant flow of gold came into India from Europe and Egypt.

The flow of Venetian sequins into India in Vijayanagar times has already received attention.[132] Around the mid-thirteenth century, Genoa and Florence started minting gold coins. The coins of Italian cities undoubtedly did come into India. The well-known Broach hoard of 1888 contained "367 Mamluk gold coins, 15 gold coins of the Il-Khans of Persia, 33 Venetian sequins, 5 Genovese quartardos." The silver coins included 226 post-Il-Khan Jalairid, 17 Armenian, and almost a thousand Mamluk coins.[133] The coins date from 1260-1380 A.D. There are no similar coin hoards in the South Indian peninsula. Nor has the outflow of gold from South India in payment for imported horses been studied, and the horse trade caused a major reverse currency drain. Nevertheless, gold undoubtedly came in. Gotein's evidence is quite clear for the eleventh and early twelfth centuries and subsequently in the thirteenth and fourteenth centuries on the west coast of the peninsula with increasing trade, particularly the export of pepper, gold flows into the country probably increased.[134] Chinese sources refer to the prohibition at the end of the thirteenth century of the export of metals particularly to the west coast of India and the Pāṇḍyan coast.[135] Earlier in Rājēndra Cōḷa's time, as already mentioned "Chīnakannakam" came into Nagapattinam.[136] No one has attempted to study the effect of this gold within India. Much of it will have ended up in royal treasuries or in temples.[137] The residue probably remained with merchants. We have no evidence that the guilds as corporate entities maintained gold reserves. But individual merchants engaged in

[130] Gotein, "Letters and Documents", p. 198. "Mostly gold and silver, in particular Egyptian gold pieces, the dollars of the period, accompanied orders for Indian goods...."

[131] F.C. Lane, "The Mediterranean Spice Trade", *American Historical Review*, 14 (1940), 587, f. n. 28, cited in Lopez et. al., "England to Egypt," p. 128. Lopez remarks, "Egypt, then, was not merely a conduit funneling Italian gold towards India, but was also contributing to this flow by its own consumption of spices and other imports from the Farther East."

[132] Abraham, "Currency System", pp. 28-29.

[133] Abraham, *op. cit.*, p. 28; O.Codrington, "On a Hoard of Coins Found at Broach", *JBBRAS*, 15 (1882), 339-370.

[134] See note on pepper in "Commodities".

[135] See f.n. 127.

[136] *ARE* 166 of 1956-57.

[137] "...and in the treasury of their palace they placed seven vessels full of money on the south-east with golden images and bronze sacrificial instruments..." c.A.D. 1454, *EC*, X, Goribidnur 22.

foreign trade had undoubtedly vast funds at their disposal some of which was utilized, as shown earlier, in urban expansion and improvement.

SECTION TWO

The Commodities of Overseas Trade Handled by the Ayyāvoḷe and Maṇigrāmam

The second section of this chapter deals with the commodities of maritime trade that were handled by the Ayyāvoḷe guild. The transport of exports to coastal centres was probably largely under their control, as was the transport of imports from the ports to the interior. The sale of these goods within Kannada and Tamil areas may also have been directly handled by them.[138] It will be noted that cotton textiles and processed iron (*wootz*) were manufactured goods of importance exported from South India. The export of iron (*wootz*) from west coast centres was important as early as the eleventh century according to Gotein's interpretation of the Geniza documents. Gotein believes it was the most important item exported from India.[139] Evidence of the transport of iron along the main export-import routes used by the Ayyāvoḷe on the east coast appears only in the thirteenth century. And it is also only in the thirteenth century that the export of textiles appears to have gained volume considerably. Spices remained important throughout the period under review but again it is from the thirteenth century onwards that the pepper-producing west coast of India became a major focal point of interest for overseas traders. One notes the commercial prominence in Vijayanagar times of the textile-producing Andhra coast and the pepper-producing Kerala and South Kanara coasts. An association similar to the Ayyāvoḷe guild and bearing the same name flourished in the textile-producing areas of Anantapur District as late as the seventeenth century.[140]

The decrease in commercial activity on the Cōḷa-Pāṇḍya coast under the first two Vijayanagar dynasties, and the increase of overseas trade coming into ports on the west coast of India is in many ways parallel to and also near contemporaneous with the movement of Sinhalese peoples away from the north of Sri Lanka to the southwest of the island, the wet zone, where opportunities existed for export trade in plantation crops such as sappanwood, areca and cinnamon. These were commodities which were in increasing demand in the markets of West Asia and Europe. The drift towards the west

[138] This observation is based on readings of the inscriptions mentioning imports.

[139] See notes on iron, textiles, pepper, in subsequent pages.

[140] See inscriptional tables, Appendix A.

coast of Sri Lanka of the Sinhalese peoples has long been an enigma. It is more than likely that one of the major reasons for this move were changes in maritime trade patterns and in commodity demand.

Aloeswood

Aquilaria aqallocha Roxb., Sk. *Agaru,* Tamil, *aghil, Aquilaria malaccensis* Lam.

The Indian aloeswood tree is found in Assam and parts of Bengal and in South Tennasserim, and parts of Bhutan. "*Agar* is regarded as a pathological product formed as the result of a fungus disease, contracted by the tree chiefly through some wound or boring in the trunk."[1] The diseased portions of the tree are heavily impregnated with resin. These portions constitute what is known in trade as *agar* or *aghil.* It is used even today for the production of incense sticks. *Agar* oil or *attar* is used in the manufacture of perfume. The oil is used in indigenous medicine and is reputed to be an aphrodisiac, carminative, an astringent,useful in diarrhoea and vomiting, and in cases of snake bite. *Agar* from India was still exported to China in the middle of this century. It was formerly exported to West Asia and Europe as well. *Aquilaria malaccensis* the product of Tennasserim, and the isthmian area of the Malaysian peninsula, and of the Indonesian islands is reputedly inferior to Indian aloeswood. This opinion finds a curious echo in medieval Chinese writings in which it is claimed that the best aloeswood came from the Indo-Chinese peninsula and from northern Malaysia.[2] The northern Malaysian aloeswood may have been from the species *agallocha.* In South India in medieval times it is included in the lists of commodities of overseas trade mentioned in the Piranmalai and Kulittalai inscriptions. It appears to have been imported most probably from Southeast Asia. In Tamil-speaking areas it was probably easier to obtain the product by sea from the east than from the northern areas of the Indian land mass where aloeswood grew.

REFERENCES

1. *The Wealth of India*, Raw Materials, Vol. I (New Delhi, 1948), p. 89.
2. Wheatley, "Commodities", pp. 69-70.

Areca Nuts, Betel Nuts
Areca catechu Linn.

Distribution in India – Coastal areas of Bengal, Madras, South Bombay, and in Assam and Mysore. Outside India it is found in Malaysia, Indonesia and the Phillippines.[1] Wheatley has an interesting list of Chinese sources of the Sung period.[2] "The Chu-fan-chih records it as an export from Hainan, Tong-king, Borneo and the Philippines, and even from as far afield as Coromandel; the *Sung Shih* (bk. 489) and *Wen-hsien-t'ung-k'ao* list it as a product of Java and Sri Vijaya." Wheatley also says: "The *Ling-wai-tai-ta* (8, p. 84) notes that the customs of Canton and Ch'üan-chou derived an annual revenue of some tens of thousands of strings of cash from the areca trade, which was carried on in foreign bottoms."[3] Areca nuts are mentioned in innumerable inscriptions of the Ayyāvoḷe guild, and also in inscriptions of this association relating to foreign trade. A brisk trade was carried on in areca nuts within the country and some of it was exported as well. *ARE* 478 of 1914, A.D. 1178, Holalu; *ARE* 157 of 1959-60, A.D. 1182, Alampur; *EC*, XI, Holalkere, 124, A.D. 1208; *EC*, XI, Davangere 105, A.D. 1218; *EC*, VII, Honnali 8, A.D. 1228; are all inscriptions (from Kannada areas) of the Ayyāvoḷe guild in which areca nuts are mentioned. Areca nuts also appear to be mentioned in *ARE* 286 of 1964-65, from Koilpatti, Kulittalai taluk, Tiruchchirapalli District, which is a major inscription of Tamil-speaking areas relating to foreign trade. They are also mentioned in the Kākatīya inscription of Ganapatidēva, A.D. 1244-45. In both these two inscriptions the bulk of the commodities listed are items of export or import and it is very likely that areca nuts were exported from these areas in medieval times.

In the early nineteenth century Buchanan notes that betel nuts were brought from the Malabar coast to Coimbatore.[4] Betel nuts were also transported from the Kannada-speaking areas of the Western Ghats and brought to trade centres such as Davangere and Bangalore, "Betel-nut is the principal article of trade at Bangalore, ..." he noted.[5] From Davangere, he said, "The most valuable trade here is that which is carried on with *Wallaja-petta.* The goods carried from here are *Betel-nut* and pepper, and those brought back are *Madras* goods, imported from Europe, China, Bengal and the Eastern Islands, together with salt, and some of the manufactures of the coast of Coromandel."[6] Buchanan's observations made in the modern period, reflect trading patterns which probably were a legacy of medieval times. Buchanan's description of Davangere as a place where draught animals were kept and betel nut was a valuable commodity of exchange is an exact replica of conditions in A.D. 1218 as reflected in the Ayyāvoḷe inscription from the same geographical area.[7]

Areca also grew abundantly in Ceylon. In a 17th century account, *Ribeiro's History of Ceilão*, it is said, "Every year there is export from the kingdom of Cotta upto a thousand *champanas* of areca: (a *champana* is a *sumaca* of forty tons) for this article is in great demand over the whole of India."[8] In the *Letters of Medieval Jewish Traders* in A.D. 1139, Gotein mentioned the export of betel nut to Aden from India[9].

REFERENCES

1. *Wealth of India,* Raw Materials, Vol.I, p. 110.
2. Wheatley, "Commodities", p. 67.
3. *Ibid.*
4. Buchanan, *A Journey from Madras,* Vol. I, p. 261.
5. *Ibid.*, Vol. II, p. 331; Vol. I, p. 201.
6. *Ibid.*, Vol. III, p. 332.
7. See transcript of *EC*, XI, Davangere 105.
8. P.E. Pieris, trans., *Ribeiro's History of Ceilão* (Colombo, 1909), p. 6.
9. Gotein, *Letters,* p. 194.

Bdellium

Commiphora mukul (Hook. ex Stocks) Engl. syn., *Balsamodendron mukul* Hook. ex Stocks, Indian Bdellium Tree, Sk. *Guggulu, Koushikaha, devadhupa,* Kannada, *Guggule,* Tamil; *Maishakshi gukkal.*[1]

Distribution—Sindh, Kathiawar, Baluchistan, Rajputana desert, parts of Karnataka, Andhra.[2]

The pale yellow, brown, or sometimes green coloured resin of this tree is purported to be an astringent, antiseptic, expectorant, an aphrodisiac, carminative, and effective for treatment of snake and scorpion bite.[3] It is still used as an incense and for perfumery. A similar resin is obtained from *Balsamodendron roxburghii* Arn. found in Assam, parts of East Bengal and Madhya Pradesh.

Yule believed that *Canarium strictum* (Roxb.) was also known as the Black Dammar of Malabar. He claimed it grew near Thana and was called there *Dhup* or *gugul.* Yule believes that it is the resin of this tree which Marco Polo refers to as Brown Incense.[4] Yule also points out that *Vateria indica* (Roxb.) was probably the same as Buchanan's *Chlorixylon Dupada* of which the resin was commonly used as incense in temples in parts of Karnataka[5] in the early nineteenth century.

Chau Ju-kua erroneously mentions dammar as an export of Cambodia and this dammar may have been the resin exuded from *Cannarium commune* Linn.[6]

Bdellium appears to have been one of the commodities carried by the Ayyāvoḷe merchants because it is mentioned in their well-known *EC,* VII, Shikarpur 118 inscription.

From an abstract of goods imported by sea in 1800 at Cannanore one learns that 9 maunds of *Googal* (bdellium) were imported.[7] Coasting vessels probably carried consignments from one port to another. The *Googal* thus imported could have been from Canara ports or from Kathiawar.

REFERENCES

1. *The Wealth of India,* Raw Materials, Vol. II, (1950), p. 313.

2. R.N. Chopra, S.L. Narayan, I.C. Chopra, *Glossary of Indian Medicinal Plants* (New Delhi, 1956), p. 75.
3. *Ibid.*
4. Yule, *Marco Polo*, Book III, pp. 396-397, f.n.2.
5. Buchanan, *A Journey from Madras*, Vol. I, p. 184.
6. Chau Ju-kua, p. 53.
7. Buchanan, *op. cit.*, Vol. III, p. xxiii.

Camphor

Cinnamomum Camphora Linn., Sk. *Karpuram, Dryobalanops aromatica* Gaertn., *Blumea balsamifera* DC.

The first is a native of Japan, Formosa and China. The second is found in Sumatra—Borneo and parts of Malaysia.[1] *Blumea balsamifera* is a native of Assam and parts of Tennasserim.[2]

In medieval trade camphor from Borneo, product of *Dryobalanops aromatica* also known as Barus camphor, was greatly valued.[3] The camphor, an oleo-resin "is found in cavities and fissures in the wood of *D. Aromatica* and is collected by scraping. It occurs in white translucent masses and closely resembles true camphor from *Cinnamomum camphora*...."[4] In Ayurvedic medicine it is considered a useful antiseptic and stimulant. It is used in cases of hysteria.[5] Camphor oil is produced by distilling the wood and leaves. The oil has medicinal properties and is used externally and internally.

It will be recalled that the Ayyāvoḷe guild had connections with Barus in the heart of the camphor producing area of Sumatra in A.D. 1088.[6] Kulōttunga I sent a trade mission to China in A.D. 1077 which carried many valuable commodities with them including fine quality camphor.[7]

Camphor is mentioned frequently in inscriptions relating to the Ayyāvoḷe guild, as for example in the twelfth century inscriptions *EC*, V, pt. 1, Belur 177 and the well-known *EC*, VII, Shikarpur 118. It is also mentioned along with imported commodities in *ARE* 277 of 1934-35 from Chintapalle in the Guntur District, *ARE* 286 of 1964-65 from Koilpatti, Kulittalai taluk, Tiruchchirappalli District and at Motupalli in *EI*, XII, No. 22, also in Guntur District, and at Piranmalai in *SII*, VIII, 442. These are all thirteenth century inscriptions. At Piranmalai camphor oil is mentioned, not camphor. At Motupalli camphor oil, Chinese camphor and ordinary camphor are mentioned separately. The Chinese camphor obviously was an import. Whether it was Chinese or from the Indonesian archipelago is not certain. The country camphor perhaps was the product of *Blumea balsamifera* from northeast India. Wheatley's analysis of Chinese accounts of the trade in camphor may throw some light on the problem. In the twelfth century compilation of Chou Ch'ü-fei, Wheatley says, camphor is mentioned erroneously as a product of the Coromandel coast.

> Possibly he was confused by the re-export thence of either Barus Camphor from Sumatra or Ngai (*Blumea*) Camphor from Tenasserim or Assam.... The other possibility is that he was referring to Patchouli Camphor, a substance homologous with Borneo camphor and prepared from *Pogostemon Patchouli,* Pellet, var. *suavis,* which occurs fairly widely in India as a cultivated plant or an escape (as in the Malay Peninsula, it is only doubtfully wild in India).[8]

If Wheatley is right then the "country" camphor of Motupalli may have been Patchouli camphor.

REFERENCES

1. *The Wealth of India,* Vol II, pp. 173-175
2. Wheatley, "Commodities", pp. 101-105.
3. *Ibid.*
4. *The Wealth of India,* Raw Materials, Vol. III (1952) p. 114.
5. Chopra, *et. al., Glossary of Indian Medicinal Plants,* p. 102.
6. See Section I.
7. *Ibid.*
8. Wheatley, *op. cit.*, p. 101.

Civet

The civet cat is found in Southeast Asia, Africa, Madagascar, South Europe and India. In India the species noted are: *Viverra zibetha* Linn. found in Bengal, Nepal, Sikkim, Bhutan and Assam and *Moschothera civettina* Blyth or the Malabar Civet a native of Kerala and Coorg. There is one other *Viverricula Indica* Geoffroy which is smaller than the others and has less developed scent glands.[1] The secretion of the sex glands of the cat is collected weekly or every month. It is used in medicine and is reputed to be an antispasmodic and aphrodisiac. It is used in the production of incense sticks. It is also mixed with oil and used to anoint images in temples.

Civet was imported into China according to Chau Ju-kua from Oman.[2] Ethiopia is considered an important source of civet. In at least two inscriptions of the Ayyāvoḷe guild in which other commodities of maritime trade are listed, civet is also mentioned but it is not possible to say whether this civet was the imported product of the African civet or Indian civet being taken to ports on the Tamil or Telugu coast for export to Southeast Asia and China.

REFERENCES

1. *The Wealth of India,* Vol. II, p. 209.
2. Wheatley, "Commodities", p. 105.

Cotton and Cotton Fabric
Gossypium Arboreum

The variety of cotton grown in the medieval period in India was *gossypium arboreum* indigenous in Gujarat. *Gossypium herbaceum* only reached South Asia in the eighteenth century.[1] In medieval times, in India and in parts of Southeast Asia where cotton fabrics were produced *gossypium arboreum* was, it is likely, the only variety known, and is to be distinguished from tree cotton or kapok, from which coarse fabrics, were produced in Southeast Asia.Paul Wheatley says that kapok was known to the Chinese as *chi-pei.*[2] L. Carrington Goodrich distinguishes between kapok produced in Southeast Asia and the fabric exported from India in Gupta times.[3]

Both Wheatley and Rockhill point out that an additional new Chinese term for describing cotton fabric was used from Sung times. This was *tou-lou-mien* based probably on "Sk. *tula*-cotton" and Chinese "*mien* downy".[4] In common currency earlier in China was the term *po-tieh* probably derived from Persian. It was used also by the Chinese in medieval times to describe a form of white muslin.[5] It is possible that the use of Persian derivatives indicates that the earliest knowledge of cotton fabrics and cotton growing came for the Chinese through the products exported from Central Asia.

Firsthand acquaintance with cotton came late for the Chinese and Mongols. In the late thirteenth century an envoy sent to Genghis Khan from China described a fabric he saw made of "wool" which grew in the ground.[6] The mid-thirteenth century account of a Taoist monk, travelling through Central Asia described a fabric he purchased at a city north of the Tarim basin, which he says was called *tu-lu-ma.* "The people say that it is woven from vegetable wool. We got seven pieces of it for winter clothes."[7] Cotton was introduced in China proper in the late Sung period.[8] From the fourteenth century, according to some, cotton weaving was not uncommon in China, but it is also held that cotton textile production was not significant till the sixteenth century.[9] Since cotton and cotton technology came so late to China one assumes that a demand for imported cotton existed.

While no quantification is possible regarding the export of Indian cotton fabrics to Southeast Asia and China there are indications available in Indian epigraphical sources and in Indian literature as well as in Chinese and Indian sources that the Indian cotton textile industry was well established in medieval times and that Indian cotton fabrics were sent eastward along the maritime route. There is also very definite evidence of the export of Indian cotton fabrics westward to Mediterranean countries and beyond. During the twelfth, thirteenth and fourteenth centuries the cotton textile trade seems to have grown steadily and cotton textiles probably were the most important of the manufactured goods to be exported from peninsular India.

In medieval times there is ample evidence of cotton cultivation and production of cotton fabrics in those areas of peninsular India relevant to this study, that is in those regions now contained within the modern states of Karnataka, Tamil Nadu and Andhra Pradesh. M.N. Katti, based on epigraphic evidence believes that cotton was grown abundantly in what is now Bijapur District and generally in the Raichur *doāb*. Weaving centres, he says, were located at Guledgud in the Badami taluk of the Bijapur District and at Ilkal in the Hungund taluk of the Bijapur District.[10] "The *Mitakṣara* specifically mentions guilds, *srenayah* of weavers...."[11] Gururajachar points out that Somēśvara in the *Abhilāṣitārtha- Cintāmaṇi* written in the twelfth century, while 'describing the royal wardrobe; "gives us a list of fabrics after their places of origin, viz. those of Nāgapaṭṭana, the Pāṇḍya country, Anilāvāta, Mūlasthāna, Kalinga, Vaṅga, Simhaladvīpa, Mahācīna and so on."[12] Some of these fabrics were, it is most likely, cotton. The mid-twelfth century Shikarpur inscription which described long-distance trade and mentioned specific imports also refers to 'local cloth' and 'foreign cloth'.[13] The Shikarpur inscription is one of the best known epigraphs relating to the Ayyāvoḷe guild.

That the technology of spinning and weaving was well-established by medieval times need not be doubted. A recent study has shown that the cotton carder's bow was in use in India and specifically South India, possibly as early as the second century.[14] The author cites medieval references to cotton ginning.[15] The spindle was used for spinning thread, she believes 'right until the thirteenth century'.[16] In the fourteenth century the spinning wheel may also have been used. The use of the spindle however continued right into modern times side by side with the wheel, and its use has been considered by some to contribute towards the quality of the thread. Inscriptional references exist proving the use of the vertical loom in the twelfth century in Karnataka. Evidence of the use of the horizontal loom appears in fifteenth century sources. And most important the draw loom possibly was in use in South India as early as the eleventh century. Certainly by the thirteenth century as inscriptional evidence suggests, the draw loom was well-known.[17] One concludes thereby that fabric with a figured weave was produced in South India from early medieval times. From the mid-twelfth century onwards increasingly cotton yarn and fabric were mentioned in inscriptions of the Ayyāvoḷe.

In epigraphs in which taxes on overseas imports are mentioned such as the major Ayyāvoḷe guild inscription of the thirteenth century found at Piranmalai, and also the thirteenth century Chintapalle and the twelfth century Shikarpur inscriptions, one notices that taxes are mentioned on yarn, thick cloth and thin cloth.[18] It is likely that overseas imports and exports were carried along certain well-defined routes. Shikarpur in Karnataka was probably situated on one such route as was Piranmalai and Chintapalle. One envisages that imports and exports to and from Southeast Asia and China were carried along the routes leading through Piranmalai and Chintapalle.

Of the transport of Indian cotton as far as China prior to the Sung period there is little evidence although there are references to Indian cotton. For example, Fa Hien in the fifth century described cotton in India. In the sixth century, it is held, cotton was sent from north India to China.[19] It is said that in Sung times "the first group of Jewish families to settle at the capital of the Northern Sung brought gifts of cotton goods from India...."[20] The 1077 Cōḷa mission to China took an array of gifts including pearls, camphor, ivory, rhinoceros teeth, incense, perfumes, rose water, medicinal plants, borax, spices and a fabric termed in Chinese *chin hwa* (Fukienese pronounciation *khin khwa* perhaps derived from Arab-Persian *khim khwab,* denoting fine brocade). Goodrich suggests this mission took cotton, but I am able from Ma Tuan-lin and the *Sung Shih* to find only a reference to *chin hwa* which is unlikely to have been pure cotton.[21] *Chin hwa* was probably a West Asian product, or rich Indian gold thread brocade which the Chinese knew by the name used by Arab-Persian traders. The *Sung Shih* however, referring to a list of imports and exports, c. 999 A.D. apparently referred to cotton imports.[22] Even if this was cotton there is no proof that it was Indian since cotton was also grown in parts of Southeast Asia.

By the late twelfth and early thirteenth centuries the Chinese were more familiar with Indian cotton products. Chau Ju-kua describes the cotton fabrics available in Malabar, Gujarat, Malwa and the Cōḷa-Pāṇḍya area. In Malabar he says "foreign cotton stuff of all colours" was available as well as *tou-lou mien.*[23] In Gujarat he referred to the large quantities of dyeing material available as well as "foreign cotton stuffs of every colour". On the Coromandel coast "cotton stuffs with coloured threads and cotton stuffs" were listed as part of the produce of the region.[24] Yet in Yüan times it is held that spices, jewels and incense were the major import items.[25] The same period was also the peak period of Pāṇḍyan power. The *Yüan Shih* has special sections on Ma-bar or the Pāṇḍyan coast, and Quilon. (See earlier text of this chapter).

It would appear that Southeast Asia may well have been a major market for Indian textiles. It was so when the Portuguese came. The Indo-Chinese peninsula, Sumatra, and Java were known to the Chinese in Sung times as areas where cotton was grown and woven.[26] These same areas were producers of cotton in the early and mid-fifteenth century. For example in the early fifteenth century Ma Huan says of the people of Sumatra: "They also have the mulberry tree, (and) people rear silk worms (but) they do not understand how to reel off silk (threads); they understand only how to make cotton."[27] In Palembang, Ma Huan notes, cloth, silk and Chinese copper coins were used for trading. One assumes this referred to a form of barter.[28] The mid-fourteenth century *Tao-i Chih-lioh* says of Palembang that its products included "cotton superior to that of any country."[29] In Jih Li which appeared to be a dependency of Annam 'chintzes' were used for trading.[30] Cotton fabrics appear to have been produced there and in addition cotton fabric, possibly of outside origin, was used in trading. This would mean it was carried from one area to another and that there was a well defined market for the specific type, Rockhill describes as "chintz". These are only scattered instances but all the Chinese accounts give the impression of a brisk trade in cottons in Southeast Asia. Even Chinese cotton from Hainan, the only early cotton producing area of China, found a market there.[31] Possible evidence of a Southeast Asian market for Indian cotton appears in the mid-fourteenth century, *Tao-i Chih-lioh,* where a fabric known to the Chinese as *pa-tu-la* was noticed in Malaysia.[32] The word, it is most likely, referred to the Indian silk or Indian silk and cotton weave *patola* of Gujarat. Further indication of the export of *patola* to Southeast Asia is the fact that today the *patola* weave and *ikat* technique are understood throughout the region. Fabrics known as *cheli* to the Chinese are also mentioned in Chinese texts, as available in Southeast Asia. The *cheli* could be the same as the Tamil word used to describe a sari either of silk or cotton and the use by the Chinese of a Tamil word is possible indication either of the provenance of the fabric or an indication that it was brought to Southeast Asia by Tamil-speaking merchants.[33] This is some evidence then that cotton fabrics were exported from India to Southeast Asia in the mid-fourteenth century, and it is also likely that this trade had been established much earlier.

One concludes, on the basis of interpretation of epigraphs that the participation of the guilds in the export of textiles is to be noticed from the mid-twelfth century onwards and more particularly in the thirteenth century. These epigraphs have been referred to both in the text and in tabular form in Appendix A. One envisages that the guilds provided the organisation for collection and for transport of goods to coastal settlements involved in the export of textiles. Both the Ayyāvoḷe and Maṇigrāmam were concerned with this trade. The Chinese texts seem to show that the acquaintance of the Chinese with Indian cotton grew steadily from the thirteenth century. Southeast Asia may have been a traditional market for Indian cotton. From the thirteenth and fourteenth centuries, the export of textiles to the East—to Southeast Asia (but not necessarily China) began to assume significant proportions. By the late fifteenth century Gujarati and Coromandel cotton textiles (from Telugu-speaking areas) were exported in large quantities to Malacca, judging from the observation in the *Suma Oriental.*[34] The importance of the Coromandel textile trade in the sixteenth century is borne out by the inscriptional evidence of the location of Telugu Ayyāvoḷe merchants in Anantapur District, a great cotton textile producing area (*ARE* 70 of 1912, *ARE* 25 of 1958-59, *ARE* 377 of 1911 and copper plate 18 of *ARE,* Appendix A, 1917). The copper plate 18 of 1917 found in Lepakshi of Hindupur taluk, Anantapur District, is clearly a record issued in an area where the textile trade was extremely important.

Export of Indian Cotton to the West

Prof. Gotein believes that "the India trade was the backbone of international economy in the Middle Ages in general and inside the Islamic world in particular". It "furthered the rise of a flourishing merchant class and created close and fruitful links between the countries of Islam and the Far East on the one hand and Europe on the other."[35] Commercial prosperity is attributed to the transit trade. Of the manufactured goods and processed raw material exchanged in this trade in the eleventh to mid-thirteenth century Gotein believes iron and steel were the most important but cotton textiles although mentioned frequently were of "secondary importance".[36]

Evidence of the export of Indian cotton textiles in the eleventh and twelfth centuries to the West is found in the documents of the Cairo Geniza written in the Arabic language and Hebrew script. These cover mainly the trade of the eleventh and twelfth centuries. Spain, Italy and France possess archival material as yet untapped for this particular purpose. According to the Geniza documents, Indian, Southeast Asian and Chinese imports on arrival in Egypt at Fustat, Old Cairo, were kept in warehouses. Other merchants then negotiated purchase and transported them further to European, and North African destinations.

On the basis of present information it is clear that silk manufactured in India and cotton textiles were exported along with iron and steel, brass and bronze vessels, pearls, beads, cowrie shells, ambergris, betel nuts, shoes, leather goods, Chinese porcelain, coconuts and other tropical produce and timber.[37] Pepper, spices and dyes, coir and aloeswood, cubeb and ginger were also exported from India. Some textiles were imported into India but in the eleventh and twelfth centuries the incoming trade from Western countries was of small market value compared to the exports.[38] The balance of trade was favourable to India. How important was the quantum of Indian silk and cotton exported to the West in early medieval and late medieval times? When one considers that the Egyptian textile industry was flourishing under the Fatimids it is hard to envisage that Indian textiles were a major import item for Egypt during Fatimid rule. It is likely that throughout the medieval period Indian cotton exports to Southeast Asia primarily and to some extent China were far more important. This is unfortunately still largely an impressionistic view but statistics to support this statement are not possible at the present stage of enquiry.

REFERENCES

1. Personal communication, Prof. Sir Joseph Hutchinson.
2. Wheatley, "Commodities" p. 59.
3. L.C. Goodrich, "Cotton in China", *Isis*, 34, 1-5 (Summer, 1944), 408-410.
4. Wheatley, *ibid.;* Hirth and Rockhill, Chau Ju-kua p. 219.

5. See Wheatley *op. cit.*, p. 59; Chau Ju-kua, pp. 218-219.
6. E. Bretschneider, *Medieval Researches,* Vol. I, pt. 1 (London, 1888), p. 31.
7. *Ibid.*, pp. 70, 71.
8. Mi Chü Wiens, "Cotton Textile Production and Rural Social Transformation in Early Modern China", *Journal of the Institute of Chinese Studies of the Chinese University of Hong Kong,* 7 (1974) 515-34.
9. Opinion of Dr. W. Atwell, April, 1980.
10. Discussion at Mysore, June, 1979.
11. S.Gururajachar, *Some Aspects of Economic and Social Life in Karnataka (A.D. 1000—A.D. 1300)* (Mysore, 1974), p. 68 ff.
12. *Ibid.*, p. 69.
13. *EC,* VII, Shikarpur 118.
14. Vijaya Ramaswamy, "Notes on the Textile Technology in Medieval India with Special Reference to the South", *IESHR,* 17, No. 2, (1981), 227-41.
15. *Ibid.*
16. *Ibid.* The rest of this paragraph is based on V.Ramaswamy's conclusions.
17. *Ibid. SII,* VII, 98 and *SII,* I, 64.
18. *SII,* VIII, 442, *ARE* 277 of 1934-35, *EC,* VII, 118.
19. Carrington Goodrich, *op. cit.*, p. 408.
20. *Ibid.*
21. Ma Tuan-lin from Hervey St. Denys. *Ethnographie,* deuxième partie, meridionaux, p. 580. *Sung Shih,* 489, 22. With generous assistance of Dr. W. Atwell, who provided oral translation of *Sung Shih* and checked translation of Ma Tuan-lin and also gave me the Fukienese dialect pronunciation of *chin hwa*. Goodrich, *op. cit.*
22. *Sung Shih,* 186, 18^b
23. Chau Ju-kua, 1, 16, 1, 19 (late 12-13 century).
24. Chau Ju-kua, 1, 16.
25. Schurmann, *Economic Structure,* p. 228.
26. Wheatley, "Commodities", 1959, p. 61.
27. J.V.G. Mills, trans. and ed., Ma Huan, *Ying-Yai Sheng-Lan, 'The Overall Survey of the Ocean's Shores',* [1433] (Cambridge, 1970), p. 119.
28. *Ibid.*, p. 102.
29. Rockhill, "Relations", (1915), p. 136 mid-fourteenth century.
30. *Ibid.*, p. 99.
31. *Ibid.*, p. 123, mid-fourteenth century.
32. Wheatley, *The Golden Khersonese,* p. 80.
33. *Ibid.* But Wheatley gives other interpretations.
34. A. Cortesão, *The Suma Oriental of Tomé Pires, an account of the East, from the Red Sea to Japan, written in Malacca and India in 1512-5, and the Book of Francisco Rodrigues, rutter of a voyage in the Red Sea, nautical rules, almanack and maps, written and drawn in the east before 1515* (London, 1944), Vol. 1, pp. 92-3; Vol. II, pp. 271-2.
35. S.D. Gotein, "Letters and Documents on the India Trade in Medieval Times", *Islamic Culture,* 37, No. 1 (1963), 188.
36. *Ibid.*, p. 196.
37. *Ibid.*
38. Gotein, *Letters,* p. 20.

Elephants

A ninth century Arab travelogue spoke of elephants in South India as part of the wealth of the king. "The Ballahra (probably the Rāṣṭrakuta king at Mankhed) makes generous gifts like the Arabs. He has horses and elephants in great number and plenty of money."[1] Another ninth century Arab account, that of Ibn Khurdadhbih said: "All the kings set great store on the elephant, and they compete for its acquisition at gold prices."[2]

Elephants were used in war though their exact function in battle, or the ratio between elephants horses and infantry in a medieval South Indian army is not clear. The head of an army, or a ruler or a prince generally went into battle mounted on an elephant. In a translation of the *Kalingattu Parani* one reads of "The prowess of one, who mounted on an elephant, conquered all the land under the sky...," Elsewhere the poet speaks of "the elephants of the Chola, drinking the waters of the Ganges...."[3] Tribute was exacted from conquered kings in elephants, camels, and precious stones and jewellery, in this period (early medieval). Elephants and horses were considered valuable booty in war. From a totally different source, the medieval Chinese account of Chao Ju-kua, one is told that; "The (Chola) government owns sixty thousand war elephants, every one seven or eight feet high."[4]

On comparing modes of warfare in South India, Sri Lanka and Burma one finds that probably the Burmese relied most heavily on the elephant in battle.[5] In an unusual and probably accurate description of a twelfth century battle formation in a war fought in South India between Cōḷa forces and Parākramabāhu of Sri Lanka, given in the *Cūlavaṃsa,* no elephants were mentioned but horses and foot soldiers were.[6] In South India and in Sri Lanka at this time probably greater use was made of infantry than of the elephant. A description, also from the *Cūlavaṃsa,* of an almost contemporaneous war between Parākramabāhu and Burma described in detail the preparations made by the Sinhalese against the war elephants of the king of Rāmañña.[7] In contrast, no such preparations were made in Parākramabāhu's war against the Cōḷas, a further indication that the use of the elephant in war was limited in South India in the twelfth and early thirteenth centuries. In many inscriptions relating to foreign trade elephants and horses are mentioned.[8] In both South India and Sri Lanka elephants were used for ceremonial purposes as well.

REFERENCES

1. Ferrand, *Relations de voyages,* pp. 47-9.
2. "Le Livre des Routes et des Provinces", p. 289.
3. V. Kanakasabhai Pillai, "Tamil Historical Texts", No. 2, "The Kalingattu Parani", *IA,* XIX, (Nov., 1890), pp. 327-345. The "Kalingattu Parani" was probably composed not later than A.D. 1113. See Canto 8, p. 331 and Canto 11.
4. Chau Ju-kua, 1, 19, p. 96.
5. W. Geiger, "Army and War in Medieval Ceylon", *The Polonnaruva Period,* ed., S.D. Saparamadu (Dehiwala, 1973), pp. 173-190.
6. *Cv.,* 20, 1.

7. Geiger, "Army and War", p. 178.
8. "The Nainativu Tamil Inscription", pp. 63-70; *EI*, XII, 22; *SII*, VIII, 442.

Horses

An anonymous Arab writer of the ninth century noted that the Rāṣṭrakūṭa king possessed a large number of horses as well as elephants.[1] Horses of quality were always imported since the rearing of horses was not understood in South India. Horse dealers are mentioned in the *Cūlavaṃsa* and it is clear they were active in both Sri Lanka and the Indian mainland in Cōḷa times.[2] It is generally accepted that by the twelfth and thirteenth centuries horses were imported on a very large scale. Gururajachar says "the (horse) trade seems to have attained phenomenal proportions in the 12th and 13th centuries *A.D.*"[3] Somēśvara said the finest horses came from Sind, Kamboja and the Yavana countries.[4] The Hoysalas used foreign horses in their armies. Reference to Kambojas appear in an inscription of the late twelfth century in Sri Lanka as well and it has been suggested that these were people settled in the Kabul valley who were perhaps horse traders.[5] A Kannada inscription of about the same period refers to 'horses from Turushka'.[6] In the early thirteenth century an inscription from Belgaum issued by the Mummuridaṇḍas in conjunction with traders from the regions of present-day Gujarat and Kerala clearly referred to the passage of horses from the north to the south.[7] Some horses may have come into peninsular India via Kabul, Tibet or through the northeast. A large number of horses also came in from ports in the west on the Konkan and Malabar coasts, and also through some ports on the southern Coromandel coast.

Marco Polo referred frequently to the trade in horses. From Persia he said dealers took horses to the shores of India from where other merchants took them further on.[8] Of southern India he said: 'Here are no horses bred, and thus a great part of the wealth of the country is wasted in purchasing horses...."[9] From the ports on the Persian Gulf and South Arabia merchants took horses on to South India. 'Cail' or Kayal, probably close to modern Kayalpattinam was a port where many horses were landed.[10] Marco Polo also said that from Amin, in the north (probably located in Yunnan), horses were sent to India.[11]

An unmistakeable reference to maritime trade and to the horse trade in particular appeared in an inscription of A.D. 1178 describing trade regulations at the island of Uratturai (Kayts), off northern Sri Lanka. A portion of the inscription reads thus:

> that foreigners should come and stay at Uratturai, that they should be protected, and that foreigners from many ports should come and gather in our ports, as we like elephants and horses, if the vessels which bring

> elephants and horses unto us get wrecked. a fourth (share of the cargo) should be taken by the treasury and the (other) three parts should be left to the owner....[12]

A parallel to this inscription is the mid-thirteenth century Motupalli pillar inscription of the Kākatīya ruler Ganapati in which it is said,

> Formerly kings used to take away by force the whole cargo, viz. gold, elephants, horses, gems etc. carried by ships and vessels which, after they had started from one country to another, were attacked by storms, wrecked and thrown on shore. But we, out of mercy, for the sake of glory and merit, are granting everything besides the fixed duty to those who have incurred the great risk of a sea-voyage with the thought that wealth is more valuable than life....[13]

Horses are also mentioned in at least three other major inscriptions of the Ayyāvoḷe guild issued in the thirteenth and early fourteenth centuries in which other commodities of overseas trade are listed. (*SII*, VIII, 442; *ARE* 286 of 1964-65 (from the transcript)). There are also inscriptional references to *kudirai-ceṭṭis* (e.g. *ARE* 322 of 1958-59).

REFERENCES

1. Ferrand, *Relations de voyages*, pp. 47-9.
2. *Cv.*, 55, 13-15.
3. Gururajachar, *Economic and Social Life*, p. 108.
4. *Ibid.*
5. *EZ*, II, 13.
6. *IA*, V, pp. 43-47.
7. *EI*, XIII, 3.
8. Yule, *Marco Polo*, Book I, pp. 83-84.
9. *Ibid.*, Book III, p. 340.
10. *Ibid.*, Book III, p. 370.
11. *Ibid.*, Book II, p. 119.
12. "Nainativu Tamil Inscription", pp. 63-70.
13. *EI*, XII, 22.

Iron and Steel: Wootz

Distribution: The major iron ore deposits of India are to be found in Bihar, Orissa, Madhya Pradesh, Maharashtra, Mysore and Tamil Nadu. In the South Indian peninsula, the area specially relevant to this study, one notes that haematite is found in Shimoga, Chikmagalur, Dharwad and Sandur in Karnataka. In Salem District, Tiruchchirappalli District and Guntur District magnetite quartz is found. Limonite and haematite are found in Kerala. Cuddapah in Andhra Pradesh has haematite and ferruginous quartz.[1]

It is believed that Indian steel was exported in the early centuries A.D. and was known even in the time of Alexander.[2] By the sixth century there is more definite evidence of the manufacture of Damascene swords and the steel used for this purpose came from India.[3] This steel was called *wootz* in early British days. In medieval Russia this steel was called 'Bulat' or 'Poulad' steel.[4] In Europe, during and after the Crusades the Damascus sword enjoyed a high reputation for its toughness and its fine cutting edge. Armour and shields were also made from this steel.

The structure of *wootz* has only recently been fully understood, The European steel manufacturers in the eighteenth and nineteenth centuries did not know how to handle *wootz*. At the end of the eighteenth century, George Pearson in the first serious study of the nature and property of *wootz* quoted from a letter sent to the President of the Royal Society, London from an Englishman in Bombay who claimed that *wootz* was far superior to steels made in Britain.[5]

Gotein believes that iron and steel were the most important exports from India carried by Jewish traders in the eleventh, twelfth and thirteenth centuries.[6] The steel he refers to is in all probability *wootz* which George Pearson described as being marketed in the shape of cakes one inch thick and five inches in diameter.[7]

The steel was made either directly from the ore, or from iron sponges with wood and charcoal for carbonization. The iron was heated at low temperatures for a long time, a process in which occasionally some of the iron remained unmelted. The finished product had a high carbon content.[8] Recent excavations at Quseir-al-Qadim on the Red Sea, show what is probably an iron forge with a Tamil inscription. The suggestion is that Indian iron workers lived there. Most probably they were processing iron into *wootz* for sale in West Asia.[9] In the thirteenth century Ayyāvoḷe inscriptions of Piranmalai and in the Kulittalai taluk inscriptions of the early fourteenth century iron is specifically mentioned along with other imports and exports.[10]

REFERENCES

1. N.R. Bannerjee, *The Iron Age in India* (New Delhi, 1965), pp. 190-191.
2. *Ibid.*, p.24, cites descriptions in the *Periplus* of Indian iron and steel in African and Ethiopian ports. N.T. Belaiew, "Damascene Steel", *Journal of the Iron and Steel Institute,* 97 (1918), 417-437, says Damascene steel was being manufactured in the time of Alexander the Great.
3. C.S. Smith, *A History of Metallography* (Chicago, 1960), p. 11. Smith cites a literary references of c. A.D. 540.
4. N.T. Belaiew, *op. cit.*
5. George Pearson, "Experiments and Observations to Investigate the Nature of a Kind of Steel, manufactured at Bombay and there called Wootz, with Remarks on the Properties and Composition of the different States of Iron", *Philosophical Transactions of the Royal Society of London,* ser. A, 85, part II (1795), 322-346.
6. S.D. Gotein, "Letters and Documents," p. 196.

7. Pearson. *op. cit.*
8. C.S. Smith, *op. cit.*, p. 21.
9. D.S. Whitcomb and J.H. Johnston, *Quseir Al-Qadim 1978 Preliminary Report, Quseir Al-Qadim 1980 Reports* (Cairo, American Research Center in Egypt Inc.), cited in *Master Dyers to the World*, M. Gittinger (Washington, 1982), p. 57.
10. *SII*, VIII, 442; *ARE* 286 of 1964-65; *ARE* 296 of 1964-65.

Musk

Musk is derived from the glands under the skin of the abdomen of the musk deer, *Moschus, moschiferus* Linn. The deer is killed and the glands removed and dried. Musk deer are found in Kashmir, Sikkim, Nepal, Tibet, China, parts of Indo-China and Siberia. It is believed to have medicinal properties and in Ayurveda is recommended for use as a diuretic, expectorant, aphrodisiac etc. It is used in perfumery. It appears to be mentioned in the Chintapalle Ayyāvoḷe inscription of the early thirteenth century. (*ARE* 277 of 1934-35). The word in the transcript translated as musk is blurred and there is a possibility that it has been misread. If it has been correctly read the musk probably arrived by land routes from Himalayan areas and may have been intended for export.

Terminalia—Myrobalan

T. Chebula Retz.

"Abundant in North India from Kangra and Kumaon to Bengal and southwards to the Deccan tablelands at 1,000—3,000 ft. and up to 6,000 ft. in Travancore, higher forests of the Bombay Ghats, Satparas, Belgaum and Kanara."[1]

T. belerica Roxb.

Available in most Indian forests below 3,000 ft.

The fruits of these species of trees are astringent and used in Ayurvedic medicine to treat a wide range of ailments. *T.chebula* is used for application to ulcers, wounds and as a tooth powder and gargle. *T. belerica* is prescribed for digestive and skin ailments and for many other diseases.

These species of myrobalan are specifically mentioned in the Piranmalai inscription (*SII*, VIII, 442), along with other commodities of overseas trade. In textile manufacture the principal use of myrobalan is as a dye, and a fixing agent. Myrobalan contain tannin, which when combined with iron assists in 'fixing' fugitive colours.

Myrobalan figures frequently in the lists of Indian exports handled by Jewish merchants. According to Gotein's assessment, in the West it was imported for medicinal purposes. A price list of the eleventh century sent by Jacob son of Ismail the Andalusian, to Egypt mentions three varieties of myrobalan, the "yellow, the "Kabuli" and the "Indian."[2] Chau Ju-kua lists them as a product of Gujarat.[3]

REFERENCES

1. Chopra, *et. al.*, *Glossary of Indian Medicinal Plants*, pp. 241-242.
2. S.D. Gotein, *Letters*, p. 118.
3. Chau Ju-kua, p. 34.

Pearls

Pearl oysters are found off the Gulf of Cambay, the south Coromandel coast, the north coast of Sri Lanka, off parts of Sumatra, Java, Malaysia, the Phillipines, parts of China and the Persian Gulf. *Pinctada vulgaris* (Schumacher) and P. *chemnitzi* (Philippi) are found in the pearl banks off the Gulf of Mannar. P. *vulgaris* is found "along the east coast (of India) from Kilakarai to Kanniyakumari...."[1]

In the early centuries A.D. the pearl fisheries of South India were located near Korkai on the Tamraparni river. Sangam literature has many references to the export of pearls and these have been carefully collected by S.Arunachalam in his monograph on the pearls of South India.[2] Arunachalam says that in later times with shifts in the configuration of the delta of the Tamraparni river, Kayal which was close to Korkai, superseded Korkai and became the main collection and distribution centre for pearls. The Pāṇḍyan coast and the Gulf of Mannar were both equally noted for pearl fisheries. Arunachaḷam also observes that the oyster beds appear to have moved periodically from the Indian coast to the Sri Lanka coast and vice versa and he believes that undercurrents and tidal waves were responsible for this phenomenon.[3]

Ibn Khurdadhbih in the ninth century refers to the pearls of Sri Lanka.[4] Marco Polo has also mentioned the pearls of Sri Lanka.[5] On the other hand Chau Ju-kua says pearls were part of the produce of the Cōḷa country.[6] In the late twelfth century a merchant prince Chaṭṭi-Seṭṭi, with connections with the Ayyāvoḷe guild is described as an importer of pearls, horses and elephants. The record of his activity is found at Arsikere in the heart of the Hoysaḷa country.[7] The pearls could have been intended for the internal market and perhaps even specifically for the Hoysaḷa court. Some pearls could also have been used in lieu of currency if records of early eighteenth century practice in the identical region are an indication. Buchanan's notes of the eighteenth century show that at Bangalore, merchants from Pune bringing shawls, saffron, musk and Persian pearls were paid either in money or in in 'Manar' pearls.[8] 'Manar' refers to the Gulf of Mannar and these were obviously Sri Lanka pearls. The mid-thirteenth century inscription found at Motupalli at the delta of the Krishna river, specified taxes on maritime imports and exports and mentioned taxes on pearls.[9]

For the Cōḷas, the control of the pearl fisheries of the Gulf of Mannar were undoubtedly important and it was likely that this was one of the calculations behind the repeated invasions of Sri Lanka from the mainland. It is held that from the early eleventh century till the beginning of the thirteenth century many South Indian Tamil inscriptions are found which contain references to donations of pearls to temples.[10] If Arunachalam is correct then the early years of the period he specifies coincide with the early years of the period of Cōḷa control of parts of northern Sri Lanka. The 1077 Cōḷa mission to China took 'pearls like peas'.[11] These would have included pearls from the coasts on either side of the straits since after the explusion of the Cōḷas in 1070 from Sri Lanka, Sri Lankan pearls were still, one imagines, stored in royal coffers or with merchant princes.

Collecting the information on this particular trade mission from the *Sung Shih* and from Ma Tuan-lin one obtains the information that 21,000 ounces of pearls were sent.[12] Assuming that these figures may not be an accurate estimate one still infers that an enormous quantity of pearls was sent, and some undoubtedly were from the Sri Lanka fisheries. One assumes in the period of Cōḷa domination of Sri Lanka that pearls were transferred in sizeable quantities to the mainland.

Pearls were cited in the *Sung Shih* as an important import into China in the late tenth century.[13] In Sung China pearls were treated as a government monopoly and one of its uses was as an exchange item to 'foreigners of the north' in return for livestock such as 'sheep, camels and horses'.[14] Of high value and low bulk pearls were easily transported and stored.The exchange of this commodity might appear at first sight irrelevant to basic needs. But in Sung China its importance was not to be underestimated. It was one of the imported items (the others being carnelian, amber, coral, ivory, frankincense and rhinoceros horn) used for the purchase of livestock, sheep which provided wool for clothing, camels and horses essential for transport and for warfare.[15]

In the thirteenth century, pearls continued to be a valuable commodity of maritime exchange. In the late thirteenth century letter of Bhuveneikabahu of Yapahuwa in Sri Lanka to Egypt, seeking trade exchanges, pearls were offered as part of the produce of Sri Lanka. "I possess a prodigious quantity of pearls...."[16] The fourteenth century *Tao-i Chih-lioh* contains a description of the sale of pearls on the west coast of India, at Jurfattan, probably located near Quilon. Here pearls were collected and sold at fixed rates by the great merchants. Individual sellers were priced out of the market.[17] Many of these pearls, it is believed, came from Sri Lanka.

In later times, the interest of the early Europeans in the pearl fisheries may be noted. The Portuguese conversions of the Parawa community in South India and the Portuguese conversions off the Mannar coast coincided with their interest in pearls. In the 1520s, the Portuguese came to the east coast of India to recover the remains of the martyred St. Thomas and with them was João Froles already appointed by the Portuguese king as Captain and Factor of the pearl fishery.[18] Just prior to the Portuguese arrival, it is believed Muslims (Arabs) rented the fisheries from the local ruler. With the Portuguese settlements in northern Sri Lanka also came Jesuit interest in Mannar. Once the fisheries were under Portuguese control the proceeds were divided, a quarter went to the king of Portugal, a quarter to the Portuguese soldiers, a quarter to the Jesuits and a quarter to the divers.[19]

The post-medieval descriptions of the pearl fisheries confirm the continuing value of pearls in trade exchanges right through to modern times unlike some commodities of maritime exchange such as aromatics which decreased in importance in post-medieval times.

REFERENCES

1. The *Wealth of India,* Raw materials, Vol. VII (1966), p. 204.
2. S.Arunachalam, *The History of the Pearl Fishery of the Tamil Coast* (Annamalai, 1952).
3. *Ibid.*, pp. 4-6.
4. Ibn Khurdadhbih, *Le Livre des Routes et des Provinces,* pp. 283-6.
5. Yule, *Marco Polo,* Book III, p. 331.
6. Chau Ju-kua, 1, 19, p. 96.
7. *EC,* V, pt. 1, Arsikere 22.
8. Buchanan, *A Journey from Madras,* Ch. IV, p. 198.
9. See text of this chapter.
10. *SII,* II, p. 398; *SII,* II, p. 399; *SII,* II, p. 346 cited in Arunachalam, *The History of the Pearl Fishery,* pp. 59, 61.
11. See p. 143.
12. See text of this chapter.
13. *Sung Shih,* 186, 18b.
14. Wheatley, "Commodities", p. 23.
15. *Ibid.*
16. See Abraham, "A Medieval Merchant Guild", p. 19. It has been pointed out that some time later in the mid-fourteenth century the Āryacakravarti ruler of the Jaffna peninsula was seen by Ibn Battuta in Puttalam examining the pearls that had been collected from his fisheries. (P.A.T. Gunasinghe, "The Political History of the Kingdoms of Yāpahuva, Kurunāgala and Gampala", Phd. Diss. Peradeniya Univ., 1980, p. 103) Gunasinghe says that the Mannar fisheries had obviously been taken over by the Āryacakravarti rulers of Jaffna and were no longer under the control of the rulers of the Singhalese south. He also says

    If the Āryacakravarti rulers of Jaffna were in possession of the pearl banks in A.D. 1344, it is a fair presumption that sixty years prior to this, their predecessors the Jāvaka kings of Jaffna were likewise interested in the pearl fishing industry.... Moreover, the Pāṇḍyan rulers who were the suzerains of the kings of Jaffna were likewise interested in this question.

The acquisition of the pearl fisheries may have been one of the many causes for the continuing Pāndyan interest in late medieval times in northern Sri Lanka and for their support of the Āryacakravartis of Jaffna.

17. Rockhill, "Relations" (1915), pp. 464-465.
18. J. Hornell, "The Indian Pearl Fisheries of the Gulf of Mannar and Palk bay", *Madras Fisheries Department Bulletin,* 16 (1922), 17. (Hornell cites from Gaspar Correa, *Lendas da India*).
19. Arunachalam, *The History of the Pearl Fishery,* p. 108.

Pepper
Piper Nigrum Linn.

In accounts of medieval Arab travellers there are many references to the pepper exports of India. In the twelfth century Yaqut (A.D. 1179-1229) says pepper was exported from Mangalore and Barakur.[1] If *The Book of the Marvels of India* may be treated as a twelfth century source one notes that it contains a story of a captain who sailed towards the "pepper-growing lands", making towards "Koulam".[2]

The Geniza papers contain references to imports of pepper at Aden. In A.D. 1149 for example, there was a specific request for pepper from Mangalore.[3] Pepper along with other spices is mentioned as one of the commodities exported from Pantalayini south of Cannanore.[4]

China in Sung times also imported pepper but apparently most of it was procured in Java.[5] In the *Chu-fan-chï* of Chau Ju-kua appears a footnote to the section on pepper which reads "some say that most of the pepper comes from the country of Wu-li-pa in Nan-p'i, and that the produce brought by the foreign traders in Shö—p'o comes from Wu-li-pa."[6] This obviously refers to Malabar pepper sold in Java but may be an interpolation of the eighteenth century editor of the text. In Yüan times the Chinese were well aware of Malabar as a source of pepper. Marco Polo also writes of the export of pepper at Quilon.[7] He also says that at the city of "Kinsay" (Hangchow) 223 lbs of pepper were consumed each day.[8] He believed more pepper came into Zayton than was sent to Alexandria.

The export of pepper westwards in the thirteenth century was handled largely by the Kārimī merchants of Egypt. Much of this was sold to Venetians at Alexandria. The average annual consumption of pepper of Venice at this time was approximately 1,150,000 pounds.[9] Much of this would have been pepper from Malabar and the pepper-growing areas of the Western Ghats. The Kārimī merchants apparently bought pepper from Indian merchants at Yemen.[10]

Evidence of the Ayyāvoḷe merchants importing or exporting pepper is noted in the thirteenth century Piranmalai inscription which lists pepper among many other articles of export and import. This pepper may have come from the west coast or may also have come from Sri Lanka. The Coromandel was not a pepper-growing area. In Ribeiro's seventeenth century account of Sri Lanka, it is said; "As for pepper, even if it is not exported in shiploads as is done in countries like Canara, Cochin, Coulão, Jambi, etc., the reason is that there it is cultivated and treated as the principal commodity. As I have already stated the local article receives no aid from human effort or cultivation...."[11] Despite this Ribeiro says pepper was exported from Sri Lanka to Bengal and the Coromandel coast. In medieval times pepper from Sri Lanka may well have been taken into India by Tamil-speaking Ayyāvoḷe merchants who were established in places like Viharehinna near the sources of pepper.[12]

In China in Ming times, enormous quantities of pepper were imported after Cheng Ho's voyages.[13] T'ien says, "During the reign of the first Ming Emperor Hung Wu, pepper and sapanwood were frequently given to subjects as a reward for services rendered – a practice first recorded in 1379."[14] He quotes the Compilation of State Regulations of the Sung Empire, ch. 139, Economics, 36, Trading of Licensed Goods; T'ai-tsu Shiu-lu, Veritable records of T'ai-tsu, ch. 1 4a, in support of his argument that in Sung times ivory and spices were already in use as currency.[15] Foreign trade in key commodities which also served as substitutes for money surely was of importance to medieval states. According to T'ien Ju Kang after the voyages of Cheng Ho "silver, paper money, cloth, sapanwood and pepper were interchangeable as currency."[16]

REFERENCES

1. Gururajachar, *Economic and Social Life,* p. 105.
2. P. Quennell trans., *The Book of the Marvels of India* (London, 1928), XLVIII, p. 80.
3. S.D. Gotein, "From Aden to India", "Specimens of the correspondence of India Traders in the Twelfth century", *JESHO*, 23, pts. i and ii (1980), 51-53.
4. Gotein, *Letters*, p. 188.
5. Wheatley, "Commodities", p. 100.
6. Chau Ju-kua, 11, 27, p. 223.
7. Yule, *Marco Polo*, Book III, p. 377.
8. *Ibid.*, Book II, pp. 234-235.
9. Subhi Labib, "Egyptian Commercial Policy", p. 73.
10. W.J. Fischel, "The Spice Trade in Mamluk Egypt", p. 161.
11. Ribeiro, "*History of Ceilão*", pp. 162-163.
12. *CTI*, I, p. 55.
13. T'ien Ju Kang, "Cheng Ho's Voyages and the Distribution of Pepper in China", *JRAS*, 2 (1981), 187.
14. *Ibid.*, p. 188.
15. *Ibid.*, p. 195.
16. *Ibid.*, p. 189.

Putchuk
Costus Linn.

Grows in many parts of India, particularly Bengal and the Konkan. It has been used as a purgative and a tonic.[1] As costus, which is the name used in commerce, it was exported to China even at the beginning of this century via Calcutta or Western India. It is mentiond in the *Chu-fan-chi* erroneously as a product of Arabia and the Somali coast but it is stated that it was available also in North India.[2]

It eighteenth century Karnataka 'costa' was used by the *Gandhaki* or drug merchants as a medicine.[3] It was one of the recognised commodities of medieval maritme trade but there is no specific mention of it in the inscriptions of the Ayyāvoḷe guild. The 1077 Cōḷa mission to China carried putchuk along with other commodities.

REFERENCES

1. *The Wealth of India*, Vol. II, p. 360.
2. Wheatley, "Commodities", p. 62.
3. Buchanan, *Travels*, Vol. I, p. 204.

Rose water

Rose water distilled from rose petals was exported from West Asia to India in medieval times.[1] It is likely that some of it was for internal consumption and some for re-consignment eastwards.[2]

REFERENCES

1. *EI*, XII, pp. 188 ff.; *SII*, VIII, 442.
2. Chau Ju-kua, 1, p. 13.

Sandalwood
Santalum album Linn

The sandalwood tree is found in Java, the eastern islands of the Indonesian archipelago and in parts of north Australia. The tree also grows in India and it is very likely that the specikes was introduced from *Survarṇadvīpa*.[1] The wood of *Pterocarpus santalinus* Linn. and *Caesalpinia sappan* Linn. was also marketed in lieu of sandalwood in medieval times.

It is still used today for the production of incense sticks and on funeral pyres. Ground into a paste it is smeared on the forehead and on the body on auspicious occasions. The oil is used in perfumery.

The sandalwood mentioned so frequently in the Ayyāvoḷe inscriptions may have been imported, since it is always mentioned along with exports and imports. Sandalwood has a wide, traditional market within the country.

REFERENCES

1. I.H. Burkill, "Habits of Man and the Origins of the Cultivated Plants of the Old World," *Proceedings of the Linnean Society of London (1951-52)*, Vol. 164, pt. 1 (London, 1953), p. 40.

Silk

Apart from silk produced from the cocoon of the silkworm reared on mulberry trees there are three other varieties of silk produced in India, *tasar, eri* and *muga.* Today most of the silk from silkworm raised on mulberry trees comes from Karnataka. *Muga* and *eri* silk come from Assam and *tassar* from Madhya Pradesh.[1] Buchanan records that in the early nineteenth century there were a few mulberry trees thriving in Mysore but he attributed their existence to Tippu Sultan's enterprise in introducing the tree. Most of the silk yarn used in Mysore came, he believed, from outside Kannada-speaking territory.[2] Buchanan says that at "Wallaja-peta" the imports from the lower Carnatic included raw silk of various kinds including varieties called "Bily China" and "Casturi China". These were undoubtedly imports from China and they were transported along with other overseas imports up the Palar valley to Wallajah and thence to interior Karnataka.[3] Buchanan's observations make it seem unlikely that the mulberry tree was known in medieval Karnataka.

The *Mānasollāsa* of the early twelfth century refers to patterned silk, apparently of local origin.[4] Whether the yarn used for weaving the fabric was local or imported Chinese yarn we do not know. Wheatley refers to the import of 'skeins of Ho-chih silk' in Malabar in the twelfth and thriteenth centuries.[5] According to Wheatley Chinese silk fabric was imported into Cōḷa and Pandya country in Sung times. There are references to "silk fabrics called *cīna* and *mahācīna*" in Somesvara, Nayasena and Harihara according to Gururajachar.[6] Gururajachar points out that in the *Mānasollāsa* already referred to fabrics coming from China are indicated – *mahācīna bhavani.*[7] Chau Ju-kua refers to "cotton stuffs with coloured silk threads" as part of the produce of the Cōḷa country.[8]

Many Ayyāvoḷe inscriptions which mention exports and imports also mention silk as the inscriptional tables show. Perhaps this was Chinese silk fabric imported for local consumption. Gotein refers to the export of "Indian silk" from west coast ports.[9] There is no indication as to whether the entire fabric including the yarn was Indian, or whether it was woven in India of Chinese silk yarn. Silk from West Asia was also probably imported into India. The *khim-khwab* referred to in the account of Kulōttunga's A.D. 1077 mission to China was probably rich brocade woven of gold and silk thread which may have come from West Asia, although Ma Huan speaks of silk woven at Kozhikode which from the description could have been brocade, *khim-khwab.*[10] Ma Huan's description is of the early fifteenth century and we do not know if this same fabric was woven in early medieval times. A mid-fourteenth century reference in a Chinese account to *'pa-tu-la'* in Malaysia most probably indicates export of fabric of Indian provenance either silk or cotton.[11] Bühler and Fischer in their decisive study of the *patola* of Gujarat conclude that in foreign literature the usage of "the word *patola*, can only be established for the late 13th or early 14th century", although there is no definite indication of what these fabrics were at that time. They also say that some references to these fabric forms (in the 16th century) allow one to conclude that " the goods might have been of either cotton or silk and patterned by the ikat or batik-mordant technique."[12] The references they speak of appear in descriptions of good from Gujarat used in sixteenth century trade in Indonesia and the Indochinese peninsula. They also say that reliable indication of the use of the word *patola* in Indian literary sources appears as early as the twelfth century and that Gujarat, and even Maharashtra and Kerala were at that time likely areas of production of the *patola*[13] Based on this analysis it would appear that we are able to specify export of a definite known woven fabric from India to Southeast Asia in medieval times. The word *patola* to-day is used to describe a particular silk fabric but the word in the fourteenth century Chinese description indicated either a silk or cotton fabric with a pattern similar to that of the true *patola.*[14]

REFERENCES

1. *The Wealth of India*, Vol IX (1972), p. 327.
2. Buchanan, *A Journey from Madras*, Ch. IV, p. 222.
3. *Ibid.*, p. 199.
4. Moti Chandra, "Indian Costumes and Textiles from the Eighth to the Twelfth Century", *Journal of Indian Textile History*, Vol. V (Ahmedabad, 1961), 21.
5. Wheatley, "Commodities", pp. 96-98.
6. Gururajachar, *Economic and Social Life*, p. 70.
7. *Ibid.*
8. Chau Ju-kua, p. 96.
9. Gotein, *Letters*, p. 196.
10. See note on "Cotton". Also Mills, *Overall Survey*, p. 143.
11. Wheatley, *The Golden Khersonese*, p. 80.
12. A. Bühler and E. Fischer, *The Patola of Gujarat*, Vol. I (Basle, 1979), p. 325.
13. *Ibid.*
14. Bühler and Fischer, *The Patola*, p. 312.

Wax
Wax and Honey

These were forest products. S. Chandrasekhara Sastri, speaking of Hoysaḷa times notes that apart from forests under control of the king's officials, *nāḍus* and villages owned forest land. Honey and wax were a source of income.[1] In the Piranmalai inscription they are noted along with exports and imports (*SII*, VIII, 442). Wheatley remarks that Chau Ju-kua mentions Cambodia, parts of the Malaysian peninsula, Srivijaya, Borneo, the Phillippines and Hainan as sources of beeswax.[2]

REFERENCES

1. S. Chandrasekhara Sastri, "Economic Conditions under the Hoysalas", *Half-yearly Journal of the Mysore University*, 2, No. 2 (1928), 314.
2. Wheatley, "Commodities", p. 125.

APPENDIX A

Inscriptions of Ayyāvoḷe

Date	*Findspot*	*Inscription Number*	*Script*	*Language*	*Remarks*
8th or 9th century on paleographic grounds.	In Lad Khan temple, Aihole, Hungund taluk, Bijapur Dt.	*IA*, VIII, LIX and *IA*, VI, p. 138 f.n.	Kannada	Kannada	Record of a grant made in favour of the Five Hundred *Caturvēdis* of Āryapura.
c. 8th century.	On a beam in Gaudaragudi, Aihole, Hungund taluk, Bijapur Dt.	*BK* 289 of 1927-28 or *KR* 94 of 1941-42.	Kannada	Kannada	Mentions *mahācaturvidya-samudāya* of 500 *Mahājanas* 8 *nagaras* and 120 *ūraḷis* of Āryapura. A land grant to to goddess Durgābhagavatī.
c. end 9th century, Cōḷa Parakēśarivar-maṉ, prob. Vijayālaya, Year 20.	On a slab lying by tank in Muna-sandal, Tiru-mayam taluk, Pudukkottai Dt.	*PSI*, 61.	Tamil	Tamil	Incomplete. Endowments for repair of tank named after *aiññūṟṟuvar*.
10th century.	Ukkirankottai, Tirunelveli taluk, Tirunelveli Dt.	*EI*, XXIII, 45.	Grantha, Vaṭṭe-ḻuttu	Sanskrit, Tamil	*Nagarattār* trading commu-nity and a member of the Ayyapoḻil Aiññūṟṟuvar

Date	*Findspot*	*Inscription Number*	*Script*	*Language*	*Remarks*
					guild in fortress of Karavan-dapuram. Record of construction of verandah for shrine.
10th century on paleographic grounds, Cōḷa Rājakēśarivarman, Year-8. (K.G. Krishnan agrees with dating.)	Valikandesvara temple, Valikandapuram, Perumbalur taluk, Tiruchchirappalli Dt.	*ARE* 308 of 1964-65.	Tamil	Tamil	This inscription mentions Valañjiyar, *aiññūṛṛuvar* and Maṇigrāmmattār. Gold given to temple.
Parāntaka Cōḷa, 907-955, Year 22.	Gangaikonda-colapuram, Thanjavur Dt.	Record now lost. No number assigned.	Tamil	Tamil	Tax exemption by king for Valañjiyar *aiññūṛṛuvar* to settle in Irumudu Colan Big Street in Thanjavur. Gift made at request of Nagan Mangala Udaiyan, guardian of the Thanjavur palace.

Date	*Findspot*	*Inscription Number*	*Script*	*Language*	*Remarks*
956-985, Ariñjaya or Uttama Cōḷa.	Wall of Manavalesvara temple, Tiruvalangadu, Mayavaram taluk, Thanjavur Dt.	*ARE* 131 of 1926, and *ARE* 121 of 1926, *SII*, XIX, 170.	Tamil	Tamil	Valañjiyar and Tiśai-Āyirattaiññūṟṟuvar communities join with others in construction of temple. (Tiruvēlvikkudi or Gangaikoṇḍasōḷanallūr in later inscriptions). 121 of 1926 of a later date in the same temple records the donation of a ***nānādēśi*** merchant, gift placed in charge of ***aiññūṟṟuvar***. (See also 586 of 1907).
Saka 888 (976 A.D.)	Slab near Siva temple, Punganur, Arcot taluk, North Arcot Dt.	*ARE* 13 of 1940-41.	Tamil	Tamil	Resident of ***Tiśaiyāira[t] taiññūṟṟunagara*** (as public service) paid gold, probably in lieu of taxes or other encumbrances on village lake or tank.
Uttama Cōḷa?	South wall, central shrine, Umamahesvara,	*ARE* 622 of 1909, *SII, XIX*, 280.	Tamil	Tamil	Land bought and given to temple for maintenance of perpetual lamp in

Date	*Findspot*	*Inscription Number*	*Script*	*Language*	*Remarks*
	Koneriraja-puram, Thanja-vur taluk, Thanjavur Dt.				Tirunallam, *brahmadeya*, by Venkāḍan Śingam, Diśai-yāyirattaiññūṛṛuvan.
Śaka 931 c. A.D. 1000, Iriva-bedaṅga Satyāś-raya, Caḷukya.	Copper plates found in Bedkihal, Chikodi taluk, Belgaum Dt.	*KI*, V, 55.	Kannada	Kannada	Bedkihal Plates with seal affixed bearing figure of Mahiśāśūramardini; re-gisters punitive action of guild.
Rājarāja I?	Slab near Pungavanattaman temple, Veeralur, North Arcot Dt.	*ARE* 349 of 1912.	Tamil	Tamil	Mutilated record. Gift by a guild of *nānādēśi*. May refer Ayyāvoḷe.
Probably Rājarāja I.	Slab near Jaina temple, Setti-patti, Kulattur taluk, Puduk-kottai Dt.	*PSI*, 1083.	Tamil	Tamil	Mentions *aiññūṛṛuva perumpaḷḷi*.
May refer to Rājēndra Cōḷa,	South wall, central shrine,	*ARE* 253 of 1907, *SII*, IX, 4.	Tamil	Tamil	Mentions Kaikkōḷa *perum-badai* and *aiññūṛṛuvar*.

Date	Findspot	Inscription Number	Script	Language	Remarks
Year 2.	Mahalingasvami, Tiruvidaimarudur, Kumbakonam taluk, Thanjavur Dt.				Expansion and improvement of *maṇḍapa* named after the *aiññūṟṟuvar* by the Kaikkōḷa.
c. 1015-1016, Rājēndra Cōḷa.	On a stone in front of Sivaratresvara *maṭha* Suttur, Nanjangud taluk, Mysore Dt.	*EC*, III (new), Nanjangud 213.	Kannada	Tamil and Kannada	Sale of tax free land by *sabha* in return for which the buyer makes an endowment to temple. Mentions Mudigoṇḍasōḷamaṇḍalam. Refers to Brahmaseṭṭis of Ayyapoḷal. The donation is protected by a Brahman, the *nānādēśis* and the Brahmaseṭṭis.
c. 1021, Jatāvarman Sundara Cōḷa-Pāṇḍyadēva.	Ramasvami temple Cheranmahadevi, Ambasamudram taluk, Tirunelveli Dt.	*ARE* 700 0f 1916.	Tamil	Tamil	Land transfer to a member of *aiññūṟṟuvar* association for purpose of maintaining temple ritual, using revenue from land.

Date	*Findspot*	*Inscription Number*	*Script*	*Language*	*Remarks*
11th century on paleographic grounds.	Stone in Siva *devale* Polonnaruva, Sri Lanka.	1280 of 1934, Archaeological Dept. of Sri Lanka, *CTI*, II, 2.	Tamil	Tamil	Refers clearly to *tiśai-āyiravar-aiññūṟṟuvar* and to a Buddhist *vihāra*. The stone may have been transferred from a *vihāra* to temple.
Rājēndra Cōḷa.	South wall, central shrine, Mahalingasvami temple, Tiruvidaimarudur, Kumbakonam taluk, Thanjavur Dt.	*ARE* 253 of 1907.	Tamil	Tamil	Window, door, door post and steps in front of *maṇḍapa* of temple constructed by Kaikkōḷa and gift placed under protection of *aiññūṟṟuvar* merchants.
1033, Rājēndra Cōḷa, Year 22.	Stone near shrine of Banesvara temple, Belathur, Heggadadevankote, Mysore Dt.	*EC*, III (new), Heggadadevankote 59.	Kannada	Kannada	Slight change in *praśasti*.

Date	Findspot	Inscription Number	Script	Language	Remarks
11th century script, probably Rājēndra Cōḷa.	Virrirunda Perumal temple, Kattur, Ponneri taluk, Chengalpattu Dt.	*ARE* 256 of 1912.	Tamil	Tamil	Decision to convert Kattur into a ***vīrapaṭṭinam*** by a group of Ayyapoḷal merchants.
11th century script.	Loose stone kept in Kalaimagal Kalvi Nilayam, Erode, Erode taluk.	*ARE* 215 of 1976-77.	Tamil	Tamil	Refers to *tiśaiyāyirattaiññūṛṛuva nānādēśi* group.
11th century script.	Near village tank, Kandagala, Gundlupet taluk, Mysore Dt.	*EC*, III (new), Gundlupet 154.	Tamil	Tamil	"...mentions *Āyiramadi-aiññūṛṛuvandan* and *Valangai āndān, vīranānādēsi Uya[ko]ndan* and "right-hand division of the army."
11th century script.	Stone south of Arkesvara temple, Hale Aluru, Chamrajnagar taluk, Mysore Dt.	*EC*, IV (new), Chamrajnagar 193.	Tamil	Tamil	Fragmentary. Mention of guild only. Could be early eleventh century.

Date	*Findspot*	*Inscription Number*	*Script*	*Language*	*Remarks*
11th century script.	Stone in front of Bhogesvara temple, Mangala, Chamrajnagar taluk, Mysore Dt.	EC, IV (new), Chamrajnagar 133.	Tamil	Tamil	Could be early eleventh century.
11th century script.	Siva temple, Mudigonda, Kollegal taluk, Mysore Dt.	EC, IV (new), Kollegal 100.	Kannada	Tamil	Gift of food for offerings. Mentions Mudigoṇḍasōḷapuram. Could be early eleventh century. Commodities mentioned, betel leaf, paddy.
11th century script.	Siva temple, Mudigonda, Kollegal taluk, Mysore Dt.	*EC*, IV (new), Kollegal 101.	Kannada	Kannada	Payment of wages in form of land by *aiññūṟṟuvan*.
11th century script.	Siva temple, Mudigonda, Kollegal taluk, Mysore Dt.	*EC*, IV (new), Kollegal 104.	Kannada	Tamil	Gift by *tiśai āyiratt-aiññūṟṟuvar* of the eighteen countries and *nagarattār* of Mudigoṇḍasōḷapuram. Ornaments to be made for

Date	Findspot	Inscription Number	Script	Language	Remarks
					king and for merit of the *nagaram*. Pepper is mentioned as a commodity on which cess is levied. Could be early eleventh century.
11th century.	Stone in front of Laksminarayanasvami temple, Kollegal, Kollegal taluk, Mysore Dt.	*EC*, IV (new), Kollegal 2.	Tamil	Tamil	Fragmentary. *Dēśi-tiśaiāyirattai ubhaya [nānādēśi]* Valañjiyar are mentioned.
11th century script.	Stone in front of Kenkere tank, Honnur, Yelandur taluk, Mysore Dt.	*EC*, IV (new), Yelandur 17.	Tamil	Tamil	A *dēvadāna* grant to Periyanagarisvaram-udai(yar). Vadakarai *nāḍ* mentioned, also *nānādēśiya-ambalam* of Ponnur, in Gangaikoṇḍasōḷavalanāḍ. Likely first half of eleventh century.
c. 11th century.	Stone in field, Mudlakoppal, Krishnarajanagara taluk, Mysore Dt.	*EC*, IV (new), Kn. 116.	Tamil	Tamil	Contains fragments of *praśasti* of Ayyāvoḷe of Tamil country, also mentions merchant groups such as *ubhaya-nānādēśi*, those

Date	*Findspot*	*Inscription Number*	*Script*	*Language*	*Remarks*
					of the "eighteen countries", the Valañjiyar, and a mercenary body the ***vīrakodi.***
11th to 12th century script.	On stone south of village, Kerehalli, Chamrajnagar taluk, Mysore Dt.	*EC*, IV (new), Chamrajnagar 353.	Tamil	Tamil	Fragmentary, opening lines of Ayyāvoḷe *praśasti.*
Cōḷa Rājādhirāja?	Sitesvara temple, Kanchipuram, Kanchipuram taluk, Chengalpattu Dt.	*ARE* 264 of 1955-56.	Tamil and Grantha	Tamil	Mentions Valañjiȳar and *nānādēśi tiśai-āyiratt-aiññūṟṟuvar maṭha.*
Cōḷa Rajādhirāja, Year 30.	Angisvara temple, Tamaraippakkam, Chengam taluk, North Arcot Dt.	*ARE* 173 of 1973-74.	Tamil	Tamil	*Ūrār* grant or sell land to *aiññūṟṟuvar* for purpose of maintaining a *śālai.*

Date	*Findspot*	*Inscription Number*	*Script*	*Language*	*Remarks*
1050, Cōḷa Rajādhirāja, Year 32.	On a slab in a field at Basinikonda, Madanapalli, Chittoor Dt.	*ARE* 342 of 1912.	Tamil and Grantha	Tamil	Convert Siravalli into an *erivīrapaṭṭinam*. *Nāḍu*, *nagara*, *nānādēśi* and *āyirattaiññūṟṟuvar* meet as well as some semi-military groups, Valaṅgai weavers etc.
Cōḷa Rajādhirāja, Year 33.	Subramanya shrine of Tirumanisvara temple, Kalasapakkam, Polur taluk, North Arcot Dt.	*ARE* 291 of 1938-39.	Tamil	Tamil	Land endowment by *nānādēśis* for feeding people at festival time in *nānādēśiyanśālai* and *aiññūṟṟuvan ambalam*.
Cōḷa Rajādhirāja, Year 34.	On a stone in a field, Malaippanahalli, Kolar taluk, Kolar Dt.	*EC*, X, Kolar 19.	Tamil and Grantha	Tamil	Mentions *aiññūṟṟuvan* Aravamudu.
Undated. May contain reference	Stone near Mulasthanesvara	*EC*, IV (new), Chamrajnagar	Tamil and Grantha	Sankrit and Tamil	"...convert the village called Velur, alias Rajādhi-

Date	*Findspot*	*Inscription Number*	*Script*	*Language*	*Remarks*
to Rajādhirāja I (1018-1054).	temple, Kempanapura, Chamrajnagar taluk, Mysore Dt.	146.			rāja-caturvēdimangalam, in Padināḍ, in Gangaikoṇḍasōḷavalanāḍ, in Mudigoṇḍasōḷamaṇḍalam into an *erivīrapaṭṭinam....*"
1054, Rajādhirāja, Year 36.	Base of *maṇḍapa* central shrine, Arkesvara temple, Karshanapalle, Chittoor Dt.	*ARE* 321 of 1912.	Tamil	Tamil	Muttukur declared an *erivīrapaṭṭinam*. May be Ayyāvoḷe—or even another association of merchants.
1055, Parakēšarivarman Rājēndradēva, Year 3.	North wall, central shrine, Devisvaramudaiyar temple, Cheranmahadevi, Ambasamudram taluk, Tirunelveli Dt.	*ARE* 651 of 1916.	Tamil	Tamil	*Sabhā* assigns street with houses to *aiññūṟṟuvar*, for use as residences or warehouses.
1055-56, Parakēśarivarman Uḍai-	On a rock which forms the north	*ARE* 359 of 1904,	Tamil	Tamil	Grant of gold for *sandhi* lamps, also mentions setting

Date	Findspot	Inscription Number	Script	Language	Remarks
yar Śri-Rājēndra [Cōḷa]-dēva, Year 4.	wall, Tirumalaik-kadambar temple, Nart-tamalai, Kulattur taluk, Pudukkot-tai Dt.	*SII*, XVII, 389.			up the image of Sangu Paramēśvari.
1055, Śaka 977.	Slab in street, Khembhavi, Shorapur taluk, Gulbarga Dt.	*ARE* 645 of 1958-59.	Kannada	Kannada	Grant of land to Nakares-vara *dēva* of *agrahāra* Elage by *nakaras* and Ayyāvoḷe.
1074, Caḷukya Somēśvara II.	Near Virabhadra temple, Holalu, Hadagalli taluk, Bellary Dt.	*SII*, IX pt. 1, 139.	Kannada	Kannada	*Mahājanas, telligas* Mummuridandas, *gavares, gātrigas, seṭṭiputra* and sixty *okkalu* and other *seṭṭis* grant land to Gavaresvara-deva. 500 *svāmis* grant cess on oil and other goods (not clear from transcript which these are).
1088.	Loboe Toewa, Barus, Sumatra.	See *TBG*, 1932, pp. 314-32.	Tamil	Tamil	Mentions *aiññūṟṟuvar* in Sumatra. Fragmentary.

Date	*Findspot*	*Inscription Number*	*Script*	*Language*	*Remarks*
c. 1090, Anantavarma, Eastern Ganga, Year 17.	On stone near Paravastu Rangacarya's house at Vishakhapatnam.	*SII*, X, 651.	Telugu	Telugu	Donor—*añjuvaṇṇattu vyāpāri* and others to *padineṭṭu* (18) *bhūmi, nagara sēnāpati* for *aiññūṟṟuva perumpaḷḷi*. *SII*, X, 211 also mentions *aiññūṟṟuva perumpaḷḷi*. See also *ARE* 97 of 1909 and 99 of 1909.
1094, Vikramāditya VI.	Kedaresvara temple, Belagavi Shikarpur taluk, Shimoga Dt.	*EC*, VII, Shikarpur 94.	Kannada	Kannada	Sculptured representation at head of inscription centre *linga*, right man and boar beyond him, left a curved sword, moon above, cow and calf beyond. For maintenance of the temple, expenses of ritual, and food for students and others at temple, tax levied on owners of shops, on vendors of betel leaves, areca nuts, oil. Taxes also on palanquin bearers, on tenants of some

Date	Findspot	Inscription Number	Script	Language	Remarks
					houses, on rent tree lands and on the shops of the Mummuri. The Nagaramummuri (here identifying themselves with Ayyāvoḷe) the *pattanassvāmi* and many representatives of groups in the city met to determine donation. Strong influence of the Kālāmukhas.
1095-96, Vikramāditya VI.	Tablet near Jain temple in fort of Hombal, Gadag taluk, Dharwad Dt.	*IA*, X, CXVI.	Kannada	Kannada	Charity to Buddhist *vihāra*. Sculptures, Tara, left hand water lily, on right cow, calf, sun, on left a figure with hands folded, two lamps, moon above.
Vikramāditya VI.	Stone near tank at entrance to fort of Kattageri, Badami taluk, Kaladgi Dt.	*IA*, VI, XXXII.	Kannada	Kannada	Sculpture at head—cow, calf in middle, above sun, *linga* overhead, curved sword and moon above left (Same device appears in

Date	*Findspot*	*Inscription Number*	*Script*	*Language*	*Remarks*
					No. XXXIII, minus sword and with additional Jinēndra figure, also at Badami, but it bears no relation to *aiññūṛṛuvar*.) Five hundred *svāmis* make donation for tank.
1098, Vikramāditya VI.	Slab, wall of Ramalinga temple, Yargal (Bhujrukh), Sindgi taluk, Bijapur Dt.	*SII*, XX, 63, *BK* 90 of 1936-37.	Kannada	Kannada	Refers to Ayyāvoḷe, damaged.
1099, Vikramāditya VI.	On a stone, Hanmanhal, Dharwad taluk, Dharwad Dt.	*SII*, XI, Pt. ii, 148.	Kannada	Kannada	Donation in betel leaves by *Tambuligas*, betel leaf vendors, given in presence of Ayyāvoḷe and others to a *gāvuṇḍa*.

Date	Findspot	Inscription Number	Script	Language	Remarks
Script about twelfth century.	Slab in front of Mariyamman temple, Sultan's Battery, Wynad taluk, Kozhikode Dt. (Kerala).	*ARE* 134 of 1961-62.	Tamil	Tamil	Privileges bestowed on *āyirattaiññūṟṟuvar*.
1102-3.	First hero stone in front of Hanumantadeva temple, Aihole Hungund taluk, Bijapur Dt.	*KR* 24 of 1952-53.	Kannada		500 *Mahājanas* of Aihole gave grant of land to a person who died in a fight over cattle.
1105-1106.	Melaikkovil, east wall of *maṇḍapa*, Kudumiamalai, Kulattur taluk, Pudukkottai Dt.	*PSI*, 125.	Tamil	Tamil	Mentions *aiññūṟṟuvar* and a group which could possibly be the militia of the guild.
1109, Vikramāditya VI.	Slab, compound of Bhairappa temple, Agar-	*SII*, XX, 71, *BK* 1 of 1937-38.	Kannada	Kannada	Gift to temple of remission of taxes on temple land, other gifts of money, in-

Date	*Findspot*	*Inscription Number*	*Script*	*Language*	*Remarks*
	khed, Indi taluk, Bijapur Dt.				come, taxes, land. Donors, preceptor of king's son, members of Silara family and 500 *svāmis* and eight *nāḍu*. 500 *svāmis* and eight *nāḍu* may have donated a cotton field.
1109.	Slab near Kanneyarahon-dada Chaudavva temple, Nulageri, Hirekerur taluk, Dharwad Dt.	*KI*, IV, 34.	Kannada	Kannada	The *Mahājanas* of the *mahāgrāma*, the Southern Ayyāvoḷe, Piriyakereyur, charity for Gavaresvara. As late as 1088 Piriyakereyur was not described as a southern Ayyāvoḷe (modern Hirekerur). Land donation to temple by Bammi-*śeṭṭi*, leader of the *Mahājanas*.
1109.	On a stone near Chandesvari temple, Mothaka-	*EC*, X, pt. 1, 247.	Kannada	Kannada	"The Five-Hundred made the Mahēndra-caturvēdi-mangala an Ayyāvoḷe."

Date	*Findspot*	*Inscription Number*	*Script*	*Language*	*Remarks*
	palli, Mulbagal taluk, Kolar Dt.				
12th century Script.	Stone west of village tank, Kandagala, Gundlupet taluk, Mysore Dt.	*EC*, III (new), Gundlupet 153.	Tamil	Tamil	Kandamangalam in [Mu]digoṇḍasōḷa-[maṇḍ alam] mentions 500 guild, fragmentary.
1113, W.Caḷukya.	Kodanganur, Davangere taluk, Chitradurga Dt.	*EC*, XI, Davangere 149.	Kannada	Kannada	"The immemorial *agrahāra* the southern Ayyāvoḷe Kodanganur."
c. 1118-35, Vikrama Cōḷa.	North wall of *maṇḍapa* in front of central shrine in Jambunatha temple, Jám-bodai, Chengam taluk, North Arcot Dt.	*ARE* 91 of 1906.	Tamil	Tamil	Man declared responsible for death of wife by *aiññūṟṟuvar* who prescribe expiatory punishment.
1119, Vikramāditya VI.	In wall of Charantigudi, Aihole, Hungund taluk,	*BK* 2 of 1928-29, I pt. ii, 168, *KR* 97 of	Kannada	Kannada	Begins with praises of *Jinaśāsna*. Speaks of Jema who was like a son to the 500

Date	*Findspot*	*Inscription Number*	*Script*	*Language*	*Remarks*
	Bijapur Dt.	1941-42.			*svāmis* of the great *agrahāra* of Aihole.
Vikramāditya VI.	On a slab near Siva temple, Shirol, Gadag taluk, Dharwad Dt.	*SII*, XI, pt. ii 172, *BK* 68 of 1926-27.	Kannada	Kannada	Gift by several bodies to temple. 500 *svāmis* appear to have donated cess on seasamum, salt, wheat, groundnut. *Gāvundas* gave land. *Ugura* 300, *lambuliga śeṭṭis* and oil merchants and *okkalu* also gave donations.
1121, Sri Vallabha Pāṇḍya	Mulasthanesvara temple, Tenkarai, Periyapalayam taluk, Madurai Dt.	*ARE* 138 of 1910	Tamil	Tamil	Mentions merchants of Ayyapoḻil.
1123-24, reference Vikramāditya VI and Rattas of Saundatti.	Stone tablet in Jaina area of Terdal, Jamkhandi taluk, Bijapur Dt.	*IA*, XIV, p. 14.	Kannada	Kannada	Lines 49ff, Ś1045. Lines 56-58 Ś1104 — 1182-83. First portion grant to Neminatha Jain temple, by Mandalika Gonkidevarasa,

Date	Findspot	Inscription Number	Script	Language	Remarks
					second records grants by 500 *svāmis*. Taxes donated on commodities such as betel leaf, oil, clay pots, 120-128 oxen, asses, rafts, buffaloes, carts, boats for temple transport of elephants and jewels.
1124, Vikramāditya VI.	Slab, Siddharamesvara temple, Hire-Bavanur, Indi taluk, Bijapur Dt.	*SII*, XX, 85, *BK* 35 of 1937-38.	Kannada	Kannada	Gift of land, money to temple *paṇḍit* by member of Silahara family. Gift of taxes to temple by *seṭṭis*, Mummuridaṇḍas, *ubhaya—nānādēśi* and 500 *svāmis*.
1127.	Slab in Isvara temple, Ragimagalwada, Harapanahalli taluk, Bellary Dt.	*SII*, IX pt. 1, 223, *ARE* 234 of 1918.	Kannada	Kannada	May refer to Ayyāvoḷe. Donations and cess for religious purposes. Commodities include pepper, areca, grain.

Date	*Findspot*	*Inscription Number*	*Script*	*Language*	*Remarks*
About 12th century script.	Nimbal, Indi taluk, Bijapur Dt. Copper plate.	*ARE* A2 of 1958-59.	Kannada	Kannada	Gift of toll incomes to temple.
1130 or 1138.	Chikka Betta, Sravanabelgola.	*EC,* II (new), 208.	Kannada	Kannada	Mentions Damiseṭṭi of Ayyāvoḷe.
1135, Silaharas of Karhad, Gangarāditya.	Jain temple, Kolhapur.	*EI*, XIX, 4A.	Kannada	Kannada prose, Sanskrit verse	Charity to Jain temple. Jain invocation. Sculptures—Jina inside a shrine, another figure, a pitcher, cow and calf, sun and moon. Commodities areca nuts, betel leaves, *ghi,* oil, cloth, gold, cotton, stools, tripods, beds, green ginger, turmeric, dry ginger, garlic, cummin, black pepper, mustard, grain, dry and fresh fruits, myrobalans, flowers.
1136.	Right side, Kadambesvara temple, Arleshwar, Hangal taluk, Dharwad Dt.	*ARE* 43 of 1950-51.	Kannada	Kannada	Gift of sesame seeds for oil for perpetual lamp by *seṭṭis* of 500 guild.

Date	Findspot	Inscription Number	Script	Language	Remarks
About mid-twelfth century, Bhūjabaḷa Cakravarti Tribhuvanamalla, Kalacuri.	Slab in Museum, Hyderabad from Gabbur, Devadurg taluk, Raichur Dt.	*ARE* 13 of 1960-61.	Telugu	Telugu	Gifts to temple of land, other incomes, and other gifts. Betel leaves mentioned. Hiriya-Gobburu is an *agrahāra*.
1142, Viṣṇuvardhana Hoysaḷa	Near Kallesvara temple, Kallengere, Arsikere taluk, Hassan Dt.	*EC*, V pt. 1, Arsikere 110.	Kannada	Kannada	Refers to Brahmans of Kellangere, which is the Hariharapura *agrahāra* considered to be the southern Ayyāvoḷe.
1142, Caḷukyas of Kalyan, Jagadēkamalla II, Year 8.	Slab in temple of Basavanna, Hagaritage, Shorapur taluk, Gulbarga Dt.	*ARE* 475 or 476 of 1959-60. (Inscription number and transcript number do not tally).	Kannada	Kannada	Donations include house site, garden and dry land, and taxes or levies on rice, sugar, asafoetida, pepper, jaggery, cummin, areca, other spices, oil, betel leaves. Contains elaborate *praśasti* of Ayyāvoḷe.

Date	*Findspot*	*Inscription Number*	*Script*	*Language*	*Remarks*
1144.	On a slab in gateway of fort, Miraj.	*EI*, XIX, 4.	Kannada	Kannada	A *mahānāḍu* at Sedambal. Sculptures—*linga* in centre, bull facing, above right ṣun and left moon. Commodities — areca nuts, betel leaves, oil, *ghi*, grain, cotton, gold (jewellery), leather sandals, pots. Toll collectors mentioned and obviously some tolls collected in gold coin.
1150.	Somesvara temple, Belagavi, Shikarpur taluk, Shimoga Dt.	*EC*, VII, Shikarpur 118.	Kannada	Kannada	Elaborate *praśasti* of Ayyāvoḷe. Many references to long-distance trade. Long list of commodities, see text, Chapter V. Priests of the Kālāmukha Pañca Linga and Tripurantaka were present when donation was specified.
12th to 13th century.	North of Kaivalyadevi temple,	*EC*, III (new), Nanjangud	Kannada	Kannada	Mentions Mudigoṇḍasōḷamaṇḍala and Rājarājapura,

Date	Findspot	Inscription Number	Script	Language	Remarks
	Kalale, Nanjangud taluk, Mysore Dt.	359.			Talakad.
Hoysaḷa Narasimha I, 1152-1173, probably.	Stone in front of Upparige Basavesvara temple, Mamballi, Yelandur taluk, Mysore Dt.	*EC*, IV (new), Yelandur 158.	Kannada	Kannada and Tamil mixed.	Mentions street *aiññūṟṟuvan perunteru* of Mamballi, "a hamlet to the west of Mudigonda", *aiññūṟṟuvar* land sale to *nānādēśis*.
Ref. Hoysaḷa Vīra Narasingadēva, 1152-1173, probably.	Lakshminarayanasvami temple, Kollegal, Mysore Dt.	*ARE* 17 of 1910.	Tamil	Tamil	Gift to temple.
1153.	Slab in compound wall of Marutesvara temple, Kallur, Manvi taluk, Raichur Dt.	*ARE* 568 of 1961-62.	Kannada	Kannada	Gift of income from taxes and a gift of betel leaves by a *mahāpradhāna* and a *heggaḍe* under direction of the *mahāmanḍalēśvara*, 500 *svāmis* are present.

Date	*Findspot*	*Inscription Number*	*Script*	*Language*	*Remarks*
1156-57, Cōḷa, Rājarāja II, Year 11.	Madisvara temple, Kallampati, Tirumayam taluk, Pudukkottai Dt.	*PSI*, 134.	Tamil	Tamil	Gift for Ai[y]yapoḻil Nācciyār by Niṣādarājan Rajēndrasōḷan Kēralan of Ponnamaravathi.
1159, Caḷukyas of Kalyan, Taila, 1149-62.	Stone east of Kallesvara temple, Bharangi, Sorab taluk, Shimoga Dt.	*EC*, VII, Sorab 328.	Kannada	Kannada	"...begins with terms of Jain cosmogony...." Donation to temple by Sovi Devarasa, *mahāmaṇḍalēśvara*, and by Chauda *gāvuṇḍa* and Keta *gāvuṇḍa* of the *okkalu* 60 of garden of 500 trees, 4 houses and one *maṭha*. Dues on grains granted by merchant in presence of Mummuridaṇḍas and 500 *svāmis*. Levies on paddy, salt, sesamum, gram, cotton, betel nut and leaves, saris, mentions Kedarīśvara Krīyaśakti *pandita-dēva* and Kalyānaśakti-

Date	Findspot	Inscription Number	Script	Language	Remarks
					pandita-dēva. Epigraph shows influence of both Jains and Kālāmukhas.
1161, Kalacurya, Bijjala.	Stone tablet incorporated into modern Hanuman temple, Managoli, Basawana taluk, Bijapur Dt.	*EI*, V, 3.	Kannada	Kannada	Ayyāvoḷe *svāmis* at a great *mahānāḍu*. Purpose, contribution for maintenance temple rites. Trade and craft associations represented. Levies granted on rubies, cotton, twelve kinds of grain, betel leaf, oil, fruit, flowers, also other levies. Mummuridaṇḍas also present.
2nd half of 12th century. Kalacurya.	Slab in temple of Basavanna, Hagaritage, Shorapur taluk, Gulbarga Dt.	*ARE* 477 of 1959-60.	Kannada	Kannada	(Transcript) Records gift of land and tamarind trees to Trikutesvara *deva*. Includes *praśasti* of Ayyāvoḷe. Second grant of 10 *maṭṭars* of land to Gavarēśvara.

Date	Findspot	Inscription Number	Script	Language	Remarks
1173 in 1163 three 1173 parts, Kadamba chiefs.	Slab before Kalamesvara temple, Golihalli, Khanapur taluk, Belgaum Dt.	*KI*, V, 64.	Kannada	Kannada	500 of Ayyāvoḷe. *seṭṭis, seṭṭiguṭṭas, aruvattokkalu* etc. make charitable grant. (1163).
1166.	Stone in house in Huilgol, Gadag taluk, Dharwad Dt.	*SII*, XV, 106.	Kannada	Kannada	500 *svāmis* at a *mahānāḍu* at Huligola, an *agrahāra* and "the foremost trading centre of the south". Includes Mummuridaṇḍas and *nānādēśis*. Gifts to temple include establishment of an *agrahāra*, details of other gifts effaced.
1167.	On a stone at village gate, Hulikere, Belur taluk, Hassan Dt.	*EC*, V pt. 1, Belur 177.	Kannada	Kannada	Commodities on which cess is levied include sandalwood, camphor, silk, horses, cloth, grain, sugar. First four articles overseas imports.

Date	Findspot	Inscription Number	Script	Language	Remarks
1168, Rajādhirāja II, Year 4.	Sukhasina Perumal temple, Tittagudi, Vriddhacalam, South Arcot Dt.	*SII*, VIII, 291, *ARE* 21 of 1903.	Tamil	Tamil	*Citramēḻi* and guilds including *aiññūṟṟuvar*. *Citramēḻi* takes precedence. Commodities mentioned paddy, *ghi*, areca nuts, pepper, betel leaves, salt, sesamum oil. Some of these donations to temples, others fees for supervisors of donation.
1170, Kalacurya, Rāyamūrāri, Sōvidēva, Year 4.	Bhalvani, Khanapur taluk, Sangli Dt.	*ARE* 38 of 1972-73.	Kannada	Kannada	Grant of flower garden to deity by *heggaḍe*, 500 *svāmis*, *seṭṭis*, *seṭṭiguṭṭas*, Mummuridaṇḍas, *nānādēśis*, grant gifts in kind on their merchandise.
1171, Rāyamurāri Sōvidēva, Year 5.	Pillar in front of Maruti temple, Adki, Sedam taluk, Gulbarga Dt.	*ARE* 135 of 1976-77.			Ayyāvoḷe *svāmis* and others, donation to Jain temple. Paddy, arecanut, oil, mentioned. *Ubhaya-nānādēśi*, Mummuridaṇḍas also present.

Date	*Findspot*	*Inscription Number*	*Script*	*Language*	*Remarks*
1172, Rāyamurāri Sōvidēva, Year 6.	Pillar in front of Maruti temple, Adki, Sedam taluk, Gulbarga Dt.	*ARE* 138 of 1976-77.	Kannada	Kannada	Charity to Jain temple.
1174.	Slab in front wall of Jain area, Khadaklat, Chikodi taluk, Belgaum Dt.	*ARE* 488 of 1961-62.	Kannada	Kannada	For maintenance of fort and *agrahāra* 500 *svāmis*, *gavares*, Mummuridaṇḍas, *ubhaya-nānādēśis* etc. meet in a *mahānāḍu*. 20 buffaloes are donated to temple. Income granted from levies on goods.
1174, Rāyamurāri Sōvidēva, Year 8.	Slab before Isvara temple, Belhod, Gadag taluk, Dharwad Dt.	*KI*, V, 37, *SII*, XV, 124, *BK*. 146 of 1926-27.	Kannada	Kannada	Gifts to temple by 500 *svāmis*. Land, oil press etc. are given.
1176.	Slab in museum, Bijapur, Bijapur Dt.	*SII*, XX, 165, *BK*. 96 of 1936-37.	Kannada	Kannada	Gift to temple by 500 *svāmis*, Mummuridaṇḍas, *nānādēśi*, and others at a

Date	*Findspot*	*Inscription Number*	*Script*	*Language*	*Remarks*
					mahānāḍu. Gifts include land, paddy, betel nut, areca.
1178.	Slab in Gaurisvara temple, Holalu, Hadagalli taluk, Bellary Dt.	*ARE* 478 of 1914.	Kannada	Kannada	Gandarādityana-Holalu, the southern Ayyāvoḷe. Areca nuts and other tolls mentioned.
1180.	At Somambudhi *agrahāra*, near Isvara temple, Kolar taluk, Kolar Dt.	*EC*, X pt.i, Kolar 170.	Kannada	Kannada	Groups mentioned along with Ayyāvoḷe merchants include *sale-gavaregas*. Ayyāvoḷe merchants clain they are allies of Cēra, Cōḷa, Pāṇḍya kings.
1181.	Wall of Neminatha-*bāsadi*, Terdal, Jamkhandi taluk, Bijapur Dt.	*KI*, V, 98.	Kannada	Kannada	*Mahānāḍu* at Teridala, a *banañjuvaṭṭana*. Donation to Jain foundation by Ayyāvoḷe merchants, *gavares gātrigas, seṭṭis* etc.

Date	*Findspot*	*Inscription Number*	*Script*	*Language*	*Remarks*
1181, may be Vikramāditya II, Gutta chief.	Beam in Mallikarjunasvami temple, Kuruvatti, Harapanahalli taluk, Bellary Dt. (formerly)	*SII*, IX pt. 1, 391, *ARE* 216 of 1918.	Kannada	Kannada	500 *svāmis* of Ayyāvoḷe with *nānādēśis* and Mummuridaṇḍas.
1182, Kalacurya, Āhavamalla, Year 4.	Pillar in Suryanarayana temple, Alampur, Alampur taluk, Mahbubnagar Dt.	*ARE* 157 of 1959-60.	Kannada	Kannada	Income from taxes for temple 500 *svāmis*, *nānādēśis*, Mummuridaṇḍas, present at *mahānāḍu* at Dakṣina-Varanasi (Alampur). Levies on grain, betel leaf, areca. Purchase of pepper mentioned.
1184, Hoysaḷa Vīra Ballāla Dēva.	Stone near Mallikarjuna temple, Duggalapura, Tarikere taluk, Kadur Dt.	*EC*, VI, Tarikere 10.	Kannada	Kannada	Land grant to temple. Important *seṭṭis* mentioned.

Date	Findspot	Inscription Number	Script	Language	Remarks
1185.	A pillar in a field, Kunigalughatta, *Honnali taluk*, Shimoga Dt.	*EC*, VII, Honnali 91, Shimoga *Dt.*	Kannada	Kannada	"All the Brahmans of the immemorial *agrahāra* Kollinganaghata, a refuge for all the *nānādēśis* from Ayyāvalage etc." Oil and looms mentioned.
1185, Somēśvara IV.	On a stone in village Konnur, Bilgi Petha, Bijapur Dt.	*SII*, XV, 65, *BK*. 82 of 1928-29.	Kannada	Kannada	Gift by 500 *svāmis* for temple. The *agrahāra* of Jambukhandi and its *Mahājanas* mentioned. Many details effaced. Among associates are *nānādēśis*.
1186, Somēśvara IV.	Slab upright in temple, Sirasangi, Saundatti taluk, Belgaum Dt. (formerly).	*KI*, I, 25.	Kannada	Kannada	A *mahānādu*. The *mahāprabhu* makes land donation to temple. Gifts to temple by 500 *svāmis*, *seṭṭis*, *seṭṭiguṭṭas*, *Mummuri-daṇḍas*, *Ubhaya-nānādēśi-gal*, *birudas*, *bīravanigas*, *gavares*, *gātrigas*, fifty

Date	*Findspot*	*Inscription Number*	*Script*	*Language*	*Remarks*
					okkals, nakaras, Malayala merchants included. Tamil and Telugu also?
1188.	Stone near Banesvara temple, Banavara Arsikere taluk, Hassan Dt.	*EC,* V pt. 1, Arsikere 22.	Kannada	Kannada	Refers to long-distance trade. Chatti-seṭṭi, a Brahman and a wealthy trader performs charitable acts. Built a tank and enlarged an existing tank and added a sluice to it, also enlarged another tank. Imported horses, elephants, pearls by sea for the king. He arranged movement of commodities internally from east to west and north to south. He minted coins.
1187-1196, Kīrti Nissanka Malla.	Anaulundava. Village near Polonnaruva, Sri Lanka.	*EZ,* II, 38.	Sinhalese 12th-13th century	Sinhalese	Fragmentary but unmistakeable portion of *praśasti* of Ayyāvoḷe.

Date	*Findspot*	*Inscription Number*	*Script*	*Language*	*Remarks*
Late 12th century, dating courtesy K.G. Krishnan.	On stone by side of Vahalkada tank on Yan Oya (Kapugollewa), Sri Lanka.	*CTI*, I, pp. 53-54 and II, pp. 7-9.	Tamil	Tamil	A long inscription. Mentions Valañjiyar, *nānādēśi*, many groups of militia, Has part of *praśasti* of Ayyāvoḷe and mentions *aiññūṟṟuvar* and other merchant groups.
1190, Kulōttunga III, Year 13, Niṣādarājan chief.	Madisvara temple, Kallampati, Tirumayam taluk, Pudukkottai Dt.	*PSI*, 148.	Tamil	Tamil	Grant to temple of Aiyyapoḷiya Nācciyār.
1196.	Slab in front of Venkatesvara temple, Mevundi, Mundargi taluk, Dharwad Dt.	*SII*, IV, 211.	Kannada	Kannada	Charity for Billesvara temple. Goats, cows buffaloes, salt mentioned.
1198.	Jalakantesvara temple, Vibhutipura, Kolar taluk, Kolar Dt.	*EC*, X, Kolar 131.	Tamil	Tamil	Mentions *ādi-vāṇikēśan* who "settled" people in the great city of Kuvalalam (Kolar). His son or friend

Date	*Findspot*	*Inscription Number*	*Script*	*Language*	*Remarks*
					Vikkirama Gangan donated land to the temple.
1200.	Haragadde, Anekal taluk, Bangalore Dt.	*EC*, IX, Anekal 67.	Tamil	Tamil	Mentions 500 and right-hand class.
Possibly 13th century. Dating courtesy M.N. Katti.	Stone fragment in wall of Mallaya temple, Hire-Hasarur, Ling-sugur taluk, Raichur Dt.	*ARE* 349 of 1957-58.	Kannada	Kannada	Grant of income from levies on betel nut, leaves etc., Mentions Ayyāvoḷe 500.
1203-04, Hoysaḷa Vīra Ballāla II.	Slab in front of Isvara temple, Alwandi, Koppal taluk, Raichur Dt.	*ARE* 419 of 1904-05.	Kannada	Kannada	Permission granted by 400 *Mahājanas* of *agrahāra* of Alvandi for grant of houses and land including black cotton soil to temple, 500 *svāmis*, Mummuridaṇḍas and *nānādēśis* are present. 500 *svāmis* are described as *cakravarti-prasamnaru*,

Date	Findspot	Inscription Number	Script	Language	Remarks
					Alavandi is a southern Ayyāvoḷe.
1205.	On a *vīrakal* at Narasimha temple Vignasanthe, Tiptur taluk, Tumkur Dt.	*EC,* XII, Tiptur 43.	Kannada	Kannada	"Alambur, like a warehouse to the southern Ayyāvoḷe." Customs dues from fair donated for maintenance of temple ritual.
1207, Yādava Singhana, Year 8.	Slab in Hanuman temple, Kandgal, Hundgund taluk, Bijapur Dt.	*SII,* XV, 156, *BK.* 51 of 1928-29.	Kannada	Kannada	Charity by 500 *svāmis* and others to Telligesvara constructed by Telliga-*ayvattokkalu*. *Prabhus* of Kandgal gave land and house site. Levies granted on oil mills and commodities of sale.
1208.	Stone in Sankaralinga temple, Kandgal, Hungund taluk, Bijapur Dt.	*SII,* XV, 157.	Kannada	Kannada	Fragmentary, brief.

Date	Findspot	Inscription Number	Script	Language	Remarks
1208.	Stone east of Isvara temple at Chikkayagatti, Hosdurga taluk, Chitradurga Dt.	*EC*, XI, Holalkere 124.	Kannada	Kannada	Nalli *seṭṭi*, probably member of "Mummuridaṇḍas of Ayyāvoḷe" gave dry land and wet land to temple. It is possible land was personal grant of *seṭṭi*. Some form of cess also granted on betel nuts, betel leaf, turmeric and pepper.
1215.	Slab in Ramalinga temple, fort, Mudgal, Lingsugur taluk, Raichur Dt.	*ARE* 253 of 1953-54.	Kannada	Kannada and Sanskrit	For temple, gift of land, oil mill and proportion of income from commodities imported into area. 500 *svāmis*, Mummuridaṇḍas, *ubhaya-nānādēśi*, *seṭṭi-guṭṭas*, the headman of the town and the agent of feudal ruler were all present.
1218, Yādava Singhāna, Year 19.	Pillar in shrine behind Gopalasvami temple,	*ARE* 519 of 1960-61.	Kannada	Kannada	*Mahānāḍu* at Mudinir. Present 500 *svāmis*, Mummuridaṇḍas, *seṭṭi-*

Date	Findspot	Inscription Number	Script	Language	Remarks
	Mudnur, Shorapur taluk, Gulbarga Dt.				*guṭṭas*, *ubhaya-nānđēśi*, 36 *bidu* etc.
1218. Yādava Singhana.	Another pillar, Gopalasvami temple, Mudnur, Shorapur taluk, Gulbarga Dt.	*ARE* 515 of 1960-61.	Kannada	Kannada	Money from certain tolls granted to temple by 500 *svāmis* and others.
1218, Hoysaḷa Vīra Ballāla Dēva.	On a stone in garden, Kundavada, Davangere taluk, Chitradurga Dt.	*EC*, XI, Davangere, 105.	Kannada	Kannada	A weekly fair is established by order of Hoysaḷa queen. Merchants including 500 *svāmis*, Mummuridaṇḍas, *ubhaya-nānādēśi*, as well as representatives of the four *nāḍ* and of the *maṭhas* met to determine dues to temple. Grant included levies on paddy, betel nuts, betel leaves and oil. A proportion of this granted to *paṭṭanasvāmi*. In addition 100 bullocks were given to

Date	*Findspot*	*Inscription Number*	*Script*	*Language*	*Remarks*
					temple and 30 to *paṭṭana-svāmi*, and 30 to an important *gāvuṇḍa*. A *banajiga* donated land as compensation to a bereaved family.
1220, Yādava Singhana, Year 21.	Slab in compound, Hanuman temple, Kándgal, Hungund taluk, Bijapur Dt.	*SII*, XV, 164, *BK*. 50 of 1928-29.	Kannada	Kannada	For maintenance of Jain temple and for expenses of ritual and feeding of ascetics, land donated. Also donated some income on betel leaves by *gātrigas*. Mummuridaṇḍas donate some income (in cash or kind) on areca nuts and pepper. Important *prabhus* present at this *mahānāḍu*.
1220, Hoysaḷa.	On a stone in front of Jain area, Arsikere, Hassan Dt.	*EC*, V pt. 1, Arsikere 77.	Kannada	Kannada	Arsikere, the southern Ayyāvoḷe. A Jain endowment.

Date	Findspot	Inscription Number	Script	Language	Remarks
1223, Yādava Singhana.	On a slab in house, Kolhur, Bagewadi taluk, Bijapur Dt.	*SII*, XV, 169, *BK*. 94 of 1929-30.	Kannada	Kannada	*Mahājanas* and chief *prabhus* of *agrahāra*, 500 *svāmis* and Mummuri-daṇḍas give gifts for god installed by Kuruba-Seniga Dasagauda and *koṭṭalis* of the village.
1225.	Stone in Kalle-svara temple, Pura, Gubbi taluk, Tumkur Dt.	*EC*, XII, Gubbi 11.	Kannada	Kannada	Speaks of the southern Ayyāvoḷe.
1225, Māravar-man Sundara Pāṇḍya, Year 7+1.	Wall of Valisvara temple, Tiruvali-svaram, Amba-samudram taluk, Tirunelveli Dt.	*ARE* 360 of 1916.	Tamil	Tamil	
Probably same ruler, c.1226	Wall of verandah in front of Ganesa shrine, cave of Kasi Visvanatha	*ARE* 150 of 1935-36.	Tamil	Tamil	Mentions street of the *aiññūṟṟuvar* in Enkarik-kudi and colony of Raja-narayanapuram. Probable

Date	*Findspot*	*Inscription Number*	*Script*	*Language*	*Remarks*
	temple, Pillai-yarpatti, Tirup-pattur taluk, Ramanatha-puram Dt.				indication these merchants were Nattukottai Chettiars.
1226, Hoysaḷa Narasimha Dēva.	Stone north of Mallikarjuna temple, Honnali, taluk, Shimoga Dt.	*EC*, VII, Honnali 8.	Kannada	Kannada	Ayyāvoḷe *svāmis* donate areca nuts. Grants of land by others.
1228, Yādava Singhana.	Slab in Hanuman temple, Hagari-tage, Shorapur taluk, Gulbarga Dt.	*ARE* 474 of 1959-60.	Kannada	Kannada	Mentions *aiññūṟṟēśvara-dēva* deity of the *aiññūṟṟu-var*.
1228, Hoysaḷa.	Stone north of Narayana temple, Hunuvinadu, Hosdurga taluk, Chitradurga Dt.	*EC*, XI, Holal-kere 104.	Kannada	Kannada	Land grant by a merchant who was local official and also probably member of the *aiññūṟṟūvar*. Wet land, dry land, garden land and other cultivable land

Date	*Findspot*	*Inscription Number*	*Script*	*Language*	*Remarks*
					donated, probably on behalf of, or in honour of, ruler.
1233..	On tiers round central shrine, Malaikolundi-svara temple, Tirumalai, Siva-ganga taluk, Ramanatha-puram Dt.	*ARE* 10 of 1924.	Tamil	Tamil	Mentions *aiññūṛṛuvar tirukkāvanam.*
1235, Rājāraja III, Year 19.	Slab in floor of entrance of Visve-svara temple, Anbil, Lalgudi taluk, Tiruch-chirappalli Dt. (Keelambil)	*SII,* VIII, 198, *ARE* 601 of 1902.	Tamil	Tamil	*Citramēḻi* and *aiññūṛṛuvar*
1240, Rājarāja III, Year 24.	*Ardhamaṇḍapa.* south wall, Veda-	*ARE* 146 of 1956-57	Tamil	Tamil	

Date	*Findspot*	*Inscription Number*	*Script*	*Language*	*Remarks*
	purisvara temple, Irunjur, hamlet of Anaikkudi, Nagapattinam taluk, Thanjavur Dt.				
1240.	On stone near Siddesvara temple, Neeragunda, Hosdurga taluk, Chitradurga Dt.	*EC*, XI, Holalkere 121.	Kannada	Kannada	At Neeragunda, the southern Ayyāvoḷe. Temple, tank and *agrahāra* require funds. The *nāyaka* and prominent merchant make land grants of wet land, garden land and sandy soil. King appears to have converted black cotton soil area into an *agrahāra* and also granted dues on fairs. Commodities mentioned, paddy, betel leaf, betel nut, oil, salt.
1245.	Kaitabhesvara	*EC*, VII, Sorab	Kannada	Kannada	A southern Ayyāvoḷe is both

Date	*Findspot*	*Inscription Number*	*Script*	*Language*	*Remarks*
	temple, Devasthanadahakkalu, Sorab taluk, Shimoga Dt.	268.			an *agrahāra* and a *banañja–paṭṭinam*–a trader's town. Deprecates traditional caste distinctions.
About mid-thirteenth century.	On a pillar in field, Chintapalle, Sattenapalle taluk, Guntur Dt.	*ARE* 277 of 1934-35.	Telugu	Telugu, some Kannada in portion on trade guilds.	For merit of Chagi chiefs who at this time may have been brought under control of Kākatīyas. 500 *svāmis, ubhaya-nānādēśi,* Mummuridaṇḍas, are mentioned. Gift of toll incomes on sesame, cotton, paddy, betel nuts, turmeric, jaggery, ginger, dry ginger, salt, onions, cotton yarn, clothing (sari?), pepper, mustard seed, grain, sandalwood, camphor, musk, civet, other incense. Commodities mentioned include overseas exports and imports. Transcript and

Date	Findspot	Inscription Number	Script	Language	Remarks
					estampage contain most of the information.
About mid-thirteenth century or later.	South wall of Sokkanatha temple, Piranmalai, Tiruppattur taluk, Ramanathapuram Dt. (borders Pudukkottai).	*SII*, VIII, 442.	Tamil	Tamil	*Citramēḻi* and *aiññūṟṟuvar*, a major inscription. Commodities, salt, paddy, rice, green gram, beans, *tuvarai dal*, castor seed, areca nuts, pepper, dry ginger, onion, mustard seed, cummin seed, chebulic myrobalans, embellic myrobalans, iron, cotton, yarn, thick cloth, thin cloth, thread, wax, honey, sesamum seed, gunny, sandalwood, aloes-wood, silk, rose water, yak's tail, civet, camphor oil, horses, elephants. Overseas exports and imports included.

Date	*Findspot*	*Inscription Number*	*Script*	*Language*	*Remarks*
13th century.	Door post, Kadali-Narasingaperumal temple, Ammayanayakkanur, Nilakottai taluk, Madurai Dt.	*ARE* 489 of 1958-59.	Tamil	Tamil	Mentions *aiññūṟṟuvan–taṭṭan*.
1250, Yādavas of Devagiri	Stone in Basavesvara temple, Mamadapur, Gokak taluk, Belgaum Dt.	*EI*, XIX, 3.	Kannada	Kannada and Sanskrit lines 1-46 Sanskrit mostly verse, lines 47-66 Kannada prose.	Specific Jain invocation in *praśasti*. Commodities, bullocks, buffaloes, ivory(?), rubies.
About mid-13th century. Dating, courtesy K.G. Krishnan.	Stone slab near Padaviya tank, Sri Lanka.	2241 of 1953, Archaeological Dept., Sri Lanka, *CTI*, II, pp. 19-20.	Tamil	Tamil	Refers to *aiññūṟṟuvar* merchants and to a settlement named after them.

Date	*Findspot*	*Inscription Number*	*Script*	*Language*	*Remarks*
About mid-13th century. Daṭing, courtesy K.G. Krishnan.	Slab near Padaviya tank, Sri Lanka or Padavi, near Hettipola, Kurunegala Dt. Sri Lanka.	*CTI*, I, pp. 54-55.	Tamil	Tamil	Ayyāvoḷe merchant inscription.
About mid-13th century. Dating courtesy K.G. Krishnan.	Stone slab found at Viharehinna, Sri Lanka.	*CTI*, II pp. 55-56.	Tamil	Tamil	Ayyāvoḷe inscription.
About mid-13th century.	Near *dagoba* at Detiyamulla in Kurunegala Dt., Sri Lanka.	*CTI*, II pp. 15-18, 2200 of 1951, Archaeological Dept. of Sri Lanka	Tamil	Tamil	Ayyāvoḷe inscription.
1260, Jatāvarman Vīra Pāṇḍya I	Agamasilisvara temple, Pillamangalam, Tirumayam taluk, Pudukkottai Dt.	PSI, 363.	Tamil	Tamil	Sale of tank called *aiññūṟṟuvan*.

Date	Findspot	Inscription Number	Script	Language	Remarks
1262, Reference Yādavas of Devagiri.	Slab in Kotesvara temple, Kotihalu, Hadagalli taluk, Bellary Dt.	*SII*, IX pt. 1, 327, *ARE* 446 of 1914.	Kannada	Kannada	Kauravagrāma, a southern Ayyāvoḷe.
1267, Jatāvarman Vīra Pāṇḍya I, Year 15.	Temple at Kuttalam, Tenkasi taluk, Tirunelveli Dt.	*ARE* 437 of 1917.	Tamil	Tamil	Mentions *aiññūṛṛuvan bhaṭṭan*.
1267, Hoysaḷa, first first portion of inscription.	On stone in fort, Dod-Ballapur, Bangalore Dt.	*EC*, IX, 31.	Kannada (later Persian of time of Aurangzeb)	Kannada (Persian)	Claim to be connected with Cōḷa *kula* and of Caḷukya descent. 500 *svāmis* including some important *seṭṭis* by name, and *ubhaya-nānādēśi, nakaras,* Mummuridaṇḍas, etc. fix dues on grain, cotton, turmeric, jaggery, betel leaves.
1269.	Enamadala, Guntur taluk, Guntur Dt.	*SII*, IV, 935.	Telegu	Telugu	Uses part of *praśasti* of of Ayyāvoḷe to describe guild of Pekkamdru. Commodities, areca, sesame, cotton, betel leaves. Not to

Date	*Findspot*	*Inscription Number*	*Script*	*Language*	*Remarks*
					be classified with the Ayyāvoḷe of Kannada and Tamil area.
1277.	Slab at entrance, Arkesvara temple, Hale Aluru, Chamrajanagar taluk, Mysore Dt.	*EC*, IV (new), Chamrajanagar 188.	Kannada	Kannada	Alur, the southern Ayyāvoḷe.
1278.	Stone in *maṇḍapa* on bank of Swarnavathi, Hale Aluru, Chamrajnagar taluk, Mysore Dt.	Ec, IV (new), Chamrajanagar 195.	Kannada	Kannada	A southern Ayyāvoḷe, Alur. Jain invocation, renovation of *basadi*. *Sthānapatis* of Siva and Visnu temples are witnesses.
1279, Telugu-Choda.	Siddesvara temples, Krishnapatnam, Nellore taluk, Nellore Dt.	*ARE* 78 of 1963-64, *NDI*, pt. 1, Gudur 45.	Tamil	Tamil	In Kollittarai (or Gandagopalapattinam), *Añju-vaṇṇa-vāṇigar, nānādēsip-padinen-bhūmi samasta paradēsigal* of *nāḍu*,

Date	Findspot	Inscription Number	Script	Language	Remarks
					nagaram and Malaimandalam met at *aiññūṛṛuvatirukkāvanam*. In 1256-57, Year 18 Virarajēndra Cōḷa, *NDI*, I (1963-64) Gudur 78, also refers to trade and *padinenbhūmi samasta paradēśigal*. Chief commodity at that time was cloth. Involvement of *samasta paradēśigal* probably indicates participation in foreign trade.
1280, Jatāvarman Sundara-Pāṇḍya.	Bilvanesvara temple, Virachilai, Tirumayam taluk, Pudukkottai Dt.	*PSI*, 421.	Tamil	Tamil	
1281, Māravarman Kulasēkhara I? Pāṇḍya.	South wall of Siva shrine, cave of Kasi Visvanatha temple, Pillaiyarpatti, Tirupattur taluk, Ramanathapuram Dt.	*ARE* 147 of 1935-36.	Tamil	Tamil	Refers to *aiññūṛṛuvar nagarattār*. These merchants were probably Nattukottai Chettiars.

Date	*Findspot*	*Inscription Number*	*Script*	*Language*	*Remarks*
c.1283, Māravarman Kulasēkhara I Pāṇḍya.	Bilvanesvara temple, Vira-chilai, Tiru-mayam taluk, Pudukkottai Dt.	*PSI*, 393.	Tamil	Tamil	Mentions *aiññūṟṟuva peraraiyar* and *aiññūṟṟuva devan* and sale of land called *aiññūṟṟuvamangalam.*
1285, Kongu-Cōḷa, Vikrama Cōḷa	Muruganatha temple, Tiru-muruganpundi, Avanasi taluk, Coimbatore Dt.	*ARE* 97 of 1915.	Tamil	Tamil	
1292.	Tripurantake-svara temple, Tripurantakam, Kurnool Dt.	*ARE* 180 of 1905.	Telegu	Telugu	Mentions Vīra Balañja merchants and Ahich-chatra. May be Ayyāvoḷe guild.
1299, Kākatīya Pratāparudra-dēva.	Slab in museum, Alampur, Alampur taluk, Hyderabad Dt.	ARE 60 of 1960-61. *Telengana Inscriptions,* I, pp. 88 ff and II, pp. 135 ff.	Telugu	Telugu	Uses part of *praśasti* of Ayyāvoḷe to describe *vīra balañju samaya* and leader Mummadi Brammiśeṭṭi.

Date	*Findspot*	*Inscription Number*	*Script*	*Language*	*Remarks*
14th century Pāṇḍya.	Slab fixed to right and left sides of door of Masjidul-Barkatain, Kayalpattinam, Tiruchchendur taluk, Tirunelveli Dt.	*ARE* 250 of 1976-77.	Tamil	Tamil	Mentions *padineṇ-bhūmi tisaiya*...
1305, Pāṇḍya	Rajarajacoli-svaramudaiyar temple, Koilpatti, Kulittalai taluk, Tiruchchirappalli Dt.	*ARE* 286 of 1964-65.	Tamil	Tamil	*Citramēḻi* and Ayyāvoḷe. A major inscription. Refers Maṇigrāmam of Kodumbalur, and Kulōttungasōlapaṭṭinam. Tolls levied on commodities such as pepper, areca, clothing, horses, camels(?), aloeswood, yak's tail, sandalwood, camphor, *avarai, tuvarai dal*, mustard seed, rice, salt, tamarind, wire (steel?). Overseas exports and imports included in this list.

Date	*Findspot*	*Inscription Number*	*Script*	*Language*	*Remarks*
1307.	Kallesvara temple, Honnekere, Holalkere taluk, Chitradurga Dt.	*EC*, XI, Holalkere 137.	Kannada	Kannada	Appointment of *nāḍ—heggaḍe* by Ayyāvoḷe merchants, *paṭṭana-svāmi*, priests and other merchants. The *nāḍ-heggaḍe* is paid by levies from villages and through tolls of the fair.
1323.	Laksminarayana temple, Mudigonda, Kollegal taluk, Mysore Dt.	*EC*, IV (new), Kollegal 97.	Kannada	Kannada	Mentions pavilion called *Aiññūṟṟuvan*.
Probably 14th century.	Thiruvarankurichi, Kulittalai taluk, Tiruchchirappalli Dt.	*ARE* 296 of 1964-65.	Tamil	Tamil	Ayyāvoḷe and *citramēḻi*. Grant of levy on commodities such as salt, pepper, rice, *tuvarai dal* other pulses, pepper, dry ginger, saris, cotton, castor seeds, iron, tamarind, yak's tail, elephants, horses, camels, turmeric, honey, wax. Note

Date	Findspot	Inscription Number	Script	Language	Remarks
					overseas imports and exports included in this list.
1382, Vijayanagara, reference Harihara.	Copper plate, Eni Ranganatha temple, Belur, Hassan Dt.	*EC*, V pt. 1, Belur 75.	Kannada	Nagari	New merchant groups and probably new association using name of old Ayyāvoḷe. Change of deity in *praśasti*. Mentions (new) Salu-Mule Banañju sect of merchants. Commercial area outlined includes South Kanara coastal towns, as well as approaches to Coromandel coast through Palar valley—i.e. Mulbagal and Kanchipuram.
1398, Vijayanagara, reference Harihara.	Entrance of Basavesvara temple, Singanallur, Kolle-	*EC*, IV (new), Kollegal 55.	Kannada	Kannada	New deities again mentioned in new form of *praśasti*. 500 *svāmis*, *ubhaya-nānādēśis* grant

Date	Findspot	Inscription Number	Script	Language	Remarks
	gal taluk, Mysore Dt.				tolls. Areca nuts, betel leaves, cotton, salt, yarn, saris, pepper, *vilanga* (Embelica ribes) a medicinal substance.
1397.	Slab in courtyard, Basavesvara temple, Singanallur, Kollegal taluk, Mysore Dt.	*ARE* 18 of 1910.	Kannada	Kannada	A gift for feeding members of their community.
1405.	On pillar near Anjaneya shrine at Appapuram, Bapatla taluk, Guntur Dt.	*ARE* 402 of 1915.	Telugu	Telugu	Refers Katuri Vallabhisetti, lord of Ayyāvaḷipura.
1502.	Precincts of Virabhadra temple, Hulikunte, former Maddagiri taluk, Tumkur Dt.	EC, XII, Maddagiri 35.			

Date	Findspot	Inscription Number	Script	Language	Remarks
1538, Vijayanagara Vīrapratāpa Achyutadēva	South wall, *prakāra*, Laksmi-devi temple, Gowrivaripalle, near Hindupur, taluk, Anantapur Dt.	*ARE* 70 of 1912.	Telugu	Telugu	Chiefs of *ubhaya-nānā-dēśis* of Ayyāvoḷe and other *seṭṭis* and *paṭṭanasvāmis* make gift to temple of income from taxes levied at weekly fair.
1549, Vijayanagara, Sadāsiva.	Slab near Siva temple, Rayal-cheruvu, Tad-patri taluk, Anantapur Dt.	*ARE* 25 of 1958-59.	Telugu	Telugu	
1551, Vijayanagara, Sadāsiva.	Slab in wall of Virabhadresvara temple, Pedda—mudiyam, Jam-malamadugu taluk, Cudappah Dt.	*ARE* 349 of 1905, *SII*, XVI, 179.	Telugu	Telugu	Lines 22-24 "*Ayyāvoḷe mukhyamaina chalumula-samasta—pekkamdru*" mentioned.
1620.	*Gopura* of Kalyāna Venka-tesaperumal	*SII*, XVI, 315. *ARE* 377 of 1911.	Telugu	Telugu	Gift of tolls on cloth, areca, pepper, *jaggery*, tamarind etc. by chiefs of Ayyāvoḷe

Date	Findspot	Inscription Number	Script	Language	Remarks
	temple, Nara-yanavanam, Put-tur Division, Chittoor Dt.				headed by (it is claimed), Prithiviśeṭṭi Rāyanamantri Bhāskara, who may have been a Brahman.
1628.	Ranganatha temple, Balla-purade-pete, Bangalore.	*EC*, IX, Bangalore 1	Telugu	Telugu	Chief men of Ayyāvoḷe, *Salumūla* of *ubhaya-nānādēśis* of Pekkonda, Penugonda, as well as of Kannada-speaking areas and also of Kaveripatti-nam are mentioned.
1680.	Copper plate, Lepakshi, Hindu-pur taluk, Anantapur Dt.	*ARE* 18 of 1917, Appendix A.			Gift of rates on pack bullocks, shops, looms; refers to Brahman minister of Golçonda king Abdul Hassan, Kutb Shahi; village headman, *paṭṭanasvāmis*, merchants, *bhūmi-prabhu* of 4 Reddi families, crafts-men, including weavers and dyers of textiles, tailors, pot-ters, shoe makers, cowherds

Date	*Findspot*	*Inscription Number*	*Script*	*Language*	*Remarks*
					and keepers of pack bullocks, hunters, washermen and barber were present when donation was decided.
S 1620	Copper plate, Kolar Dt.	EC, XVII, (supplement to X), 257.	Telugu	Telugu	List of townships in inscription includes both Kannada-and Telugu-speaking areas. These towns straddle the peninsula from Belur and its environs to Coromandel coast. The commodities on which levies are made include cloth, blankets, *ghi*, oil, sugar.
not yet dated.	By road on stone from Kasireddipalli to Gorantla, Hindupur taluk, Anantapur Dt.	ARE 818 of 1917.	Kannada	Kannada	Mentions merchants of Ayyāvoḷe.

Date	*Findspot*	*Inscription Number*	*Script*	*Language*	*Remarks*
not yet dated.	South wall, central shrine, Manavalesvara temple, Tiru-valangadu, Maya-varam taluk, Thanjavur Dt.	*ARE* 121 of 1926, *SII*, XIX, 170.	Tamil	Tamil	Gift to temple entrusted to *tiśai-yāyiratainnūṟṟuvan.*
not yet dated.	On a pillar in *maṇḍapa* in front of central shrine Vedaranyesvara temple, Vederan-yam, Tirutturai-pundi taluk, Thanjavur Dt.	ARE 436 of 1904, *SII*, XIX, 216.	Tamil	Tamil	Gift of 90 sheep for a per-petual lamp on behalf of a merchant of Karuvur (Karur), by *aiññūṟṟuvar*.

APPENDIX B

Inscriptions relating to Maṇigrāmam

Date	*Findspot*	*Inscription Number*	*Script*	*Language*	*Remarks*
9th or early 10th century.	Copper plates in possession of Syrian Christians in Kerala.	*TAS*, II, 9.	Vaṭṭeḻut-tu Kufic, Hebrew, Pahlavi.	Tamil, Arabic, Persian.	Known as Sthāṇu Ravi plates. An impressive and elaborate contract drawn, formalizing relationship between local authority and foreign trader in Quilon, Kerala.
9th century. Probably Pallava Nandivarman III.	Takuapa, Thailand, (Isthmus of Kra)	*JMBRAS*, 22, pt. 1 (1949), 25-30.	Tamil	Tamil	Refers to a tank under protection of Maṇigrāmam.
928-29, tentative dating courtesy K.G. Krishnan.	Slab in courtyard of Narayankannur temple,	*ARE* 474 of 1926.	Archaic Vatteḻuttu	Tamil	Mentions members of Maṇigrāmam of Ilangop-paṭṭinam.

Date	*Findspot*	*Inscription Number*	*Script*	*Language*	*Remarks*
	Ramantali, Chirakkal taluk, former Maľabar Dt.				
10th century, dating courtesy K.G. Krishnan.	North wall of Korangunathan temple, Srinivasanallur, Musiri taluk, Tiruchchirappalli Dt.	*ARE* 597 of 1904, *SII*, XIII, 26.	Tamil	Tamil	Member of Maṇigrāmam is signatory to land sale-cum-donation to temple.
928, Dating courtesy K.G. Krishnan.	Kuttalanathasvamin temple, Kuttalam, Tenkasi, Tirunelveli Dt.	*ARE* 439 of 1917, *SII*, XIX, 417.	Vaṭṭeḻutu	Tamil	Gift of 26 cows for maintaining a lamp in temple by member of Maṇigrāmam.
10th century, dating courtesy K.G. Krishnan and K.V. Ramesh.	Rock in front of Jambunatha temple, Tiruvellarai, Tiruchchirappalli taluk, the same district.	*ARE* 519 of 1905, *SII*, XIII, 28.	Tamil	Tamil	Endowment of 50 *kaḷañju* of gold for feeding a Brahman by a member of Maṇigrāmam.

Date	Findspot	Inscription Number	Script	Language	Remarks
First half of 11th century dating courtesy K.G. Krishnan and K.V. Ramesh.	On a slab now in compound of Roman Catholic church, Talakkad, Mukundapuram taluk, former Cochin State.	*ARE* 358 of 1927.	Vaṭṭeḻutu	Tamil	Describes founding of a market and privileged position of two members of Maṇigrāmam.
11th century, on paleographic grounds, K.G. Krishnan agrees.	On a step at entrance of shrine of goddess at Sukhavanesvara temple, Salem, same district.	*SII*, IV, 147, *ARE* 47 of 1888.	Tamil	Tamil	Mentions donation of Merchant from Maṇigrāmam of Kodumbalur.
11th century, or early 12th 12th century.	Wall of Tirukkotisvara temple, Tirukkodikaval, Kumbakonam taluk, Thanjavur Dt.	*ARE* 46 of 1930-31.	Tamil	Tamil	Member of Maṇigrāmam makes gold donation to temple.

Date	*Findspot*	*Inscription Number*	*Script*	*Language*	*Remarks*
1180 or 1183.	Rajarajacoli-svaramudaiyar temple, Koil-patti, Kuliṭtalai taluk, Tiruch-chirappalli Dt.	*ARE* 288 of 1964-65.	Tamil	Tamil	Mentions Kodumbalur Maṇigrāmam.
First quarter 13th century.	Kottayam Plate of Vīra-Rāghava, now in possession of Syrian Chris-tian church, Kerala.	*EI*, IV, 41.	Vaṭṭeḻutu and Malaya-lam	Tamil with some slight Malaya-lam	Describes trade at Kodun-gallur on west coast.
1268, Jatāvarman Vīrapāṇḍya I.	Rajarajacoli-svaramudaiyar, Koilpatti, Kulittalai taluk, Tiruchchirappalli Dt.	*ARE* 283 of 1964-65.	Tamil	Tamil	Mentions merchant of Maṇigrāmam of Kodumbalur.
1269, Jatāvarman Vīrapāṇḍya I.	Base south wall of *maṇḍapa* in front of Siva	*ARE* 598 of 1926-27.	Tamil	Tamil	Mentions merchants of Sri Lanka and Kaikkōḷas. Merchandise taxed

Date	Findspot	Inscription Number	Script	Language	Remarks
	temple, Tittandatanapuram, Tiruvadanai taluk, Ramanathapuram Dt.				probably included textiles.
13th century, probably second half.	On the south wall of Sokkanatha temple, Piranmalai, Tiruppattur taluk, Ramanathapuram Dt.	*SII*, VIII, 442.	Tamil	Tamil	A major inscription listing many commodities of overseas trade. Mentions Maṇigrāmam of Kodumbalur.
1305.	Rajarajacolisvaramudaiyar, Koilpatti, Kulittalai taluk, Tiruchchirappalli Dt.	*ARE* 286 of 1964-65	Tamil	Tamil	Another major inscription along with Ayyāvoḷe, *citramēḻi periyanāṭṭavar* and many trading groups including Maṇigrāmam. Many important commodities of overseas trade are mentioned.

APPENDIX C

Pudukkoṭṭai Inscriptions

Date	*Findspot*	*Inscription Number*	*Script*	*Language*	*Remarks*
c. 870	On a slab by tank, Munasandal, Tirumayam taluk.	*PSI*, 61.	Tamil	Tamil	*Aiññūṟṟuvar* tank.
Prob. Rājarāja Cōḷa I.	Slab near Jaina temple, Settipatti, Kulattur taluk.	*PSI*, 1083.	Tamil	Tamil	Mentions *aiññūṟṟuva perumpaḷḷi*.
1055-56.	On rock, Tirumalaikkadambar temple, Narttamalai, Kulattur taluk.	*ARE* 359 of 1904.	Tamil	Tamil	Grant of gold for lamps. Installation of image.
1105-1106.	East wall of Melaikkovil,	*PSI*, 125.	Tamil	Tamil	Mentions *Paliyili aiññūṟṟuvar*.

Date	*Findspot*	*Inscription Number*	*Script*	*Language*	*Remarks*
	Kudumiamalai, Kulattur taluk.				
1156-57, Rājarāja II, 11th Year.	North wall of Madisvara temple, Kallampatti, Tirumayam taluk.	*PSI*, 134.	Tamil	Tamil	Gift to temple of Aiyyapoḻi[l] Nācciyār by Niṣādarājan chief Rajēndra Cōḻan Kēralan.
1190-91, Cōḻa, Kulōttunga III, 13th Year.	Madisvara temple, Kallampatti, Tirumayam taluk.	*PSI*, 148.	Tamil	Tamil	Grant to temple of Ayyapoḻiya Nācciyār by Niṣādarājan chief.
1260, Pāṇḍya.	Agamasilisvara temple, Pillamangalam, Tirumayam taluk.	*PSI*, 363.	Tamil	Tamil	Sale of tank called Aiññūṟṟuvan.
1280	Bilvanesvara temple, Virachilai, Tirumayam taluk.	*PSI*, 421.	Tamil	Tamil	Land sale mentions *aiññūṟṟuva perarāiyar*.

Date	*Findspot*	*Inscription Number*	*Script*	*Language*	*Remarks*
1283.	Bilvanesvara temple, Vira-chilai, Tiru-mayam taluk.	PSI, 393.	Tamil	Tamil	Mentions *aiññūṛṛuva peraraiyar* and *aiññūṛṛuva dēvan* and sale of land called *aiññūṛṛuvamangalam*.
	Rock near Tiru-malaikkadambar temple, Nartta-malai, Kulattur taluk.	*PSI*, 621.	Tamil	Tamil	Distribution of temple land, mentions *aiññūṛṛuva bhaṭṭan*.
	Bilvanesvara temple, Vira-chilai, Tiru-mayam taluk.	*PSI*, 534.	Tamil	Tamil	Sale of land mentions *aiññūṛṛuva perarāiyar*.
	On pillar in ruins of Siva temple, Tenmavur, Kulat-tur taluk.	PSI, 576.	Tamil	Tamil	Gift of pillar by *aiññūṛṛuvar*.
	Slab near Kailasa-natha temple, Valara-manikkam.	PSI, 1022.	Tamil	Tamil	'The village is called... *Ainjūṛṛuvanallūr* in *Memiyarru(-nāḍu)*'.

Date	*Findspot*	*Inscription Number*	*Script*	*Language*	*Remarks*
13th century, probably latter half.	Sokkanatha temple, Piran-malai, Tirupattur taluk, Rama-nathapuram District, borders Pudukkottai tract.	*SII*, VIII, 442.	Tamil	Tamil	A major incription lists cess on commodities, issued in conjunction with *citramēḻi*.

Bibliography

Epigraphy: General

Epigraphia Indica. Delhi/Calcutta, 1892-
Indian Antiquary. Bombay, 1872-1923.

Epigraphy: South India

Annual Report on (South Indian) Epigraphy. Madras, 1887-
South Indian Inscriptions. Madras, 1890-
South Indian Temple Inscriptions. Ed.Subramaniam, T.N. 3 vols. Madras, 1953-7.
A Topographical List of the Inscriptions of the Madras Presidency, collected till 1915, with Notes and References. Ed. Rangacharya, V. 3 vols. Madras, 1919.

Epigraphy: Pudukkottai

Chronological List of Inscriptions of the Pudukkottai State arranged according to Dynasties. Pudukkottai, 1929.
Inscriptions in the Pudukkottai State, translated intc English. Srinivasa Aiyar, K.R.Pts. i and ii. Pudukkottai, 1941, 1946.
Inscriptions (Texts) of the Pudukkottai State arranged according to Dynasties. Pudukkottai, 1929.

Epigraphy: Andhra

A Collection of the Inscriptions on Copper-Plates and Stones in the Nellore District. Ed. Butterworth, A. and V. Venugopal. 3 pts. Madras, 1905.
Epigraphia Andhrica. Hyderabad, 1969-
Telengana Inscriptions. 2 vols. Hyderabad, 1935, 1960.

Epigraphy: Karnataka. Maharashtra

Annual Report of the Mysore Archaeological Department. Mysore, 1905-
Epigraphia Carnatic. Mysore, 1889-
Inscriptions from Nanded District. Ed. Ritti, Shrinivas and G.C. Shelke. Nanded, 1968.

Inscriptions in Northern Karnataka and Kolhapur. Ed. Kundankar, K.G. Kolhapur, 1939.

Karnatak Inscriptions. Dharwad, 1941-

Epigraphy: Kerala

Travancore Archaeological Series. 9 vols. Travancore, 1910-41.

Epigraphy: Sri Lanka

Ceylon Tamil Inscriptions. Ed. Velupillai, A. Pts. i; ii. Peradeniya, 1972.

Epigraphia Tamilica. Ed. Indrapala, K. Jaffna, 1971-

Epigraphia Zeylanica. Colombo, 1941-

Epigraphy: Indonesia

Corpus of the inscriptions of Java (Corpus inscriptionum Javanicarum) (up to 928 A.D.). Ed. Sarkar, H.B. Calcutta, 1971.

Epigraphy: Thailand

Recueil des Inscriptions du Siam. Ed. Coedès, G. Pt. ii. Bangkok, 1961.

Epigraphy: Articles. Analyses. Books

AIYER, K.V. SUBRAHMANYA. "The Larger Leiden plates (of Rājarāja I)". *EI*, XXII, 34.

BALASUBRAHMANIAM, S.R. "Āyirattaiññūṟṟuvar and the Municandai Record." *TBG*, deel 74 (1934), 613-8.

Burnell, A.C. "On Some Pahlavi Inscriptions in South India". *IA*, 3 (Nov. 1874), 308-316.

__________. "The Original Settlement-Deed of the Jewish Colony at Cochin". *IA*, 3 (Dec. 1874), 333-334.

DANIEL, K.N. "Kottayam Plate of Vira-Raghava Chakravarti". *IA*, 53 (1924), 185-196, 219-229, 244-251.

__________. "An Inscription of Iraya Chinka (Rāja Simha) Perumal". *IA*, 58 (1929), 158-159.

__________. "The Anchuvannam and the Manigramam of the Kottayam Plates of Tanu Iravi or the Jews and Christians of Malabar." *IA*, 52 (1924), 257-261.

GUNASINGHAM, S. "A Tamil Slab Inscription at Nilāveli". *SLJH*, 1, No. 1 (1975), 61-71.

__________. "Two Inscriptions of Cōḷa Ilankēśvara Dēva". *Trincomalee Inscriptions*, Series No. 1. Privately printed.

———————. "Three Cōḷa Inscriptions from Trincomalee". *Trincomalee Inscriptions*. Series No. 2. Privately printed.

GUNDERT, REV. H. "Translation and Analysis of the ancient documents engraved on copper in possession of the Syrian Christians and Jews of Malabar". *MJLS*, 13, No. 30, pt. i(1844), 115-46.

———————. "Hebrew version of the Jewish Sasanam with translation into English; together with a notice of an ancient Malayalim Poem, called the Song or Legend of Payanūr." *MJLS*, 13, No. 31, pt. ii (1844), 11-16.

HOSTEN, REV. H. "Thomas Caṅa and his Copper-Plate Grant." *IA*, 56 (1927), 121-128, 147-155.

HOSTEN, REV. H. and T.K. JOSEPH. "Thomas Cana and his Copper-Plate Grant." *IA*, 56 (1927), 177-185.

HULTZSCH, E. "Motupalli Pillar Inscription of Ganapatidēva A.D. 1244-45." *EI*, XII, 22.

INDRAPALA, K. "The Nainativu Tamil Inscription of Parākramabahu I." *UCR*, 21, No. 1 (April 1963), 63-70.

———————. "An Inscription of the Tenth Year of Cōḷa Laṅkēśvara dēva from Kantalai, Sri Lanka." In *Senarat Paranavitana Commemoration Volume*. Eds. L. Prematilleke, K. Indrapala, J.E. Van Lohuizen-de-Leeuw. Leiden, 1978, pp. 81-97.

JOSEPH, T.K. "A Pahlavi Inscription Round a Persian Cross at Katamarram, Travancore." *IA*, 53 (1924), 122-123.

JOSEPH, T.K. "A Rājasimha Inscription at Tāḷekkād in Cochin." *IA*, 57 (1928), 24-31.

———————. "The Malabar Christian Copper-Plates." *Kerala Society Papers*, 4 (1930), 201-204.

KARASHIMA, N., Y. SUBBARAYALU and TORU MATSUI. *A Concordance of the Names in the Cōḷa Inscriptions*. 3 vols. Madurai, 1978.

KIELHORN, F. "The Date of the Kottayam (Syrian Christians') Plate of Vira-Raghava." *EI*, 6 (1900-1), 83-4.

MAHADEVAN, I. "Corpus of the Tamil-Brahmi Inscriptions." In *Seminar on Inscriptions*. Ed. R. Nagaswamy. Madras, 1966, pp. 57-68.

———————. "Tamil-Brahmi Inscriptions of the Sangam Age." In *Proceedings of the Second International Conference Seminar of Tamil Studies*. Vol. I. Madras, 1971, pp. 73-106.

NAIR, K.K. "Memorandum on the Syrian and Jewish Copper Plates of Malabar." *MJLS*, 21, No. 9, n.s. (1859), 30-55.

RAO, T.A. GOPINATHA. "A Note on Maṇigrāmmattār Occuring in Tamil Inscriptions." *EI*, XVII, pp. 69-73.

———————. "Three Inscriptions of Sthāṇu Ravi." *TAS*, II, 9.

SASTRI, K.A. NILAKANTA and T.N. SUBRAMANIAM. "Hemavati Pillar Inscription of Kulottungachola (III), Year 21." *EI*, XXXI, 37.

SASTRI, K.A. NILAKANTA. "A Tamil Merchant-guild in Sumatra." *TBG*, deel lxxii (1932), 314-27.

___________. "Foreign Trade under the Kakātīyas". *JOR*, 8, Madras (1934), 315-320.

___________. "Takuapa and its Tamil Inscription." *JMBRAS*, 22, pt. 1 (1949), 25-30.

SUBRAMANIAM, T.N. ed. "Tamil Inscriptions in other Countries." *Handbook*. World Tamil Conference, Madras (1968). [Tamil]

TAN, YEOK SENG. "The Śri Vijayan Inscription of Canton (A.D. 1079)." *JSEAH*, 2 (1964), 17-24.

VENKAYYA, V. "Kottayam Plate of Vīra-Rāghava." *EI*, IV, 41.

WEST, E.W. "Inscriptions Around Crosses in South India." *EI*, IV, pp. 174-176.

Other Primary Sources in Original and in Translation

ABBELOOS, J.B. *Acta Sancti Maris Assyriae, Babyloniae ac Persidis Seculo I Apostoli*. Syriace Sive Aramaice. Leipzig, 1885.

AIYAR, C., ed. *Konecar Kalvettu*. Jaffna, 1909. [Tamil]

ALBUQUERQUE, B. de. *The Commentaries of the Great Afonso Dalboquerque*. 4 vols. Trans. and ed. W.de Gray Birch. London, 1875-84.

BARBOSA, DUARTE. *A Description of the Coasts of East Africa and Malabar in the Beginning of the Sixteenth Century*. Trans.and ed. H.E.J. Stanley. London, MDCCCLXVI.

BEVAN, A.A. trans. *The Hymn of the Soul* contained in *The Syriac Acts of St. Thomas*. In *Texts and Studies, Contributions to Biblical and Patristic Literature*. Ed. J. Armitage Robinson. Vol. V. Cambridge, 1899.

BOSTOCK, J., and H.T. RILEY, trans. *The Natural History of Pliny*. 6 vols. London, MDCCCLV.

BRETSCHNEIDER, E.V. *Medieval Researches from Eastern Asiatic Sources*. Fragments towards the knowledge of the Geography and History of Central and Western Asia from the 13th to the 17th Century. London, 1888. 2 vols. rpt. London, 1967.

BROWN, C.C., trans. "The Malay Annals." *JMBRAS*, 25, pts. ii and iii (1952), 6-276.

"*Conga desa Rajakal*". Trans. Rev. W. Taylor. *MJLS*, 14, pt. 1 (1847), 1-66.

CORTESÃO, A. *The Suma Oriental of Tome Pires, an account of the East, from the Red Sea to Japan, written in Malacca and India in 1512-5, and the Book of Francisco Rodrigues, rutter of a voyage in the Red Sea, nautical rules, almanack and maps, written and drawn in the east before 1515*. 2 vols. London, 1944.

Cūlavaṃsa. Trans. W. Geiger and M. Rickmers. 2 vols. rpt. Colombo, 1953.

CHETTIAR, C.M. RAMACHANDRAN, ed. *Kongadēsa Rājākkaḷ*. Madras, 1950. [Tamil]

——————. ed. *Cōḷan Pūrvapaṭṭaiyam.* Madras, 1950. [Tamil]

DIKSHITAR, V.R., trans. and ed. *The Silappadikāram.* Oxford, 1939.

FAUSBØLL, V., ed. and T.W. Rhys Davids, trans. *Jātakatthavaṇṇanā. Text.* Vol. III, London, 1883.

FERRAND, G. *Relations de voyages et textes géographiques, arabes, persans et turks relatifs à l'Extrême-Orient du VIIIe au XVIIe siècles.* 2 vols. Paris, 1913-4.

HANDIQUI, K.K., trans and ed. *Yasastlilaka and Indian Culture.* Sholapur, 1949.

HIRTH, FREDERICK, and W.W. ROCKHILL, trans. and eds. *Chau Ju-kua, His work on the Chinese and Arab trade in the twelfth and thirteenth centuries, entitled Chu-fan-chï.* St. Petersburg, 1911. rpt. New York, 1966.

LAND, J.P.N., ed. *Anecdota Syriaca.* Vol. 1. Leiden, 1862.

MAÇOUDI. *Les Prairies d'Or.* Vol. I, III. Paris, 1861, 1864.

MCCRINDLE, J.W., trans. and ed. *The Christian Topography of Cosmas an Egyptian Monk.* London, 1897.

——————. *The Commerce and Navigation of the Erythraean Sea and Arrian's Account of the Voyages of Nearkhos.* London, 1879.

MEYNARD, C. BARBIER de., trans. "Le Livre des Routes et des Provinces." *JA,* sixième série, tome V (1865), 5-127; 227-96; 446-532.

MILLS, J.V.G., trans. and ed. Ma Huan. *Ying-yai Sheng-lan 'The Overall Survey of the Ocean's Shores'* [1433]. Cambridge, 1970.

Palm-Leaf Gazetteer of the Pudukkoṭṭai State. Otherwise referred to as the *Statistical Account* of 1813. Government Museum, Pudukkottai.

PENZER, N.M., ed. *The Ocean of Story: being C.H. Tawney's translation of Somadeva's Kathā Sarit Sāgara.* 10 vols. London, 1924.

PILLAI, T.P.P., ed. *Kappal Sattiram.* Madras, 1950. [Tamil]

PILLAI, V. KANAKASABHAI, trans. "Tamil Historical Texts," No. 2, "The Kalingattu Parani". *IA,* 19 (1890), pp. 327-345.

QUENNELL, P., trans. *The Book of the Marvels of India.* London, 1928.

ROCKHILL, W.W. "Notes on the relations and trade of China with the Eastern Archipelago and the coasts of the Indian Ocean during the fourteenth century." *T'oung Pao,* 14 (1913), 473-6; 15 (1914), 419-47; 16 (1915), 61-159, 236-71, 374-92, 435-67, 604-26.

SAINT-DENYS, D'HERVEY DE, MARQUIS., trans. *Ethnographie des peuples étrangers à la Chine. Traduit pour la première fois du Chinois avec un commentaire perpétuel par le Marquis d' Hervey de Saint-Denys. Deuxième partie,* Geneva, 1883.

SASTRI, K.A. NILAKANTA, ed. *Foreign Notices of South India; from Megasthenes to Ma Huan.* Madras, 1939.

SAUVAGET, J., trans. and ed. *'Ahbār as-Sīn wa'l-Hind; relation de la Chine et de l 'Inde, rédigée en 851.* Paris, 1948.

SCHOFF, W.H., trans. and ed. *The Periplus of the Erythraean Sea*. Philadelphia, 1912.

SCHURMANN, F. *Economic Structure of the Yüan Dynasty*. Translation of Chapters 93 and 94 of the Yüan Shih. Cambridge, 1967.

TAYLOR, REV. W. *The Catalogue Raisonné of Oriental Manuscripts in the Government Library*. Vol. III. Madras, 1862.

THIRUVENKATACHARI, S., trans. *Madhurā-Vijayam of Gaṅgā Devī*. Annamalai, 1957.

YULE, H., trans., rev. 3rd. ed., H. Cordier. *The Book of Ser Marco Polo, the Venetian Concerning the Kingdoms and Marvels of the East*. 2 vols., London, 1903.

YULE, SIR HENRY, trans. and ed., rev. ed., H. Cordier. *Cathay and the Way Thither*. 3 vols. London, 1913.

Select Bibliography. Books. Theses. Articles.

Secondary Works.

ABRAHAM, M. "The Currency System and Monetisation in Karnataka in Vijayangar "Times." *QJMS*, 69 (Jan-June 1978), 12-39.

———————. "The Ayyāvoḷe Guild of Early Medieval South India." M. Phil. Diss. Jawaharlal Nehru Univ., 1978.

———————. "A Medieval Merchant Guild of South India." *Studies in History*, 4, No. 1 (1982), 1-26.

ADAMS, ROBERT MCC. "Anthropological Perspectives on Ancient Trade." *Current Anthropology*, 15, No. 3 (1974), 239-258.

AGUR, C.M. *Church History of Travancore*. Madras, 1903.

AIYAR, S. RADHAKRISHNA. *A General History of the Pudukkottai State*. Pudukkottai, 1916.

AIYER, K.V. SUBRAHMANYA. "Largest Provincial Organisations in Ancient India." *QJMS*, 45 (July, 1954), 29-47; 45 (Oct. 1954), 70-98; 45 (April, 1955), 270-286.

APPADORAI, A. *Economic Conditions in Southern India, 1000-1500 A.D.* 2 vols. Madras, 1936.

AROKIASWAMI, M. *The Early History of the Vellar Basin*. Madras, 1954.

———————. *The Kongu Country*. Madras, 1956.

ARUNAÇHALAM, S. *The History of the Pearl Fishery of the Tamil Coast*. Annamalai, 1952.

ASHTOR, E. *A Social and Economic History of the Near East in the Middle Ages*. London, 1976.

AYYAR, A.S. RAMANATHA. "A New Persian Cross from Travancore." *The Ceylon Antiquary*, 9, pt. iv (1924), 188-196.

BANNERJEE, N.R. *The Iron Age in India*. New Delhi, 1965.

BELAIEW, N.T. "Damascene Steel." *Journal of the Iron and Steel Institute*, 97 (1918), 417-437.

BRIGGS, LAWRENCE PALMER. "The Khmer Empire and the Malay Peninsula." *The Far Eastern Quarterly*, 9, No. 3 (Nov. 1949 — Aug. 1950), 257-305.

BROHIER, R.L. *Ancient Irrigation Works in Ceylon*. Colombo, 1934.

BRONSON, BENNETT. "The Archaeology of Sumatra and the Problem of Srivijaya." In *Early South East Asia*. Eds.R.B. Smith and W. Watson. New York, 1979, pp. 395-405.

BROWN, L.W. *The Indian Christians of St. Thomas*. Cambridge, 1956.

BUCHANAN, FRANCIS. *A Journey from Madras through the Countries of Mysore, Canara and Malabar*, 3 vols. London, 1807.

BÜHLER, A. and E. FISCHER. *The Patola of Gujarat*, 2 vols. Basle, 1979.

BURKILL, I.H. "Habits of Man and the Origins of the Cultivated Plants of the Old World." *Proceedings of the Linnean Society of London 1951-52*. 164, pt. i, (London, 1953), 12-42.

BURNELL, A.C. "The Oldest Known South Indian Alphabet." *IA*, 1 (1872), 229-30.

BYRNE, EUGENE H. "Easterners in Genoa." *JAOS*, 38 (1918), 176-187.

CARSWELL, JOHN. "China and Islam in the Maldive Islands." Paper read 21 April 1976, *TOCS*, 41 (1975-76, 1976-77), 121-198.

____________. "China and Islam. A Survey of the Coast of India and Ceylon." Paper read 11 April, 1978, *TOCS*, 42 (1977-78), 25-68.

CASPARIS, J.G. de. "New evidence on cultural relations between Java and Ceylon in ancient times." *Artibus Asiae*, 24 (1961), 241-248.

CHAMPAKALAKSHMI, R. "Archaeology and Tamil Literary Tradition." *Purātattva*, 2(1975-76), 110-122.

____________. "Growth of urban centres in South India: Kudamūkku-Paḻaiyāṟai, the twin-city of the Cōḻas." *Studies in History*, 1, No. 1 (1979), 1-29.

CHANDRA, MOTI. "Indian Costumes and Textiles from the Eighth to the Twelfth Century." *Journal of Indian Textile History*, 5 (1961).

CHATTOPADHYAYA, B. *Coins and Currency Systems in South India c.* A.D. *905-1300*. Delhi, 1977.

CHAUDHURI, K.N. *Trade and Civilization in the Indian Ocean*. Cambridge, 1985.

CHOPRA, R.N., S.L.NARYAN and I.C. CHOPRA. *Glossary of Indian Medicinal Plants*. New Delhi, 1956.

CODRINGTON, O. "On a Hoard of Coins Found at Broach." *JBBRAS*, 15 (1882), 339-370.

COEDÈS, G. *The Indianized States of Southeast Asia*. Ed. W.F.Vella, and trans. S.B. Cowing. Kuala Lumpur, 1968.

Council of Scientific and Industrial Research. *The Wealth of India*, Raw Materials. Vol. I, New Delhi (1948), Vol. II (1950), Vol. III (1952), Vol. VII (1966), Vol. IX (1972).

DERIYANAGALA, S. "Archaeological Survey to Investigate Southeast Asian Prehistoric Presence in Ceylon." *Ancient Ceylon,* Vol. 1, pt. ii, Colombo (1972).

DERRETT, J.D.M. *The Hoysaḷas.* London, 1957.

DESAI, P.B. *Jainism in South India and some Jaina Epigraphs.* Sholapur, 1957.

____________. *"Trade Guilds in Karnataka and their Jaina Associations." Voice of Ahimsa* (1959).

____________. "Vajra-baisanige: Derivation and Interpretation." In *Srikanthika.* Dr. S.Srikantha Sastri Felicitation Volume. Mysore, 1973, pp. 82-91.

DIKSHIT, G.S. "The Guild of Ayyāvoḷe." Unpublished paper.

____________. "Constitution of the Trade Guilds in Medieval Karnataka." *JKUH,* 3 (1959), 53-57.

____________. *Local Self-Government in Medieval Karnataka.* Dharwar, 1964.

____________. "Mahānāḍu." In *Srikanthika.* Dr. S. Srikantha Sastri Felicitation Volume. Mysore, 1973, pp. 92-96.

DIRKS, N.B. "The Structure and Meaning of Political Relations in a South Indian Little Kingdom," Humanities Working Paper, No. 14, California Institute of Technology (October, 1978) pp. 1-70.

DUPONT, P. "Les Buddhas dit d 'Amaravati en Asia du Sud-Est." *BEFEO,* 49 (1954), 631-36.

ELLIOT, SIR W. *Coins of Southern India.* London, 1886, rpt. Varanasi, 1970.

FARQUHAR, J.N. "The Apostle Thomas in South India." *BJRL,* 11 (1927), 21-24.

FERNANDO, W.P.M. *Yapahuva.* Colombo, 1969.

FILIOZAT, JEAN. *Les Relations Exterieures de L'Inde.* Pondicherry, 1956.

FISCHEL, W.J. "The Spice Trade in Mamluk Egypt. A Contribution to the Economic History of Medieval Islam." *JESHO,* 1 (1958), 157-174.

FORD, R.I. "Barter, gift or violence; An analysis of Tewa intertribal exchange." In *Social Exchange and Interaction.* Ed. E.N. Wilmsen. Museum of Anthropology, University of Michigan, Anthropological Papers 46 (1972), pp. 2-45.

FOUCHER, A. *Etude sur l 'iconographie bouddhique de l'Inde, d' après des documents nouveaux.* 2 vols. Paris, 1900-05.

Geiger, W. "Army and War in Medieval Ceylon." In *The Polonnaruva Period.* Ed. S.D. Saparamadu. Dehiwala, 1973, pp. 173-190.

GITTINGER, M. *Masters Dyers to the World.* Washington, 1982.

GOODRICH, L.C. *"Cotton in China." Isis,* 34, 1-5 (Summer. 1944), 408-10.

GOTEIN, S.D. "New Light on the Beginnings of the Kārim Merchants." *JESHO,* 1 (1958), 175-184.

__________. "Letters and Documents on the India Trade in Medieval Times." *Islamic Culture,* 37 (Jan. 1963), 188-205.

__________. "Mediterranean Trade in the Eleventh Century: Some Facts and Problems." In *Studies in the Economic History of the Middle East from the rise of Islam to the present day,* ed. M.A. Cook. London, 1970, pp. 51-61.

GOTEIN, S.D. *Letters of Medieval Jewish Traders.* Princeton, 1973.

__________. "From Aden to India," "Specimens of the Correspondence of India Traders in the Twelfth Century." *JESHO,* 23, pts. i and ii (1980), 43-66.

GOVINDASAMY, M.S. "The Role of Feudatories in Cōḷa History." Diss. Annamalai Univ., 1974.

GRAY, BASIL. "The Export of Chinese Porcelain to India." *TOCS,* 36 (1964-65, 1965-66), 21-36.

GUNASINGHE, P.A.T. "The Political History of the Kingdoms of Yāpahuva, Kurunāgala and Gampala."Diss. Peradeniya Univ., 1980.

GUPTE, R.S. *The Art and Architecture of Aihole.* Bombay, 1967.

GURURAJACHAR, S. *Some Aspects of Economic and Social Life in Karnataka (A.D. 1000 – A.D. 1300).* Mysore, 1974.

HALL, KENNETH R. "The *'Nagaram'* as a Marketing Center in Early Medieval South India." Diss. Michigan Univ., 1975.

__________. "Khmer Commercial Development and Foreign Contracts under Sūryavaraman I." *JESHO,* 18, pt. 3 (1975), 318-336.

__________. "International Trade and Foreign Diplomacy in Early Medieval South India." *JESHO,* 21, pt.1 (1978), 75-93.

__________. "Eleventh-Century Commercial Developments in Angkor and Champa." *Journal of Southeast Asian Studies,* 10, No.2 (1979), 420-434.

__________. *Trade and Statecraft in the Age of the Cōḷas.* New Delhi, 1980.

__________. "Trade and Statecraft in the Western Archipelago at the dawn of the European age." *JMBRAS,* 54, pt.1 (1981), 21-51.

HALL, KENNETH R., and J.K. Whitmore, "Southeast Asian Trade and the Isthmian Struggle, 1000-1200 A.D. In their eds. *Explorations in Early Southeast Asian History: The Origin of Southeast Asian Statecraft.* Ann Arbor, 1976, pp. 303-341.

HAMILTON, A.W. "The Old Kedah-Pattani Trade Route." *JSBRAS,* 86 (1922), 389-92.

HAZRA, KANAI LAL. "Religious Intercourse among the Theravāda Countries from the Eleventh Century A.D. to the Sixtenth Century A.D." Diss. Peradeniya Univ., 1968.

HIRTH, F. "Chau Ju-kua; a new source of Medieeval Geography." *JRAS* (1896), 57-82.

__________. "Chao Ju-kua's ethnography: table of contents and extracts regarding Ceylon and India, and some articles of trade." *JRAS* (1896), 477-507.

HORNELL, JAMES, "The Indian Pearl Fisheries of the Gulf of Mannar and Palk Bay." *Madras Fisheries Bulletin,* 16 (1922).

HOURANI, G.F. *Arab Seafaring in the Indian Ocean in Ancient and Early Medieval Times.* Princeton, 1951.

INDRAPALA, K. "Some Medieval Mercantile Communities of South India and Ceylon." *JTS,* 2, No. 2, pt. 1 (1970), 3-15.

__________. ed. *The Collapse of the Rajarata Civilization in Ceylon and the drift to the South West.* Peradeniya, 1971.

__________. "South Indian Mercantile Communities in Ceylon, circa 950-1250." *CJHSS,* n.s. 1, No.1 (1971), 101-113.

JOSEPH, T.K. "Another Persian Cross in Travancore." *IA,* 52 (1923), 355-356.

JOSEPH, T.K. *Malabar Christians and their Ancient Documents.* Trivandrum, 1929.

__________. "The Saint Thomas Traditions of South India." *Bulletin du Comité international des Sciences historiques,* 20 (July, 1933), 560-9.

__________. "Christian and non-Christian Crosses in Ancient India." *JIH,* 28 (1950), 112-122.

KARASHIMA, NOBORU. "The Power Structure of the Chola Rule." *Proceedings of the Second International Conference Seminar of Tamil Studies.* Madras, January 1968. Vol.II, pub. 1971, pp. 233-238.

__________. *South Indian History and Society Studies from Inscriptions A.D. 850–1800.* Delhi, 1984.

KATÔ, SHIGESHI. "On the Hang or the Associations of Merchants in China, With Especial Reference to the Institution in the T'ang and Sung periods." *MTB,* No.8 (1936), 45-83.

KUPPUSWAMY, G.R. "The Role of the Mahājanas in Medieval Karnataka." *JKU,* Social Sciences 6 (1970), 61-66.

__________. *Economic Conditions in Karnataka. (A.D. 973 – A.D. 1336).* Dharwar, 1975.

KUWABARA JITSUZO. "On P'u Shou-keng, a man of the western regions who was the superintendent of the Trading Ship's office in Ch'üan-chou towards the end of the Sung dynasty, together with a general sketch of trade of the Arabs in China during the T'ang and Sung eras" *MTB,* No.2 (1928) and No. 7 (1935).

LABIB, S. "Egyptian Commercial Policy in the Middle Ages." In *Studies in the Economic History of the Middle East from the rise of Islam to the present day.* Ed. M.A. Cook. London, 1970, pp. 63-77.

LAMB, ALASTAIR. "Kedak and Takuapa: Some Tentative Historical Conclusions." *FMJ,* 6 (1961), 69-88.

__________. "Takuapa: The Probable Site of a Pre-Malaccan Entrepôt in the Malay Peninsula." In *Malayan and Indonesian Studies*. Eds. John Bastin and R.Roolvink. Oxford, 1964, pp. 76-86.

LEUR, J.C. VAN. *Indonesian Trade and Society, Essays in Asian Social and Economic History*. The Hague, 1955.

LEVI, SYLVAIN. "Ptolémée, le Niddesa et la Bṛhatkathā." *EA*, 2 (1925), 1-55, 431-2.

LEVI D'ANCONA, M. "Amarāvati, Ceylon and the Three 'Imported Bronzes'." *The Art Bulletin*, 34 (1952), 1-17.

LICERIA, SISTER M. "Emergence of Brāhmaṇas as Landed Intermediaries in Karnataka (c. A.D. 1000 – 1300)." *IHR*, 1, No. 1 (1974), 28-35.

__________. "Social and Economic History of Karnataka, c. A.D. 1000 – 1300." Diss. Patna Univ., 1972.

LO, HSIANG-LIN. "On the Voyage of Soli Samudra Chola's Envoy to China in A.D. 1015." *Proceedings of the First International Conference Seminar of Tamil Studies*. Vol. I, Kuala Lumpur, 1968, pp. 494-508.

LO, JUNG-PANG. "The Emergence of China as a Sea Power During the Late Sung and Early Yüan Periods." *Far Eastern Quarterly*, 14, No. 4 (1955), 489-503.

LOPEZ, R.S. "European Merchants in the Medieval Indies: The Evidence of Commercial Documents." *Journal of Economic History*, I (1943), 164-184.

__________. "Still Another Renaissance?" *The American Historical Review*, 57, No.1 (1951), 1-21.

LOPEZ, R.S., Harry Miskimin and Abraham Udovitch. "England to Egypt, 1350-1500: Long-term Trends and Long-distance Trade." In *Studies in the Economic History of the Middle East from the rise of Islam to the present day*. Ed. M.A. Cook. London, 1970. pp. 93-128.

LORENZEN, DAVID. *The Kāpālikas and Kālāmukhas: Two Lost Saivite Sects*. New Delhi, 1972.

MAHALINGAM, T.V. *South Indian Polity*. Madras, 1955.

__________. "*The Citramēḷi Periyanāṭṭar*." In *Dr. R.P.Sethupillai Jubilee Commemoration Volume*. Madras, 1961, pp. 195-9.

MAJUMDAR, R.C. *Corporate Life in Ancient India*. Calcutta, 1969. First pub. 1918.

__________. *Ancient Indian Colonies in the Far East*. Vol. II. Dacca, 1937.

MAXWELL, W.E. "Journey on Foot to the Patani Frontier in 1876." *JSBRAS*, 9 (1882), 1-67.

MAYERS, W.F. "Chinese Explorations of the Indian Ocean During the Fifteenth Century." *The China Review*, 3 (1874-75), 219-225, 321-331; 4 (1875-6), 61-190.

MCKINNON, E.P. Edwards. "Oriental Ceramics Excavated in North Sumatra." Paper read 16 September, 1976, *TOCS*, 41 (1975-1976, 1976-1977), 59-80.

MEDLYCOTT, A.E. *India and the Apostle Thomas. An Inquiry with a critical analysis of the Acta Thomae.* London, 1905.

MI CHÜ WIENS. "Cotton Textile Production and Rural Social Transformation in Early Modern China." *Journal of the Institute of Chinese Studies of the Chinese University of Hong Kong,* 7 (1974), 515-34.

MINES, MATTISON. *The Warrior merchants: Textiles, trade and territory in South India.* Cambridge, 1984.

MINGANA, A. "The Early Spread of Christianity in India." *BJRL,* 10, No.2 (1926), 3-82.

MODI, J.J. "A Christian Cross with a Pahlavi Inscription Recently Discovered in the Travancore State." *JBBRAS,* 2 No.1 (1926), 1-18.

MOOKERJI, RADHA KUMUD. *A History of Indian Shipping.* Allahabad, 1962. First pub. 1912.

NAERSSEN, F.H. VAN. *Orientalia Neerlandica.* Leiden, 1948.

NAGASWAMY, R. *Studies in Ancient Tamil Law and Society.* Madras, 1978.

NAINAR, S.M.H. *Arab Geographer's Knowledge of Southern India.* Madras, 1942.

O'CONNOR, S.J. *Hindu Gods of Peninsular Siam.* Ascona, MCMLXXII.

PARANAVITANA, S. "Mahayanism in Ceylon." *Ceylon Journal of Science,* Section G, 2 (Dec. 1928 – Feb. 1933), 35-71.

PATHMANATHAN, S. "Cōḷa rule in Ceylon; circa 993-1070." *Proceedings of the Fourth International Conference Seminar of Tamil Studies.* Vol.II, Jaffna, 1980, pp. 19-35.

__________. *The Kingdom of Jaffna.* Colombo, 1978.

PATABIRAMIN, P.Z. *Les fouilles d'Arikamedou (Podouké).* Pondicherry, 1946.

PEARSON, GEORGE. "Experiments and Observations to Investigate the Nature of a Kind of Steel, manufactured at Bombay and there called Wootz, with Remarks on the Properties and Composition of the different States of Iron." *Philosophical Transactions of the Royal Society of London,* Ser. 4, 85, pt. ii (1795), 332-346.

PERERA, B.J. "The Foreign Trade and Commerce of Ancient Ceylon," I, "The Ports of Ancient Ceylon." III, "Ancient Ceylon's Trade with the Empires of the Eastern and Western Worlds." *CHJ,* 1 (1951), 4 (1952).

PERLIN, FRANK. "Proto-Industrialization and Pre-Colonial South Asia." *Past and Present,* 98 (1983), 31-95.

PIERIS, P.E., trans. *Ribeiro's History of Ceilão.* Colombo, 1909.

PILLAI, ELAMKULAM KUNJAN. *Studies in Kerala History.* Kottayam, 1970. [Malayalam].

PILLAY, K.K. *A Social History of the Tamils.* Madras, 1969.

PIRENNE, HENRI. *Medieval Cities.* Princeton, 1974. First pub. 1925.

POLANYI, KARL. "Traders and Trade." In *Ancient Civilization and Trade.* Eds. J.A. Sabloff and C.C. Lamberg-Karlovsky. Albuquerque, 1975, pp. 133-154.

POSTAN, M. and E.E. RICH, eds. *The Cambridge Economic History*. Vol. III. Cambridge, 1963.

Pudukkottai Darbar Record Office. *Report on the Administration of Pudukkottai for the Year 1881-82*.

RAMASWAMY, VIJAYA. "Notes on the Textile Technology in Medieval India with Special Reference to the South." *IESHR*, 17, No.2 (1981), 227-41.

RAMESH, K.V. *A History of South Kanara*. Dharwar, 1970.

RAO, R. NARASIMHA. *Corporate Life in Medieval Andhra Desa*. Hyderabad, 1967.

RATNAGAR, S. *Encounters: The westerly trade of the Harappa civilization*. Delhi, 1981.

RENFREW, COLIN. "Trade as Action at a Distance: Questions of Integration and Communication." In *Ancient Civilization and Trade*. Eds. J.A. Sabloff and C.C. Lamberg-Karlovsky. Albuquerque, 1975, pp. 3-59.

REVERE, ROBERT B. "Ports of Trade in the Eastern Mediterranean." In *Trade and Market in the Early Empires*. Karl Polyanyi *et. al.* Glencoe, 1957, p. 38-63.

RICHARDS, J.F., ed. *Precious Metals in the Later Medieval and Early Modern Worlds*. Durham, 1983.

ROCHER, LUDO. "Jacob Mossel's Treatise on the Customary Laws of the Vellalar Chettiyars." *JAOS*, 89 (1969), 27-50.

SALETORE, B.A. *Social and Political Life in the Vijayanagara Empire (A.D. 1346-1646)* Vol. II. Madras, 1934.

__________. "Karnataka's Trans-Oceanic Contacts." Dharwar, 1956. Pamphlet.

SAMPATH, M.D. "The *Chitramēḷi*." In *Studies in Indian History and Culture*. Dharwar, 1971, pp. 314-319.

SAPARAMADU, S.D., ed. *The Polonnaruva Period*. Dehiwala, 1973.

SASTRI, CHANDRASEKHARA S. "Economic Conditions under the Hoysaḷas." *Half-Yearly Journal of the Mysore University*, 2, No.2 (1928), 196-233.

SASTRI, K.A. NILAKANTA. *The Pāṇḍyan Kingdom: From the Earliest Times to the Sixteenth Century*. Madras, 1972. First pub. 1929.

__________. *The Cōḷas*. Madras, 1975. First pub. 1935-37.

__________. "The Beginnings of Intercourse between India and China." *IHQ*, 14 (June, 1938), 380-7.

__________. *The History of Sri Vijaya*. Madras, 1949.

__________. "A Note on Vēlaikkārar." *JRAS (C)*, 4, n.s. (1954), 67-71.

__________. *A History of South India from Prehistoric Times to the Fall of Vijayanagar*. Madras, 1966. First pub. 1955.

__________. "Cōḷa invasions: Downfall of Anuradhapura." In University of Ceylon. *History of Ceylon*. Vol. I, Book III. Colombo, 1959.

SASTRY, K.R.R. *South Indian Gilds*. Madras, 1925.

SETTAR, S. *Hoysaḷa Sculptures*. Copenhagen, 1975.

SHANTHAKUMARI, S.L. "Agrahāras in Ancient Karnataka." Diss. Karnatak Univ., 1970.

SHARMA, R.S. "Social Changes in Early Medieval India (c. A.D. 500-1200)." First Devraj Chanana Memorial Lecture 1969. Delhi 1969.

SILVA, K.M. De. *A History of Sri Lanka*. Delhi, 1981.

SIRISENA, W.M. *Sri Lanka and South-East Asia*. Leiden, 1978.

SMITH, C.S. *A History of Metallography*. Chicago, 1960.

SPENCER, GEORGE. "Royal Leadership and Imperial Conquest in Medieval South India: The Naval Expedition of Rajendra Chola I. c. 1025 A.D." Diss. California Univ., Berkeley, 1967.

SPENCER, GEORGE W. "Religious Networks and Royal Influence in Eleventh Century South India." *JESHO*, 12 (1969), 42-56.

__________. "The Politics of Plunder: The Cholas in Eleventh Century Ceylon." *JAS*, 35, No.3 (1976), 405-419.

SRINIVASAN, T.M. "Irrigation and Water Supply in South India upto 1300 A.D." M.Phil. Diss. Madras Univ., 1968.

STARGARDT, JANICE. "Burma's Economic and Diplomatic Relations with India and China from Early Medieval Sources." *JESHO*, 14 (1971), 38-62.

STEIN, BURTON. "Historical Ecotypes in South India." *Proceedings of the Second International Conference Seminar of Tamil Studies*, January 1968. Vol. II. Madras, 1971, pp. 284-288.

__________. "The State and the Agrarian Order in Medieval South India: A Historiographical Critique." In *Essays on South India*. Ed. Burton Stein. Hawai, 1975, pp. 64-92.

__________. "Coromandel Trade in Medieval India." In *Merchants and Scholars*. Ed. John Parker. Minneapolis, 1965, pp. 49-62.

__________. "The Segmentary State in South Indian History." In *Realm and Region in India*. Ed. Robert Fox. Durham.

__________. "Social Mobility and Medieval South Indian Hindu Sects." In *Social Mobility in the Caste System of India*. Ed. J. Silverberg. The Hague, 1968. pp. 78-94.

__________. *Peasant State and Society in Medieval South India*. Delhi, 1980.

SUBBARAYALU, Y. *Political Geography of the Chola Country*. Madras, 1973.

SUNDARAM, K. *Studies in Economic and Social Conditions in Medieval Andhra*. Madras, 1968.

TARN, W.W. *The Greeks in Bactria and India*. Cambridge, 1951.

THAPAR, ROMILA. "Continuous beginnings." *Seminar*. (Jan. 1984).

THURSTON, E. *Castes and Tribes of Southern India*. Vol. V. rpt. Delhi, 1975.

TIBBETTS, G.R. "Early Muslim Traders in South-East Asia." *JMBRAS*, 30, pt.1 (1957), 1-46.

T'IEN JU KANG. "Chêng Ho's Voyages and the Distribution of Pepper in China." *JRAS*, 1 (1981), 186-197.

TIRUMALAI, R. *Studies in Ancient Townships of Pudukkottai*. Madras, 1981.

TISSERANT, EUGENE, CARDINAL. *Eastern Christianity in India*. Adapted and trans. E.R. Hambye. Calcutta, 1957.

VELLAN, JACOB., ed. *The Apostle Thomas in India according to the Acts of Thomas*. Kottayam, 1972.

VENKATARAMA AYYAR, K.R. *A Manual of the Pudukkottai State*. Vol. 1, Vol.II, pt. i and ii. Pudukkottai, 1940, 1944.

__________. "Medieval Trade, Craft and Merchant Guilds in South India." *JIH*, 25, pt. 1 (1947), 269-80.

VENKATARAMAN, K.R. "More about the Aiññūṟṟuvar." *Proceedings of the All-India Oriental Conference*, Tenth Session, Tirupati, 1940, pp. 349-53.

VENKATARAMANUJAM CHETTY, ed. *Revenue Settlement Report on Pudukkottai*, 1910.

WALES, H.G.Q. "A Newly Explored Route of Indian Cultural Expansion." *IAL*, 9, No.1 (1935), 1-35.

WANG, GUNGWU. "The Nanhai Trade." *JMBRAS*, 31, pt. 2 (1958), 1-135.

WATSON, ANDREW M. "Back to Gold-and Silver." *The Economic History Review*, 2d. ser. 20, No.1 (1967), 2-34.

WEERASOORIA, W.S. *The Nattukottai Chettiar Merchant Bankers in Ceylon*. Dehiwala, 1973.

WHEATLEY, PAUL. "Geographical Notes on some Commodities involved in Sung Maritime Trade." *JMBRAS*, 32, pt. 2 (June 1959), 5-140.

__________. *The Golden Khersonese*. Kuala Lumpur, 1966.

__________. "Satyānṛta in Suvarṇadvīpa From Reciprocity to Redistribution in Ancient Southeast Asia," In *Ancient Civilization and Trade*. Eds. J.A. Sabloff and C.C. Lamberg-Karlovsky. Albuquerque, 1975, pp.227-283.

WHEELER, R.E.M. "Arikamaedu: An Indo-Roman Trading Station on the East Coast of India." *Ancient India*, 2 (July, 1946), 17-124.

WHITEHOUSE, T. *Lingerings of Light in a Dark Land*. London, 1873.

WICKREMASINGHE, S. "Ceylon's Relations with South-East Asia. With Special Reference to Burma." *CJHS*, 3, No. 1 (1960), 38-58.

WIJETUNGA, W.M.K. "Some aspects of Cōḷa Administration of Ceylon in the Eleventh Century." *UCR*, 23, Nos. 1-2 (1965), 67-81.

__________. "South Indian Corporate Commercial Organizations in South and South-East Asia." *Proceedings of the First International Conference Seminar of Tamil Studies*. Vol. I, Kuala Lumpur, 1968, pp. 494-508.

WOLTERS, O.W. "*Tāmbralinga.*" *BSOAS*, 21 (1958), 587-707.

____________. "A note on the capital of Srivijaya during the Eleventh Century." *Artibus Asiae Supplementum 23*. Felicitation Volume presented to Professor G.H. Luce. Vol. I. Ascona, 1966, pp. 225-239.

____________. *Early Indonesian Commerce, A Study of the Origins of Srivijaya*. Ithaca, 1967.

____________. *The Fall of Srivijaya in Malay History*. Ithaca, 1971.

WONG, LIN KEN. "The Malayan Tin Industry." In *Papers on Malayan History*. Ed. K.B. Tregonning. Singapore, 1962.

YUSUF, S.M. "Ceylon and the Arab Trade." University of Ceylon, *History of Ceylon*. Vol. I, pt.2. Colombo, 1960, pp. 703-710.

Index